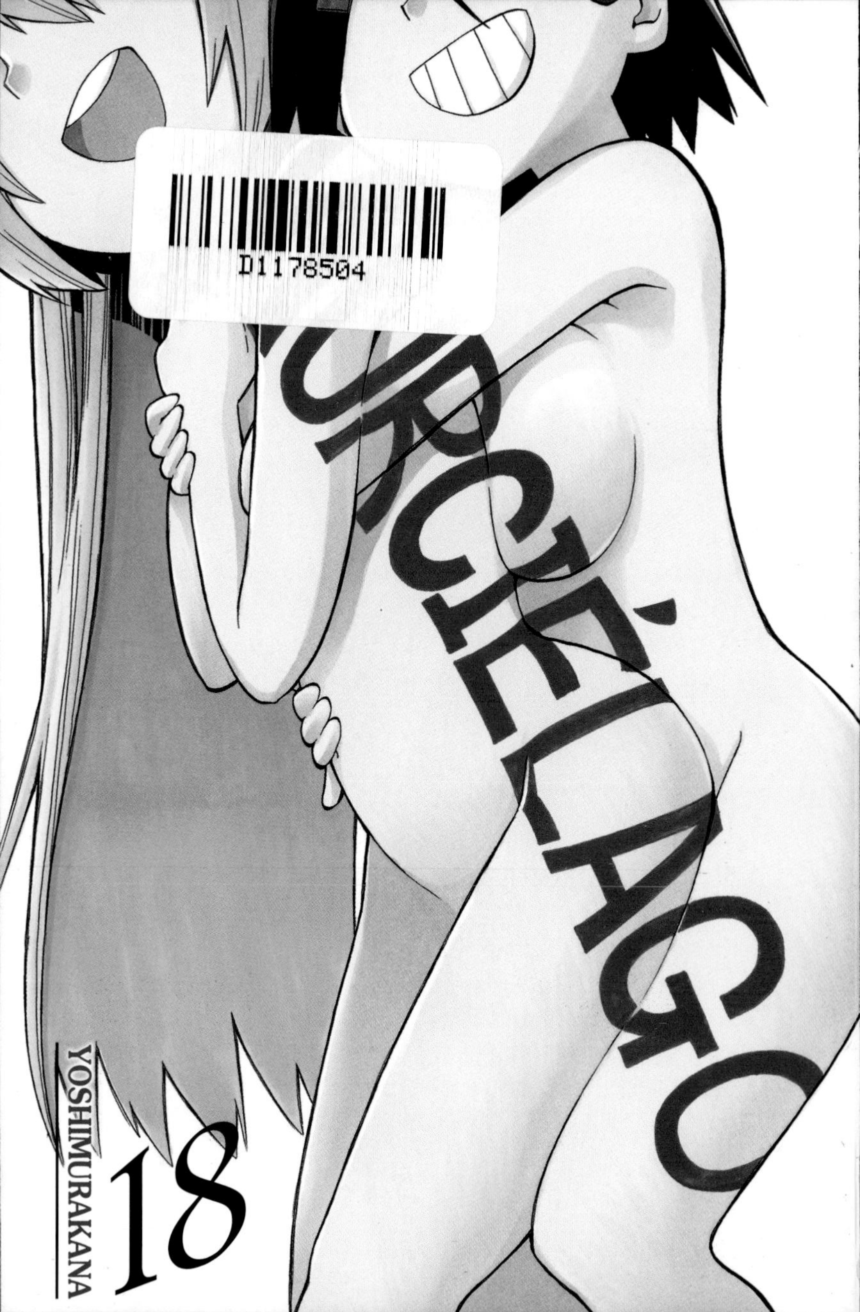
RCIÉLAGO
YOSHIMURAKANA
18

MURCIÉLAGO

18

CONTENTS

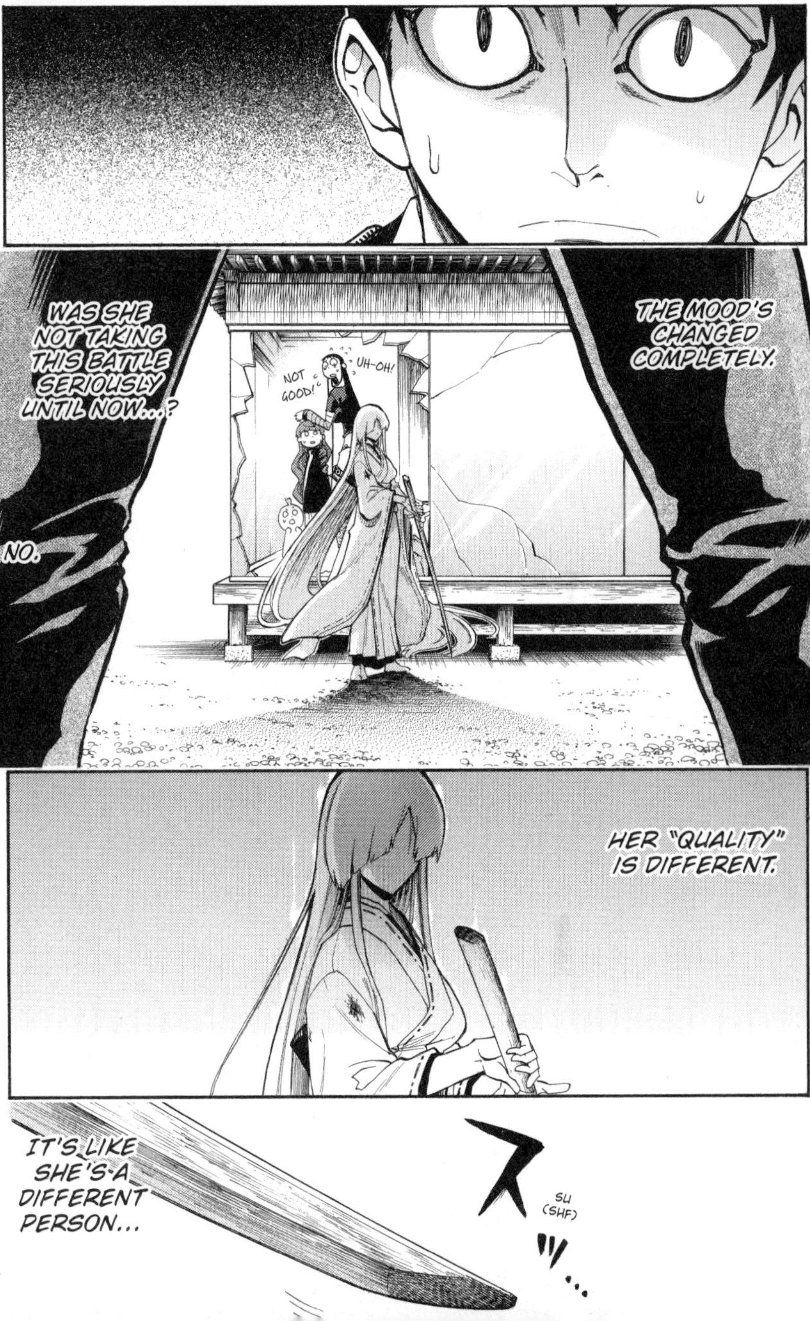
THE MOOD'S CHANGED COMPLETELY.
UH-OH!
NOT GOOD!
WAS SHE NOT TAKING THIS BATTLE SERIOUSLY UNTIL NOW...?
NO.
HER "QUALITY" IS DIFFERENT.
SU (SHF)
IT'S LIKE SHE'S A DIFFERENT PERSON...

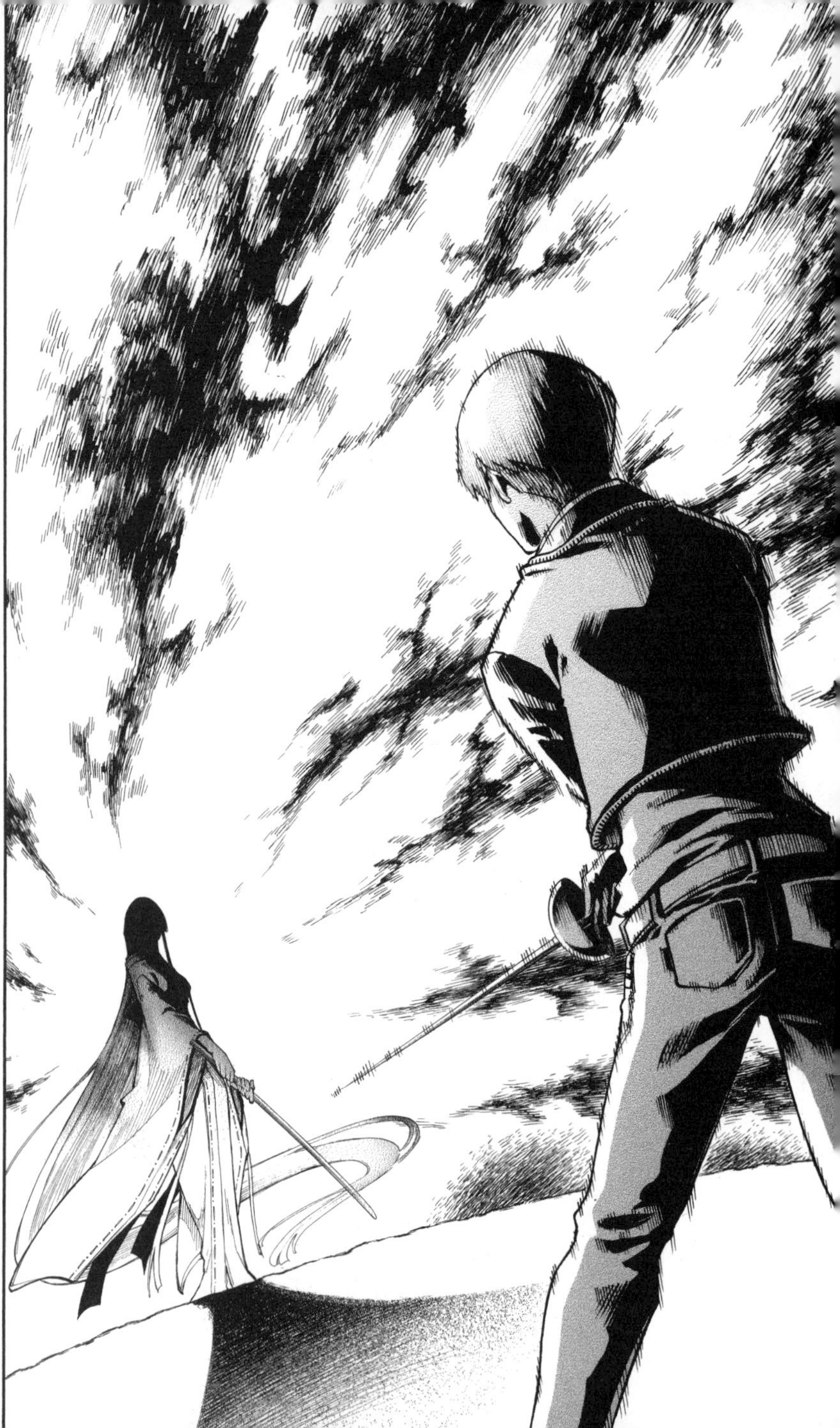

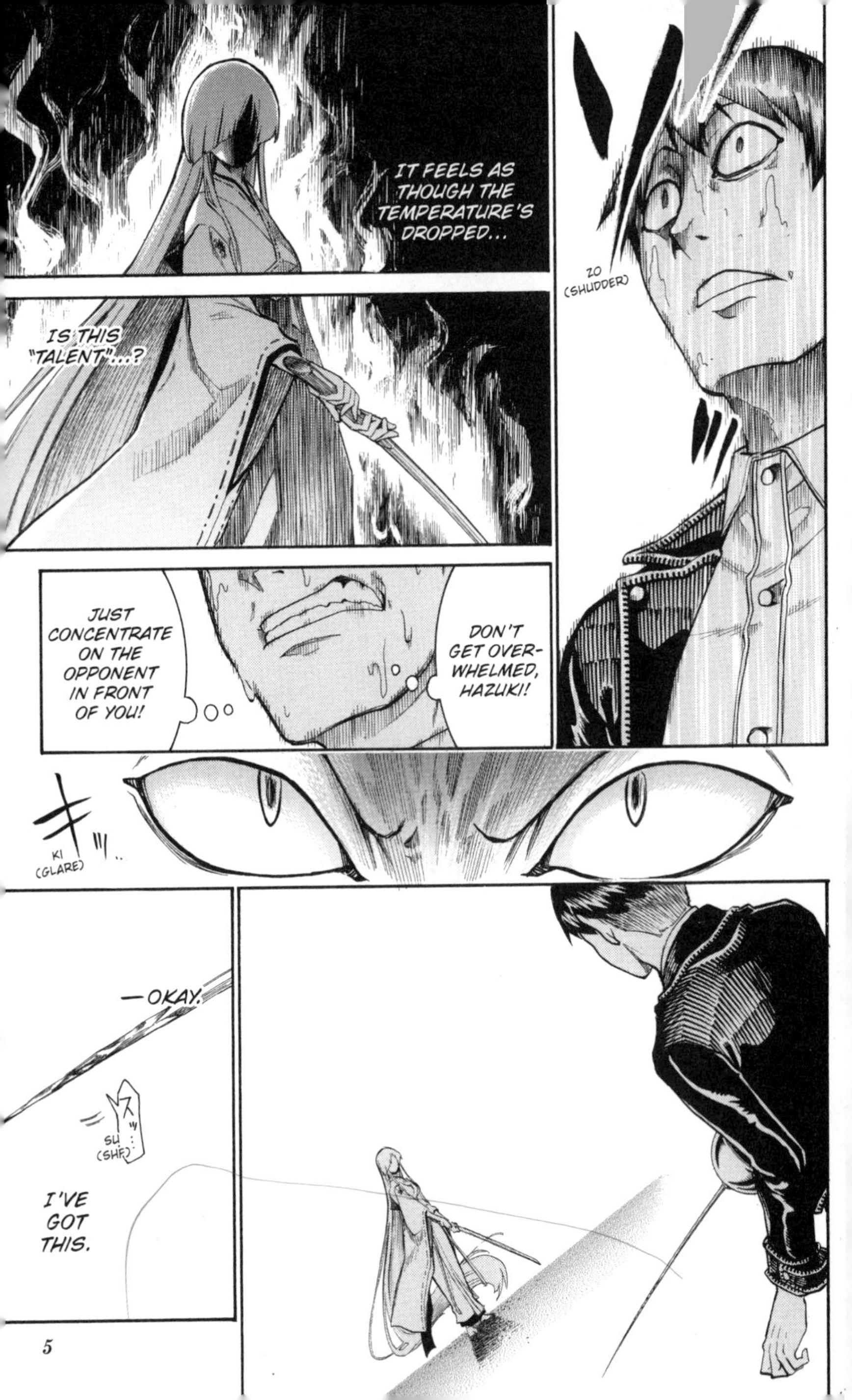
ZO
(SHUDDER)
IT FEELS AS THOUGH THE TEMPERATURE'S DROPPED...
IS THIS "TALENT"...?
DON'T GET OVER-WHELMED, HAZUKI!
JUST CONCENTRATE ON THE OPPONENT IN FRONT OF YOU!
KI
(GLARE)
—OKAY.
SU
(SHF)
I'VE GOT THIS.

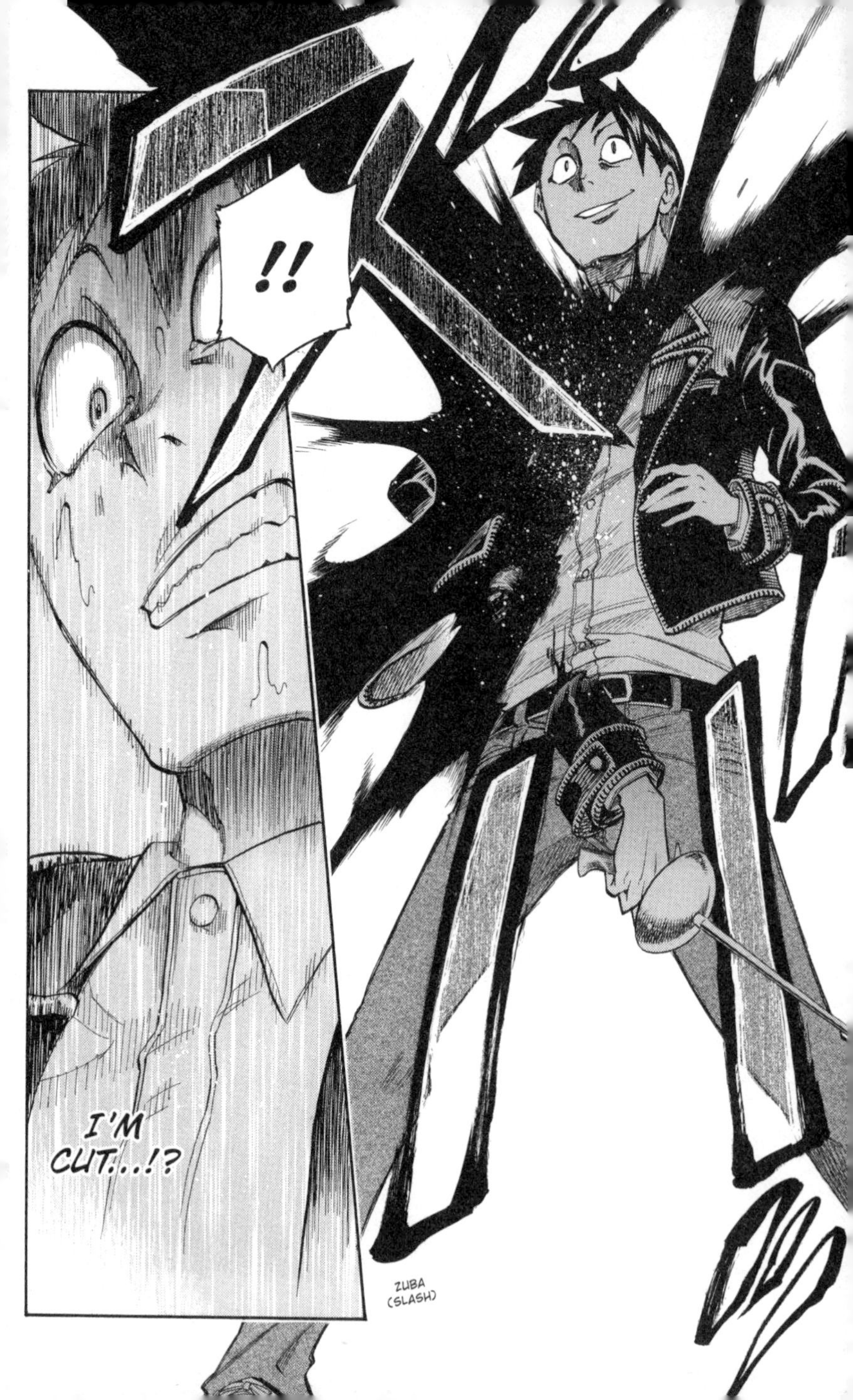
ZUBA
(SLASH)
!!
I'M CUT...!?

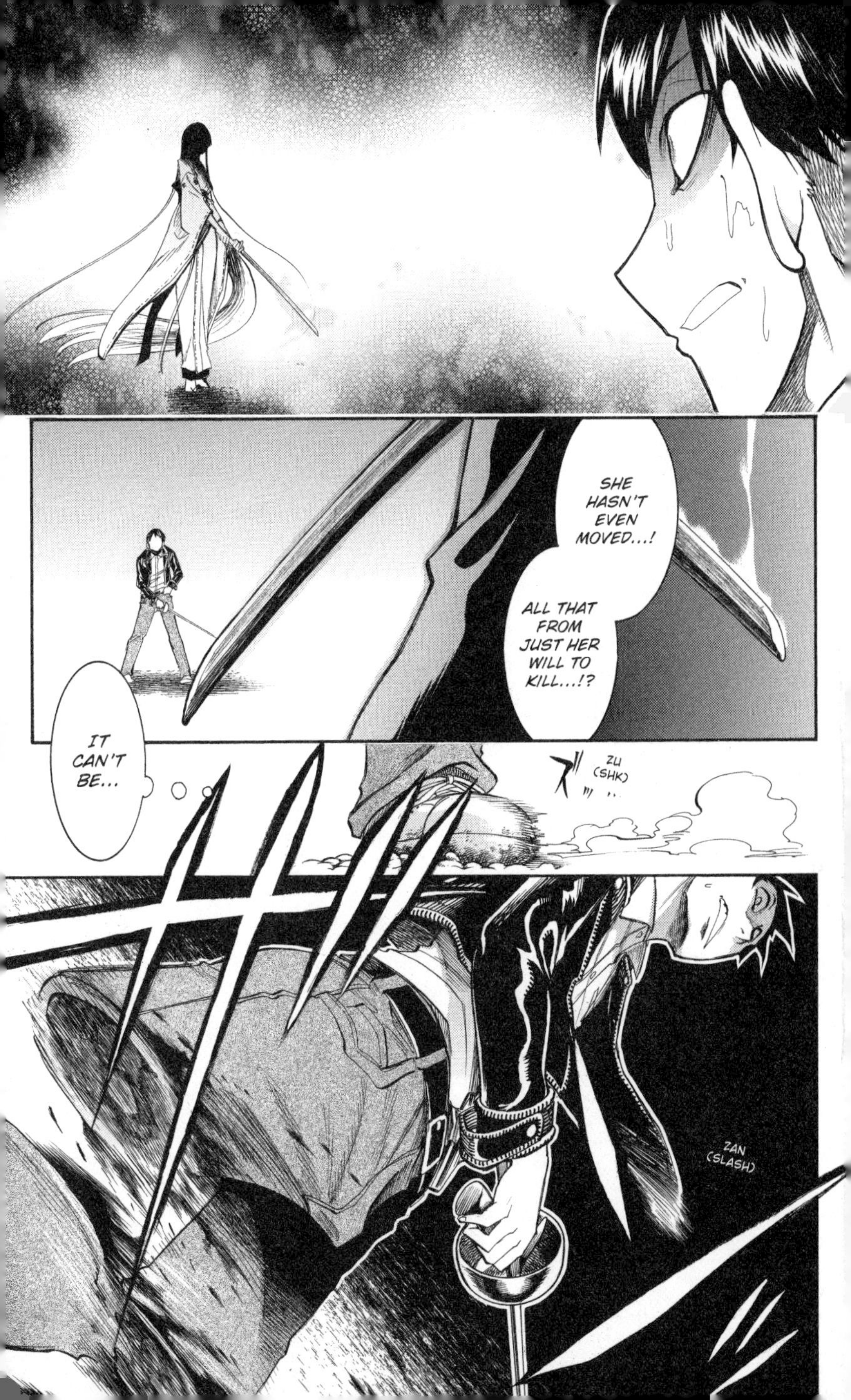
SHE HASN'T EVEN MOVED...!
ALL THAT FROM JUST HER WILL TO KILL...!?
IT CAN'T BE...
ZU (SHK)
ZAN (SLASH)

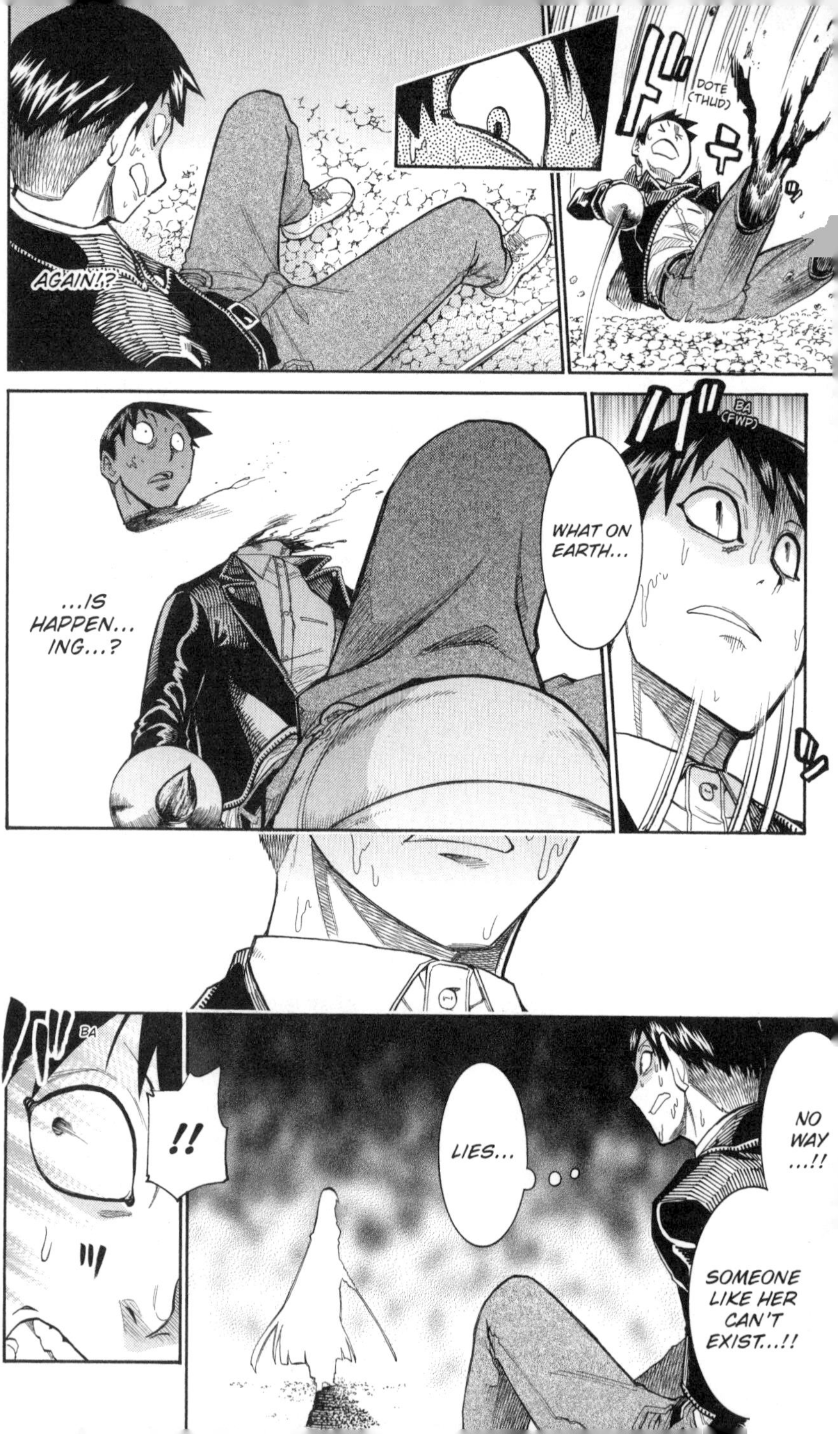
DOTE (THUD)
AGAIN!?
BA (FWP)
WHAT ON EARTH...
...IS HAPPEN... ING...?
NO WAY ...!!
SOMEONE LIKE HER CAN'T EXIST...!!
LIES...
BA
!!

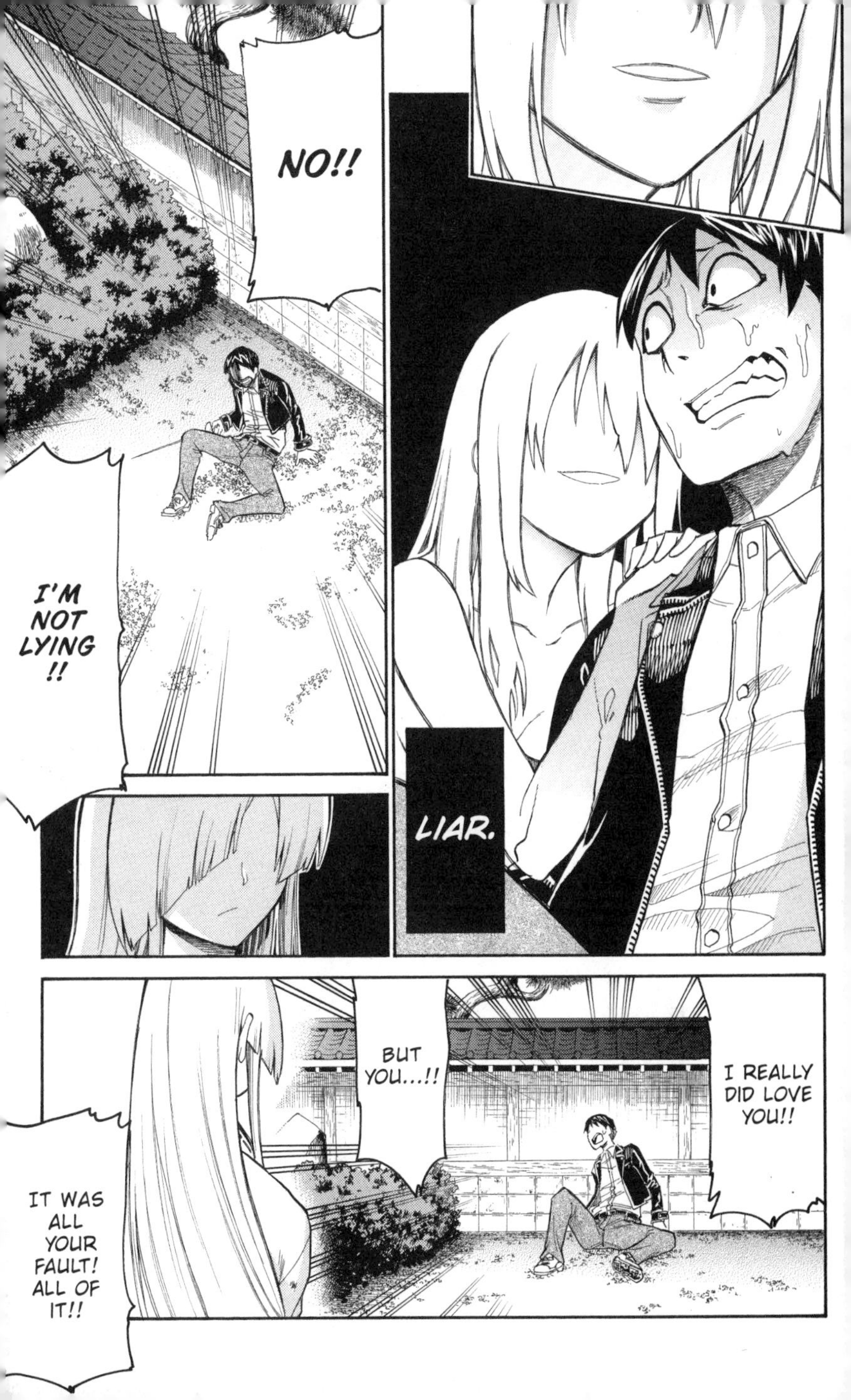
LIAR.
NO!!
I'M NOT LYING!!
I REALLY DID LOVE YOU!!
BUT YOU...!!
IT WAS ALL YOUR FAULT! ALL OF IT!!

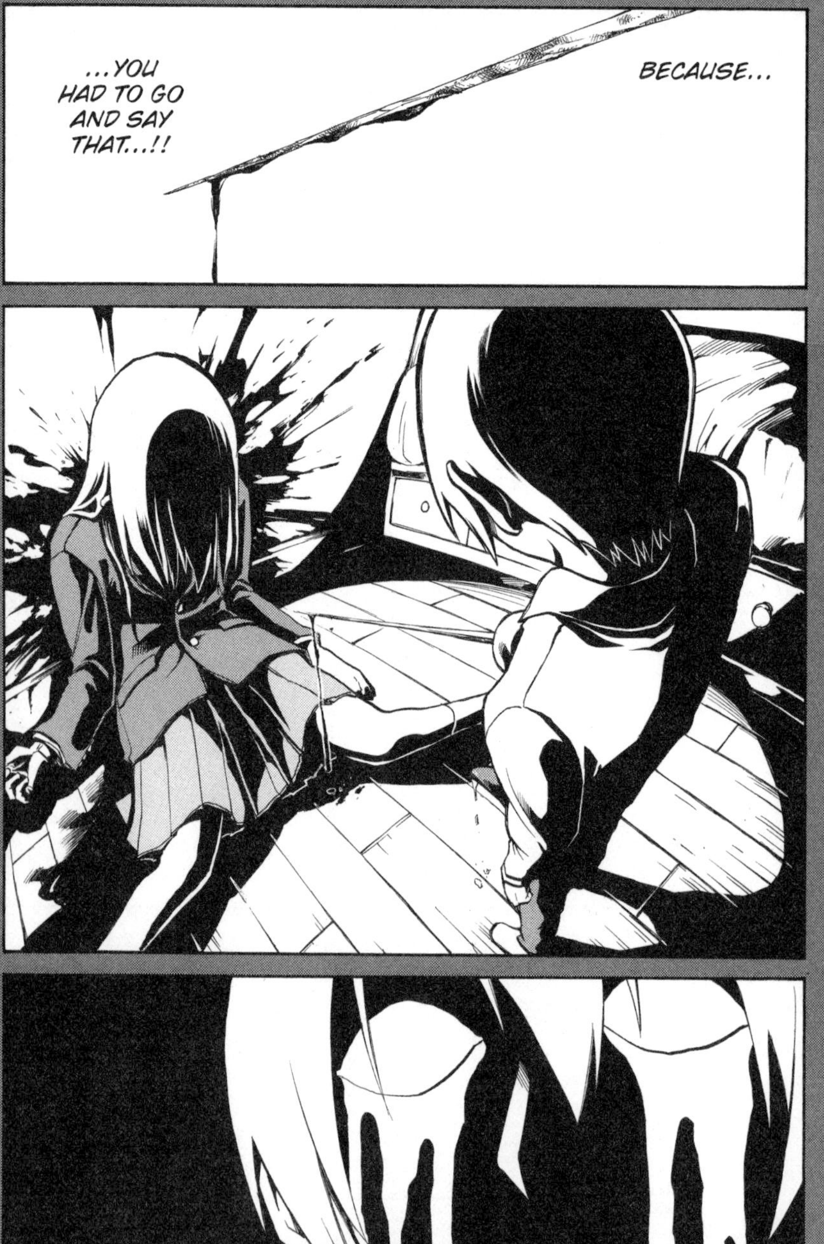
BECAUSE...
...YOU HAD TO GO AND SAY THAT...!!

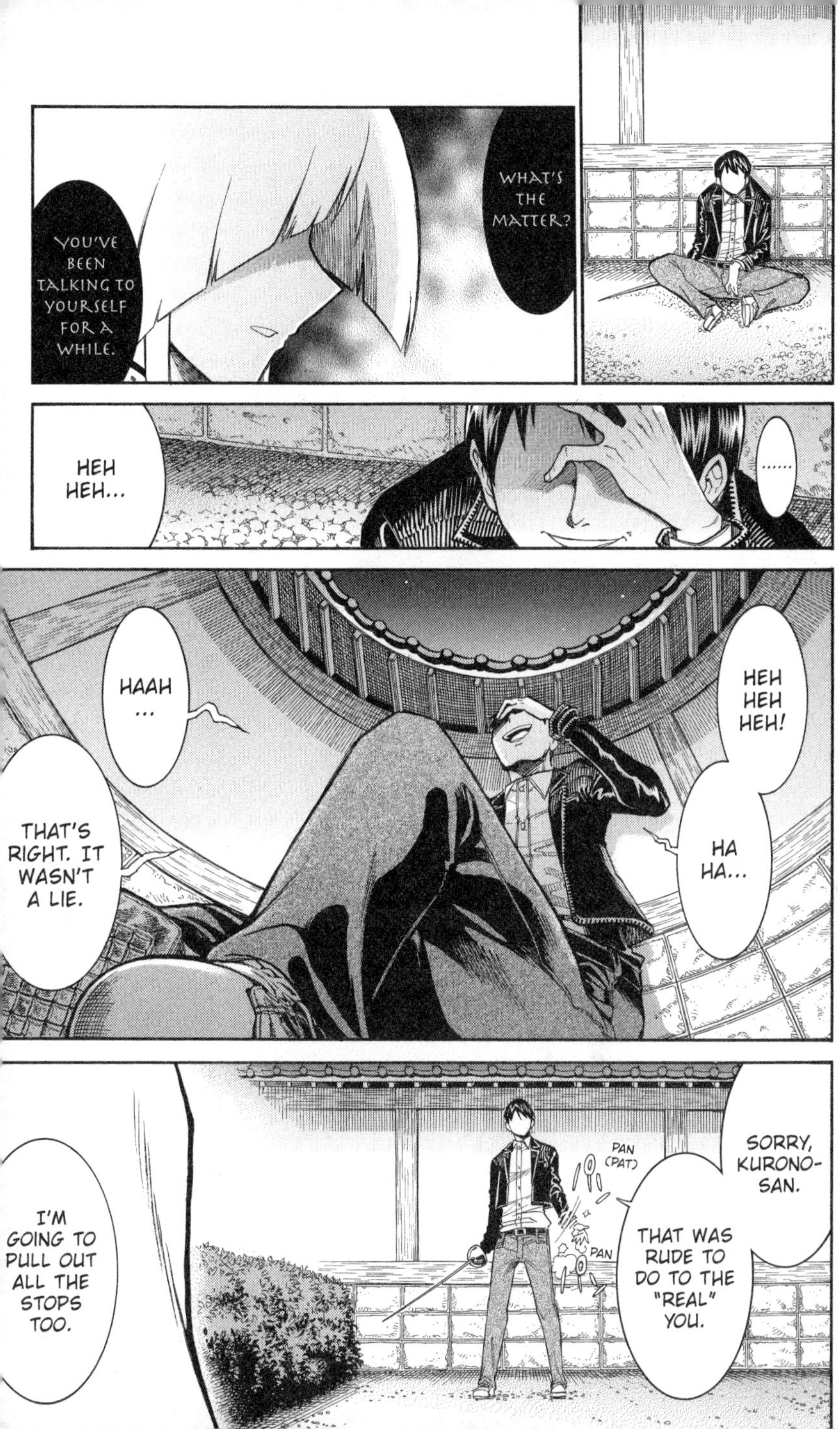
WHAT'S THE MATTER?
YOU'VE BEEN TALKING TO YOURSELF FOR A WHILE.
......
HEH HEH...
HEH HEH HEH!
HA HA...
HAAH ...
THAT'S RIGHT. IT WASN'T A LIE.
SORRY, KURONO-SAN.
THAT WAS RUDE TO DO TO THE "REAL" YOU.
PAN (PAT)
PAN
I'M GOING TO PULL OUT ALL THE STOPS TOO.

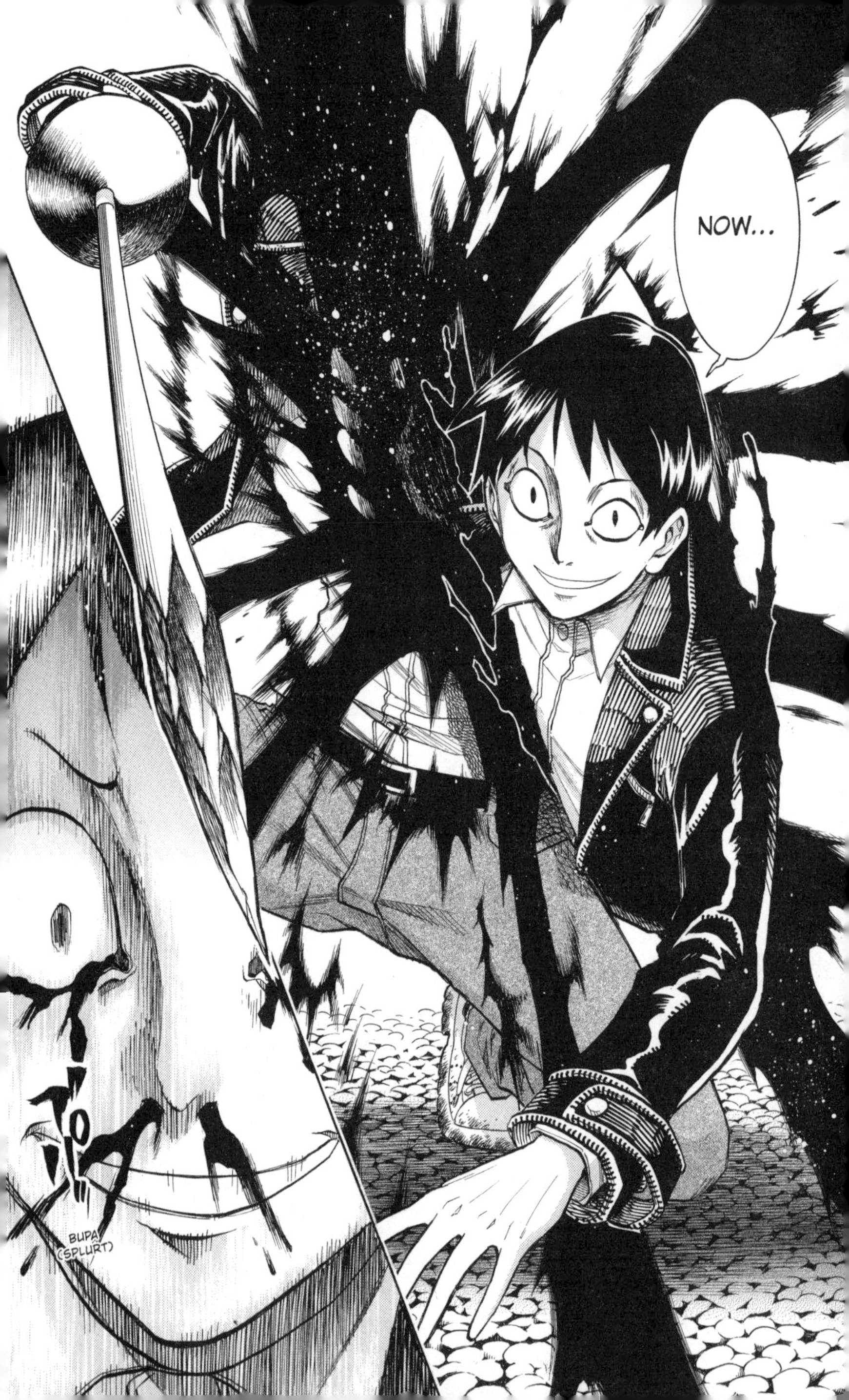
NOW...
BUPA
(SPLURT)

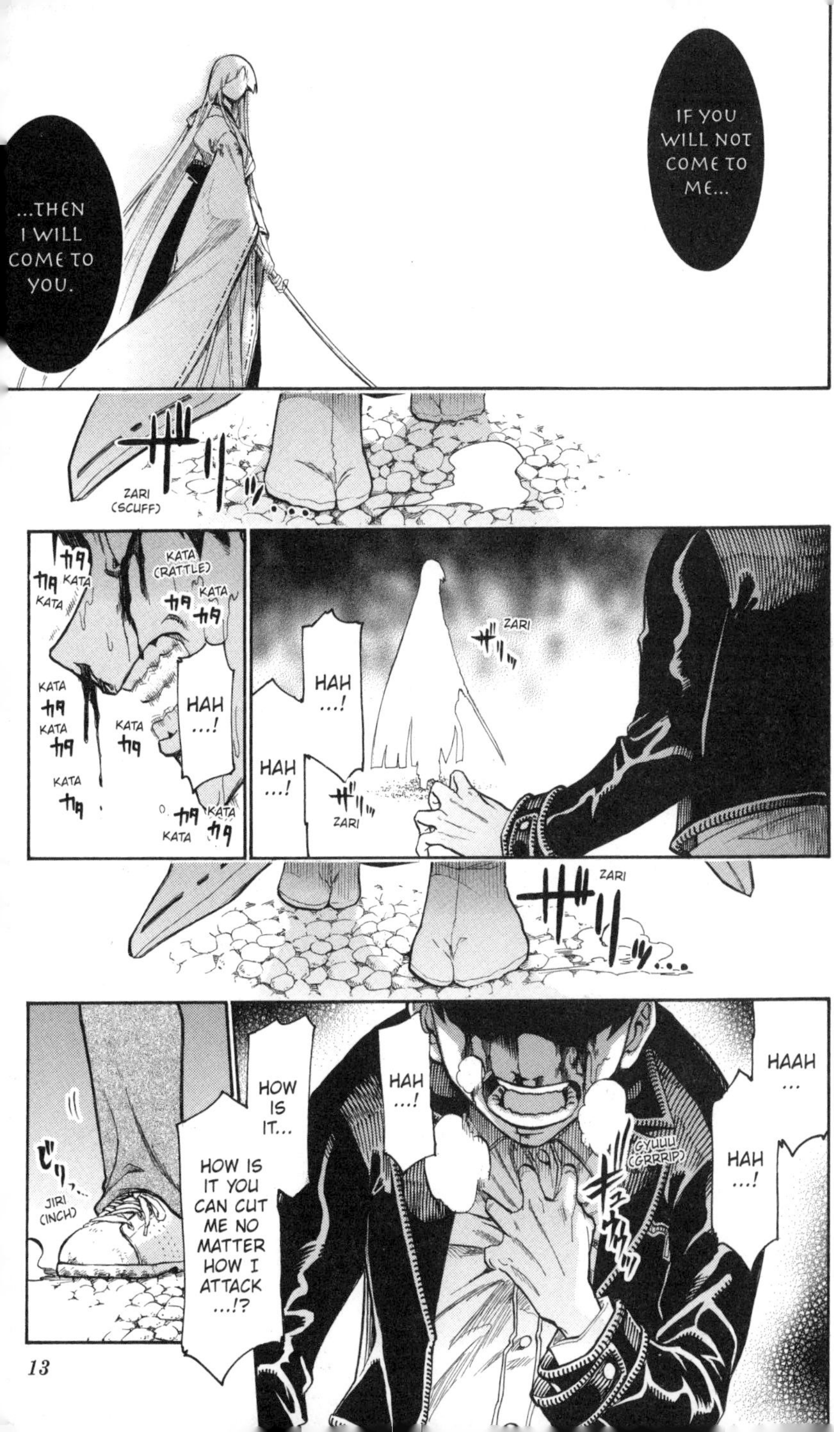

IF YOU WILL NOT COME TO ME...
...THEN I WILL COME TO YOU.
ZARI (SCUFF)
ZARI
HAH ...!
HAH ...!
ZARI
KATA (RATTLE)
KATA
KATA
KATA
HAH ...!
KATA
KATA
KATA
KATA
KATA
KATA
ZARI
HAAH ...
HAH ...!
GYUUU (GRRRIP)
HAH ...!
HOW IS IT...
HOW IS IT YOU CAN CUT ME NO MATTER HOW I ATTACK ...!?
JIRI (INCH)

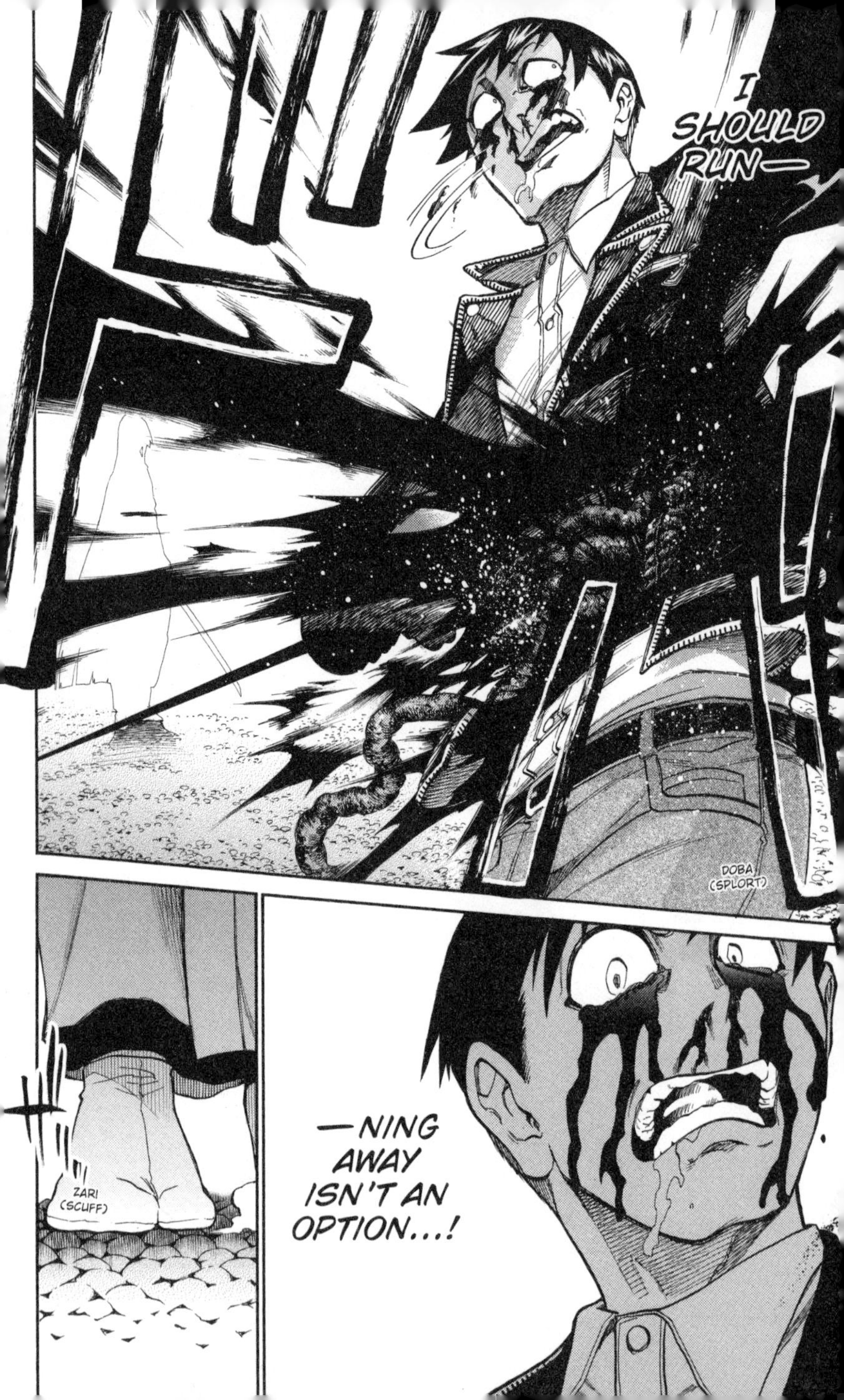
I SHOULD RUN—
DOBA (SPLORT)
—NING AWAY ISN'T AN OPTION...!
ZARI (SCUFF)

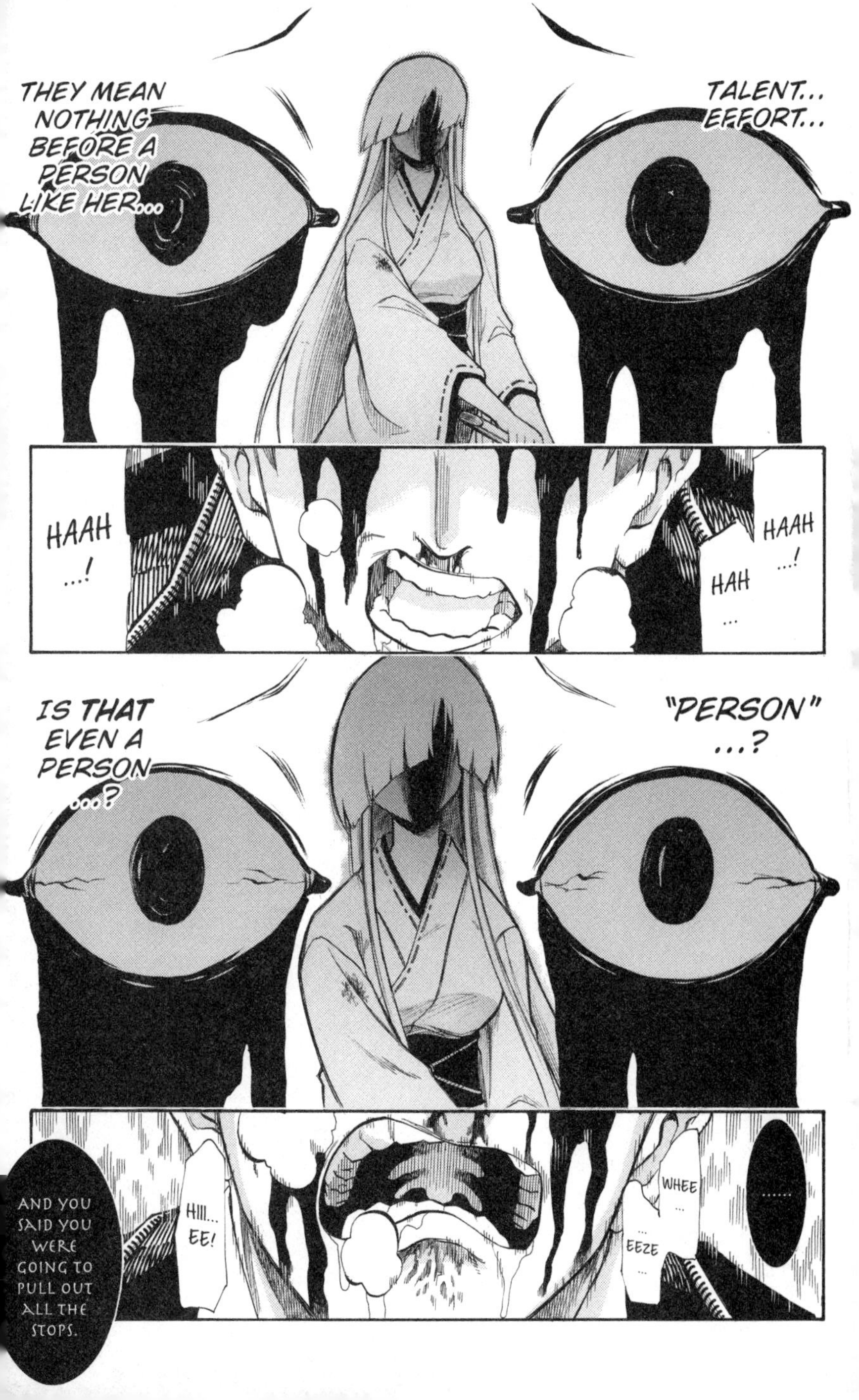
TALENT... EFFORT...
THEY MEAN NOTHING BEFORE A PERSON LIKE HER...
HAAH ...!
HAH ...
HAAH ...!
"PERSON" ...?
IS THAT EVEN A PERSON ...?
......
WHEE ... ... EEZE ...
HIII... EE!
AND YOU SAID YOU WERE GOING TO PULL OUT ALL THE STOPS.

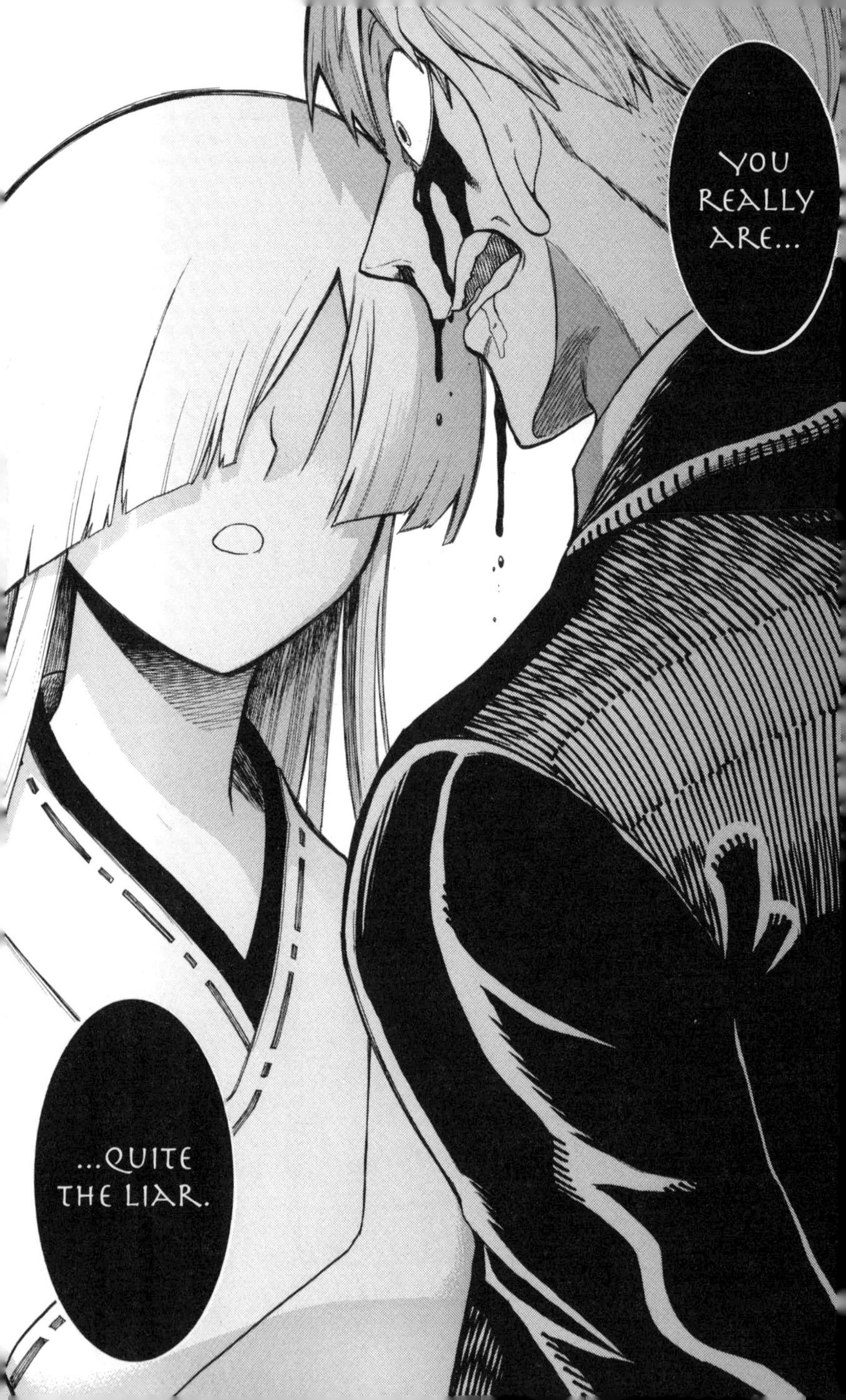
YOU REALLY ARE...
...QUITE THE LIAR.

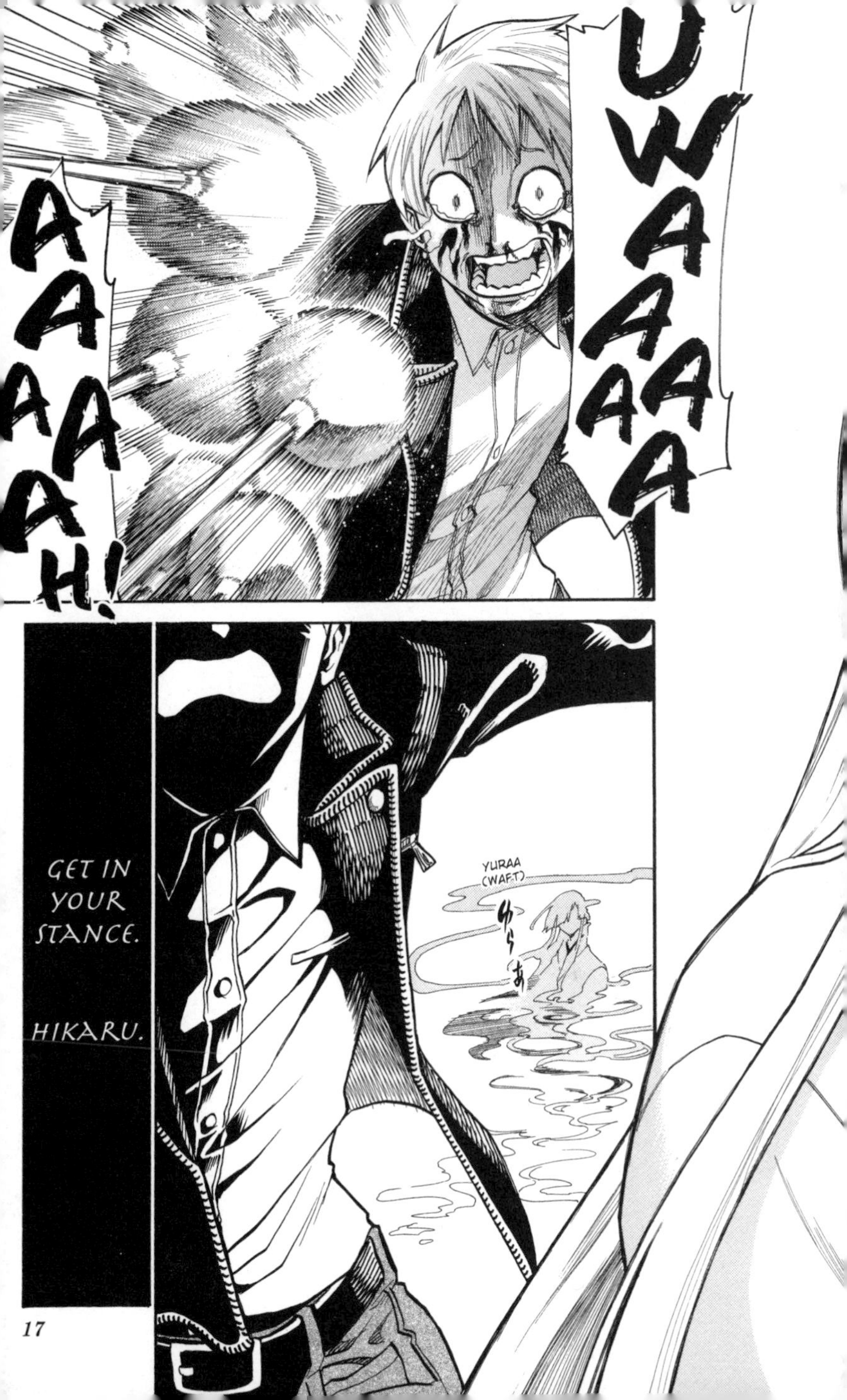

UWAAAAAA
AAAAAH!
YURAA (WAFT)
ゆらあ
GET IN YOUR STANCE.
HIKARU.

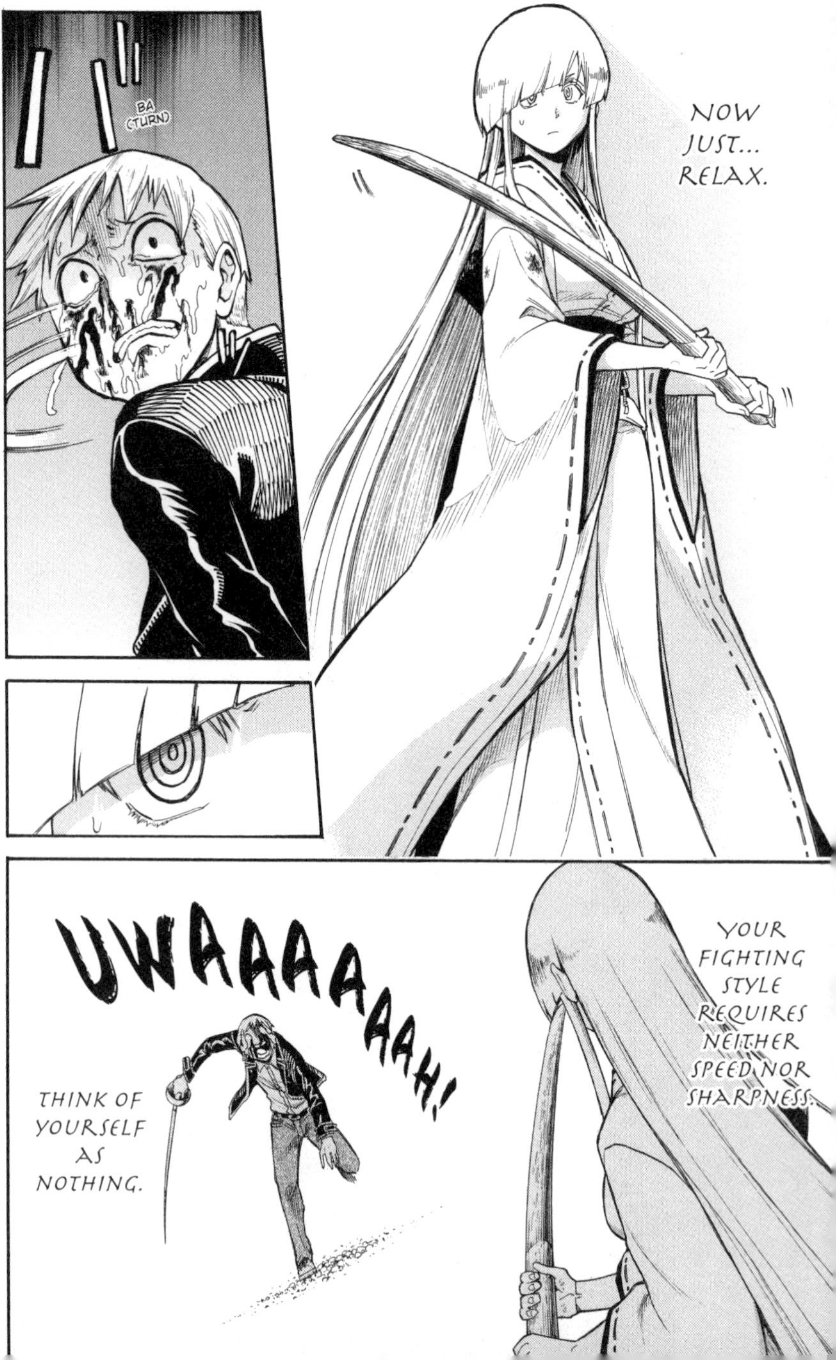
NOW JUST... RELAX.
BA (TURN)
YOUR FIGHTING STYLE REQUIRES NEITHER SPEED NOR SHARPNESS.
UWAAAAAAAAH!
THINK OF YOURSELF AS NOTHING.

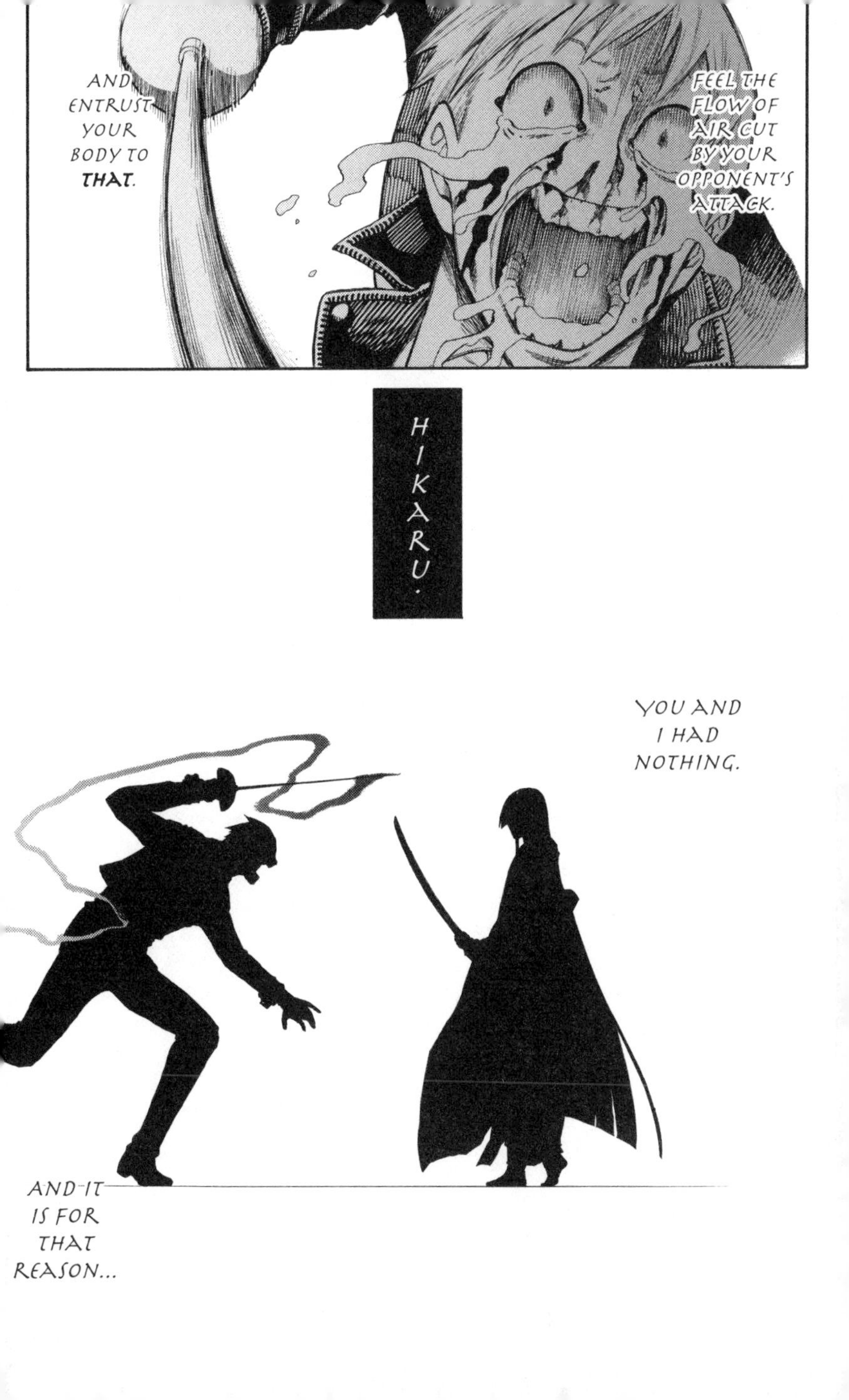
FEEL THE FLOW OF AIR CUT BY YOUR OPPONENT'S ATTACK.
AND ENTRUST YOUR BODY TO **THAT**.
HIKARU.
YOU AND I HAD NOTHING.
AND IT IS FOR THAT REASON...

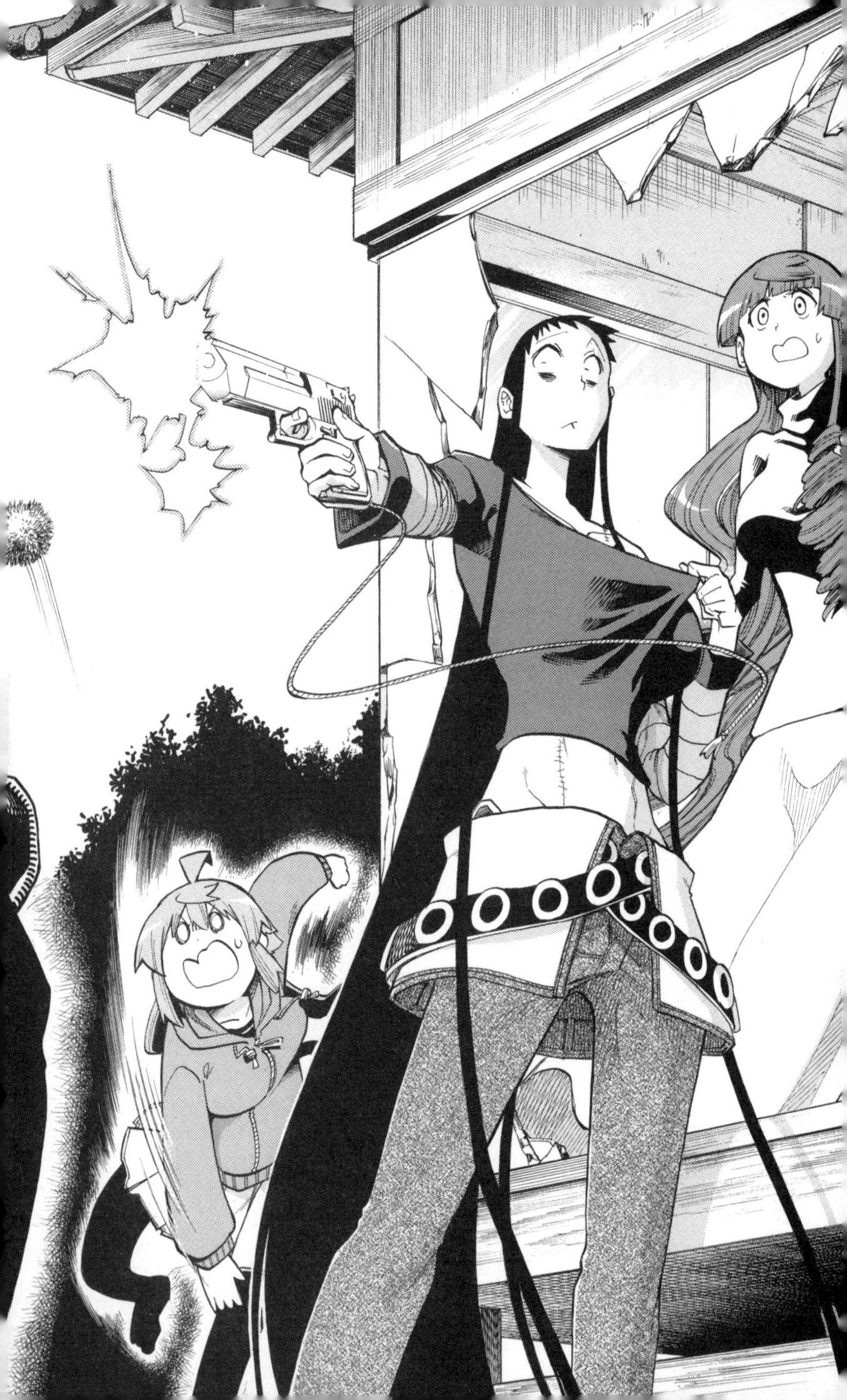

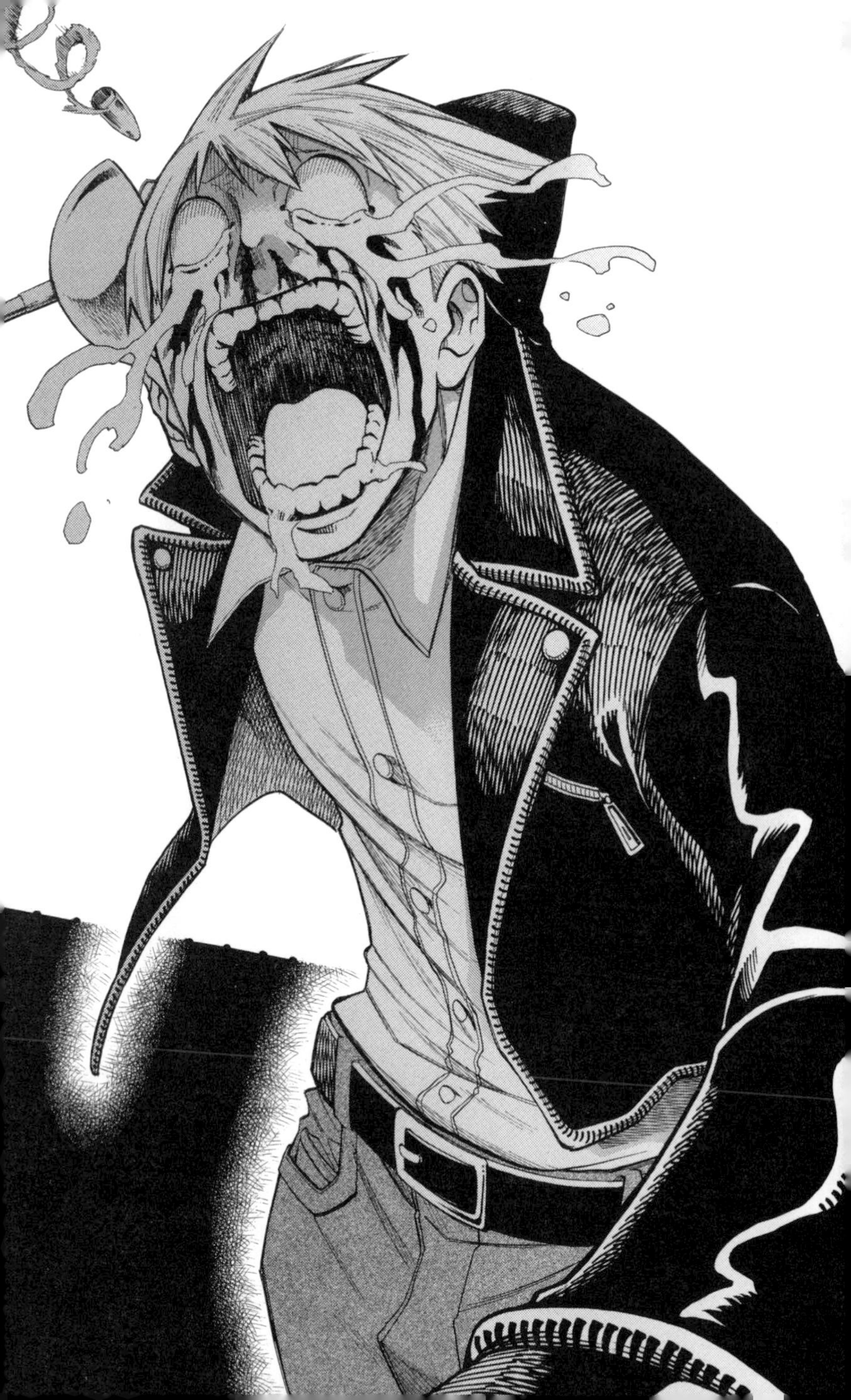

SAKU
(THUNK)

MURCIÉLAGO

Yoshimurakana

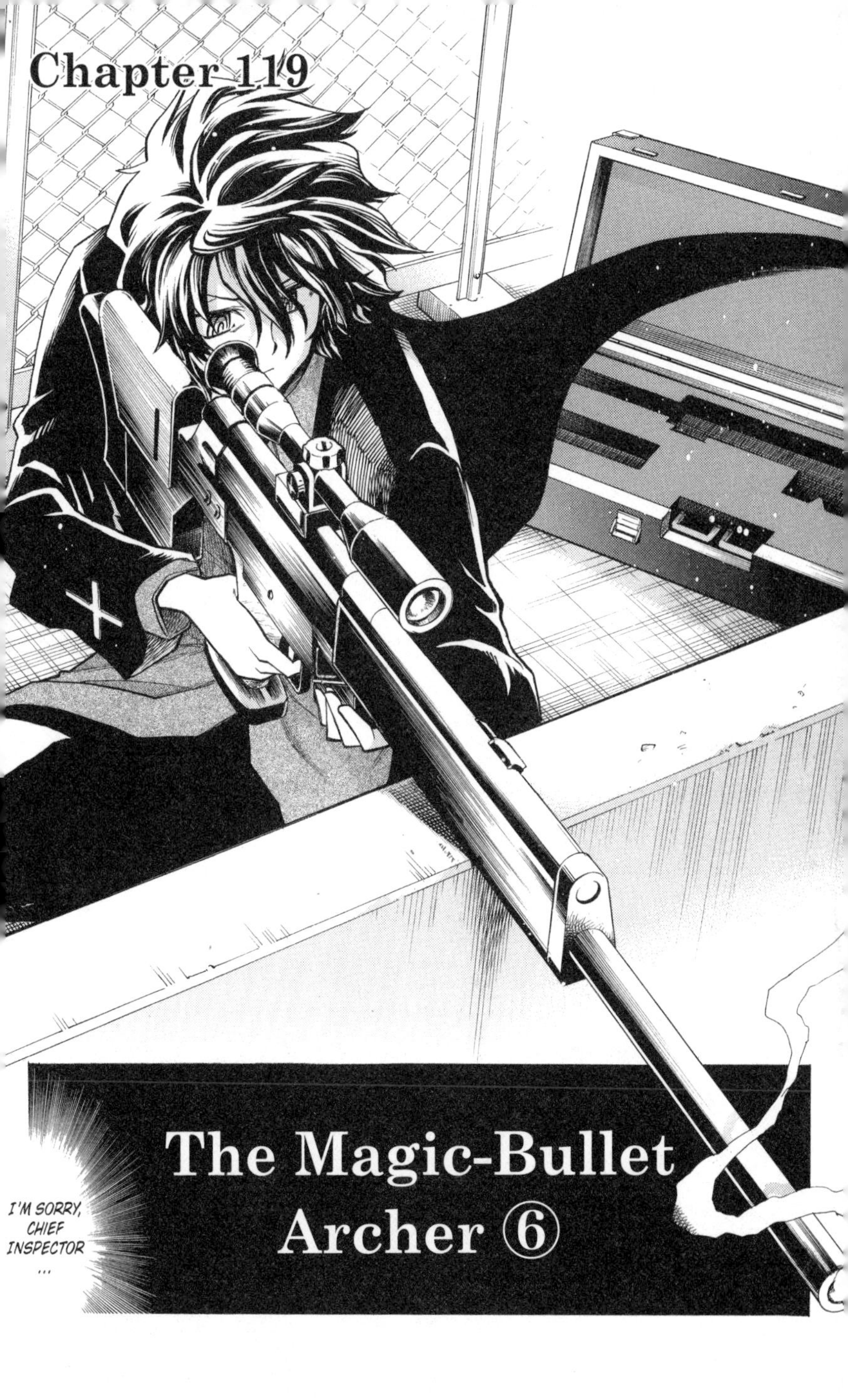
Chapter 119
The Magic-Bullet Archer ⑥
I'M SORRY, CHIEF INSPECTOR ...

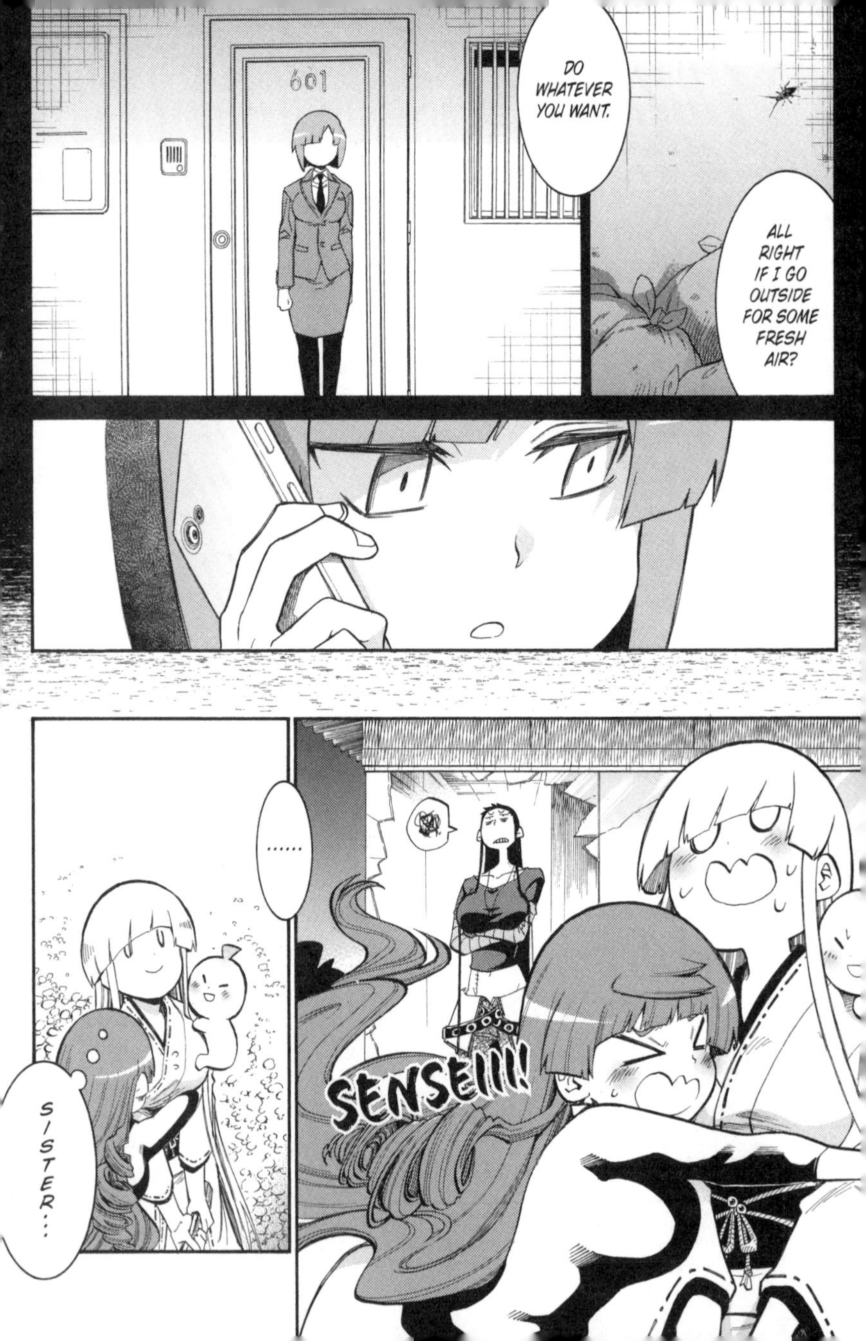
ALL RIGHT IF I GO OUTSIDE FOR SOME FRESH AIR?
DO WHATEVER YOU WANT.
......
SENSEIII!
SISTER...

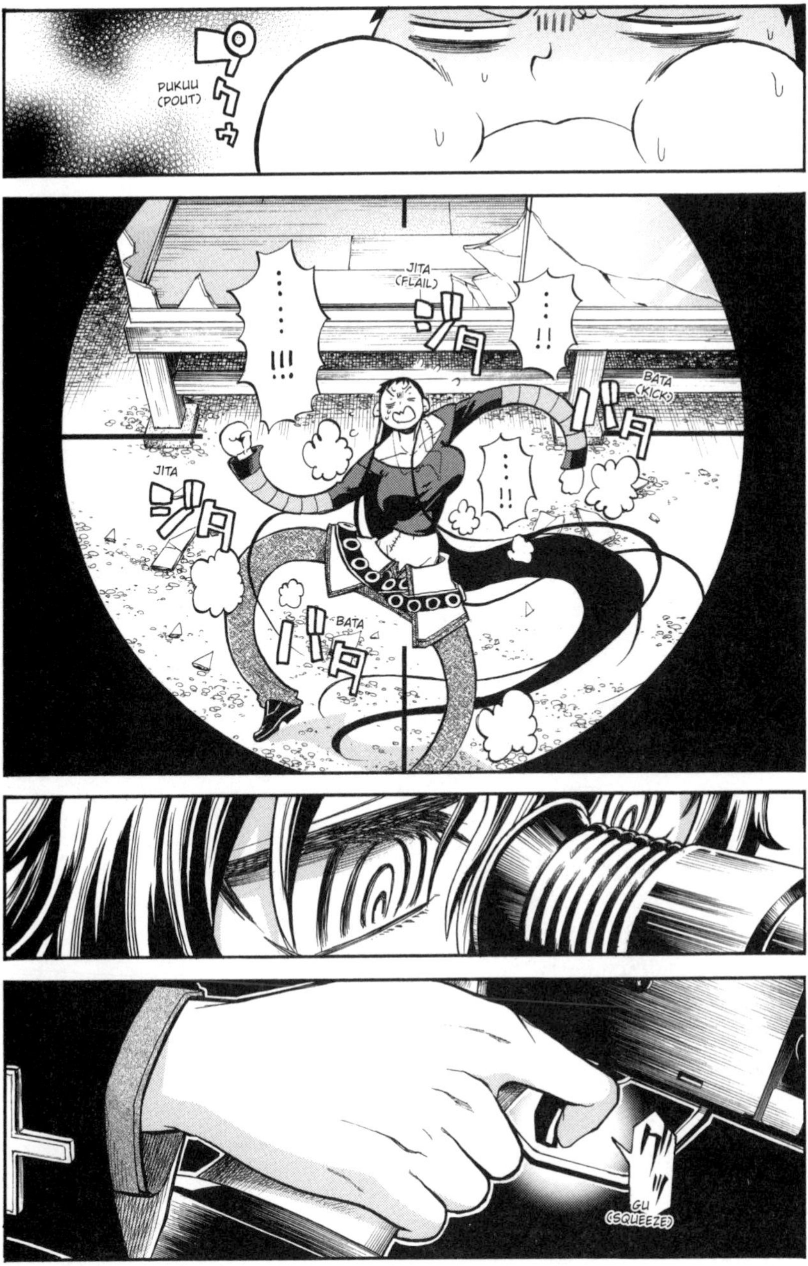

プクゥ
PUKUU (POUT)
...!!
バタ
BATA (KICK)
ジタ
JITA (FLAIL)
......!!!
...!!
ジタ
JITA
バタ
BATA
グ
GU (SQUEEZE)

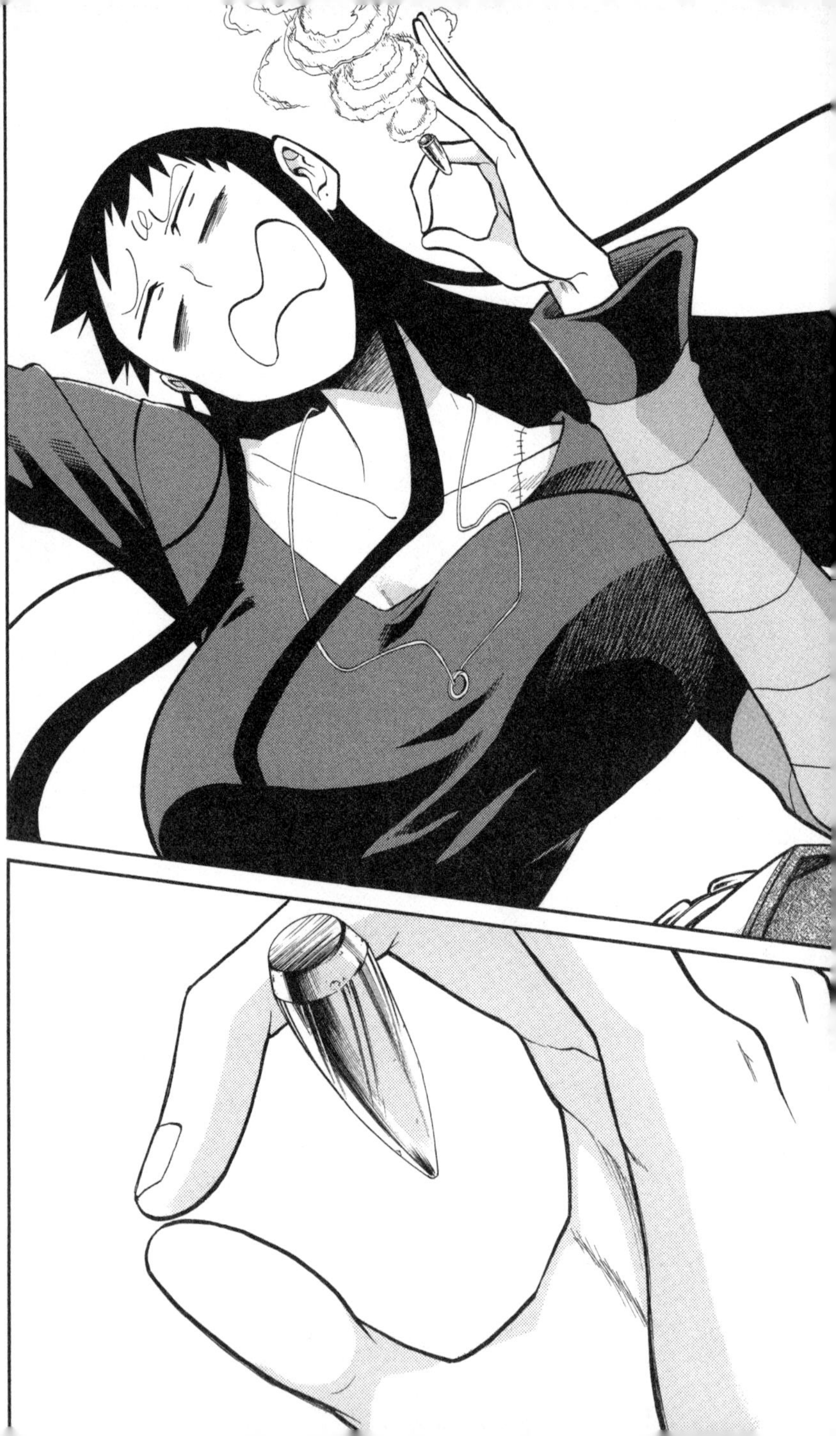

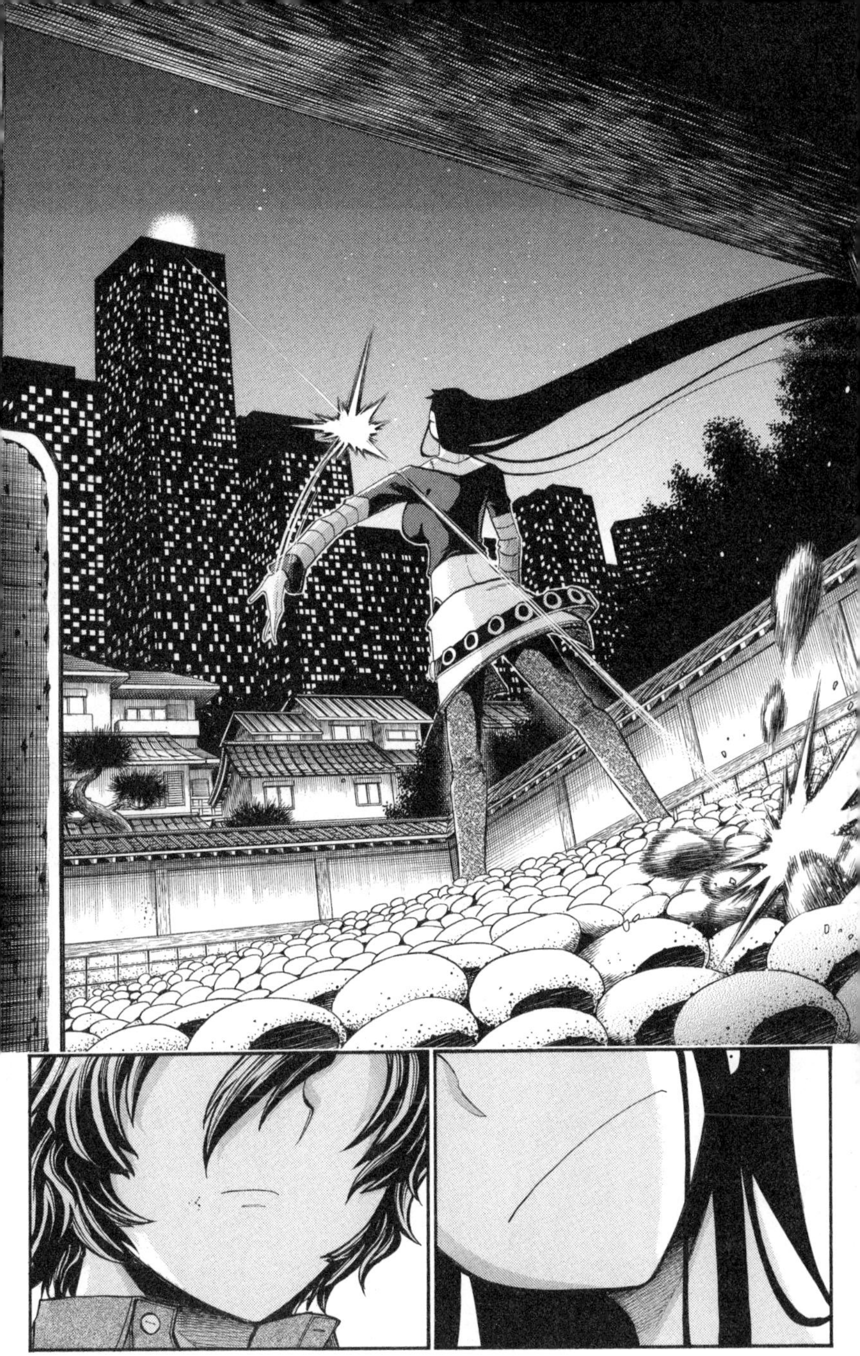

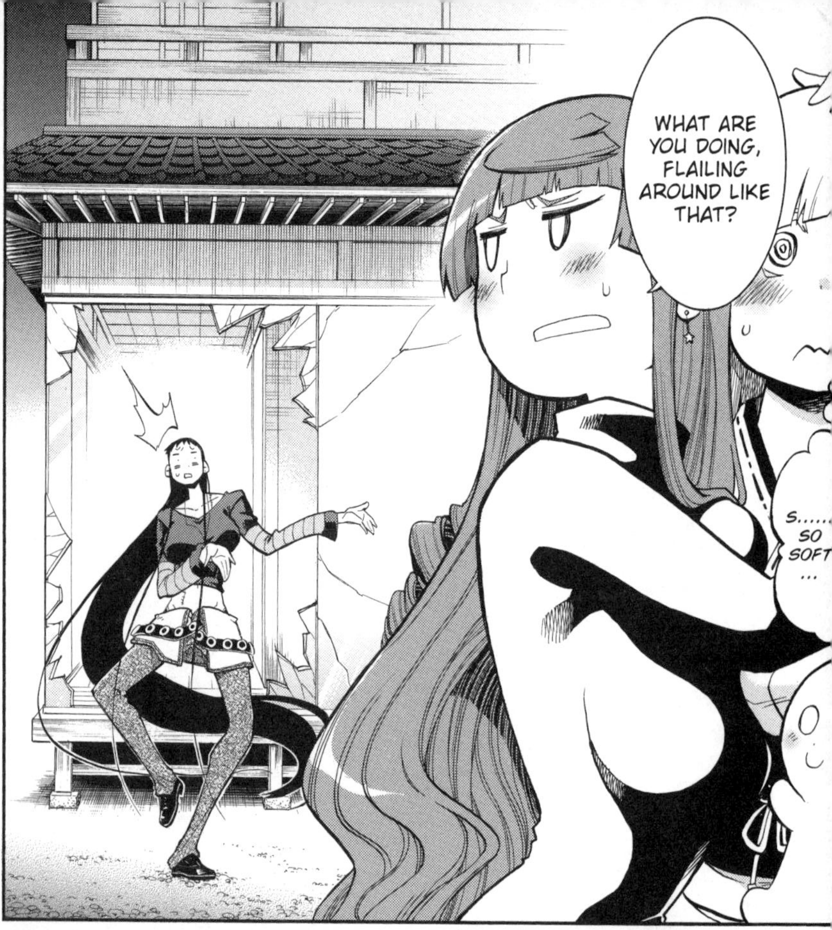
WHAT ARE YOU DOING, FLAILING AROUND LIKE THAT?
S...... SO SOFT ...

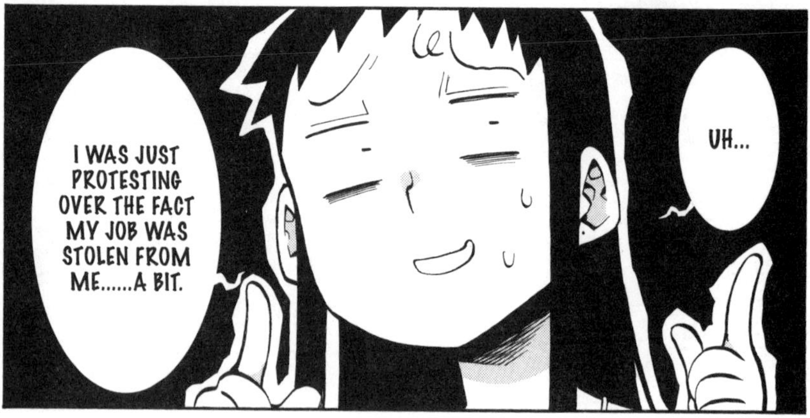
UH...
I WAS JUST PROTESTING OVER THE FACT MY JOB WAS STOLEN FROM ME......A BIT.

MURCIÉLAGO

MURCIÉLAGO

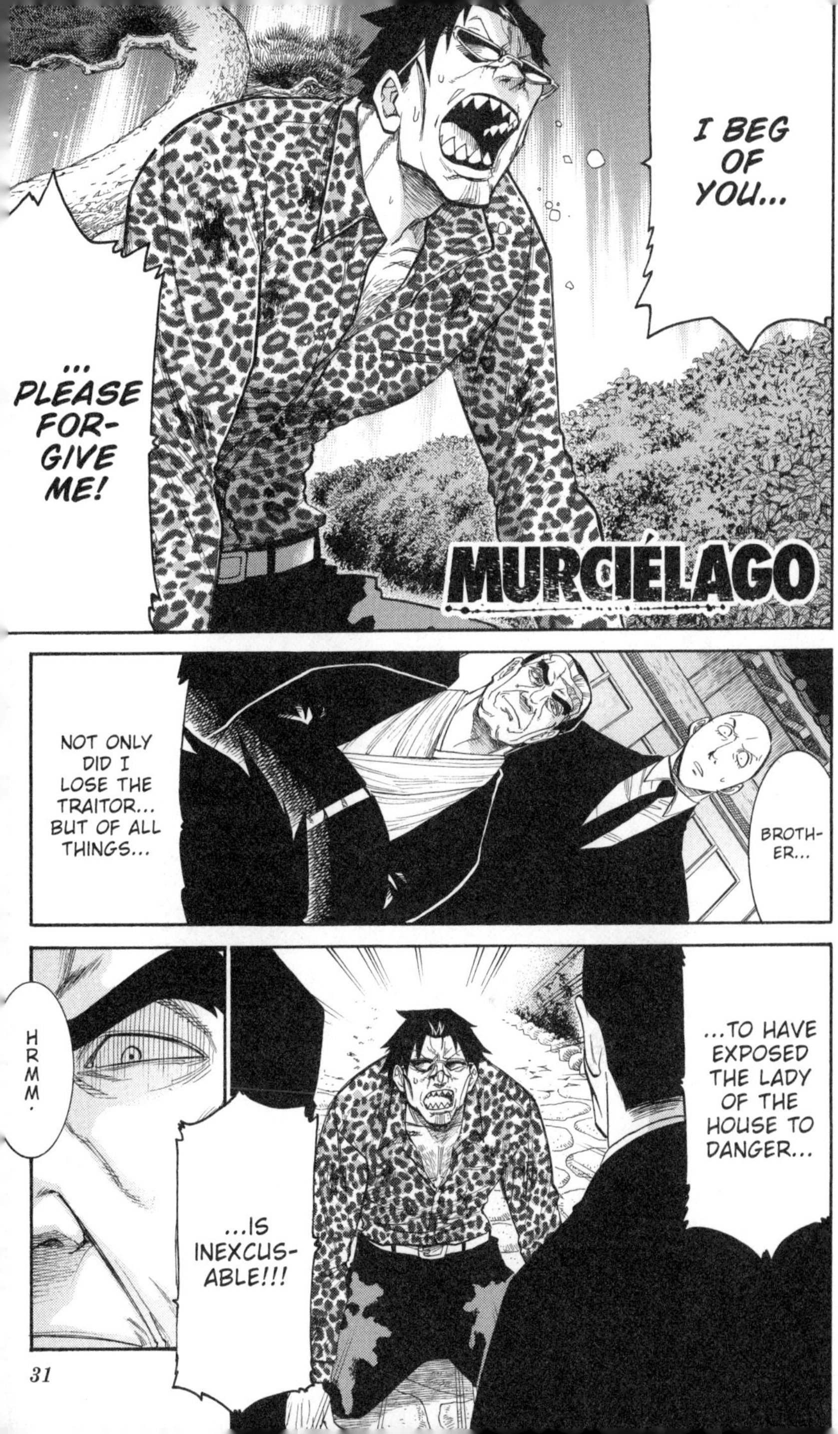
I BEG OF YOU...
...PLEASE FORGIVE ME!
MURCIÉLAGO
BROTHER...
NOT ONLY DID I LOSE THE TRAITOR... BUT OF ALL THINGS...
...TO HAVE EXPOSED THE LADY OF THE HOUSE TO DANGER...
...IS INEXCUSABLE!!!
HRMM.

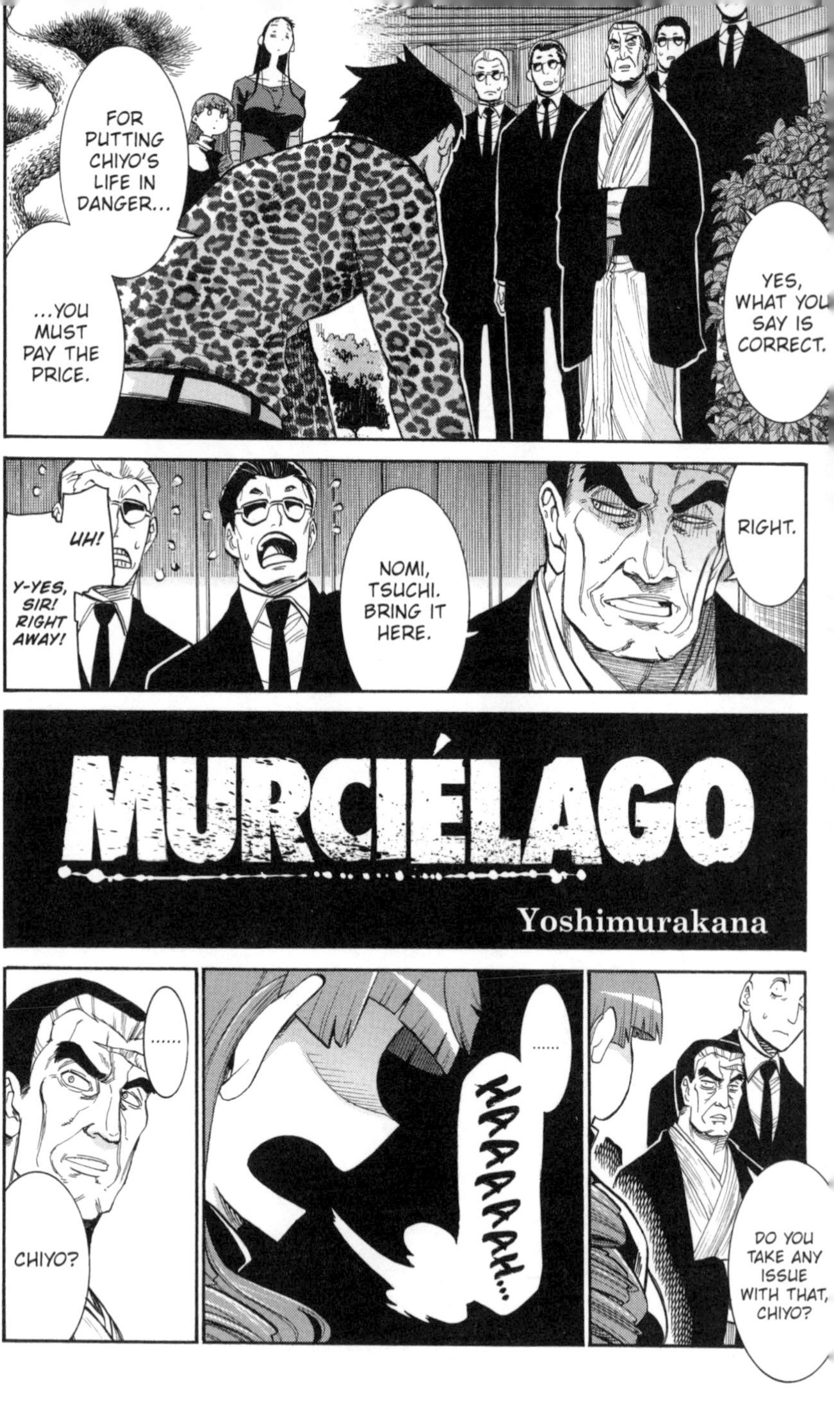
FOR PUTTING CHIYO'S LIFE IN DANGER...
...YOU MUST PAY THE PRICE.
YES, WHAT YOU SAY IS CORRECT.
RIGHT.
NOMI, TSUCHI. BRING IT HERE.
UH!
Y-YES, SIR! RIGHT AWAY!
MURCIÉLAGO
Yoshimurakana
DO YOU TAKE ANY ISSUE WITH THAT, CHIYO?
......
HAAAAAAAH...
......
CHIYO?

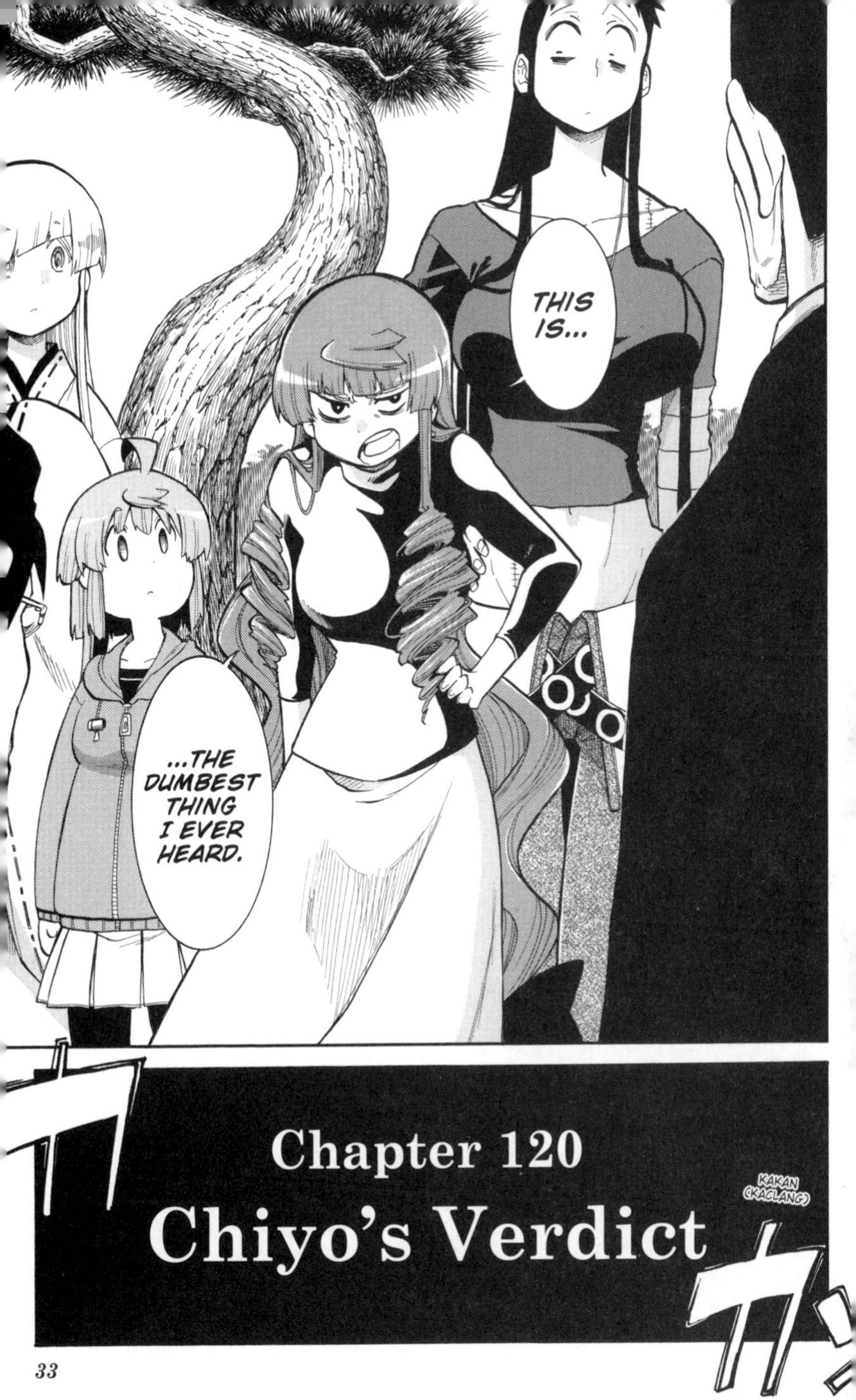
THIS IS...
...THE DUMBEST THING I EVER HEARD.
KAKAN (KACLANG)

Chapter 120
Chiyo's Verdict

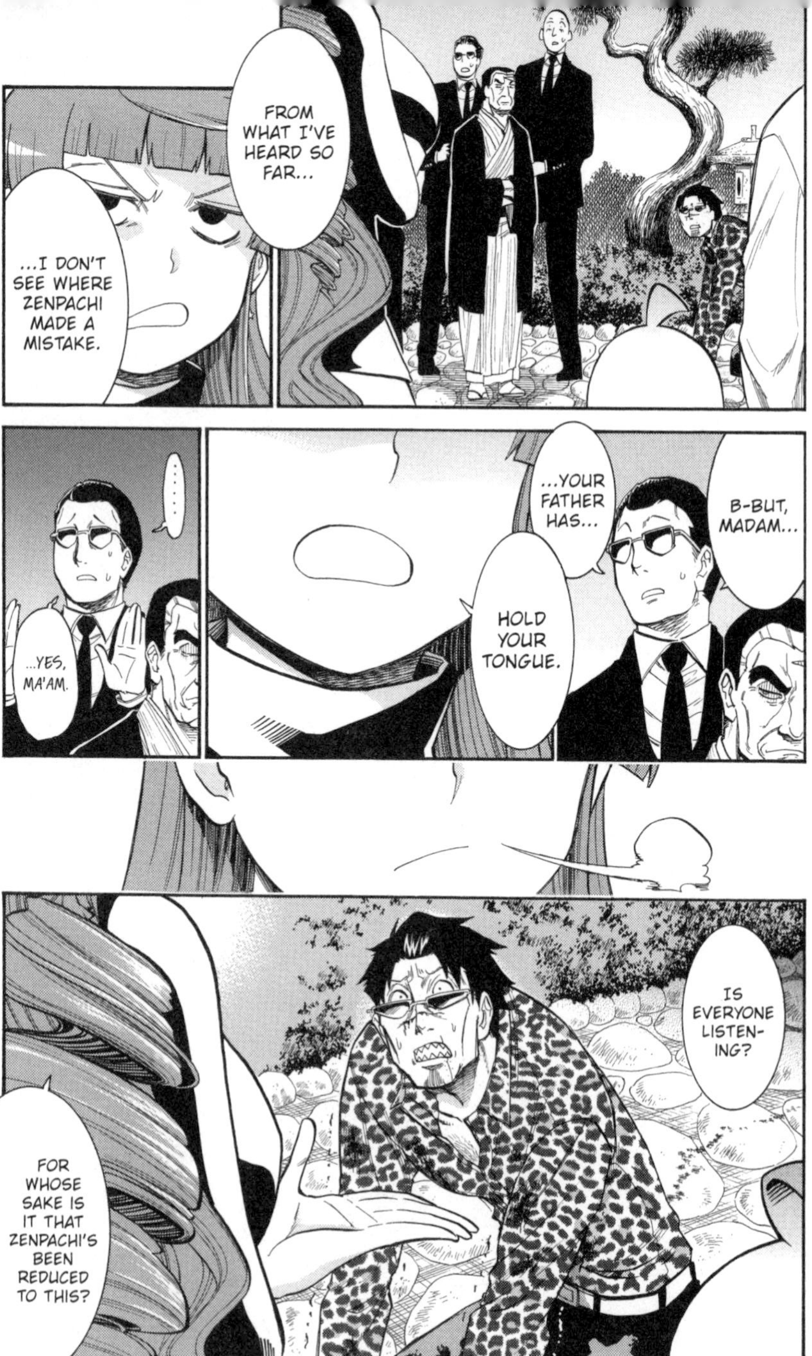
FROM WHAT I'VE HEARD SO FAR...
...I DON'T SEE WHERE ZENPACHI MADE A MISTAKE.
B-BUT, MADAM...
...YOUR FATHER HAS...
HOLD YOUR TONGUE.
......
...YES, MA'AM.
IS EVERYONE LISTEN-ING?
FOR WHOSE SAKE IS IT THAT ZENPACHI'S BEEN REDUCED TO THIS?

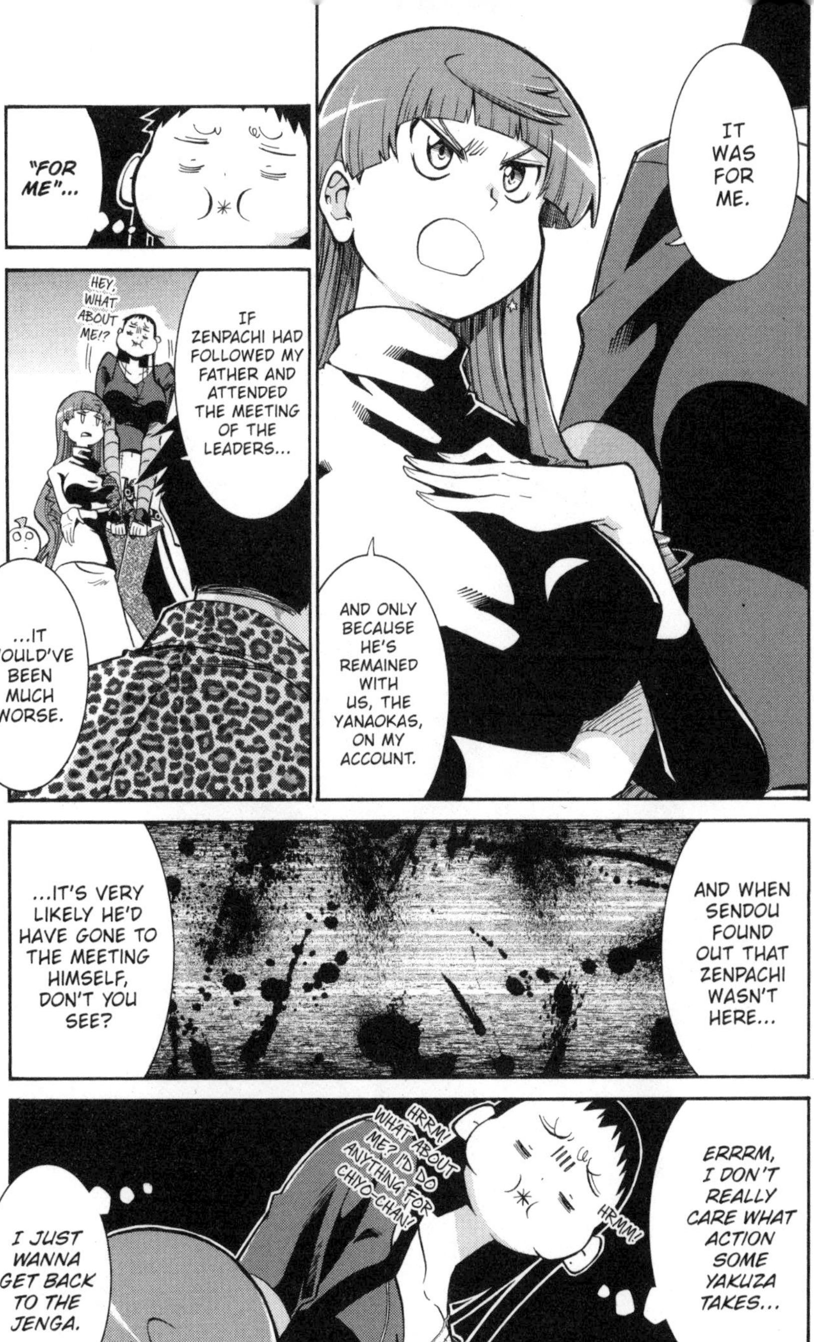
IT WAS FOR ME.
AND ONLY BECAUSE HE'S REMAINED WITH US, THE YANAOKAS, ON MY ACCOUNT.
"FOR ME"...
IF ZENPACHI HAD FOLLOWED MY FATHER AND ATTENDED THE MEETING OF THE LEADERS...
HEY, WHAT ABOUT ME!?
...IT WOULD'VE BEEN MUCH WORSE.
AND WHEN SENDOU FOUND OUT THAT ZENPACHI WASN'T HERE...
...IT'S VERY LIKELY HE'D HAVE GONE TO THE MEETING HIMSELF, DON'T YOU SEE?
ERRRM, I DON'T REALLY CARE WHAT ACTION SOME YAKUZA TAKES...
HRMM!
HRRM! WHAT ABOUT ME? I'D DO ANYTHING FOR CHIYO-CHAN!
I JUST WANNA GET BACK TO THE JENGA.

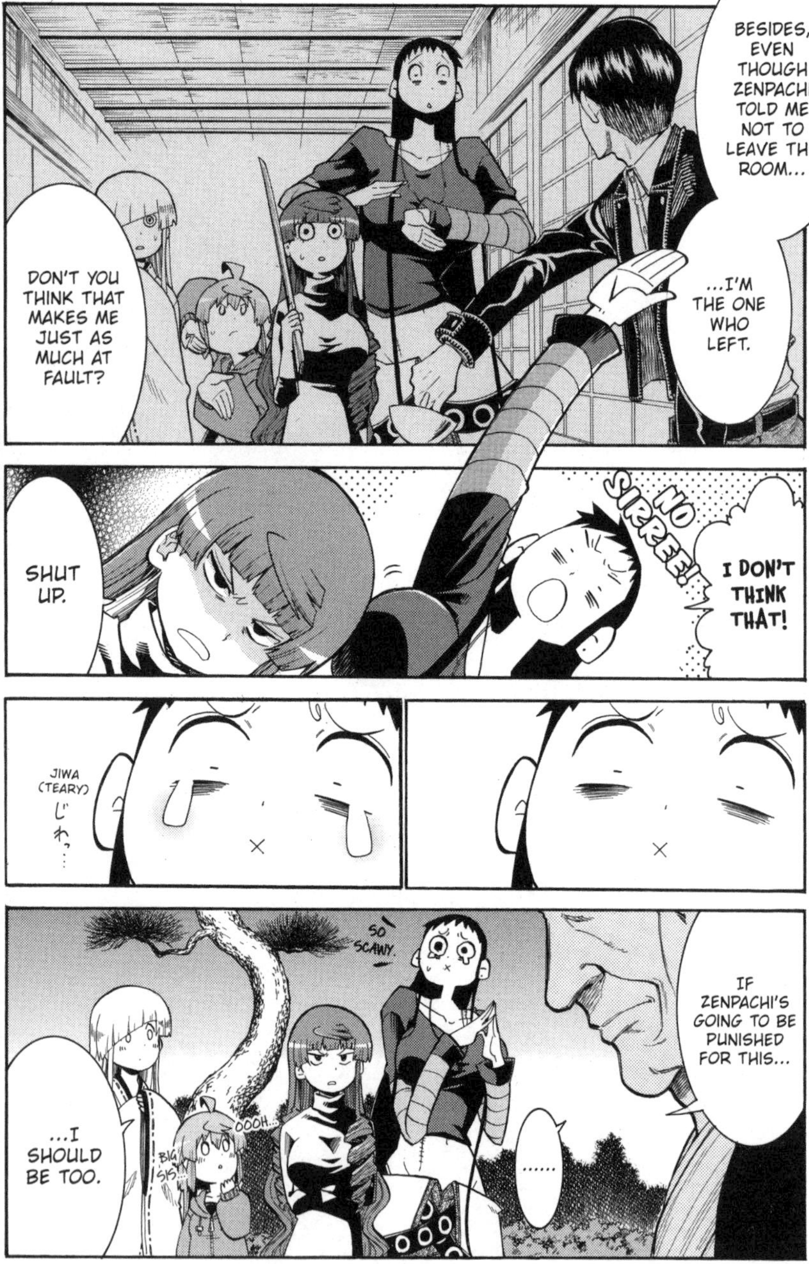
BESIDES, EVEN THOUGH ZENPACHI TOLD ME NOT TO LEAVE THE ROOM...
...I'M THE ONE WHO LEFT.
DON'T YOU THINK THAT MAKES ME JUST AS MUCH AT FAULT?
I DON'T THINK THAT!
NO SIRREE!
SHUT UP.
JIWA (TEARY)
じわ…
IF ZENPACHI'S GOING TO BE PUNISHED FOR THIS...
SO SCAWY.
......
OOOH...
BIG SIS...
...I SHOULD BE TOO.

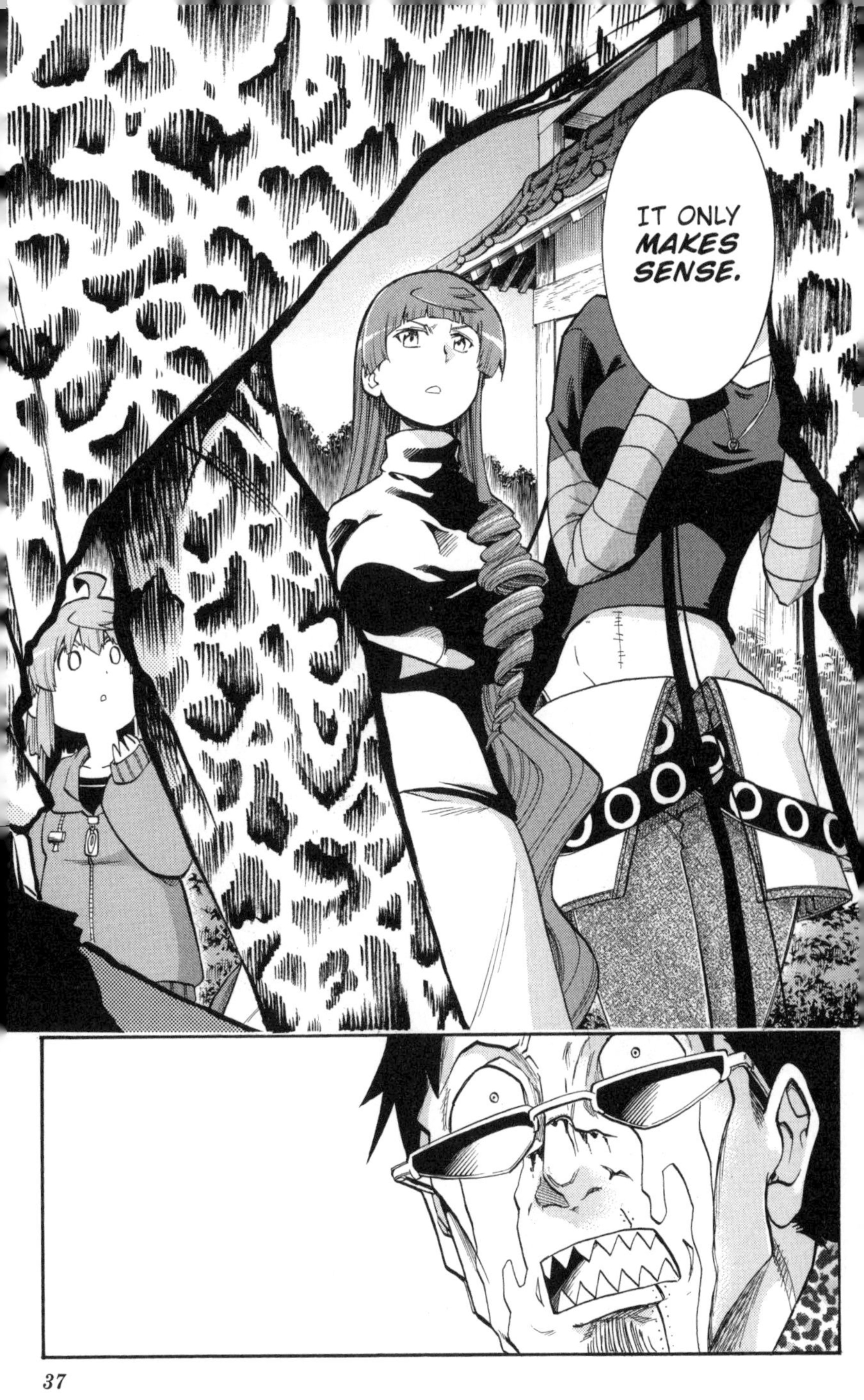
IT ONLY MAKES SENSE.

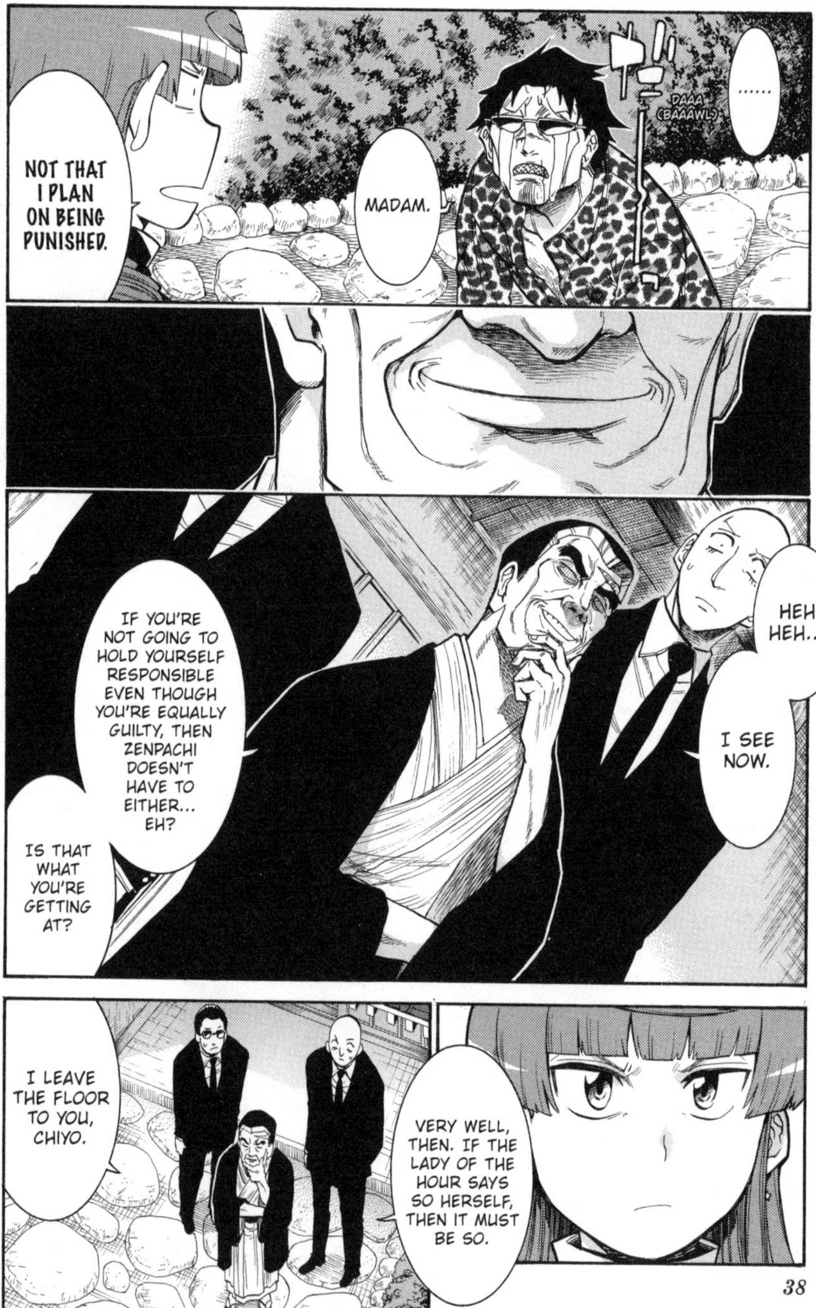
......
DAAA (BAAAWL)
MADAM.
NOT THAT I PLAN ON BEING PUNISHED.
HEH HEH...
I SEE NOW.
IF YOU'RE NOT GOING TO HOLD YOURSELF RESPONSIBLE EVEN THOUGH YOU'RE EQUALLY GUILTY, THEN ZENPACHI DOESN'T HAVE TO EITHER... EH?
IS THAT WHAT YOU'RE GETTING AT?
VERY WELL, THEN. IF THE LADY OF THE HOUR SAYS SO HERSELF, THEN IT MUST BE SO.
I LEAVE THE FLOOR TO YOU, CHIYO.

AH! BUT BOSS...

IT'S ABOUT TIME I GOT SOME SHUT-EYE.

GARARA (SLIDE)

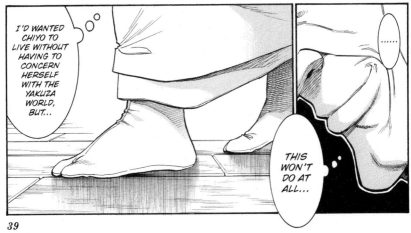

I'D WANTED CHIYO TO LIVE WITHOUT HAVING TO CONCERN HERSELF WITH THE YAKUZA WORLD, BUT...

......

THIS WON'T DO AT ALL...

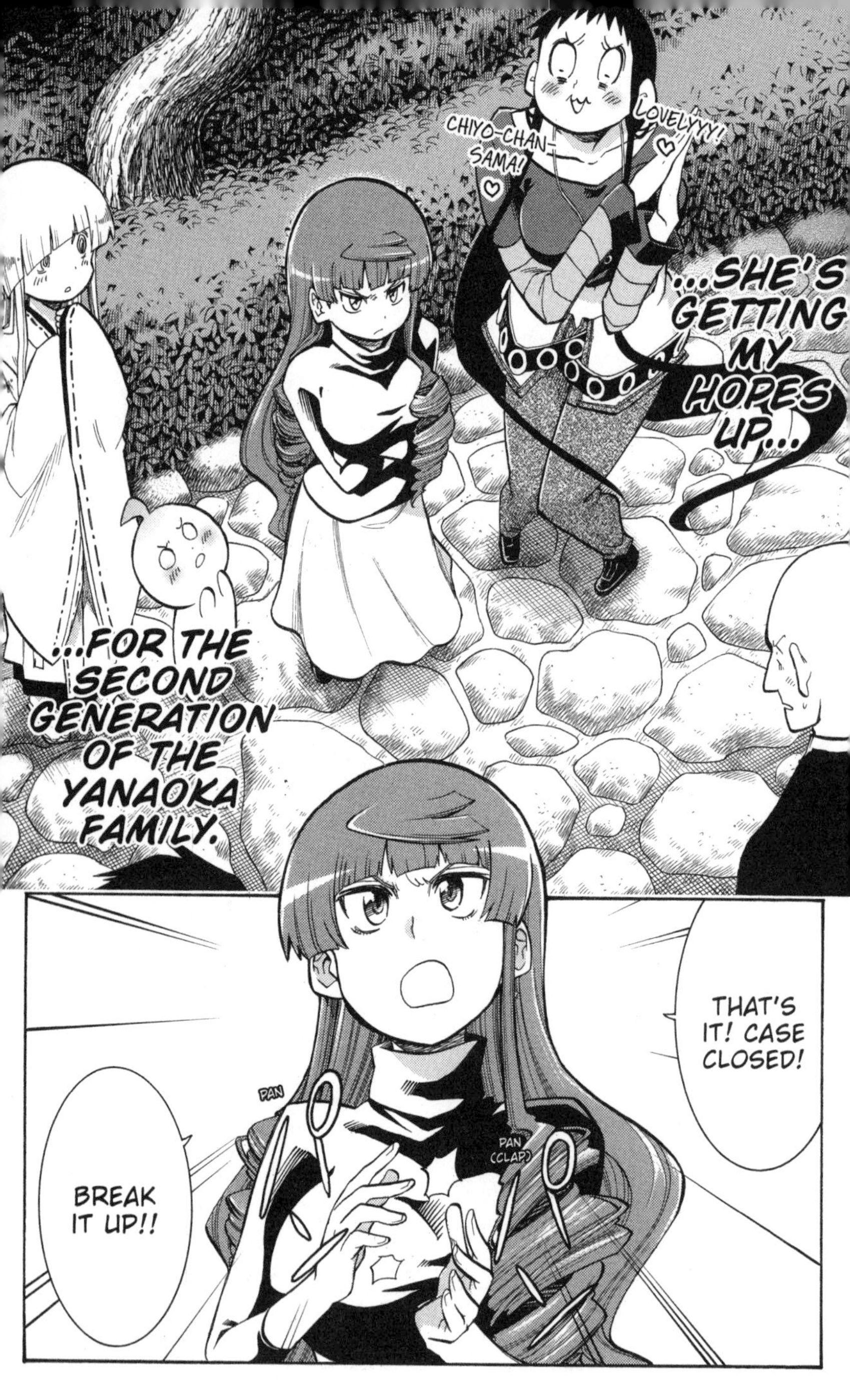
LOVELYYY!
CHIYO-CHAN-SAMA!
...SHE'S GETTING MY HOPES UP...
...FOR THE SECOND GENERATION OF THE YANAOKA FAMILY.
THAT'S IT! CASE CLOSED!
PAN (CLAP)
PAN
BREAK IT UP!!

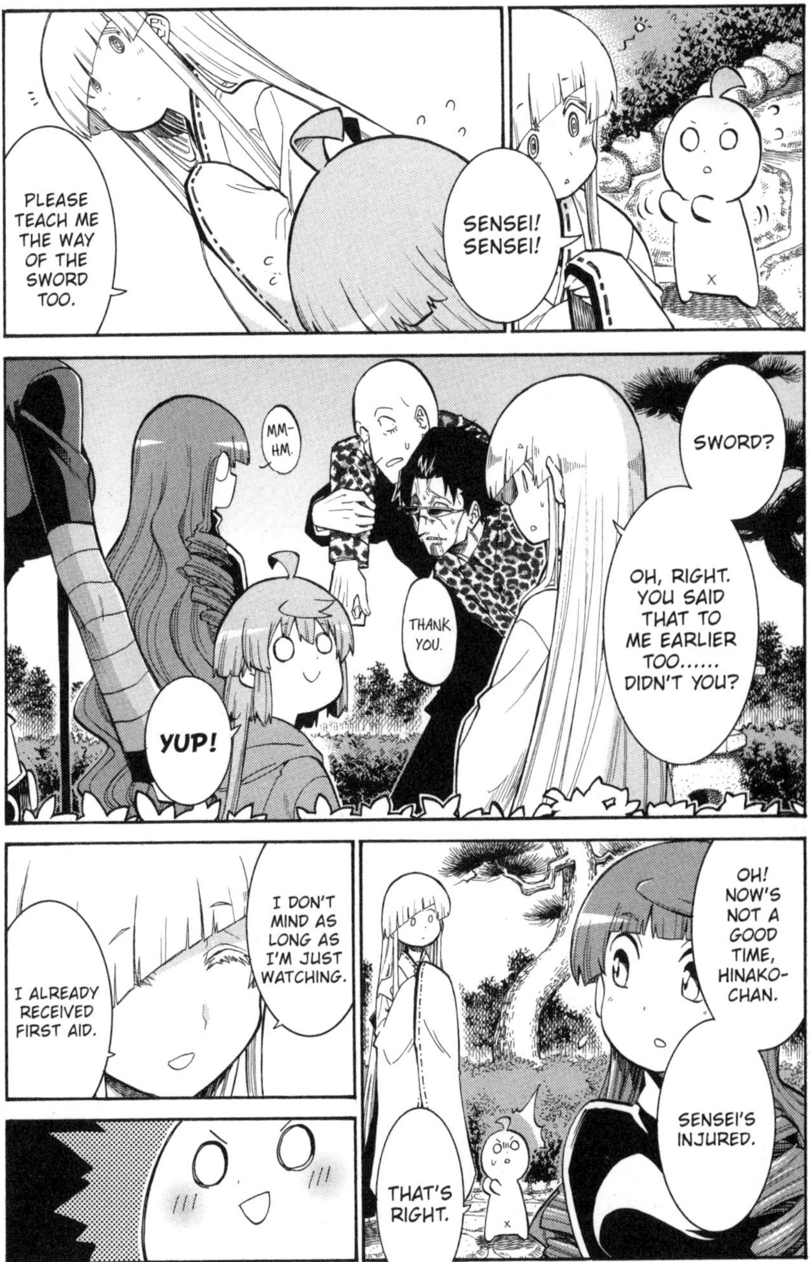
SENSEI! SENSEI!
PLEASE TEACH ME THE WAY OF THE SWORD TOO.
SWORD?
OH, RIGHT. YOU SAID THAT TO ME EARLIER TOO...... DIDN'T YOU?
THANK YOU.
MM-HM.
YUP!
OH! NOW'S NOT A GOOD TIME, HINAKO-CHAN.
SENSEI'S INJURED.
THAT'S RIGHT.
I DON'T MIND AS LONG AS I'M JUST WATCHING.
I ALREADY RECEIVED FIRST AID.

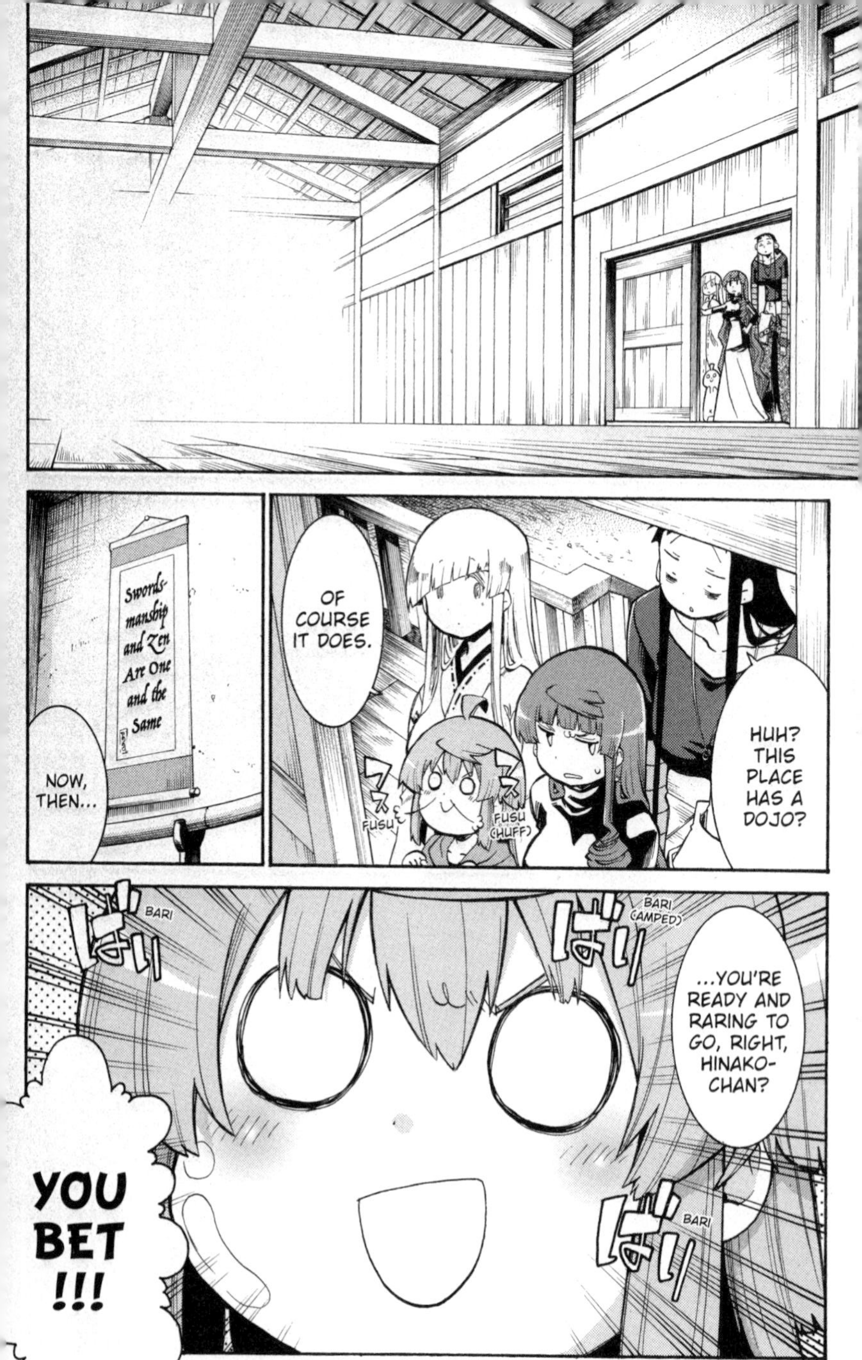
HUH? THIS PLACE HAS A DOJO?
OF COURSE IT DOES.
FUSU (HUFF)
FUSU
Swordsmanship and Zen Are One and the Same
NOW, THEN...
BARI (AMPED)
...YOU'RE READY AND RARING TO GO, RIGHT, HINAKO-CHAN?
BARI
BARI
YOU BET!!!

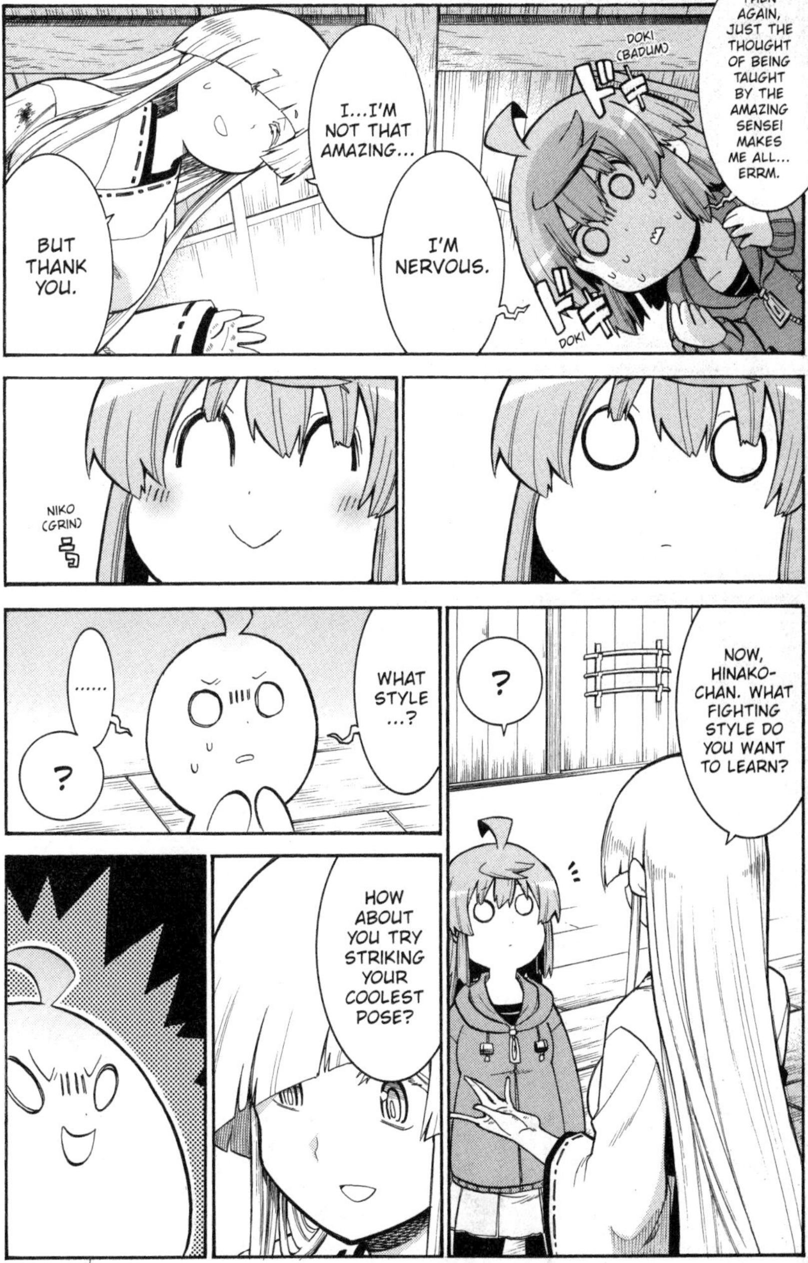
THEN AGAIN, JUST THE THOUGHT OF BEING TAUGHT BY THE AMAZING SENSEI MAKES ME ALL... ERRM.
DOKI (BADUM)
I'M NERVOUS.
DOKI
I...I'M NOT THAT AMAZING...
BUT THANK YOU.
NIKO (GRIN)
NOW, HINAKO-CHAN. WHAT FIGHTING STYLE DO YOU WANT TO LEARN?
?
WHAT STYLE ...?
......
?
HOW ABOUT YOU TRY STRIKING YOUR COOLEST POSE?

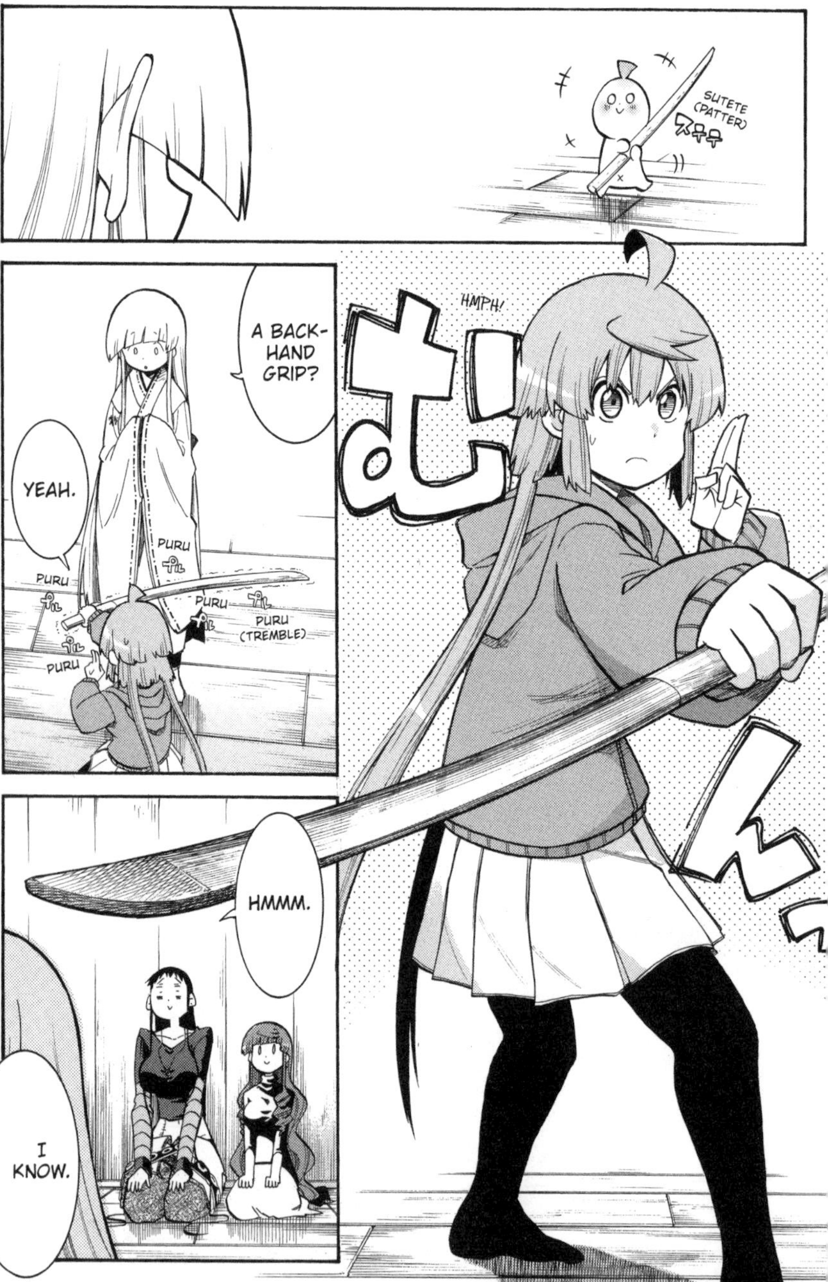
SUTETE (PATTER)
ステテ
HMPH!
む
ん
A BACK-HAND GRIP?
YEAH.
PURU
PURU
PURU
PURU
PURU (TREMBLE)
HMMM.
I KNOW.

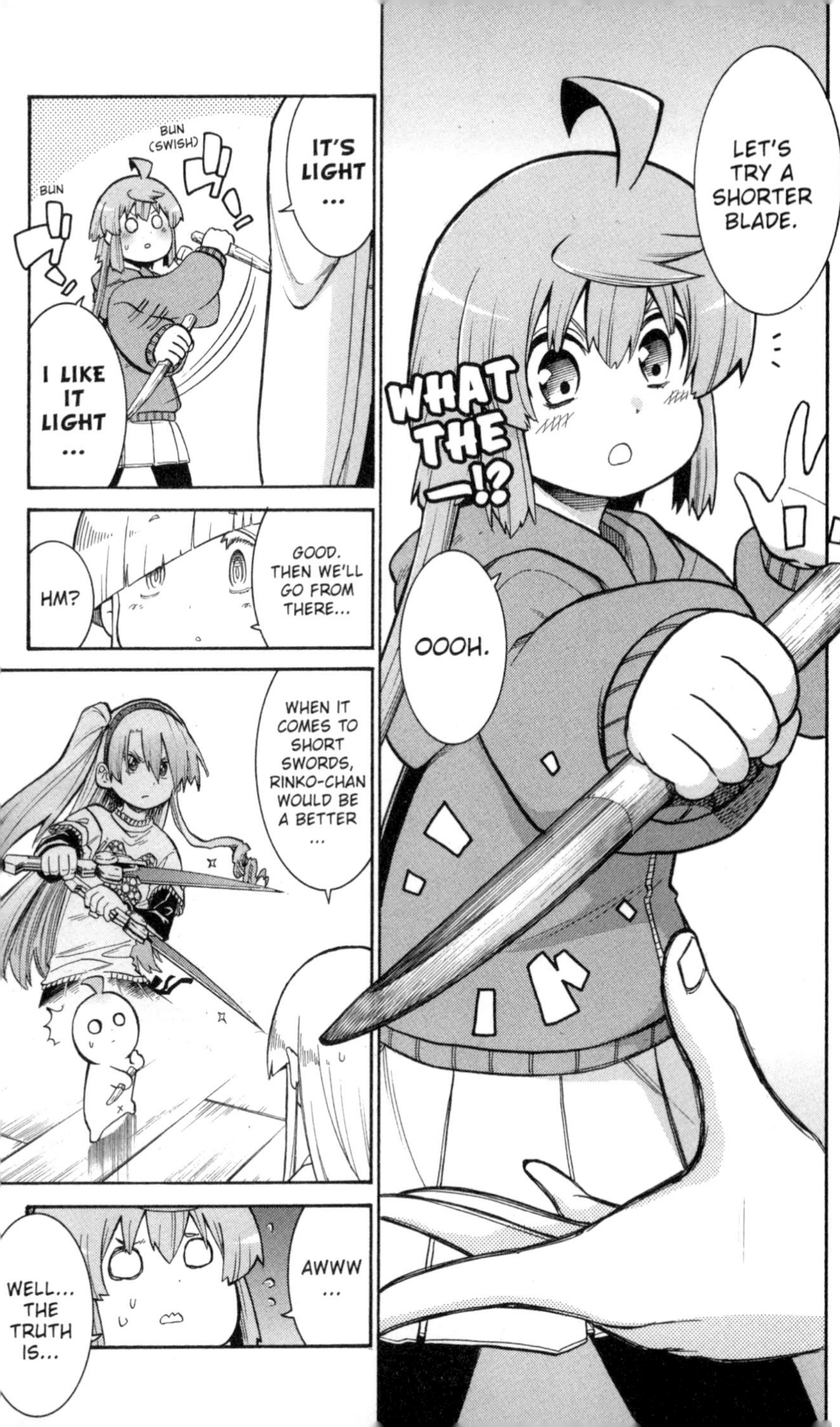
LET'S TRY A SHORTER BLADE.
WHAT THE—!?
OOOH.
IT'S LIGHT...
BUN (SWISH)
BUN
I LIKE IT LIGHT...
GOOD. THEN WE'LL GO FROM THERE...
HM?
WHEN IT COMES TO SHORT SWORDS, RINKO-CHAN WOULD BE A BETTER...
AWWW...
WELL... THE TRUTH IS...

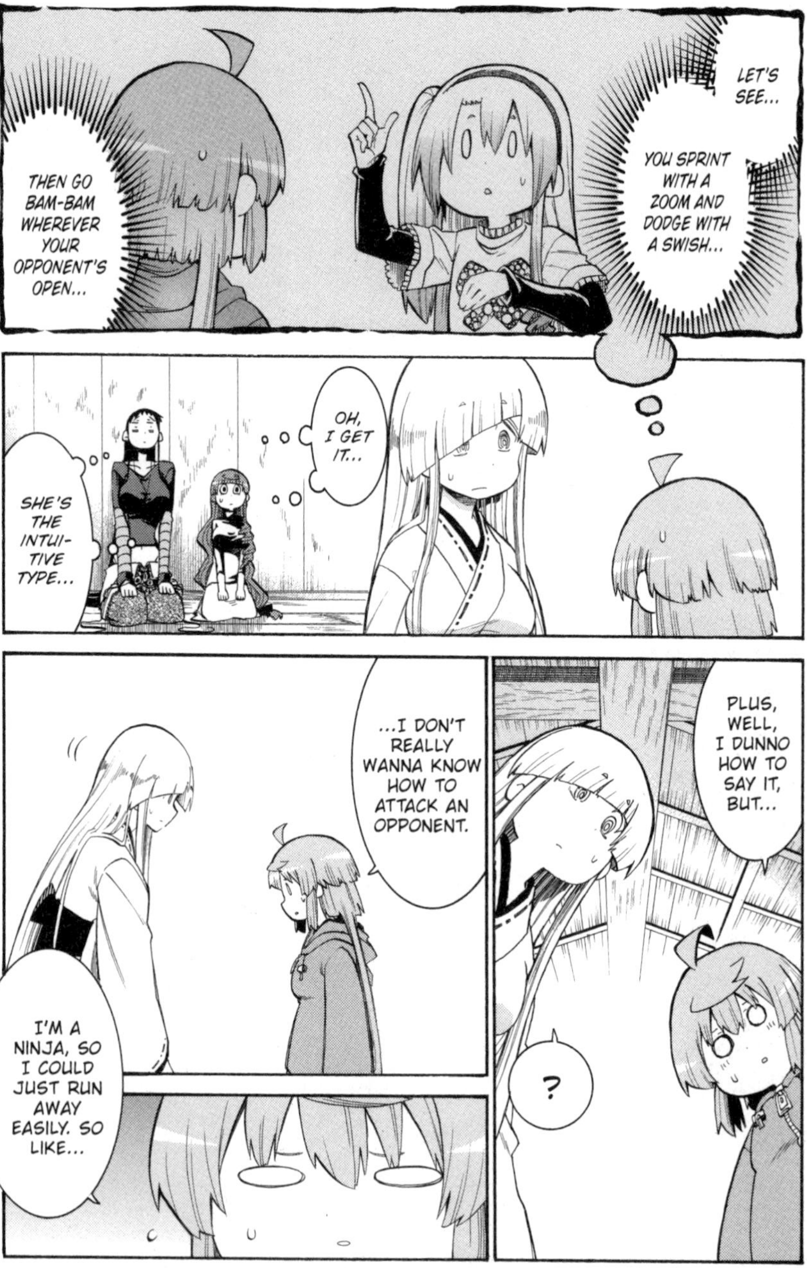
LET'S SEE...
YOU SPRINT WITH A ZOOM AND DODGE WITH A SWISH...
THEN GO BAM-BAM WHEREVER YOUR OPPONENT'S OPEN...
OH, I GET IT...
SHE'S THE INTUI-TIVE TYPE...
PLUS, WELL, I DUNNO HOW TO SAY IT, BUT...
?
...I DON'T REALLY WANNA KNOW HOW TO ATTACK AN OPPONENT.
I'M A NINJA, SO I COULD JUST RUN AWAY EASILY. SO LIKE...

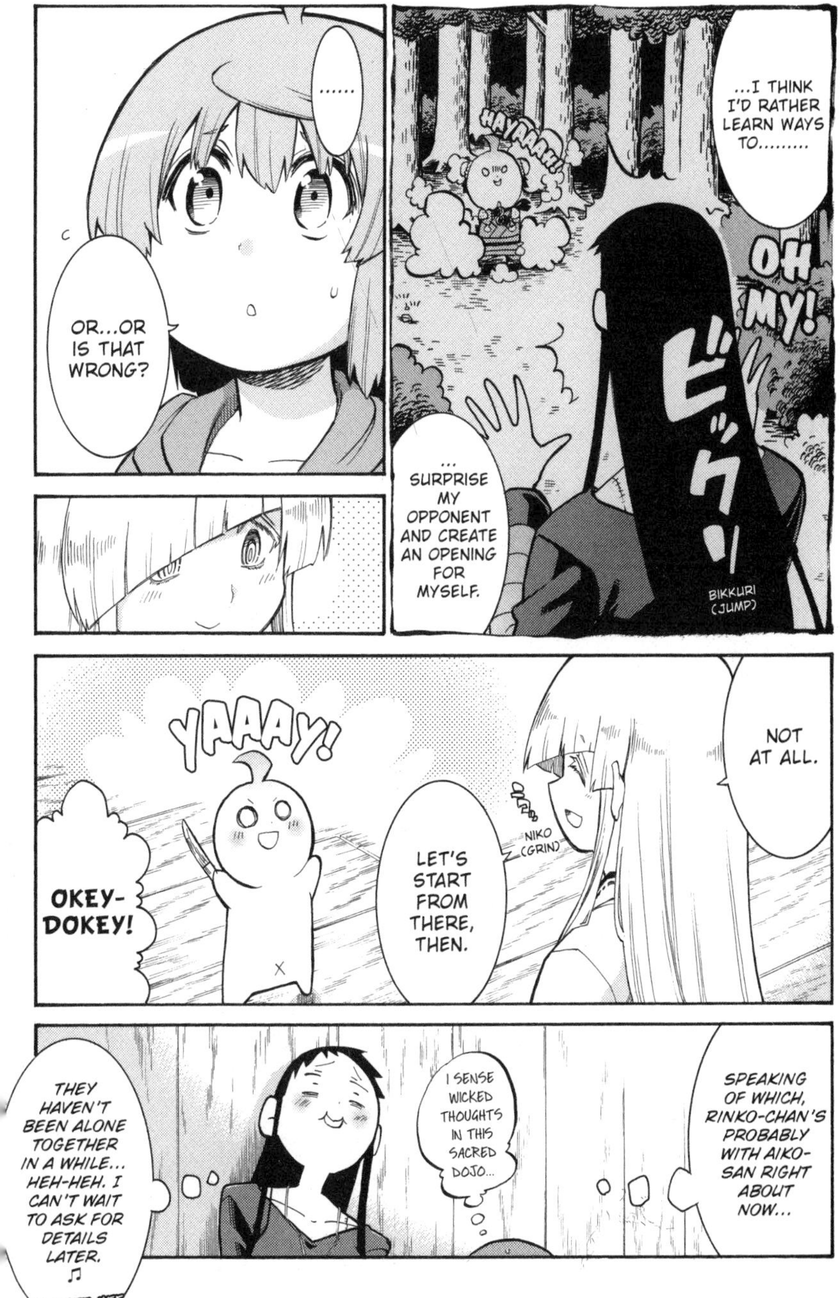
...I THINK I'D RATHER LEARN WAYS TO.........
HAYAAAH!
OH MY!
ビクッ
BIKKURI (JUMP)
... SURPRISE MY OPPONENT AND CREATE AN OPENING FOR MYSELF.
......
OR...OR IS THAT WRONG?
NOT AT ALL.
NIKO (GRIN)
LET'S START FROM THERE, THEN.
YAAAY!
OKEY-DOKEY!
SPEAKING OF WHICH, RINKO-CHAN'S PROBABLY WITH AIKO-SAN RIGHT ABOUT NOW...
I SENSE WICKED THOUGHTS IN THIS SACRED DOJO...
THEY HAVEN'T BEEN ALONE TOGETHER IN A WHILE... HEH-HEH. I CAN'T WAIT TO ASK FOR DETAILS LATER. ♫
NYEE-HEE-HEE.

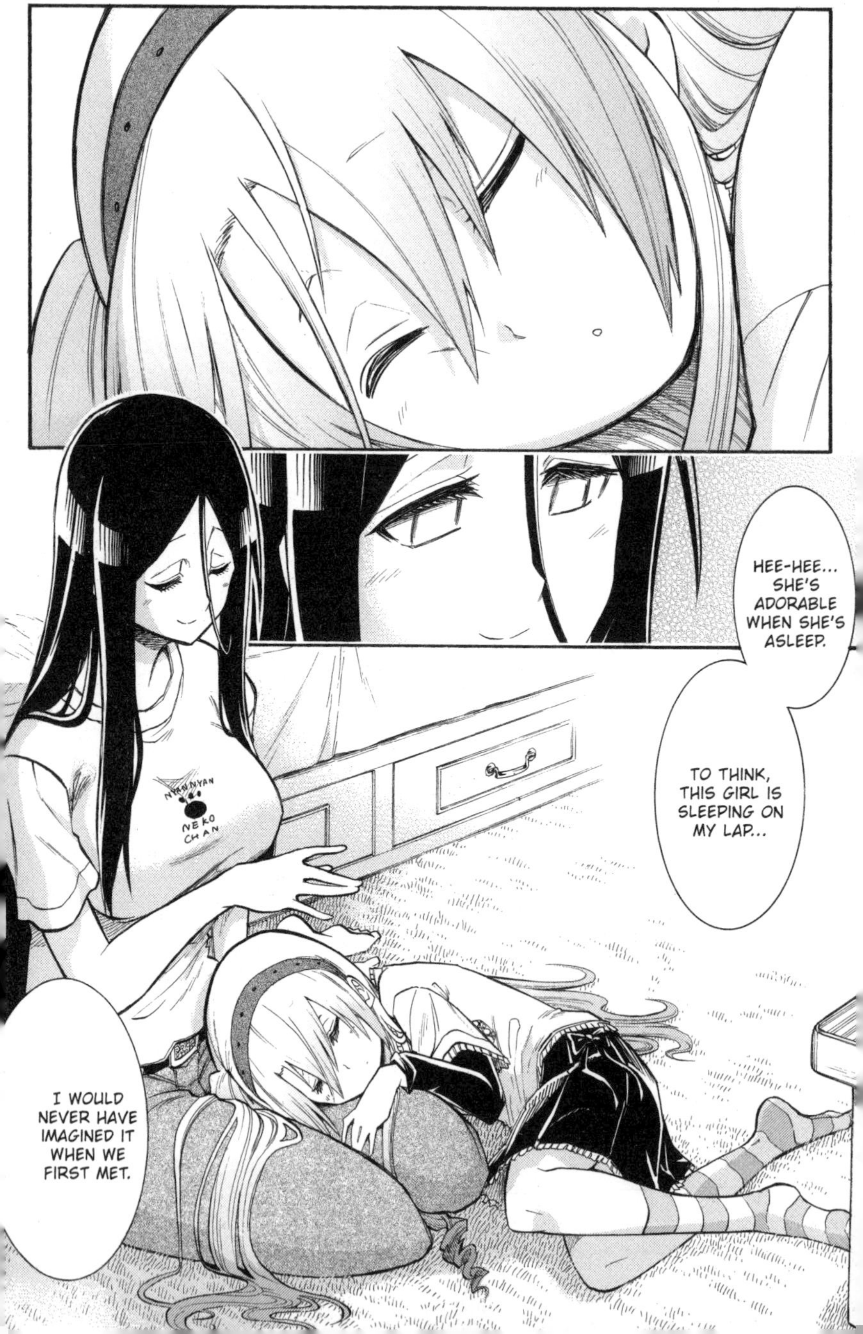
HEE-HEE... SHE'S ADORABLE WHEN SHE'S ASLEEP.
TO THINK, THIS GIRL IS SLEEPING ON MY LAP...
I WOULD NEVER HAVE IMAGINED IT WHEN WE FIRST MET.
NYAN NYAN NEKO CHAN

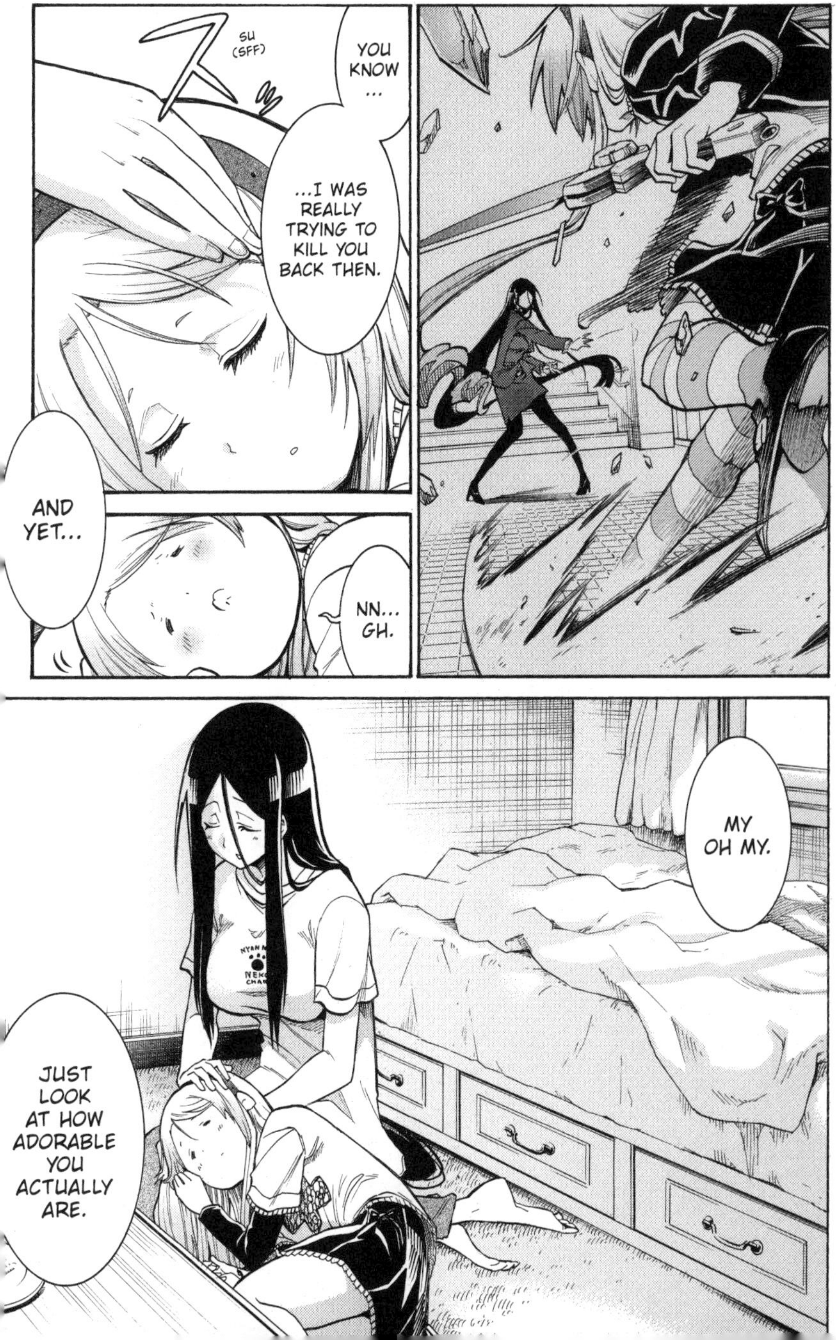
SU (SFF)
YOU KNOW...
...I WAS REALLY TRYING TO KILL YOU BACK THEN.
AND YET...
NN... GH.
MY OH MY.
JUST LOOK AT HOW ADORABLE YOU ACTUALLY ARE.

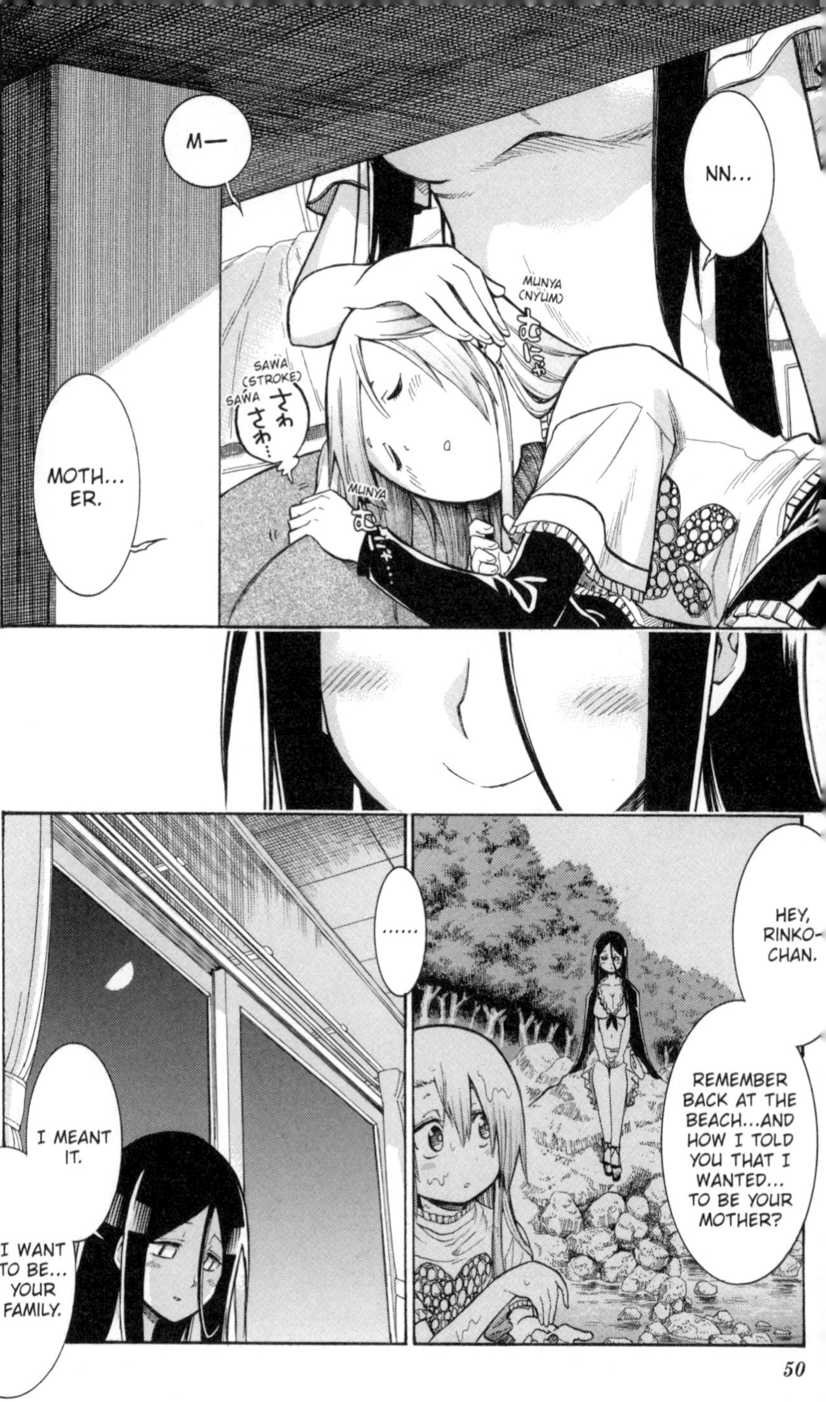
NN...
MUNYA (NYUM) むにゃ
SAWA (STROKE) SAWA さわさわ…
MUNYA むにゃ…
M—
MOTH... ER.
HEY, RINKO-CHAN.
REMEMBER BACK AT THE BEACH...AND HOW I TOLD YOU THAT I WANTED... TO BE YOUR MOTHER?
......
I MEANT IT.
I WANT TO BE... YOUR FAMILY.

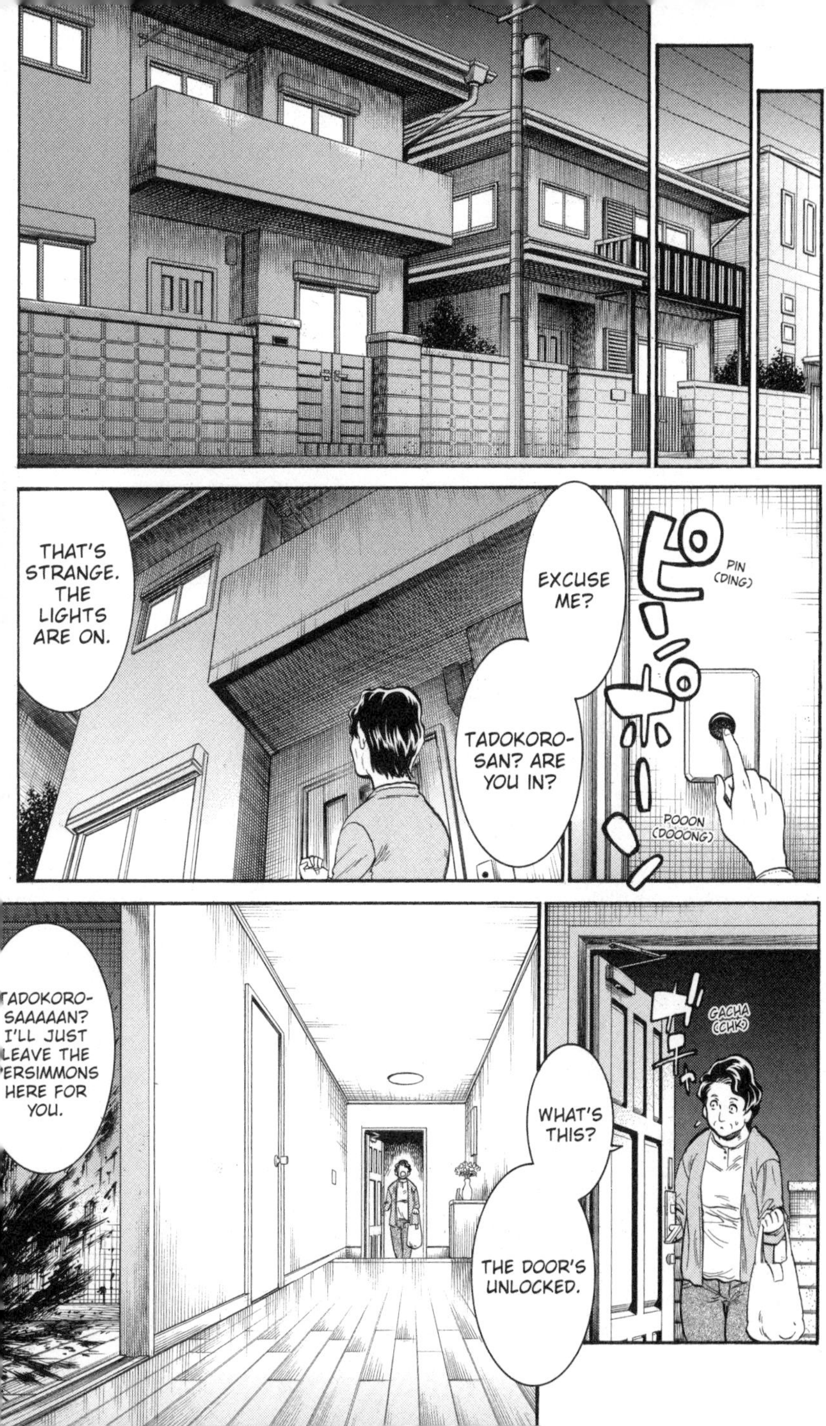
PIN (DING)
POOON (DOOONG)
EXCUSE ME?
TADOKORO-SAN? ARE YOU IN?
THAT'S STRANGE. THE LIGHTS ARE ON.
GACHA (CHK)
WHAT'S THIS?
THE DOOR'S UNLOCKED.
TADOKORO-SAAAAAN? I'LL JUST LEAVE THE PERSIMMONS HERE FOR YOU.

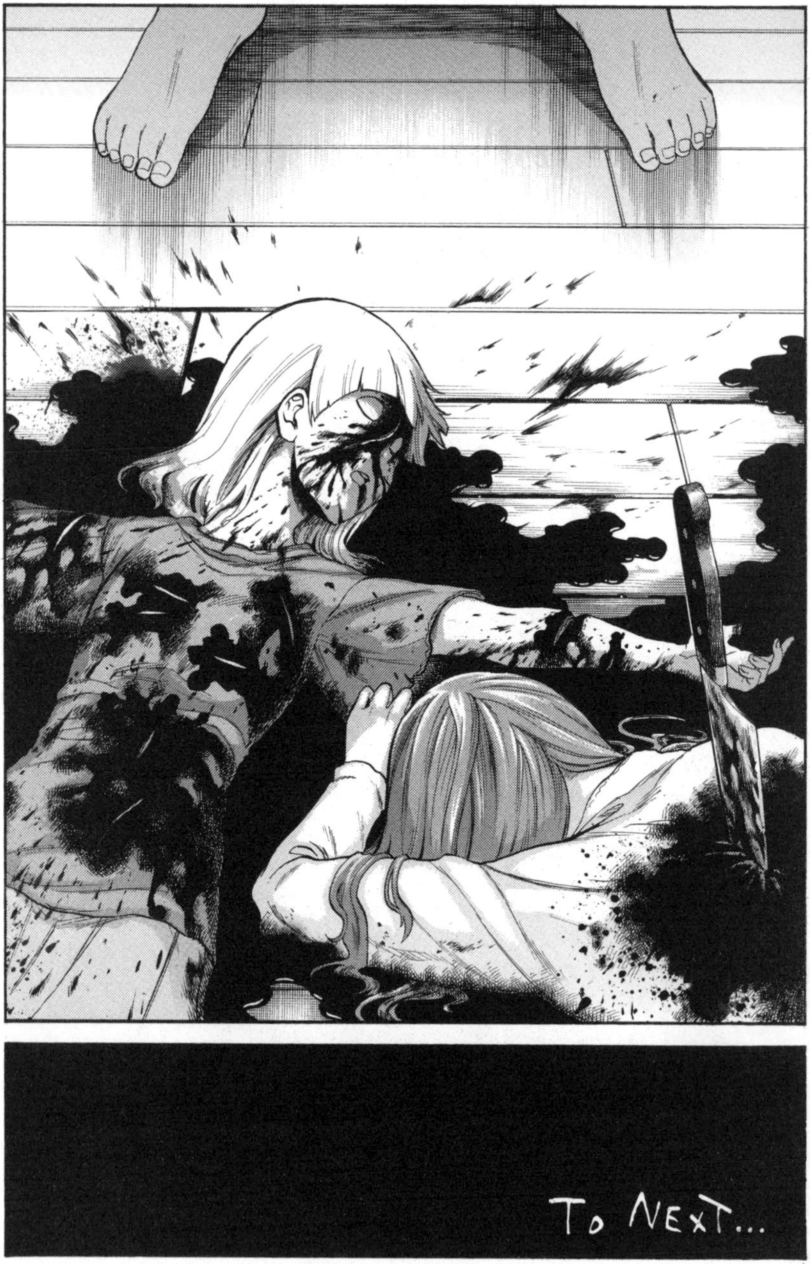
To Next...

MURCIÉLAGO

MURCIÉLAGO

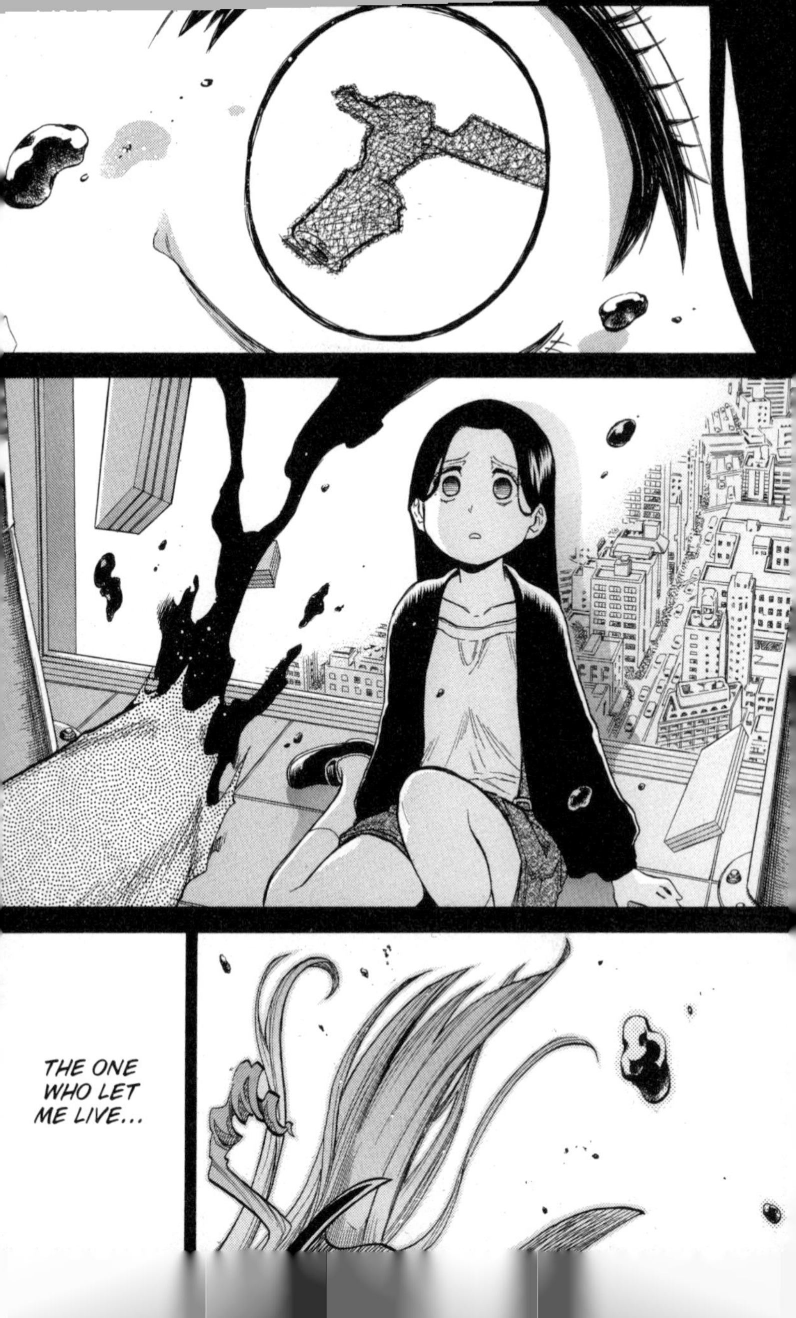
THE ONE WHO LET ME LIVE...

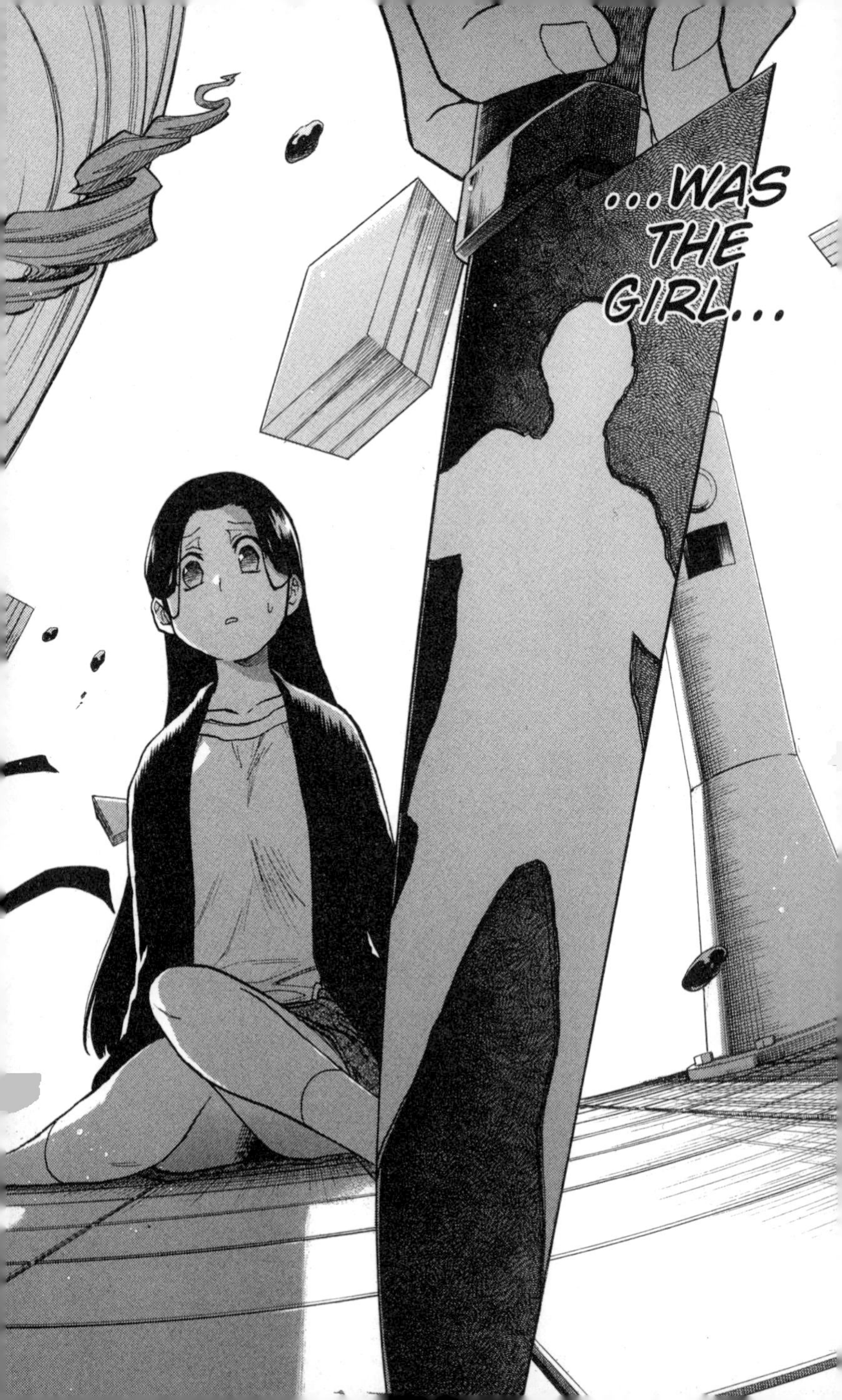
...WAS THE GIRL...

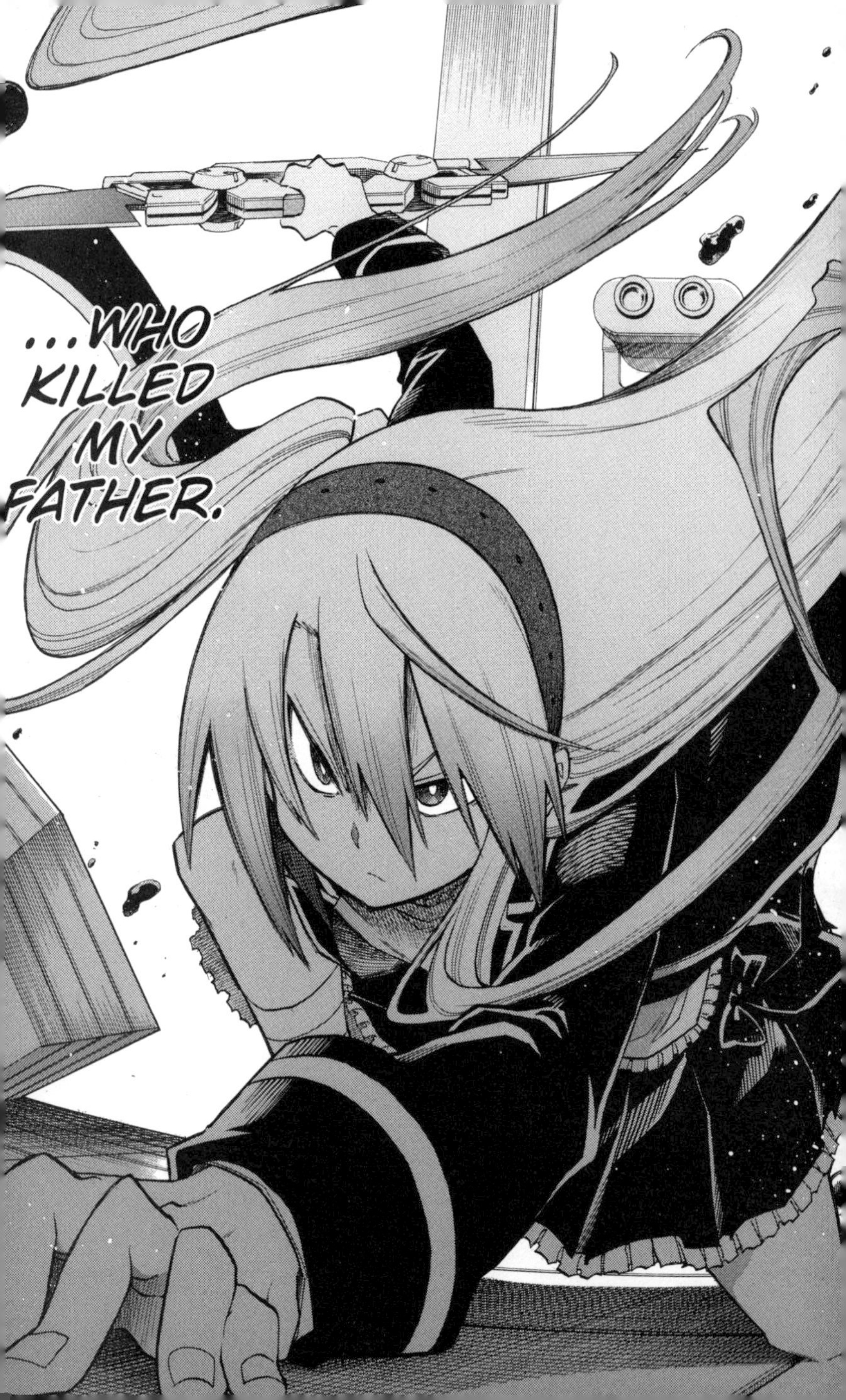
...WHO KILLED MY FATHER.

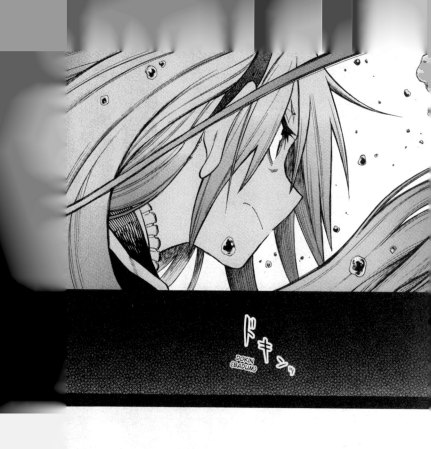

DOKIN
(BADUM)

IT WAS THE
FIRST TIME
I EVER FELL
IN LOVE.

MURCIÉLAGO

Yoshimurakana

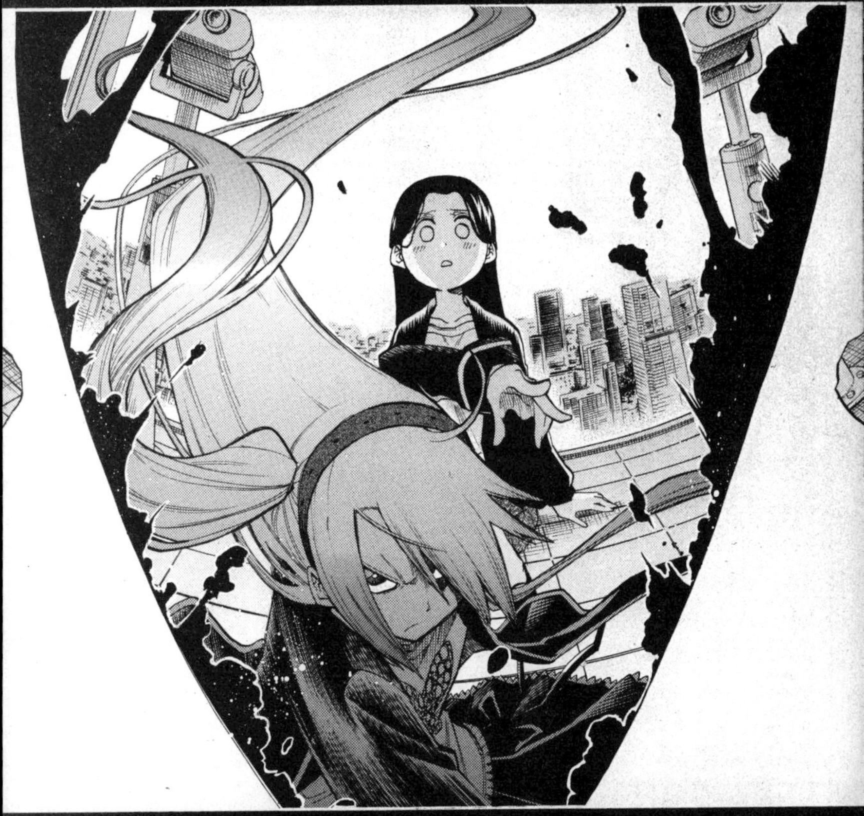

Chapter 121

Punishing Love

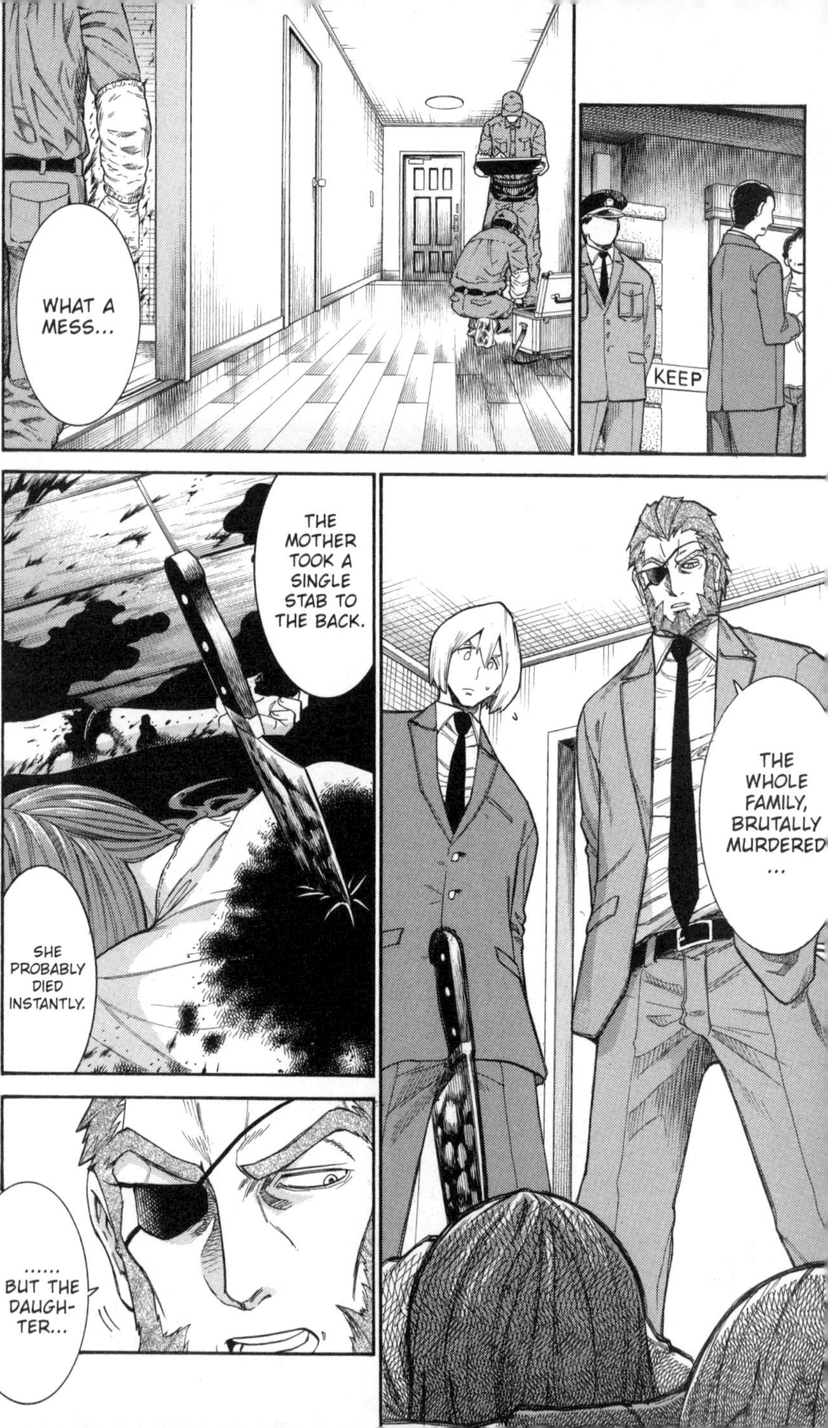
KEEP
WHAT A MESS...
THE WHOLE FAMILY, BRUTALLY MURDERED...
THE MOTHER TOOK A SINGLE STAB TO THE BACK.
SHE PROBABLY DIED INSTANTLY.
...... BUT THE DAUGHTER...

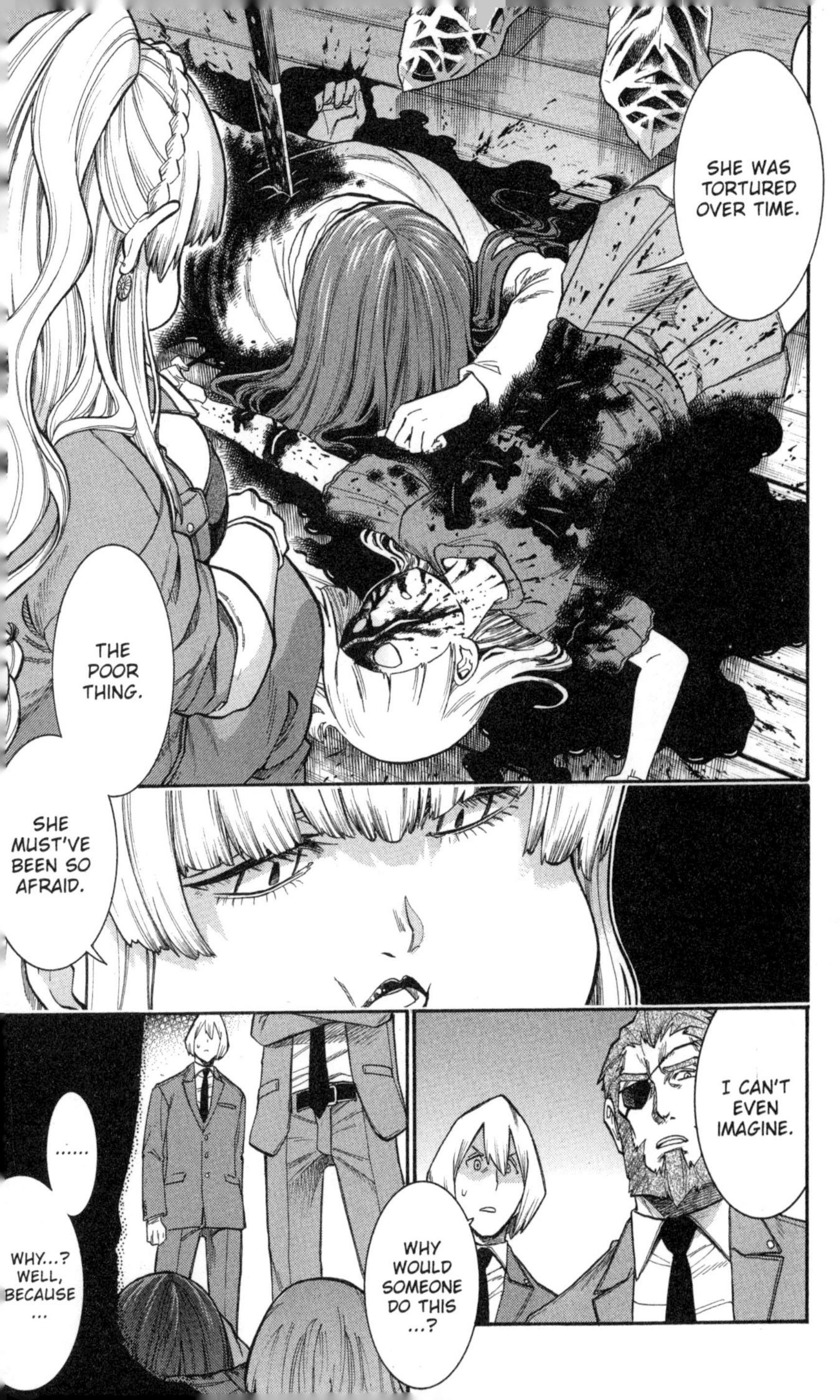
SHE WAS TORTURED OVER TIME.
THE POOR THING.
SHE MUST'VE BEEN SO AFRAID.
I CAN'T EVEN IMAGINE.
WHY WOULD SOMEONE DO THIS ...?
......
WHY...? WELL, BECAUSE ...

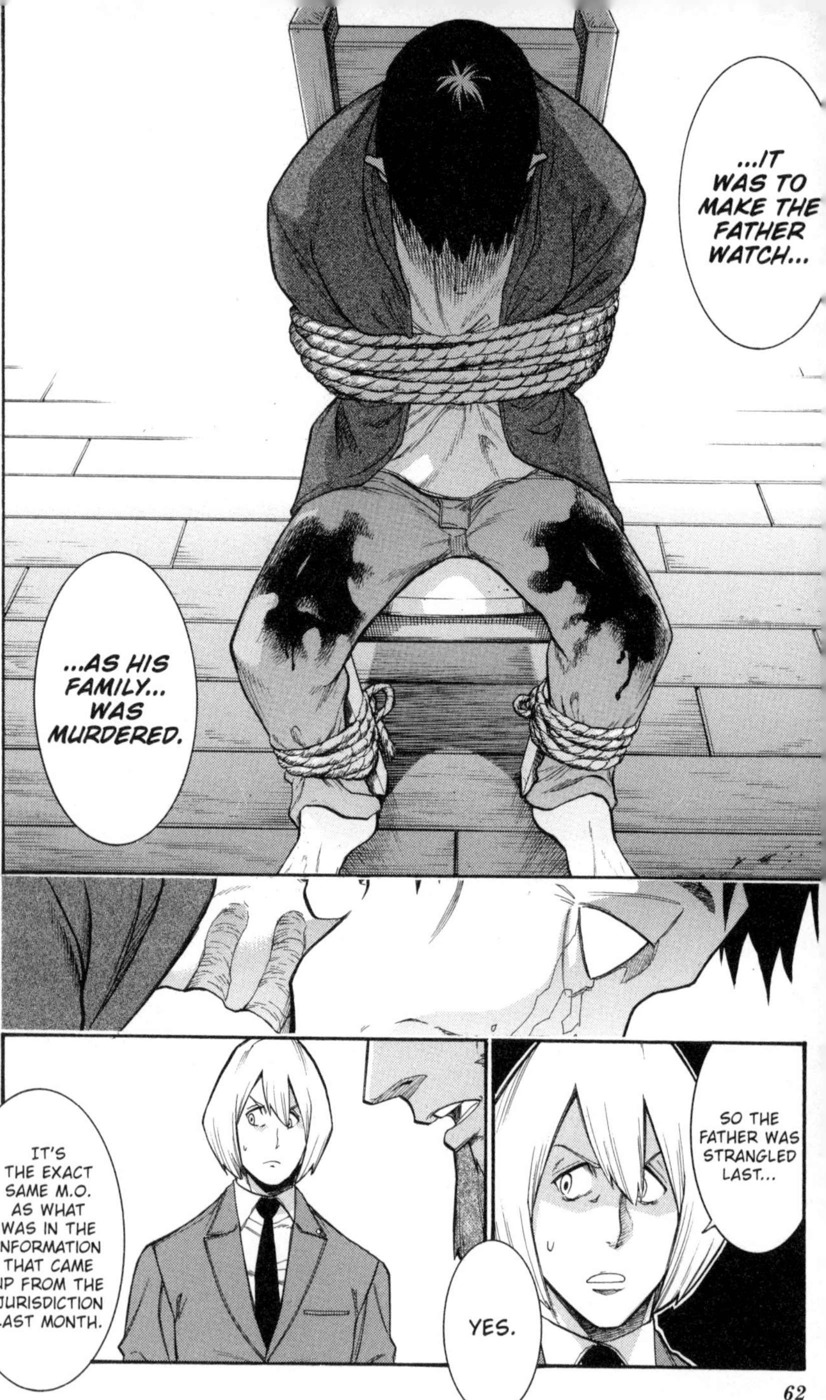
...IT WAS TO MAKE THE FATHER WATCH...
...AS HIS FAMILY... WAS MURDERED.
SO THE FATHER WAS STRANGLED LAST...
YES.
IT'S THE EXACT SAME M.O. AS WHAT WAS IN THE INFORMATION THAT CAME UP FROM THE JURISDICTION LAST MONTH.

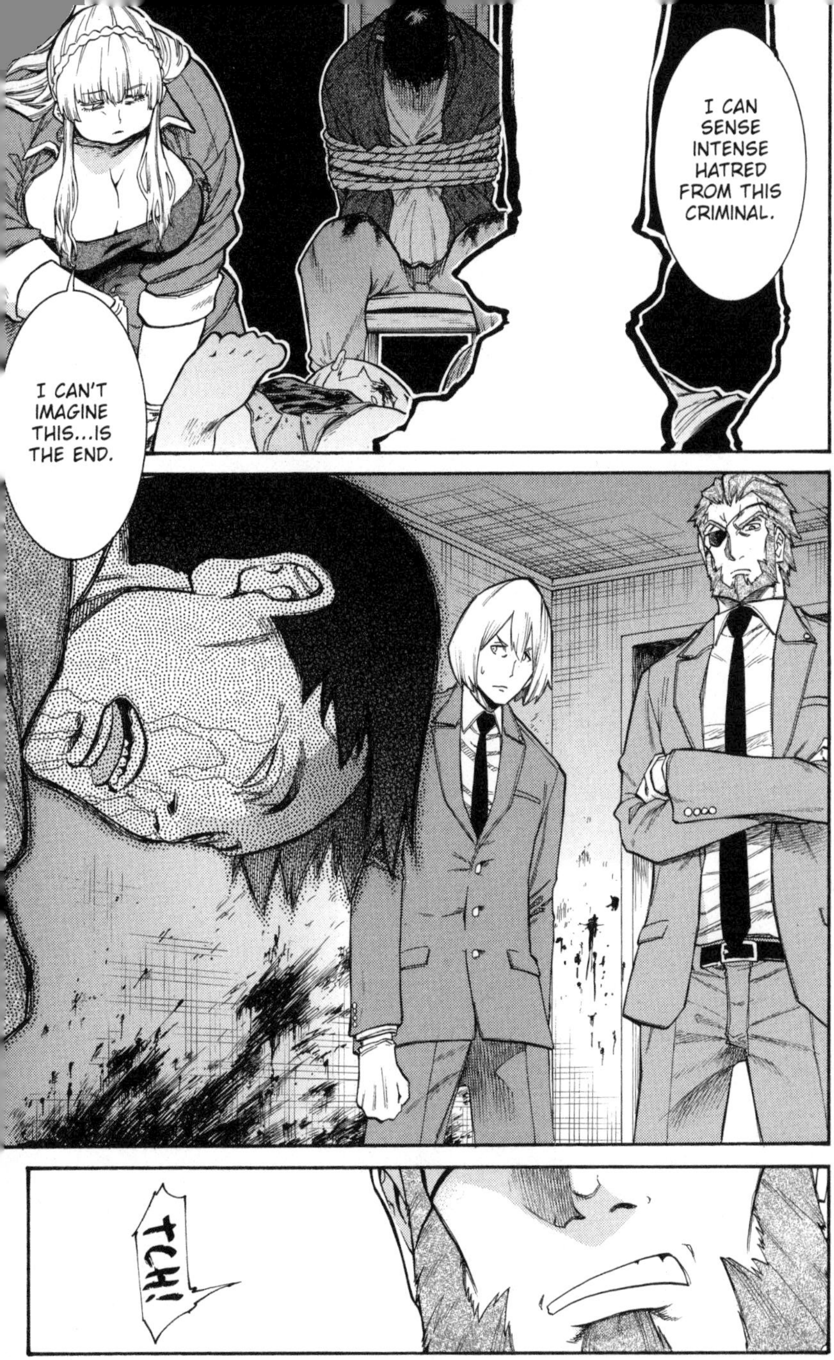
I CAN SENSE INTENSE HATRED FROM THIS CRIMINAL.
I CAN'T IMAGINE THIS...IS THE END.
TCH!

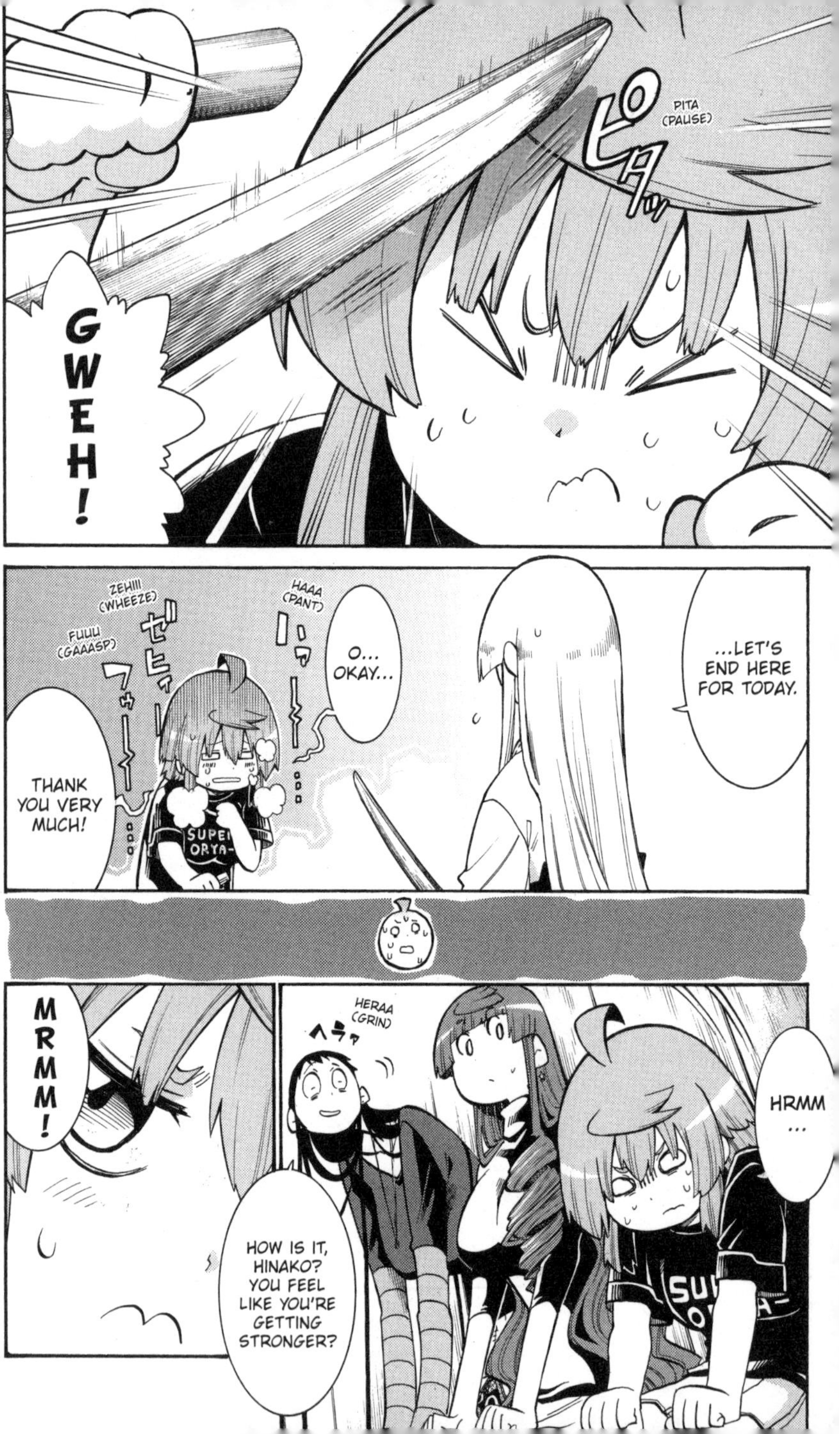

PITA (PAUSE)
GWEH!
...LET'S END HERE FOR TODAY.
O... OKAY...
HAAA (PANT)
ZEHIII (WHEEZE)
FUUU (GAAASP)
THANK YOU VERY MUCH!
HRMM...
HERAA (GRIN)
HOW IS IT, HINAKO? YOU FEEL LIKE YOU'RE GETTING STRONGER?
MRMM!

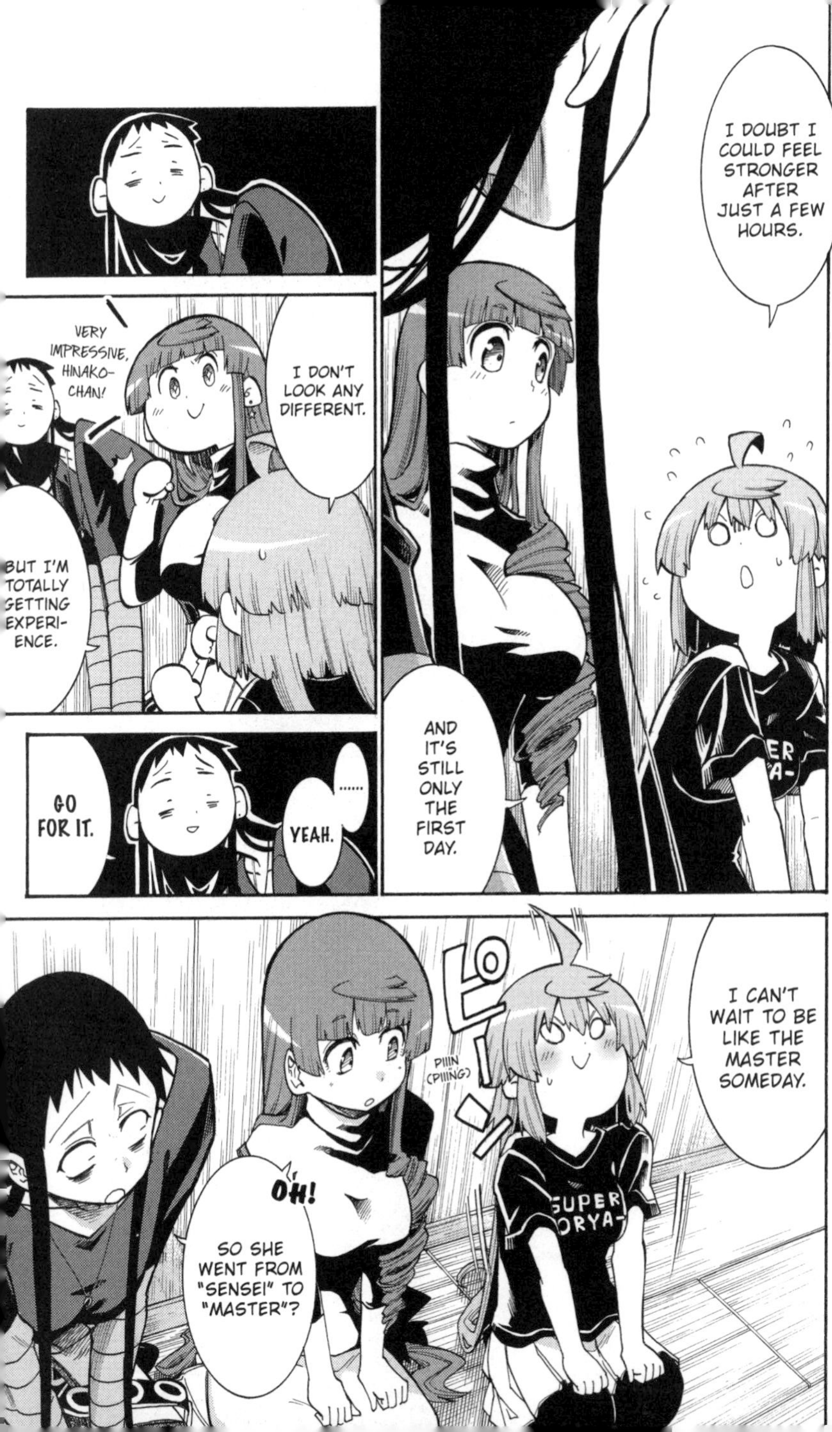
I DOUBT I COULD FEEL STRONGER AFTER JUST A FEW HOURS.
AND IT'S STILL ONLY THE FIRST DAY.
I DON'T LOOK ANY DIFFERENT.
VERY IMPRESSIVE, HINAKO-CHAN!
BUT I'M TOTALLY GETTING EXPERIENCE.
......
YEAH.
GO FOR IT.
I CAN'T WAIT TO BE LIKE THE MASTER SOMEDAY.
PIIIN (PIIIING)
OH!
SO SHE WENT FROM "SENSEI" TO "MASTER"?

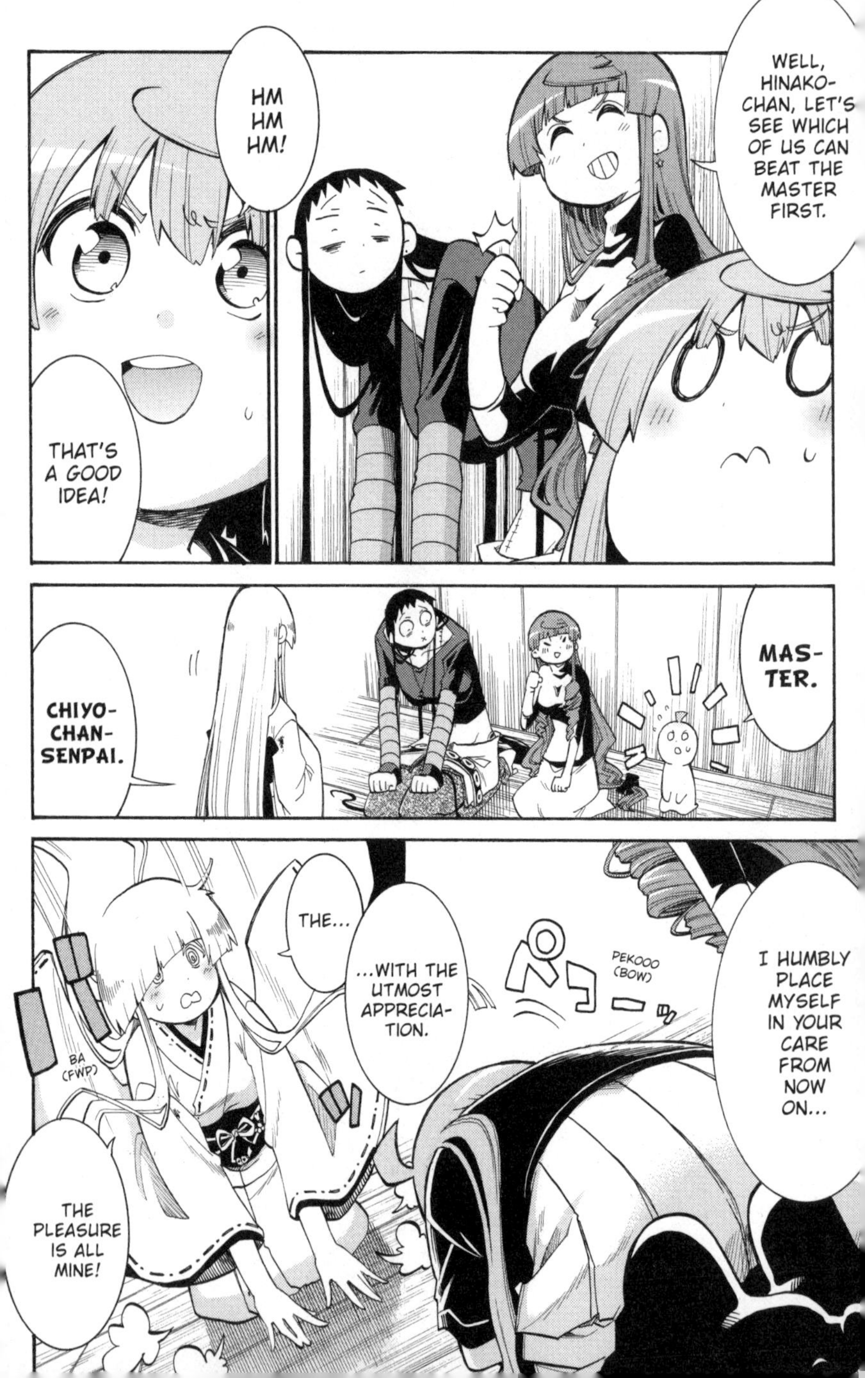
WELL, HINAKO-CHAN, LET'S SEE WHICH OF US CAN BEAT THE MASTER FIRST.
HM HM HM!
THAT'S A GOOD IDEA!
MASTER.
CHIYO-CHAN-SENPAI.
I HUMBLY PLACE MYSELF IN YOUR CARE FROM NOW ON...
PEKOOO (BOW)
...WITH THE UTMOST APPRECIATION.
THE...
BA (FWP)
THE PLEASURE IS ALL MINE!

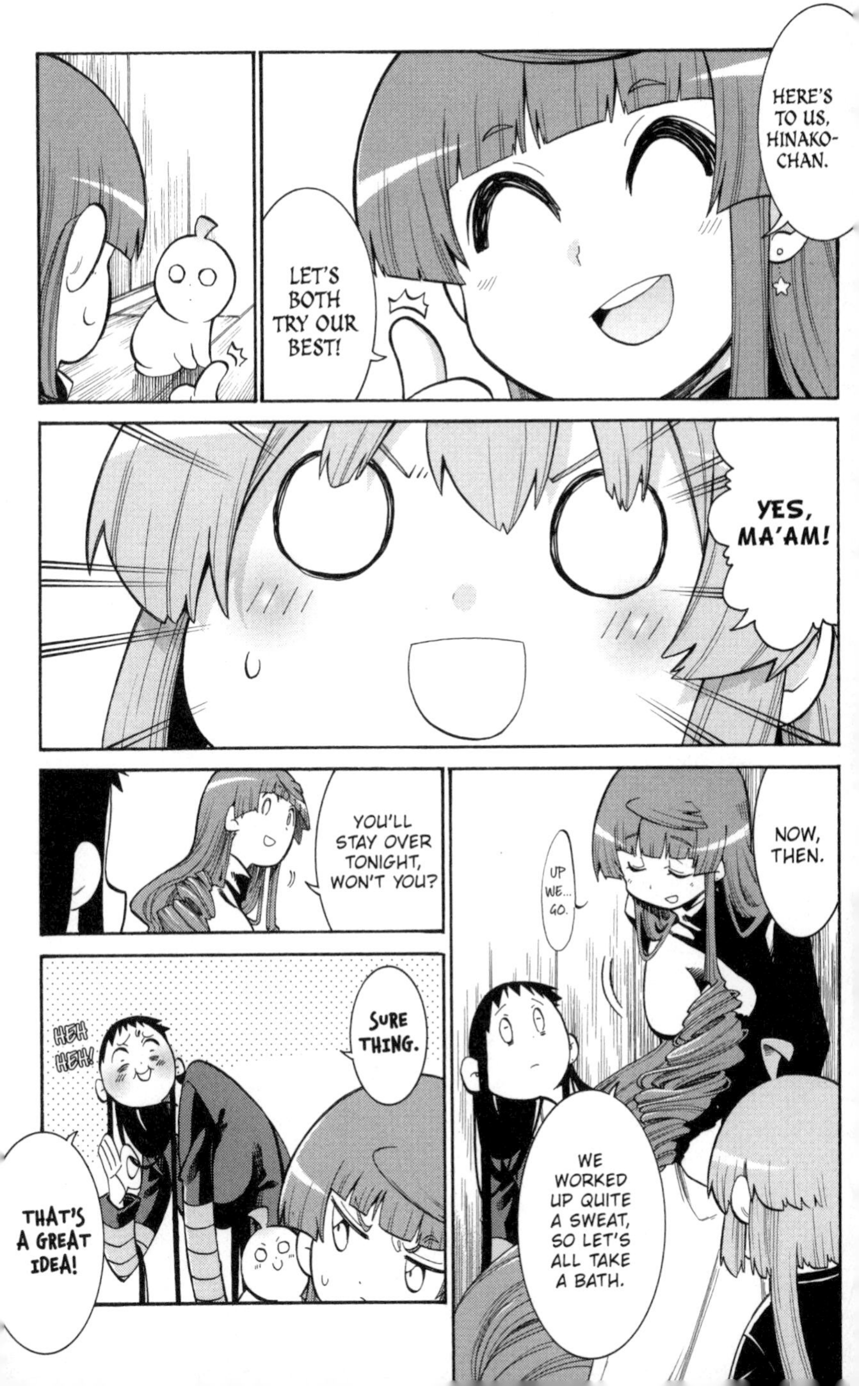
HERE'S TO US, HINAKO-CHAN.
LET'S BOTH TRY OUR BEST!
YES, MA'AM!
NOW, THEN.
UP WE... GO.
WE WORKED UP QUITE A SWEAT, SO LET'S ALL TAKE A BATH.
YOU'LL STAY OVER TONIGHT, WON'T YOU?
SURE THING.
HEH HEH!
THAT'S A GREAT IDEA!

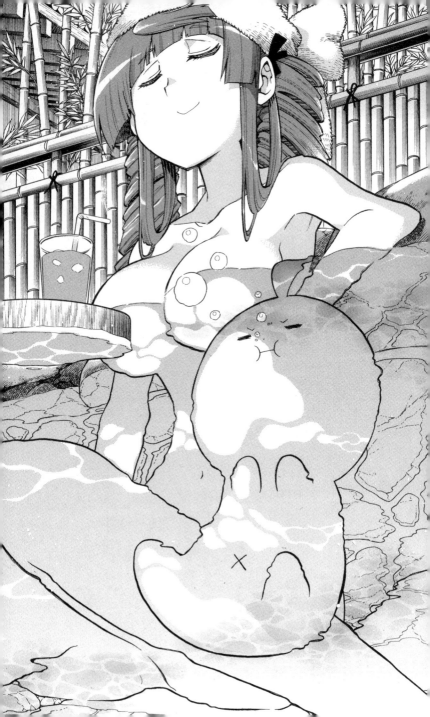

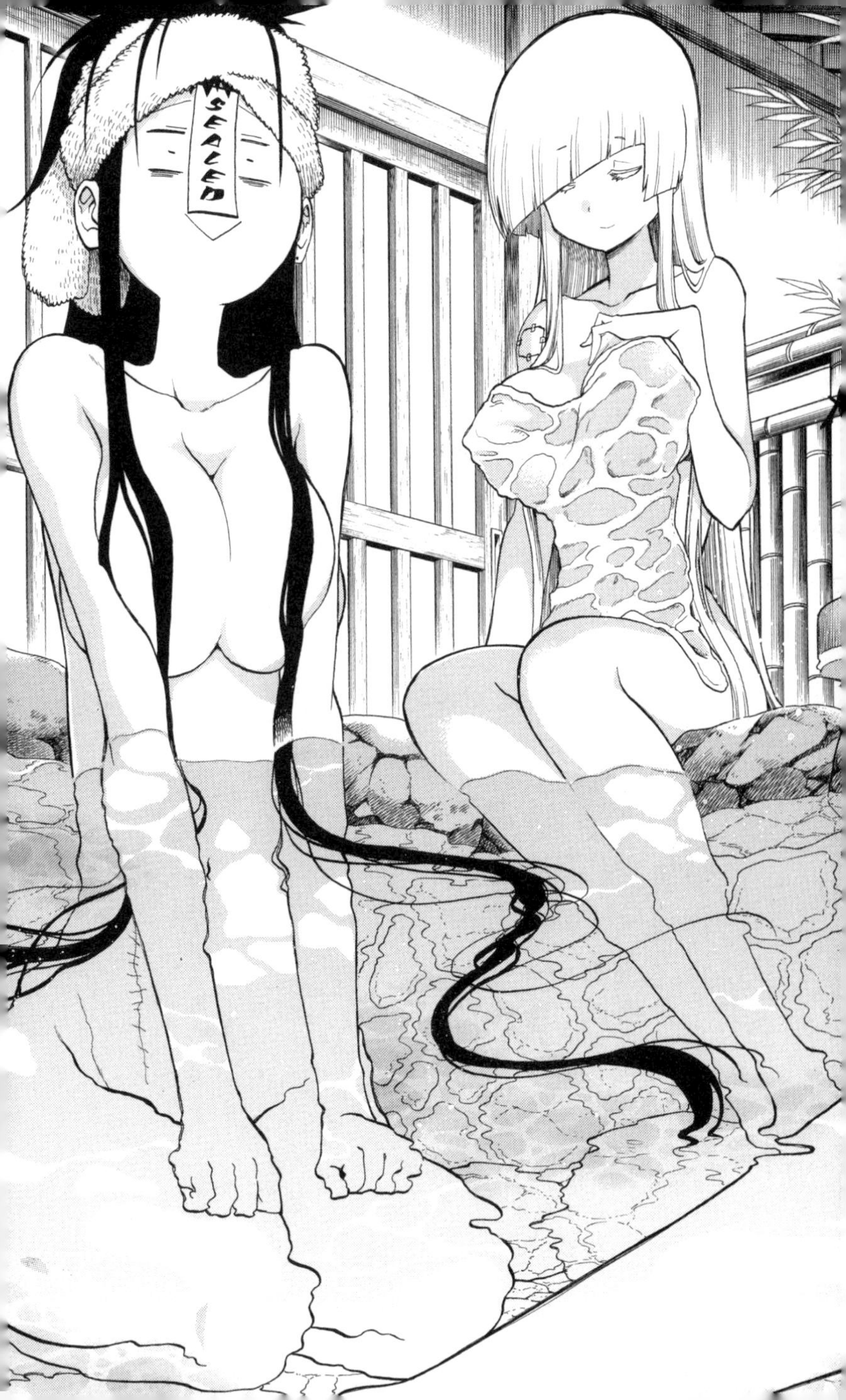
SEALED

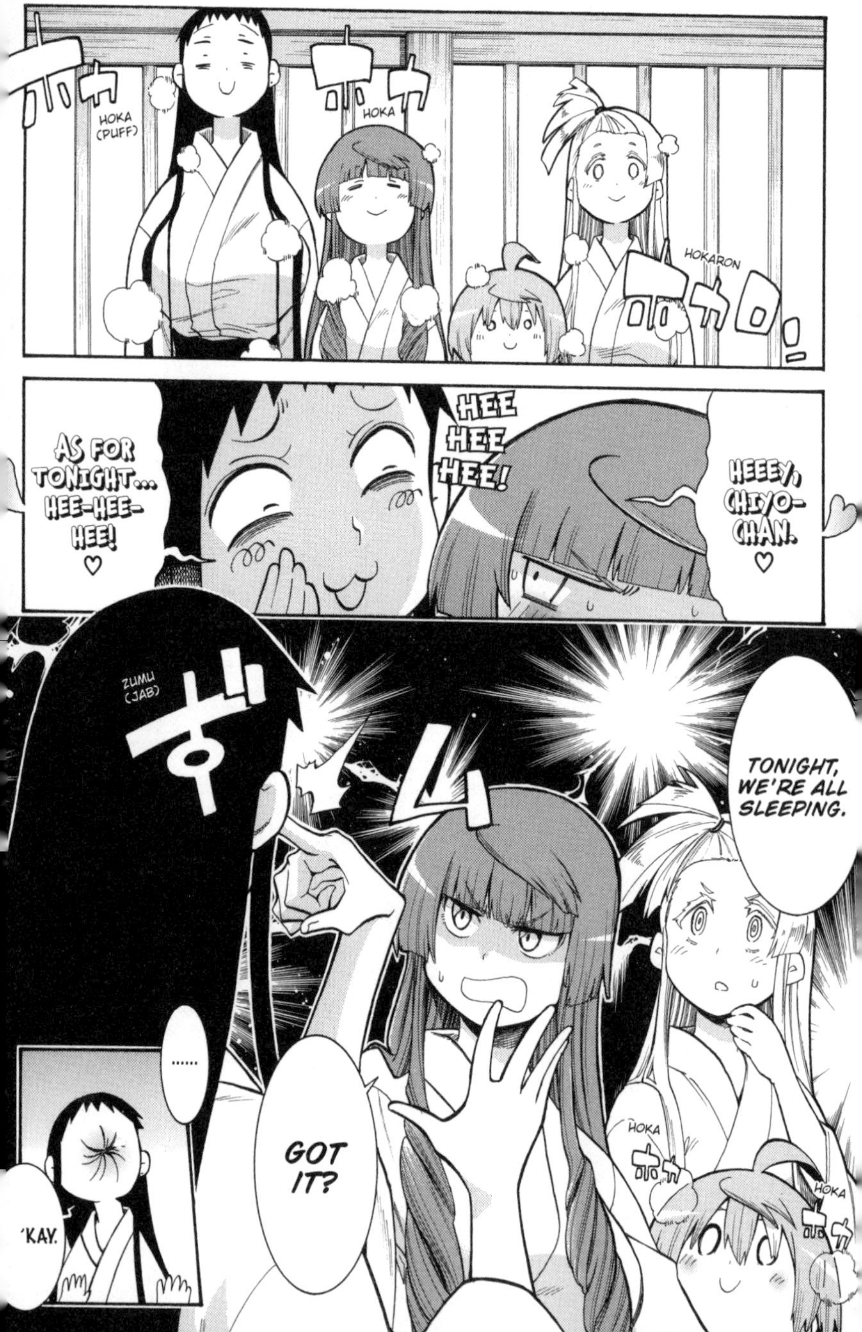
HOKARON
HOKA
HOKA (PUFF)
HEEEY, CHIYO-CHAN. ♡
HEE HEE HEE!
AS FOR TONIGHT... HEE-HEE-HEE! ♡
TONIGHT, WE'RE ALL SLEEPING.
ZUMU (JAB)
GOT IT?
HOKA
HOKA
......
'KAY.

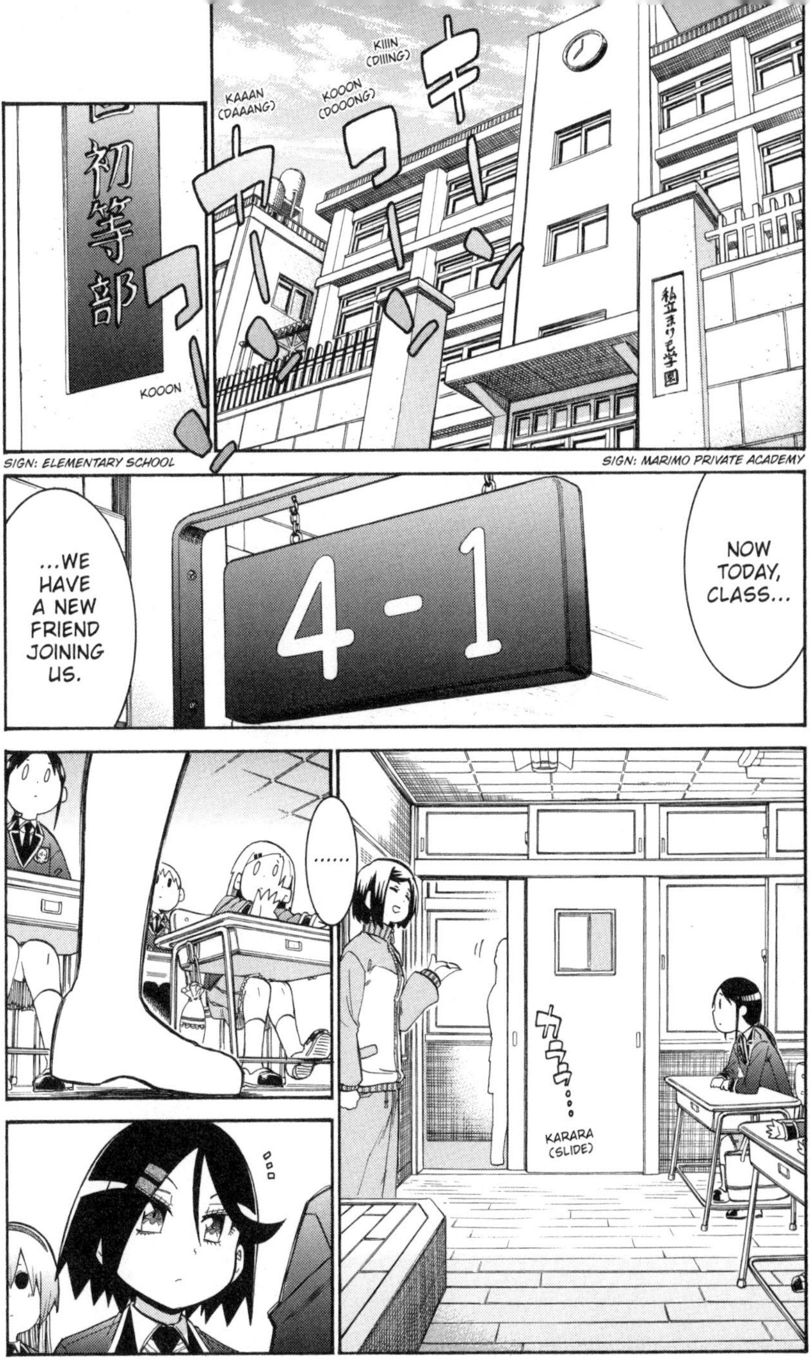
KIIIN (DIIING)
KOOON (DOOONG)
KAAAN (DAAANG)
KOOON
SIGN: MARIMO PRIVATE ACADEMY
SIGN: ELEMENTARY SCHOOL
NOW TODAY, CLASS...
...WE HAVE A NEW FRIEND JOINING US.
KARARA (SLIDE)
......

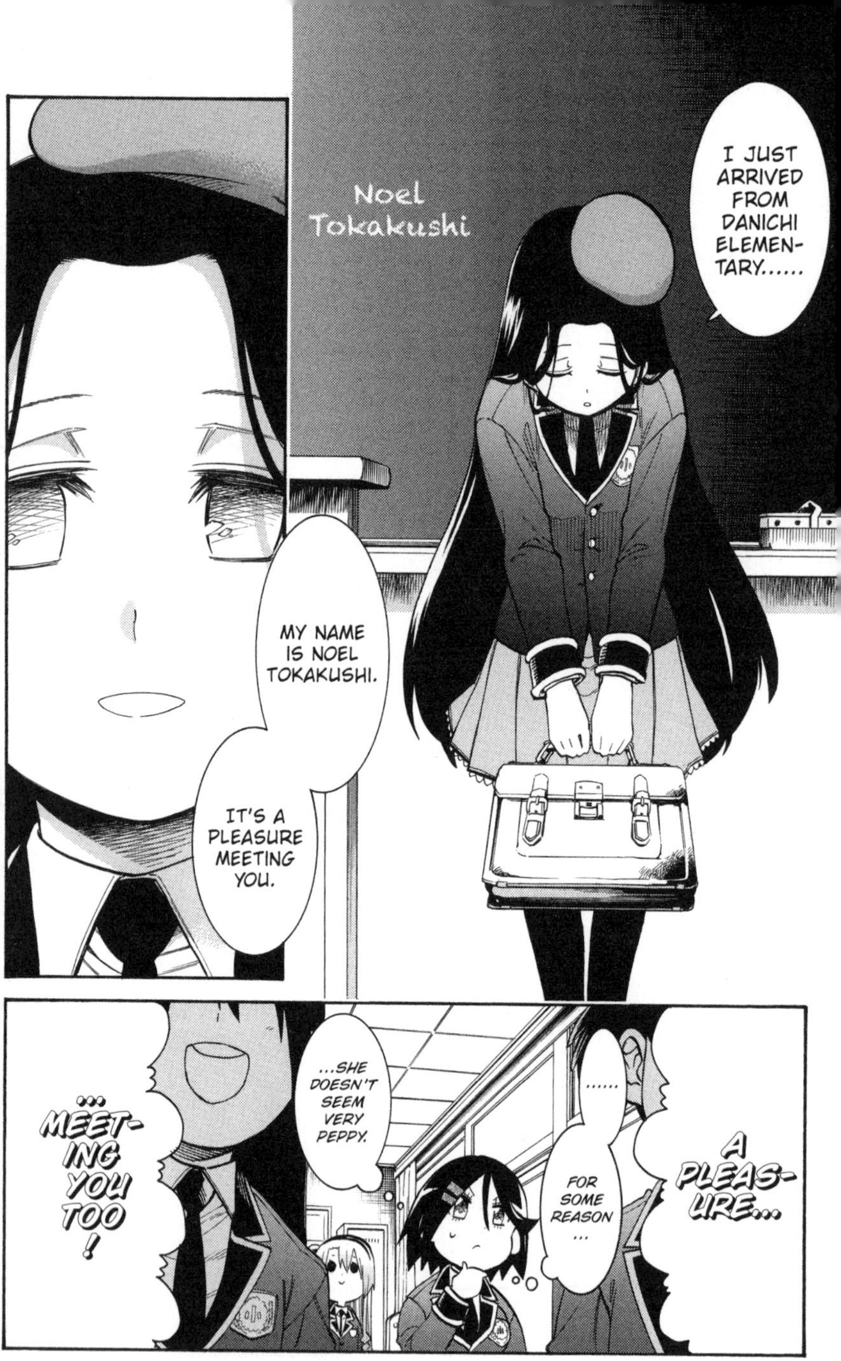
Noel Tokakushi
I JUST ARRIVED FROM DANICHI ELEMENTARY......
MY NAME IS NOEL TOKAKUSHI.
IT'S A PLEASURE MEETING YOU.
A PLEASURE...
......
FOR SOME REASON ...
...SHE DOESN'T SEEM VERY PEPPY.
...MEETING YOU TOO!

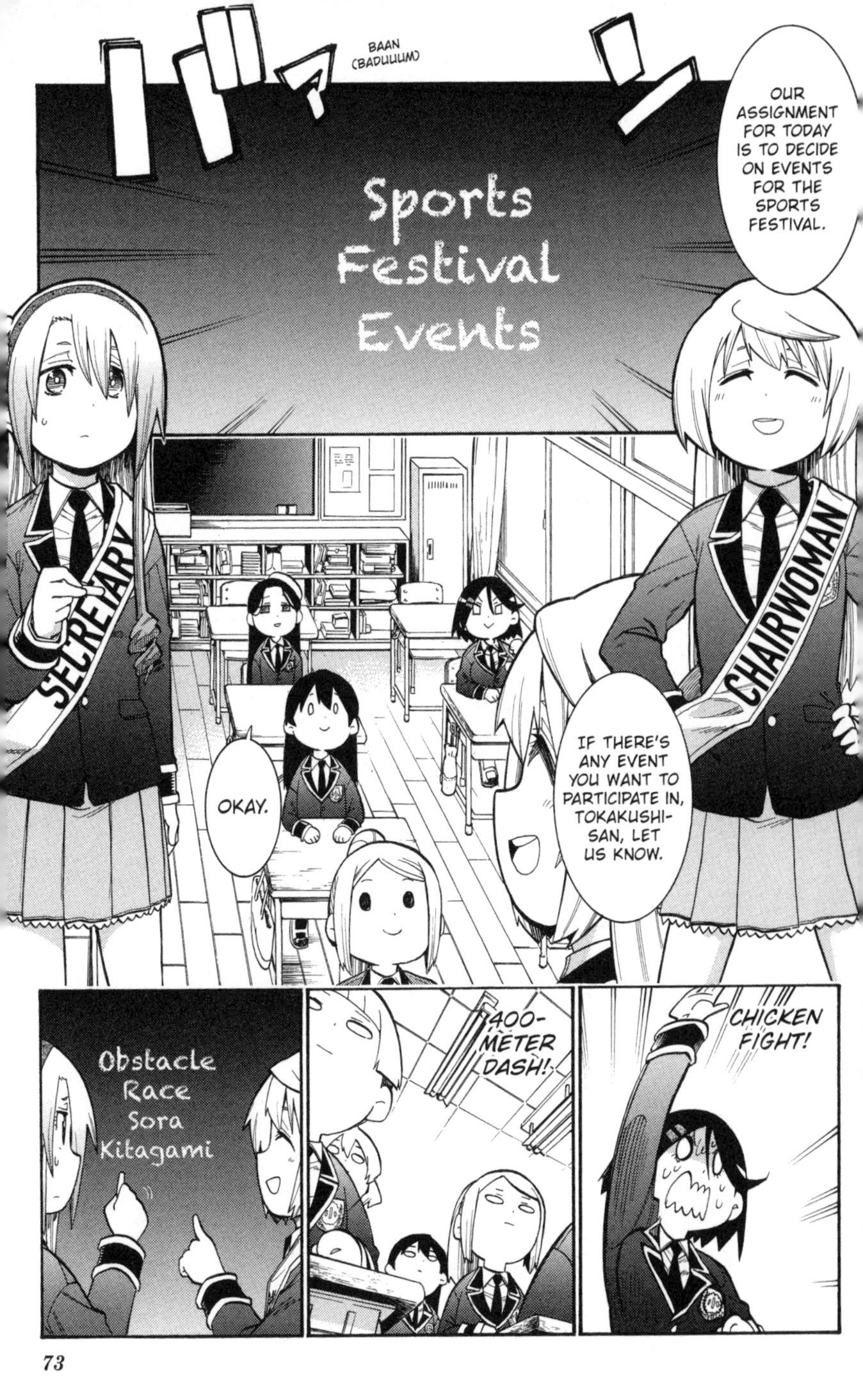
BAAN (BADUUUM)
OUR ASSIGNMENT FOR TODAY IS TO DECIDE ON EVENTS FOR THE SPORTS FESTIVAL.
Sports Festival Events
IF THERE'S ANY EVENT YOU WANT TO PARTICIPATE IN, TOKAKUSHI-SAN, LET US KNOW.
OKAY.
CHICKEN FIGHT!
400-METER DASH!
Obstacle Race Sora Kitagami

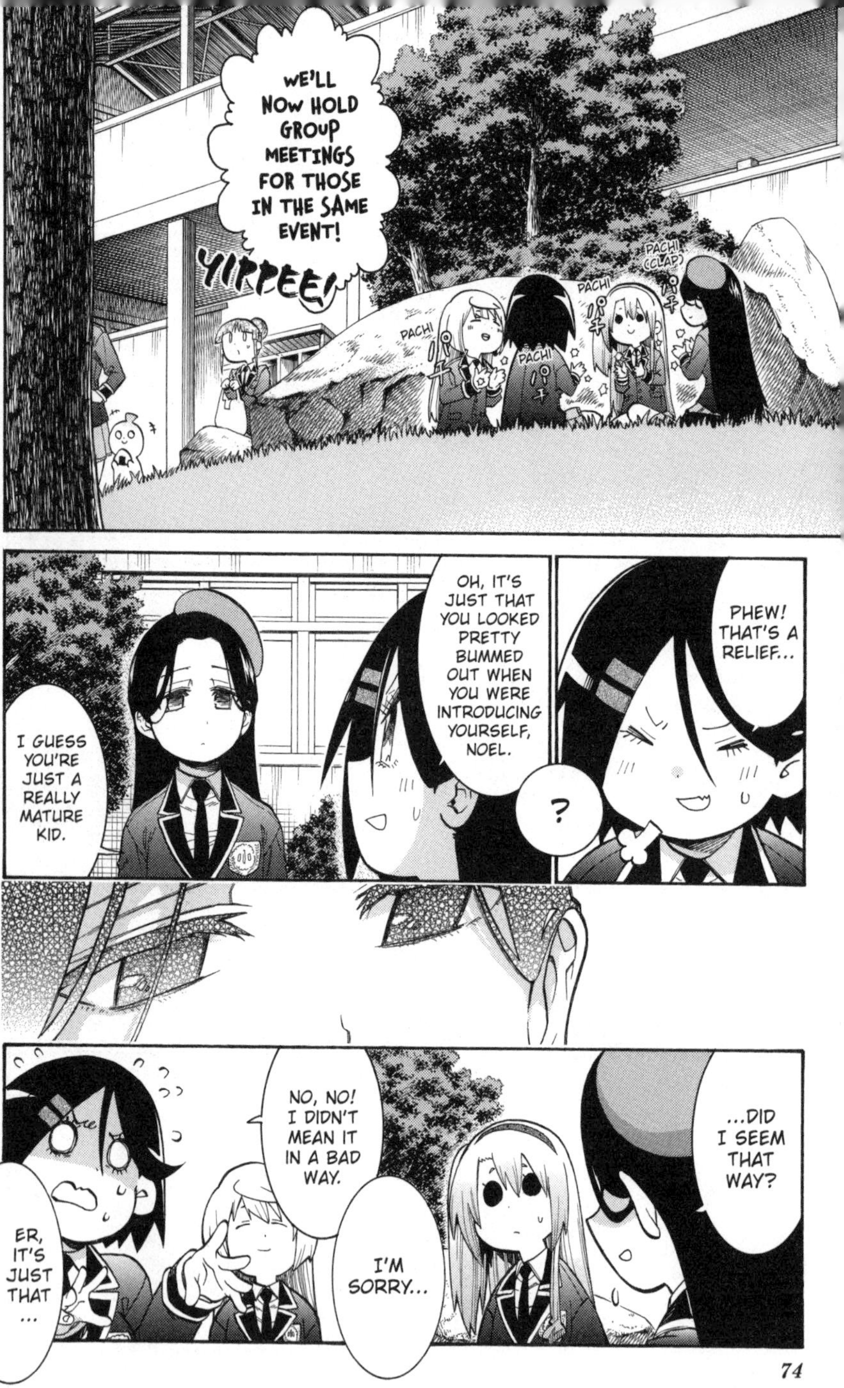
WE'LL NOW HOLD GROUP MEETINGS FOR THOSE IN THE SAME EVENT!
YIPPEE!
PACHI (CLAP)
PACHI
PACHI
PACHI
PHEW! THAT'S A RELIEF...
?
OH, IT'S JUST THAT YOU LOOKED PRETTY BUMMED OUT WHEN YOU WERE INTRODUCING YOURSELF, NOEL.
I GUESS YOU'RE JUST A REALLY MATURE KID.
...DID I SEEM THAT WAY?
I'M SORRY...
NO, NO! I DIDN'T MEAN IT IN A BAD WAY.
ER, IT'S JUST THAT...

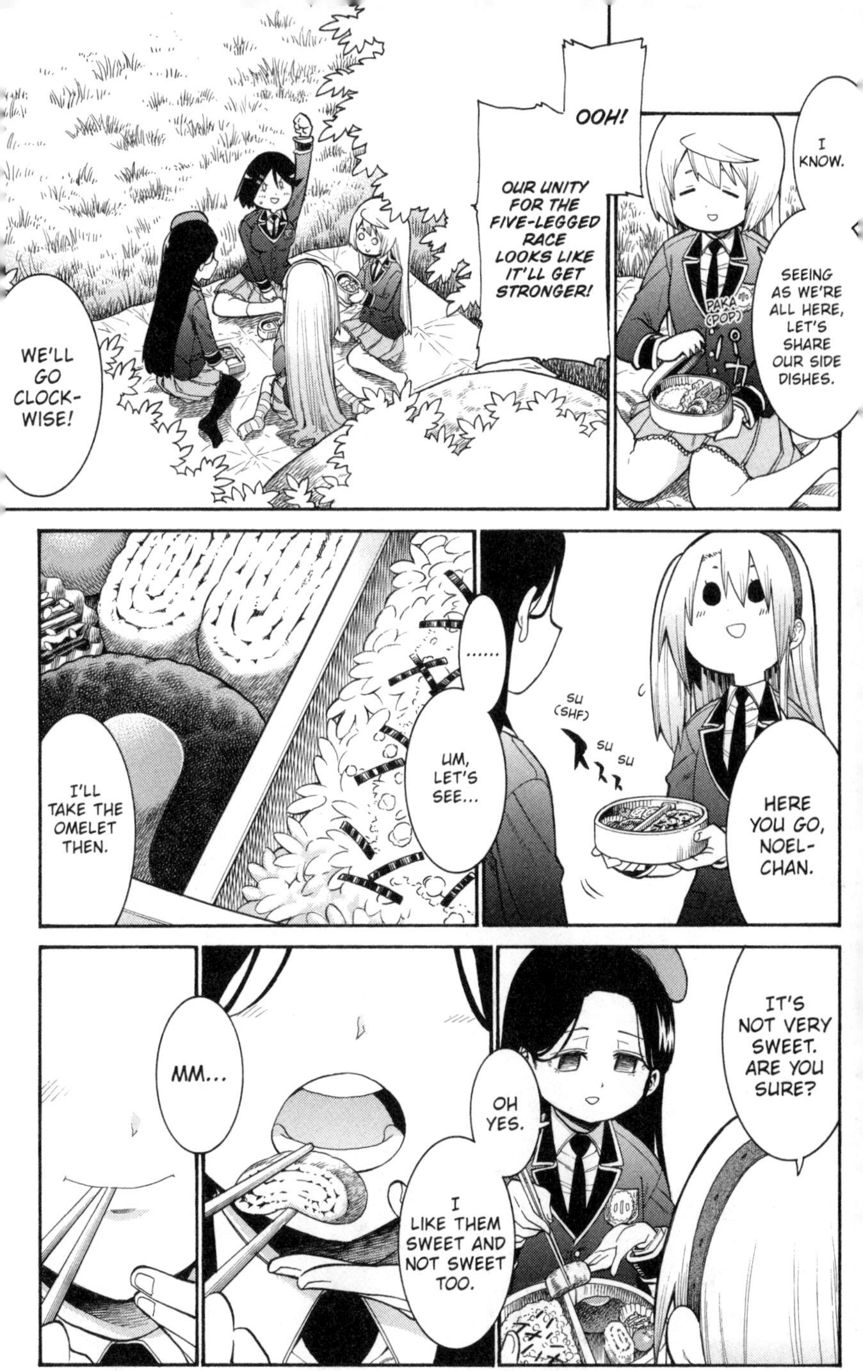
I KNOW.
SEEING AS WE'RE ALL HERE, LET'S SHARE OUR SIDE DISHES.
PAKA (POP)
OOH!
OUR UNITY FOR THE FIVE-LEGGED RACE LOOKS LIKE IT'LL GET STRONGER!
WE'LL GO CLOCK-WISE!
HERE YOU GO, NOEL-CHAN.
SU (SHF) SU SU
......
UM, LET'S SEE...
I'LL TAKE THE OMELET THEN.
IT'S NOT VERY SWEET. ARE YOU SURE?
OH YES.
I LIKE THEM SWEET AND NOT SWEET TOO.
MM...

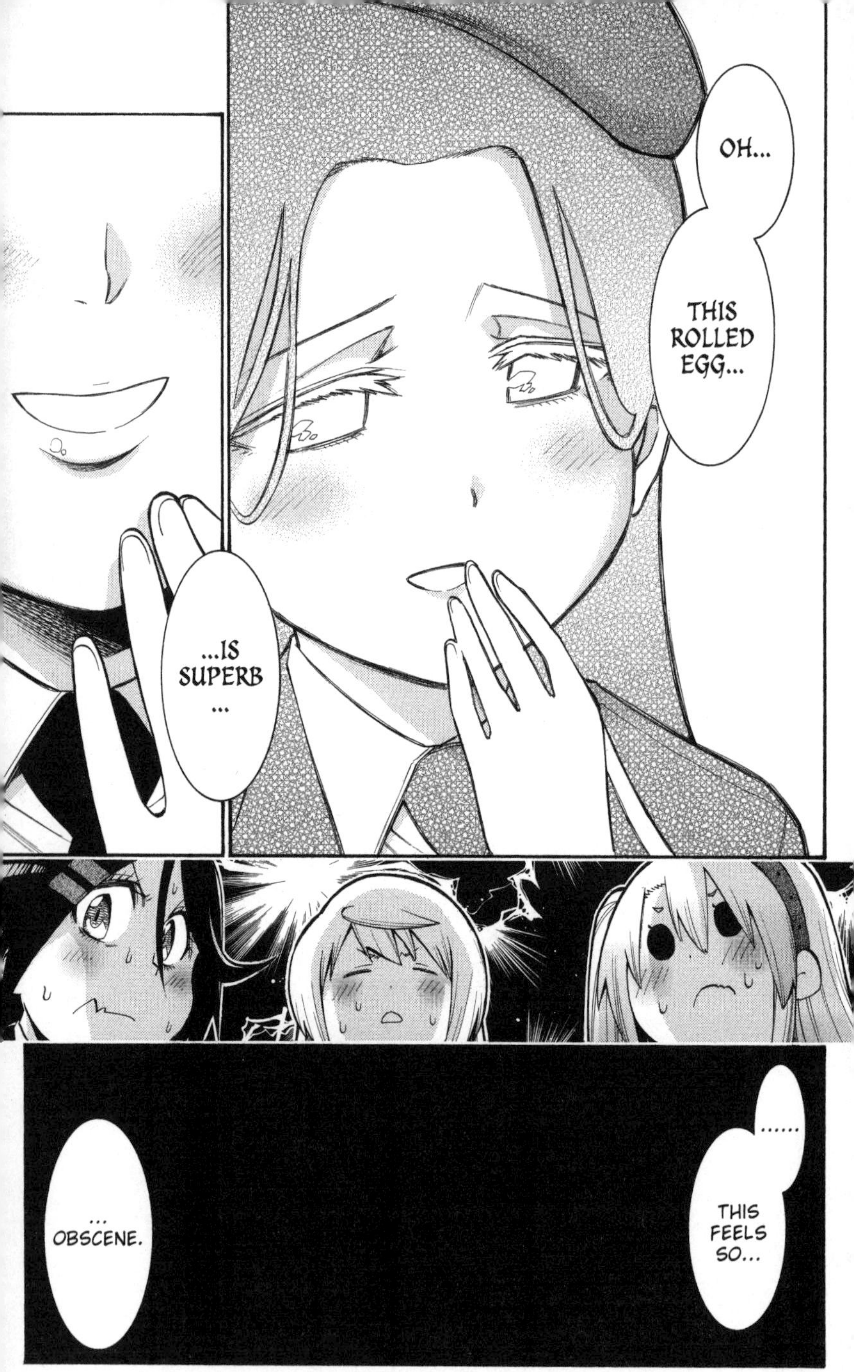
OH...
THIS ROLLED EGG...
...IS SUPERB ...
......
THIS FEELS SO...
... OBSCENE.

MURCIÉLAGO

MURCIÉLAGO

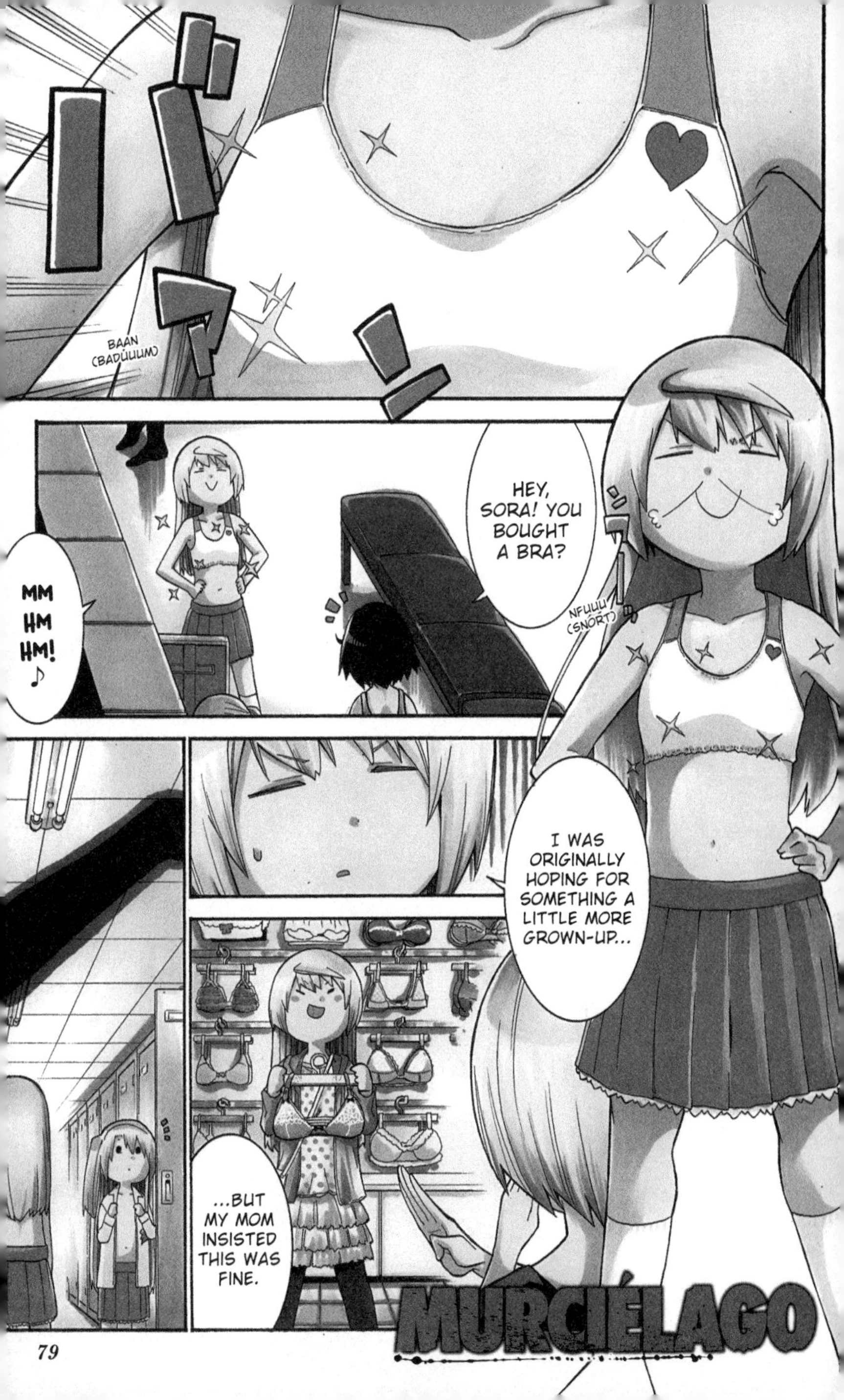
BAAN (BADUUUM)
HEY, SORA! YOU BOUGHT A BRA?
MM HM HM! ♪
NFUUU (SNORT)
I WAS ORIGINALLY HOPING FOR SOMETHING A LITTLE MORE GROWN-UP...
...BUT MY MOM INSISTED THIS WAS FINE.
MURCIÉLAGO

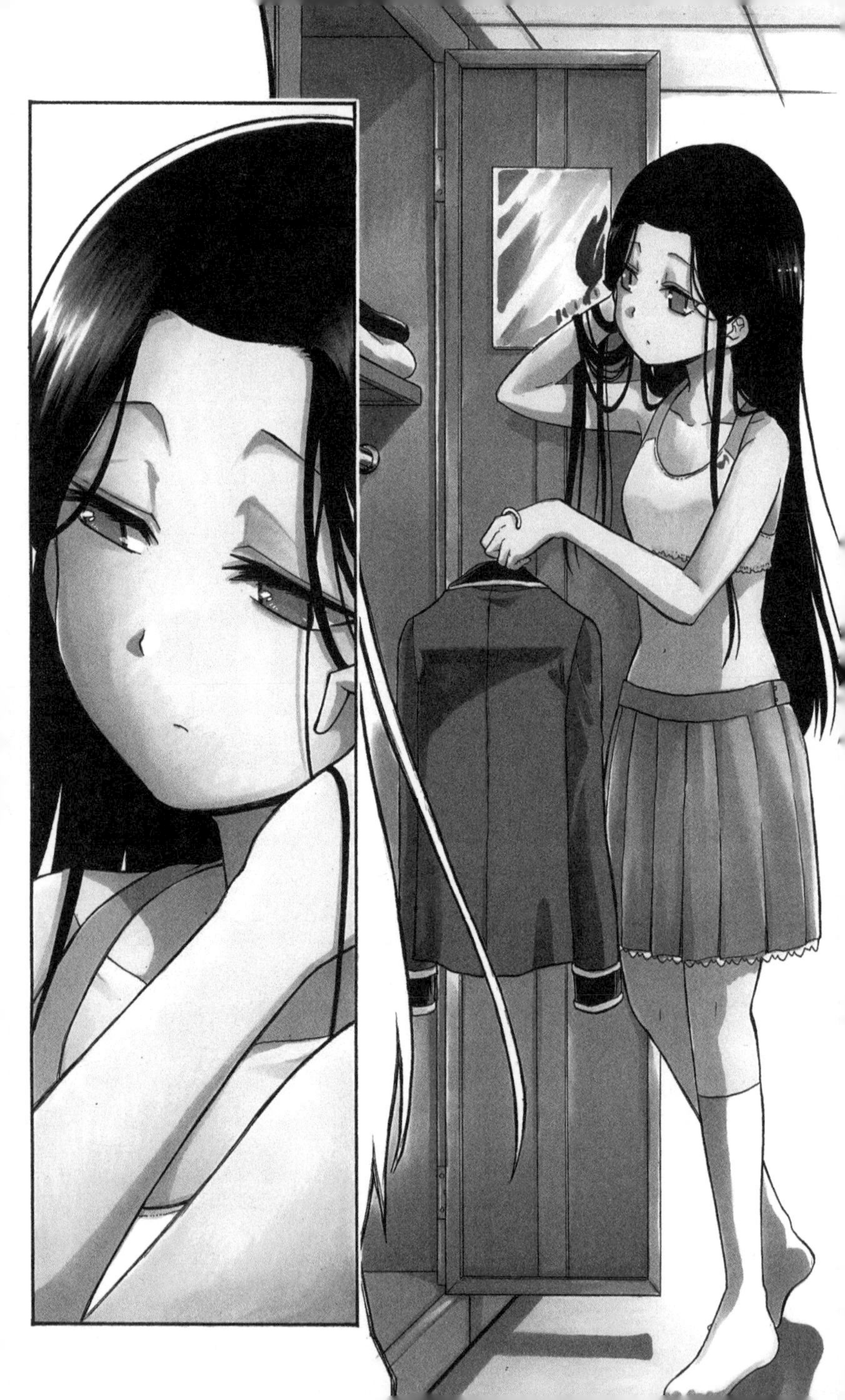

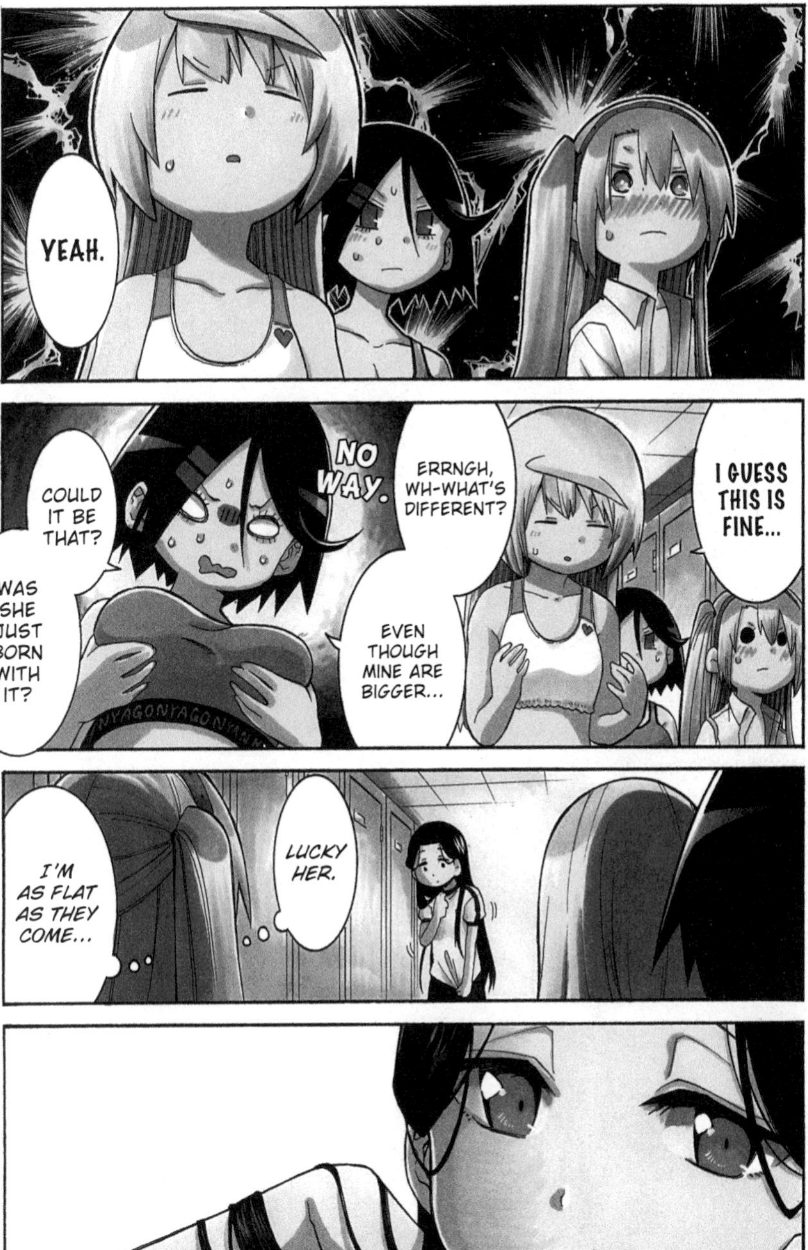
YEAH.
I GUESS THIS IS FINE...
ERRNGH, WH-WHAT'S DIFFERENT?
NO WAY.
COULD IT BE THAT?
EVEN THOUGH MINE ARE BIGGER...
WAS SHE JUST BORN WITH IT?
LUCKY HER.
I'M AS FLAT AS THEY COME...

MURCIÉLAGO

MURCIÉLAGO

Yoshimurakana

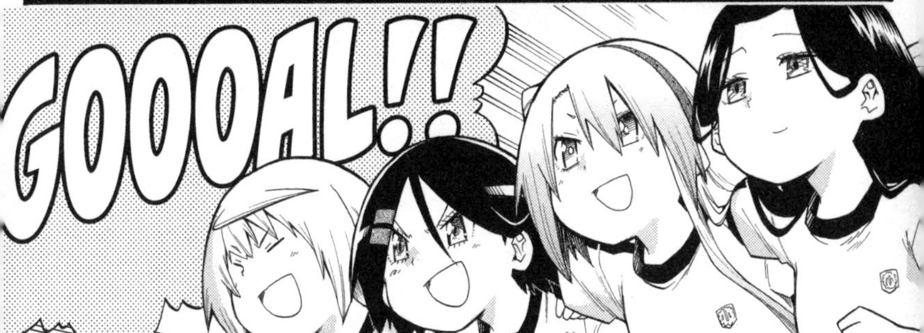
GOOOAL!!

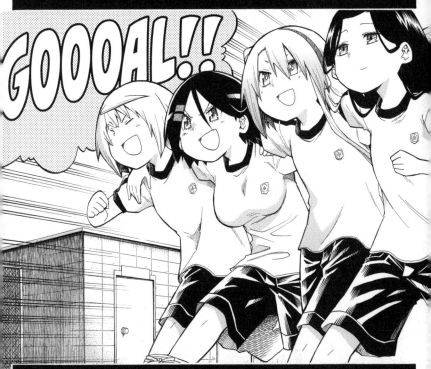

Chapter 122
Punishing Love ②

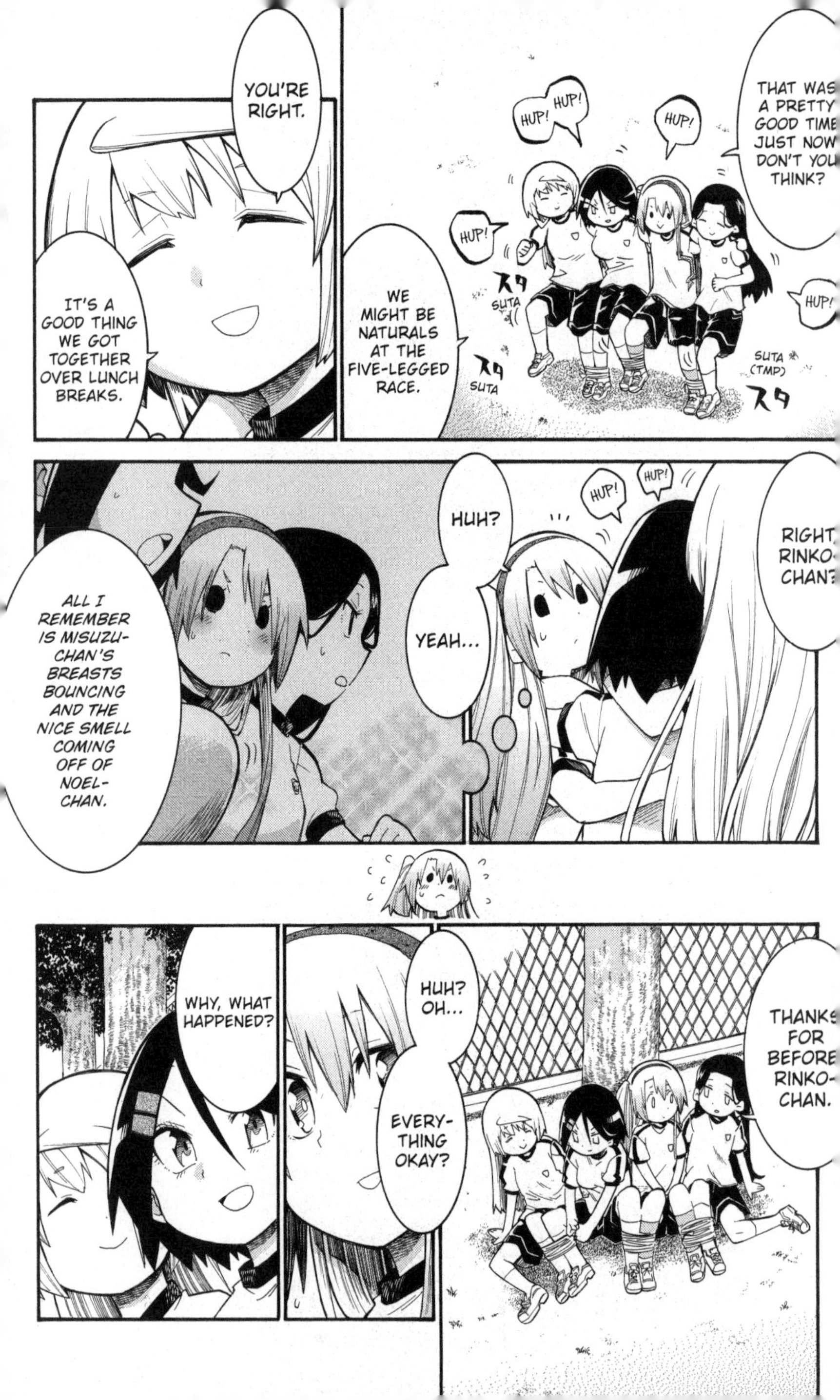
THAT WAS A PRETTY GOOD TIME JUST NOW DON'T YOU THINK?
HUP!
HUP!
HUP!
HUP!
HUP!
スタ SUTA
スタ SUTA (TMP)
WE MIGHT BE NATURALS AT THE FIVE-LEGGED RACE.
スタ SUTA
YOU'RE RIGHT.
IT'S A GOOD THING WE GOT TOGETHER OVER LUNCH BREAKS.
RIGHT, RINKO-CHAN?
HUP!
HUP!
HUH?
YEAH...
ALL I REMEMBER IS MISUZU-CHAN'S BREASTS BOUNCING AND THE NICE SMELL COMING OFF OF NOEL-CHAN.
THANKS FOR BEFORE, RINKO-CHAN.
HUH? OH...
EVERY-THING OKAY?
WHY, WHAT HAPPENED?

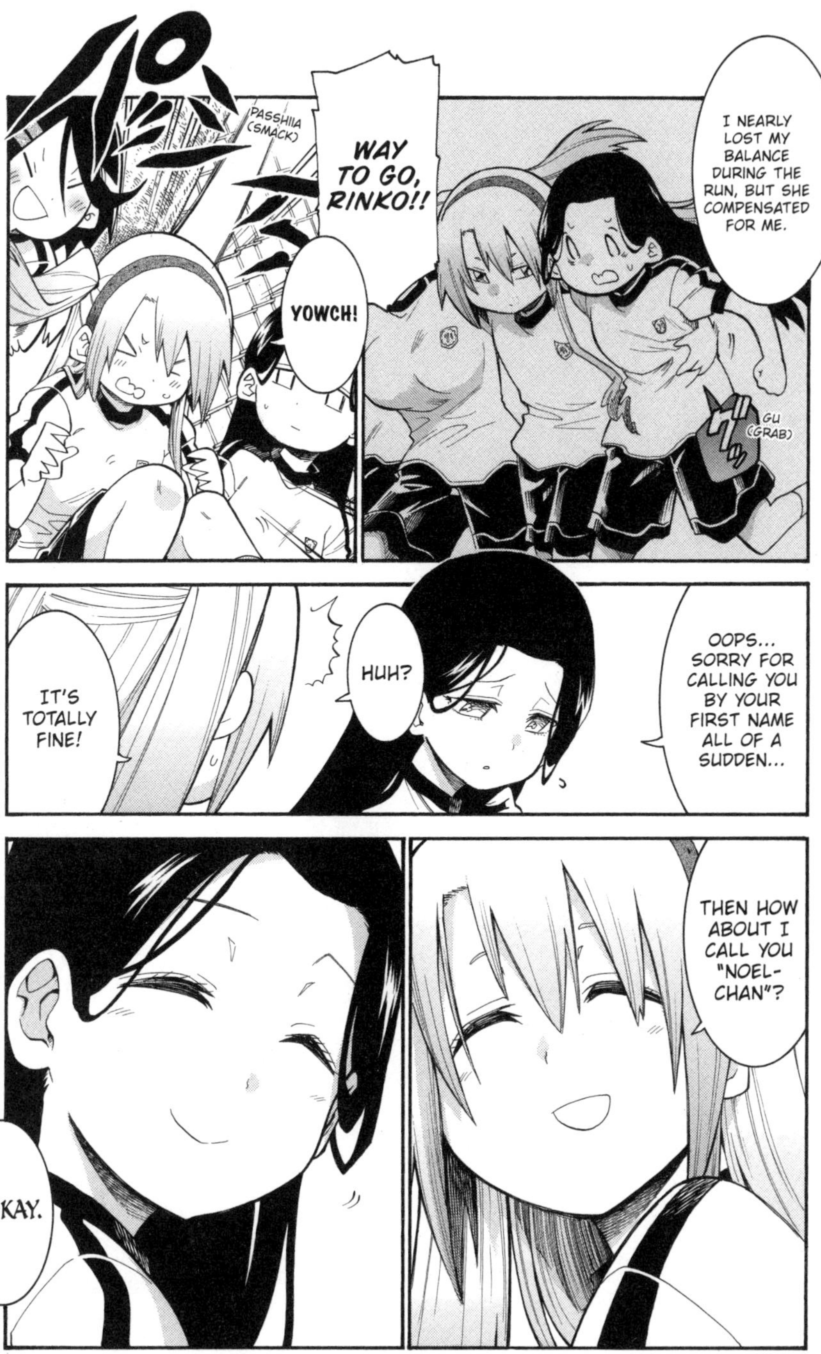
I NEARLY LOST MY BALANCE DURING THE RUN, BUT SHE COMPENSATED FOR ME.
GU (GRAB)
WAY TO GO, RINKO!!
PASSHIIA (SMACK)
YOWCH!
OOPS... SORRY FOR CALLING YOU BY YOUR FIRST NAME ALL OF A SUDDEN...
HUH?
IT'S TOTALLY FINE!
THEN HOW ABOUT I CALL YOU "NOEL-CHAN"?
OKAY.

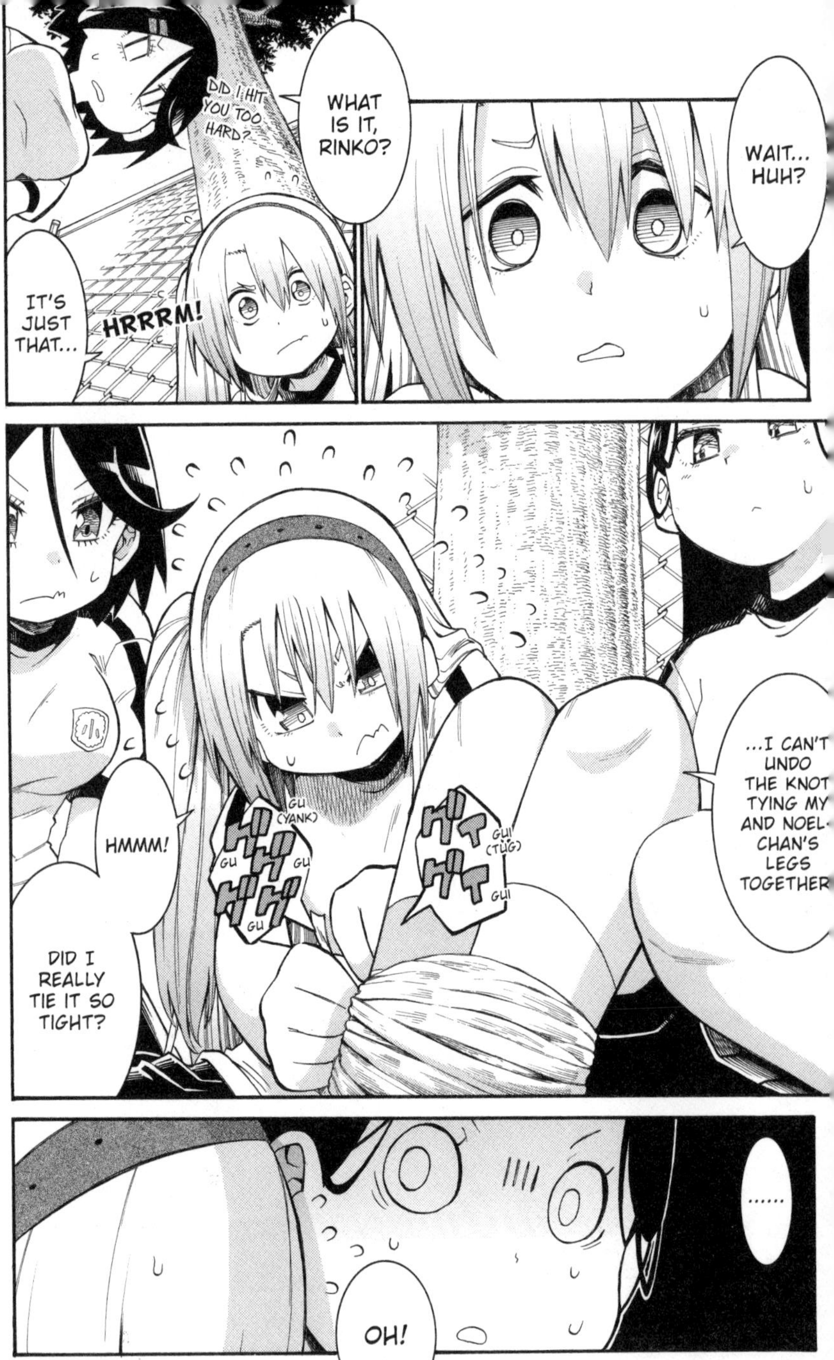
WAIT... HUH?
WHAT IS IT, RINKO?
DID I HIT YOU TOO HARD?
HRRRM!
IT'S JUST THAT...
...I CAN'T UNDO THE KNOT TYING MY AND NOEL-CHAN'S LEGS TOGETHER
GUI (TUG) GUI
GU (YANK) GU GU GU
HMMM!
DID I REALLY TIE IT SO TIGHT?
......
OH!

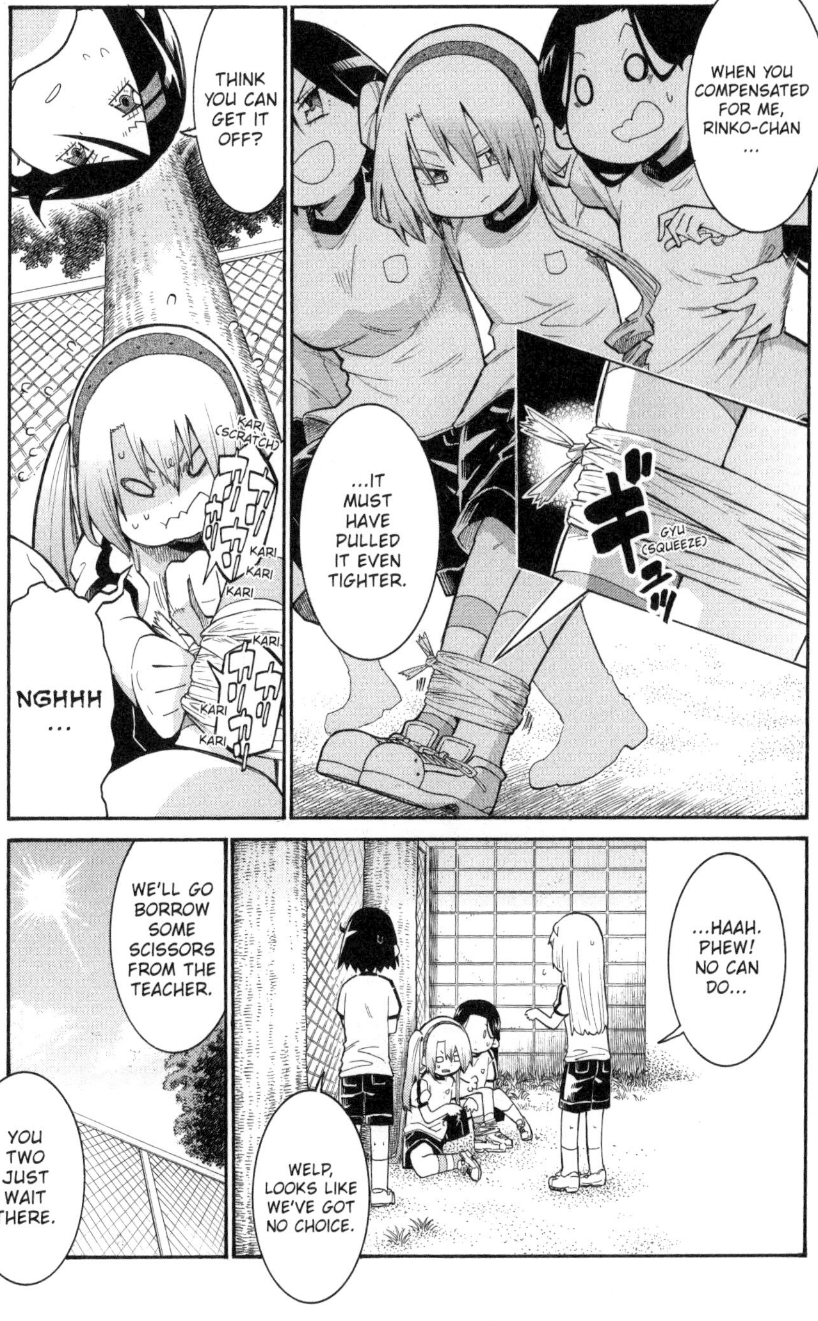
WHEN YOU COMPENSATED FOR ME, RINKO-CHAN ...
...IT MUST HAVE PULLED IT EVEN TIGHTER.
GYU (SQUEEZE)
THINK YOU CAN GET IT OFF?
KARI (SCRATCH)
KARI
KARI
KARI
KARI
KARI
KARI
NGHHH ...
...HAAH. PHEW! NO CAN DO...
WELP, LOOKS LIKE WE'VE GOT NO CHOICE.
WE'LL GO BORROW SOME SCISSORS FROM THE TEACHER.
YOU TWO JUST WAIT THERE.

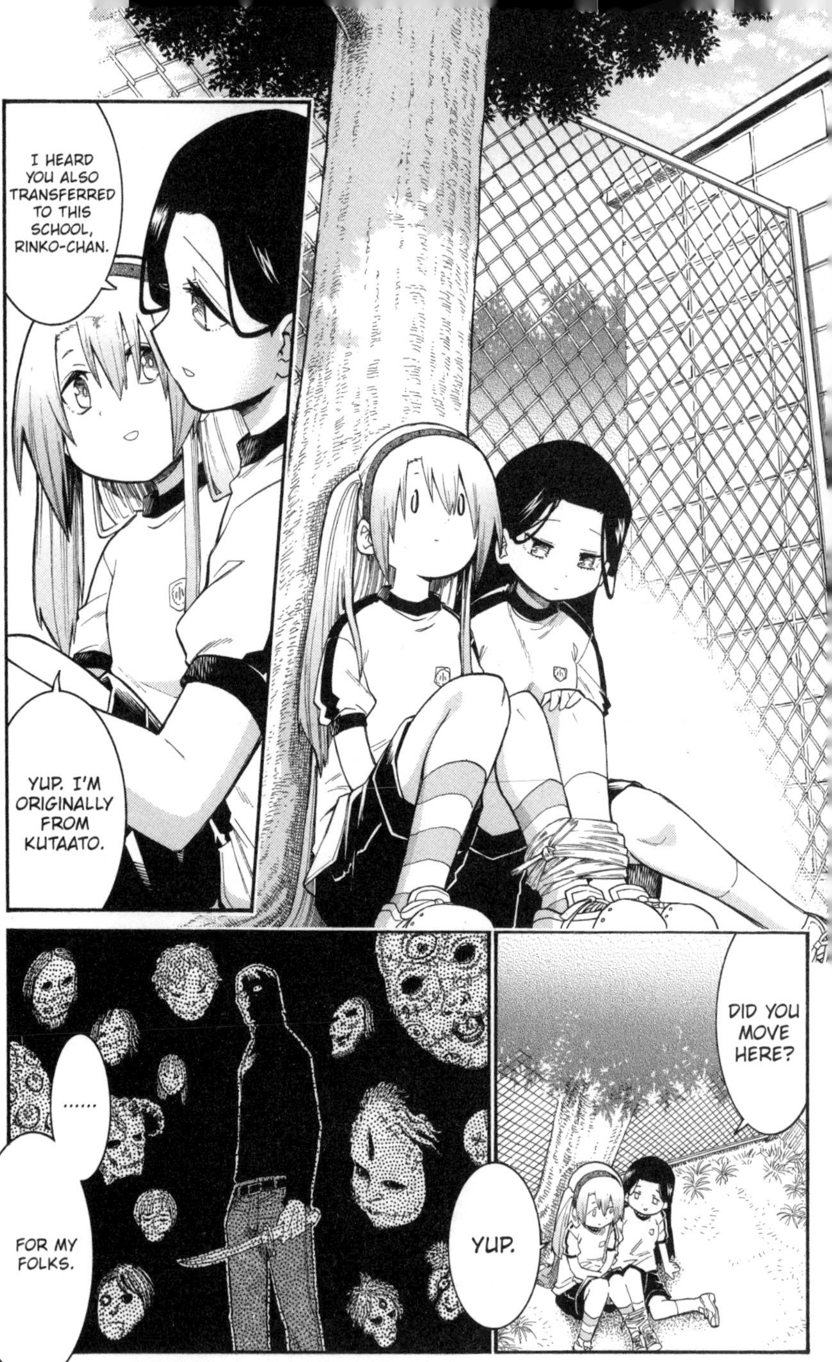
I HEARD YOU ALSO TRANSFERRED TO THIS SCHOOL, RINKO-CHAN.
YUP. I'M ORIGINALLY FROM KUTAATO.
DID YOU MOVE HERE?
YUP.
......
FOR MY FOLKS.

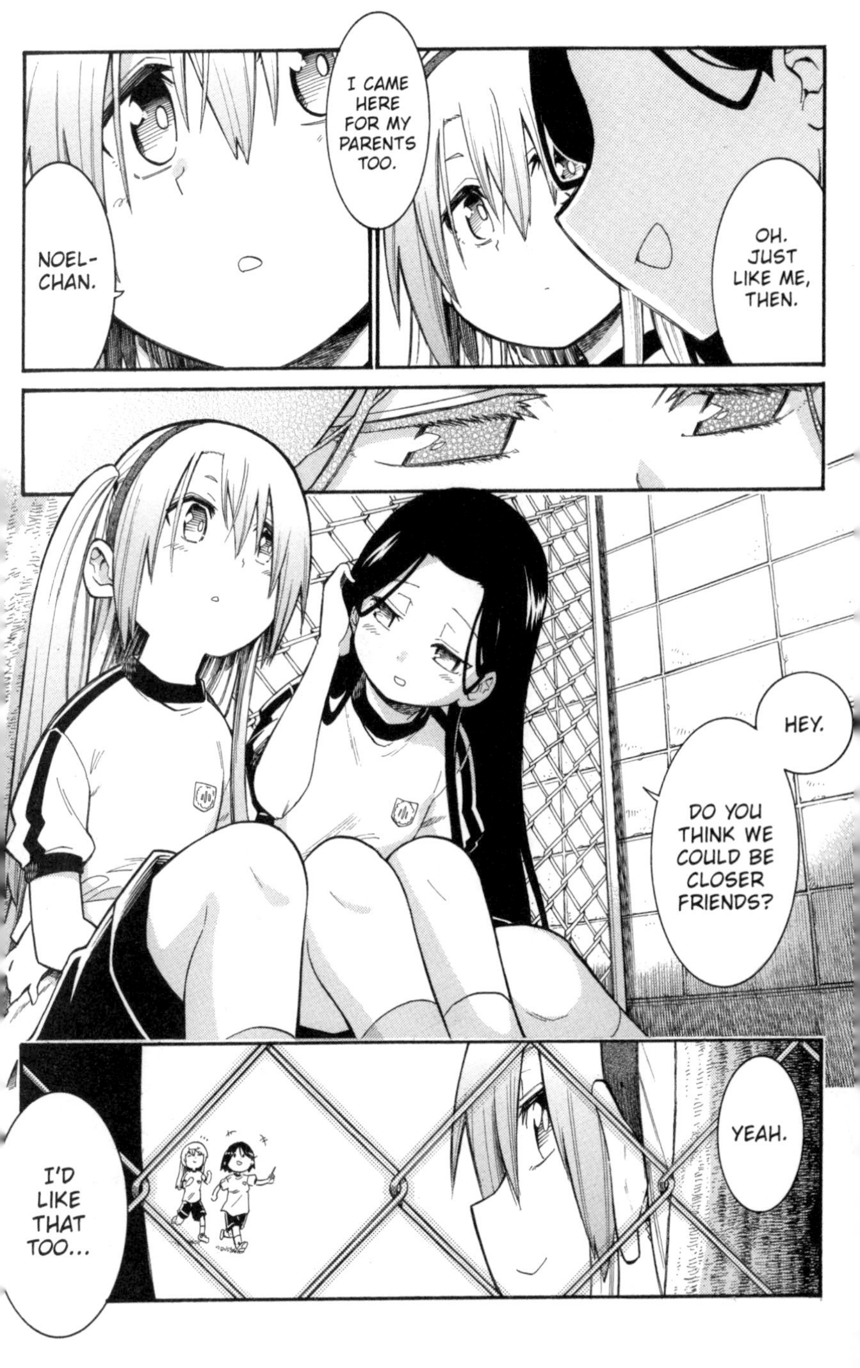
I CAME HERE FOR MY PARENTS TOO.
OH. JUST LIKE ME, THEN.
NOEL-CHAN.
HEY.
DO YOU THINK WE COULD BE CLOSER FRIENDS?
YEAH.
I'D LIKE THAT TOO...

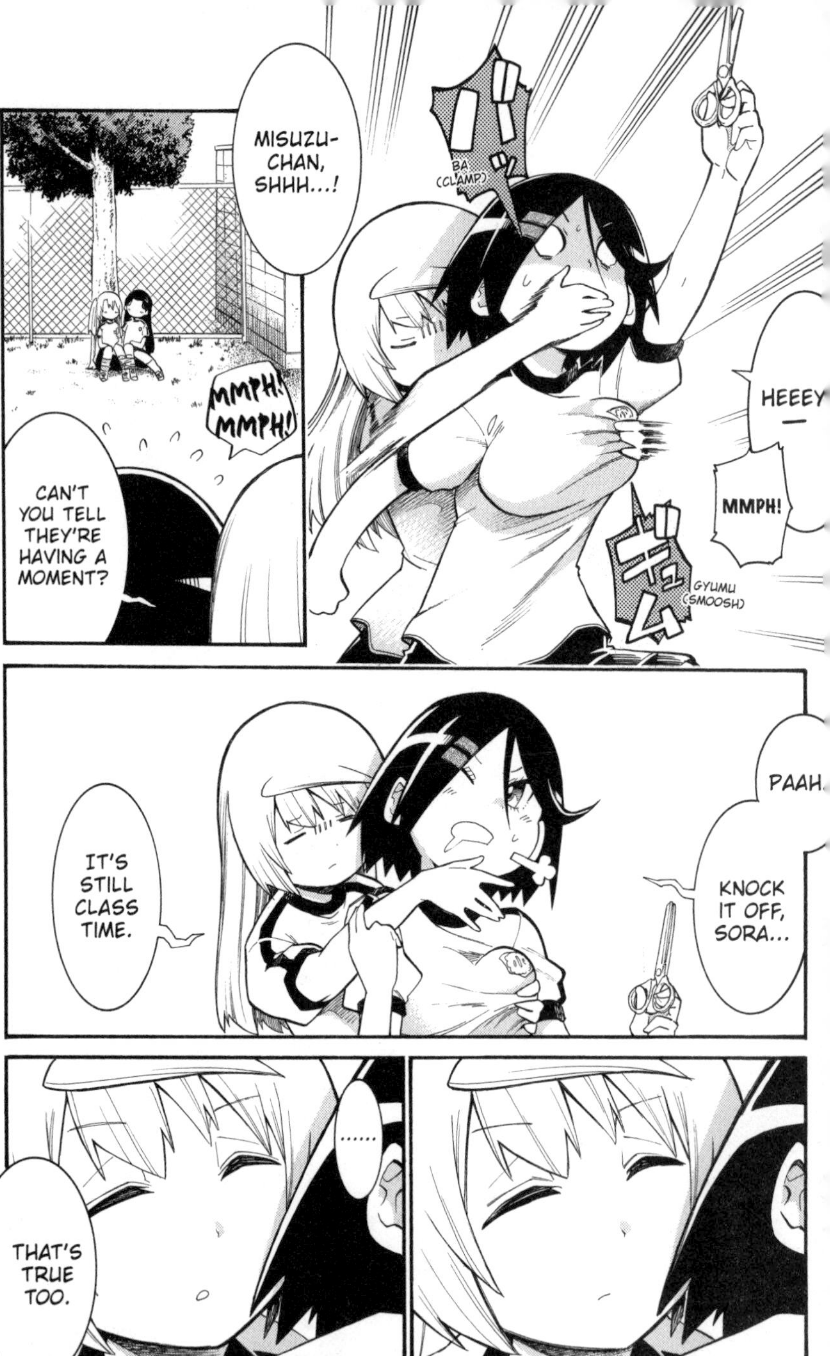
HEEEY—
BA (CLAMP)
MISUZU-CHAN, SHHH...!
MMPH!
GYUMU (SMOOSH)
MMPH! MMPH!
CAN'T YOU TELL THEY'RE HAVING A MOMENT?
PAAH.
KNOCK IT OFF, SORA...
IT'S STILL CLASS TIME.
......
THAT'S TRUE TOO.

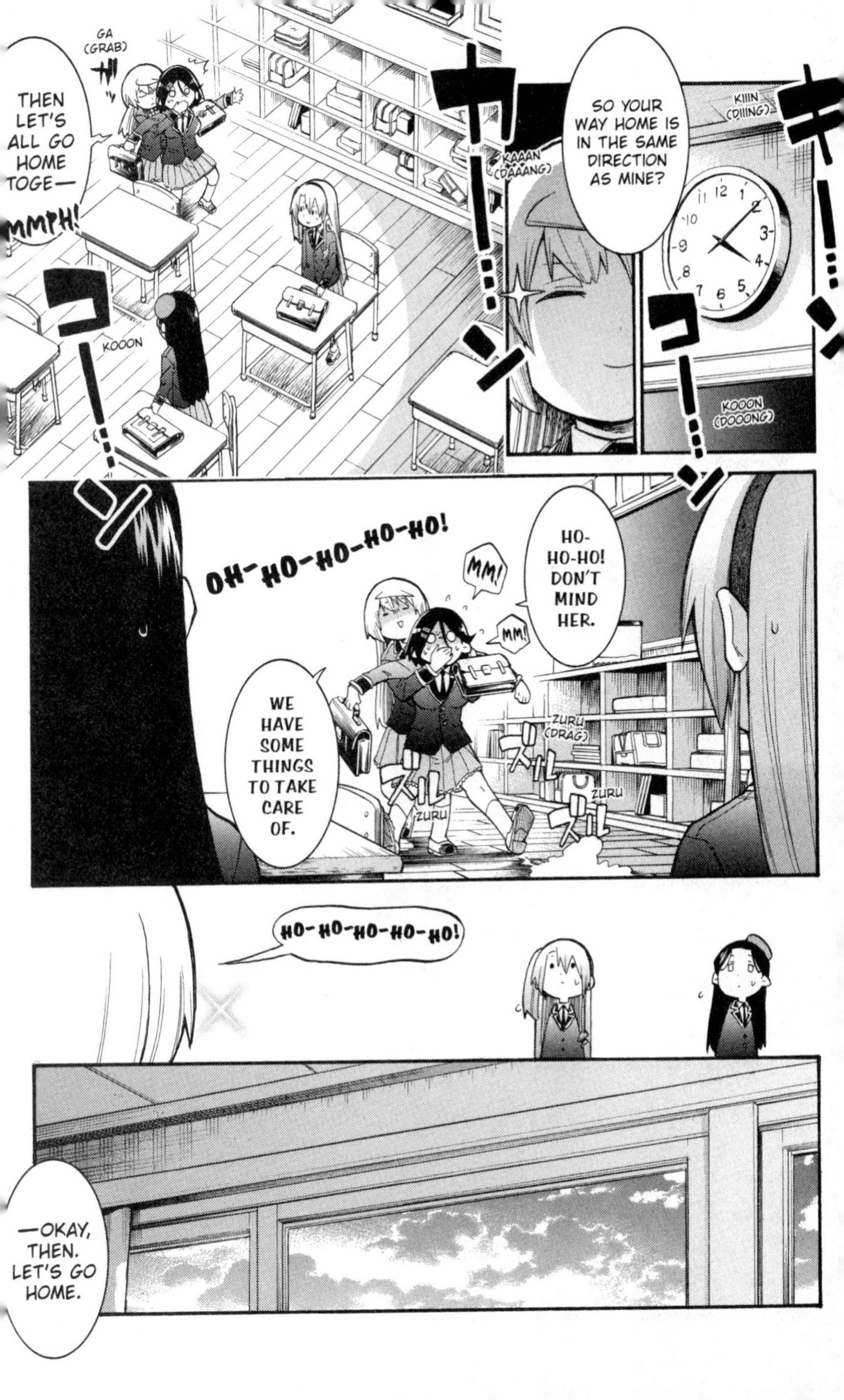
KIIIN (DIIING)
SO YOUR WAY HOME IS IN THE SAME DIRECTION AS MINE?
KAAAN (DAAAANG)
KOOON (DOOONG)
GA (GRAB)
THEN LET'S ALL GO HOME TOGE—
MMPH!
KOOON
HO-HO-HO! DON'T MIND HER.
MM!
MM!
OH-HO-HO-HO-HO!
WE HAVE SOME THINGS TO TAKE CARE OF.
ZURU (DRAG)
ZURU
ZURU
HO-HO-HO-HO-HO!
—OKAY, THEN. LET'S GO HOME.

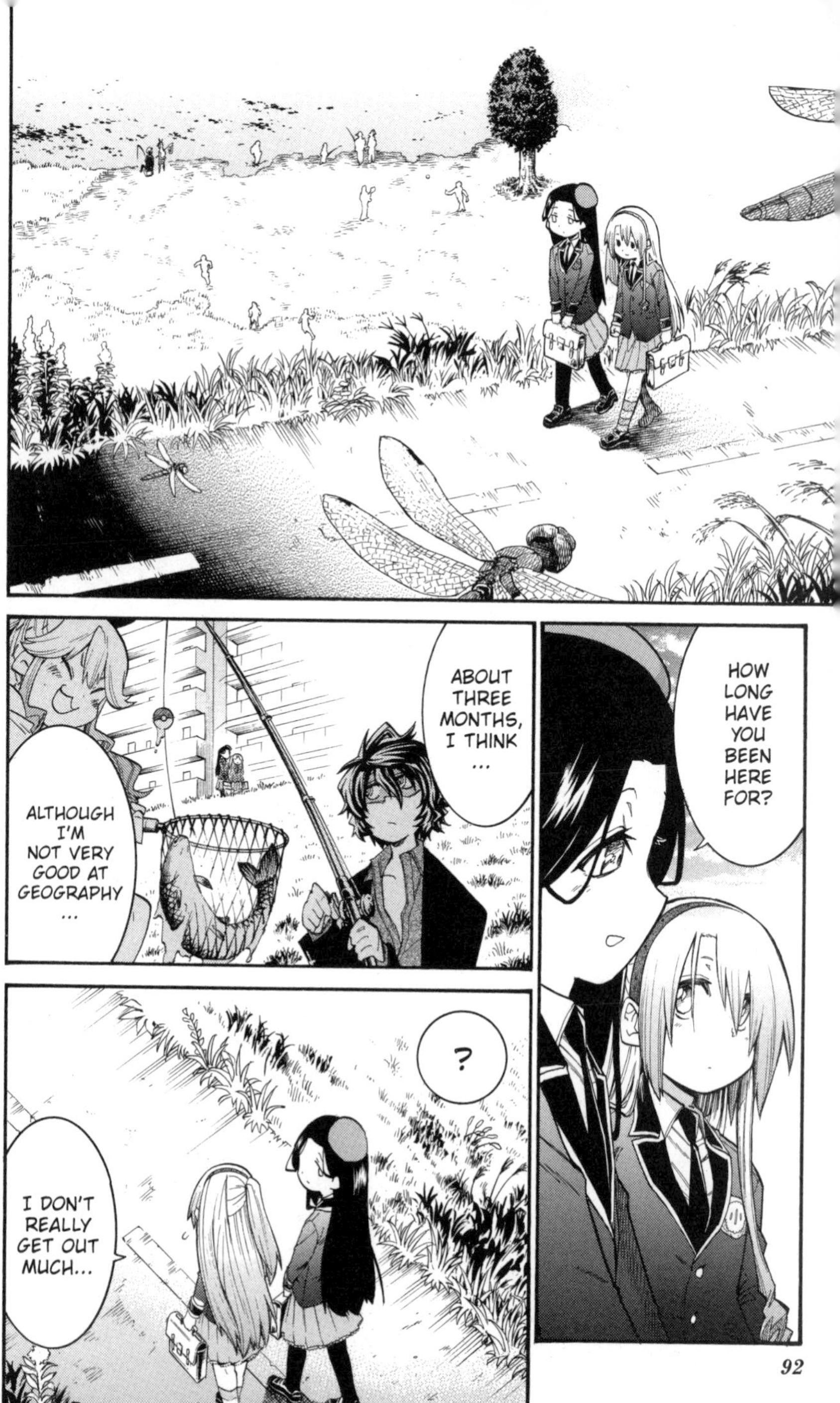
HOW LONG HAVE YOU BEEN HERE FOR?
ABOUT THREE MONTHS, I THINK...
ALTHOUGH I'M NOT VERY GOOD AT GEOGRAPHY...
?
I DON'T REALLY GET OUT MUCH...

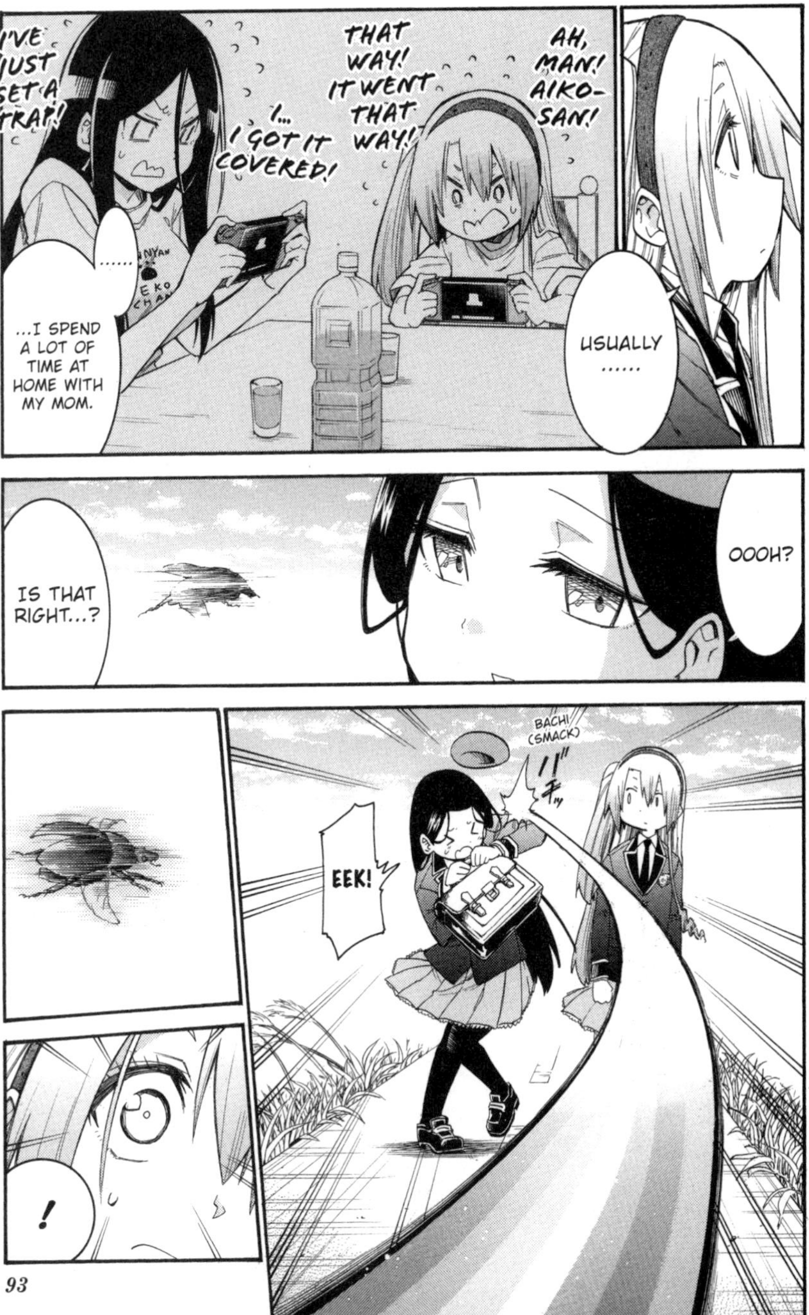
USUALLY ......
AH, MAN! AIKO-SAN!
THAT WAY! IT WENT THAT WAY!
I... I GOT IT COVERED!
I'VE JUST SET A TRAP!
......
...I SPEND A LOT OF TIME AT HOME WITH MY MOM.
OOOH?
IS THAT RIGHT...?
BACHI (SMACK)
EEK!
!

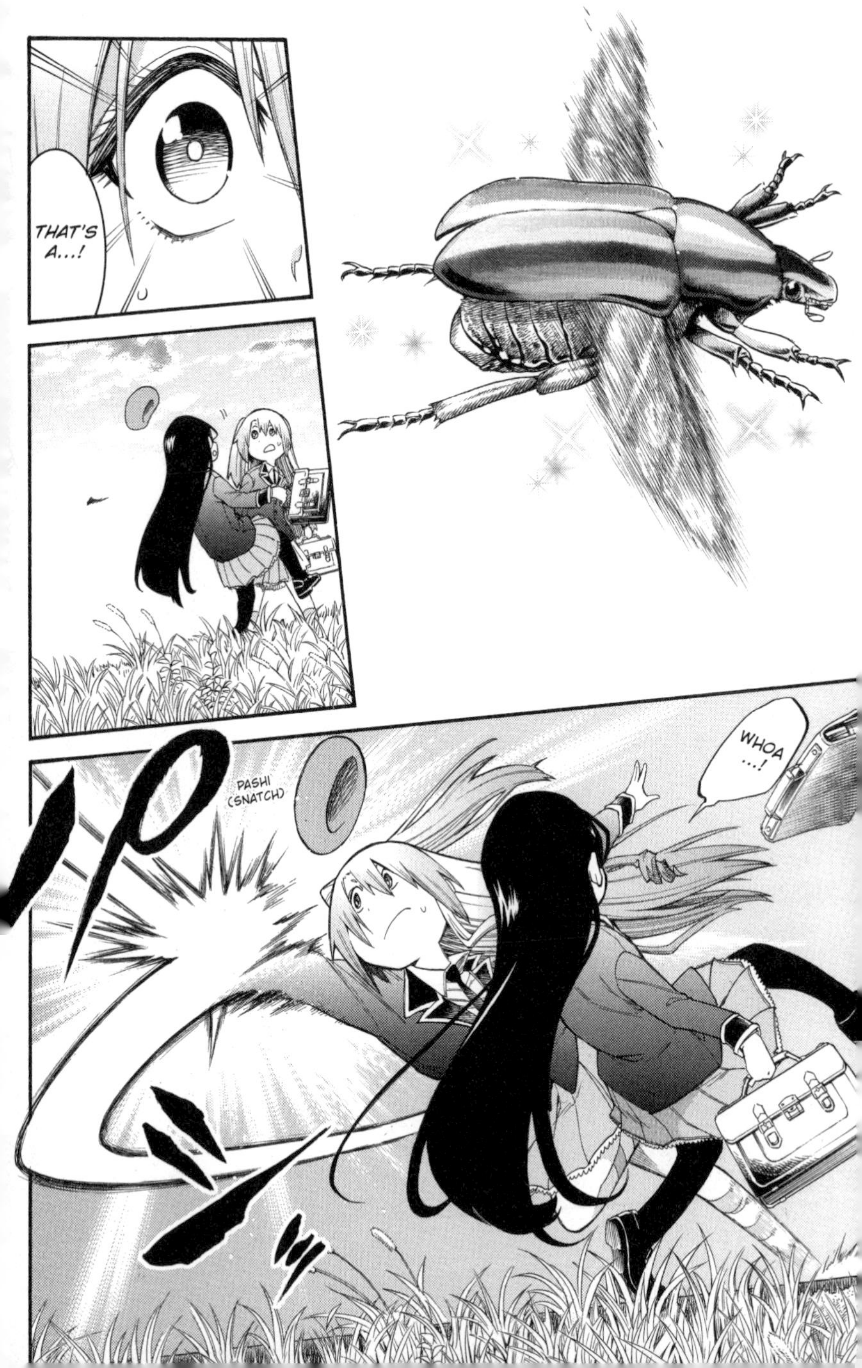
THAT'S A...!
WHOA...!
PASHI (SNATCH)

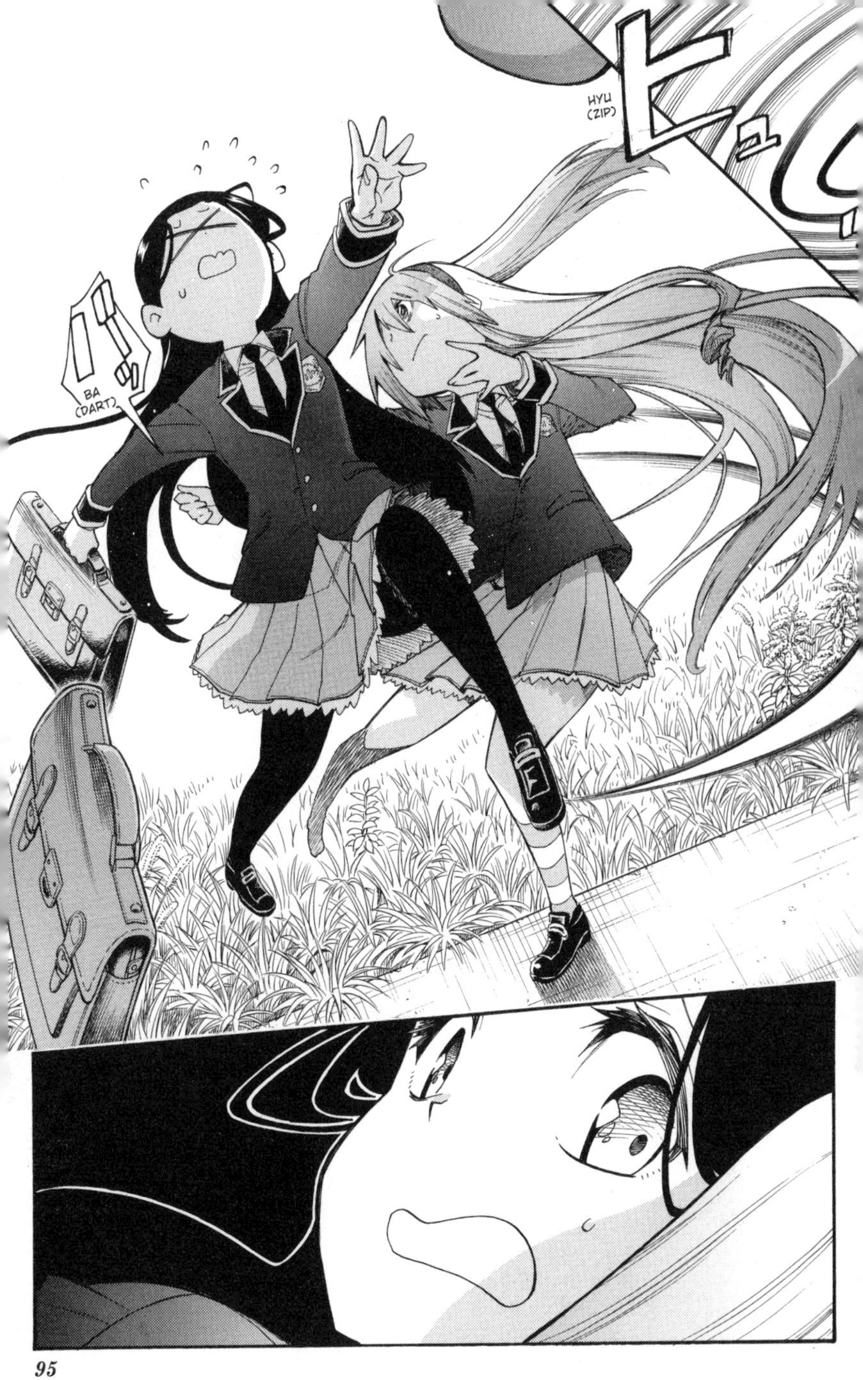
HYU
(ZIP)
BA
(DART)

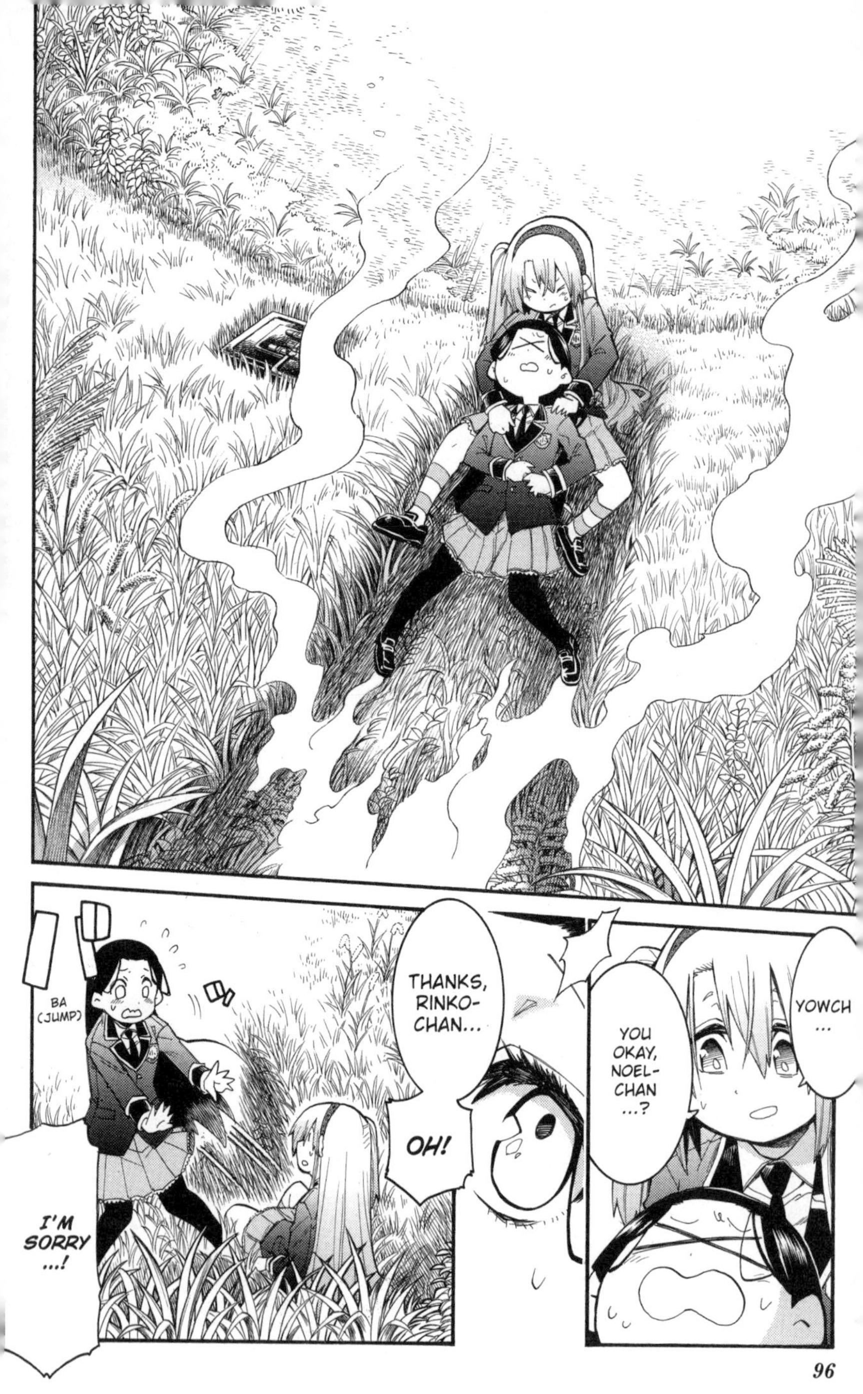
YOWCH ...
YOU OKAY, NOEL-CHAN ...?
THANKS, RINKO-CHAN...
OH!
BA (JUMP)
I'M SORRY ...!

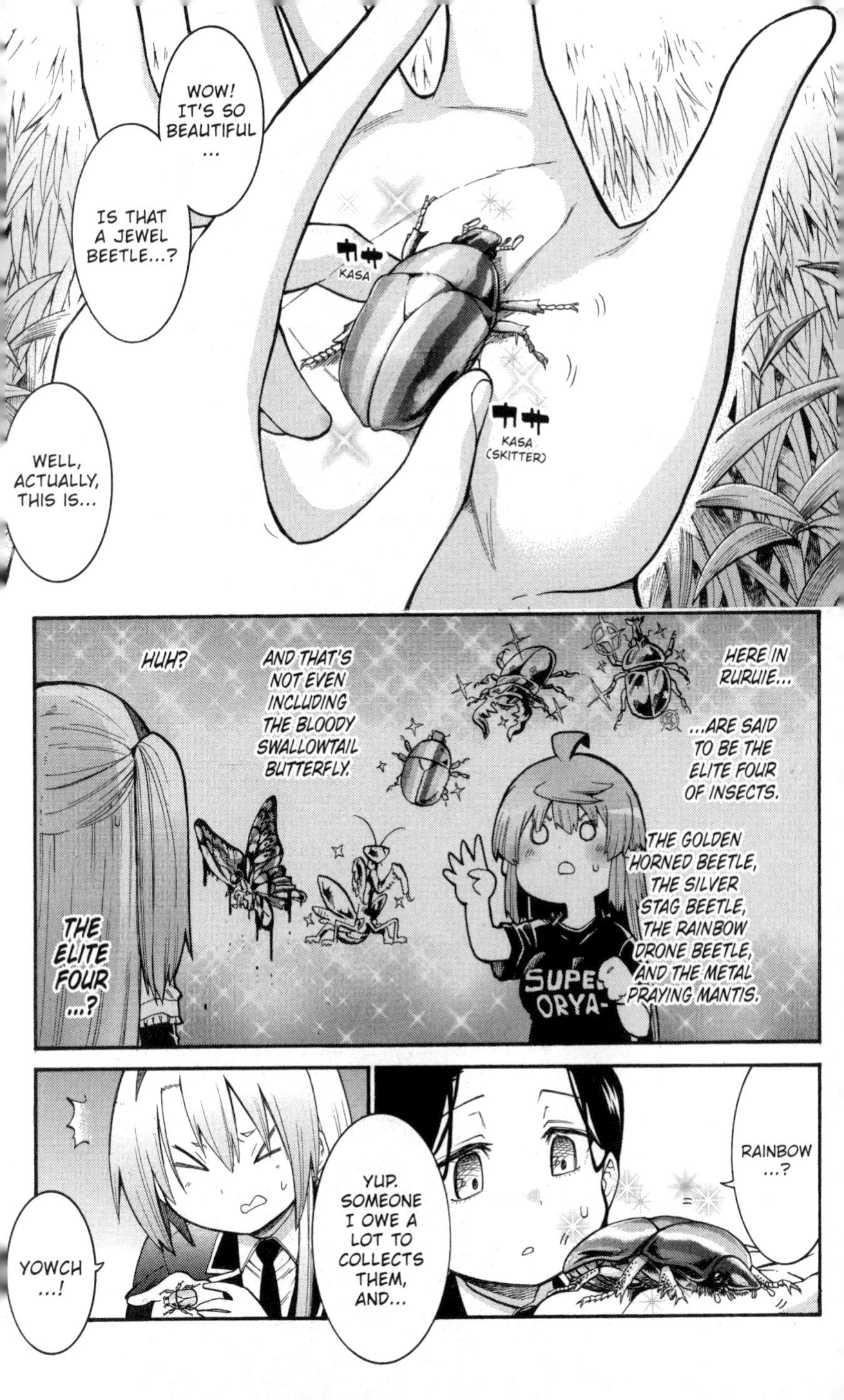
WOW! IT'S SO BEAUTIFUL ...
IS THAT A JEWEL BEETLE...?
KASA
KASA (SKITTER)
WELL, ACTUALLY, THIS IS...
HERE IN RURUIE...
...ARE SAID TO BE THE ELITE FOUR OF INSECTS.
THE GOLDEN HORNED BEETLE, THE SILVER STAG BEETLE, THE RAINBOW DRONE BEETLE, AND THE METAL PRAYING MANTIS.
AND THAT'S NOT EVEN INCLUDING THE BLOODY SWALLOWTAIL BUTTERFLY.
HUH?
THE ELITE FOUR ...?
SUPER ORYA-
RAINBOW ...?
YUP. SOMEONE I OWE A LOT TO COLLECTS THEM, AND...
YOWCH ...!

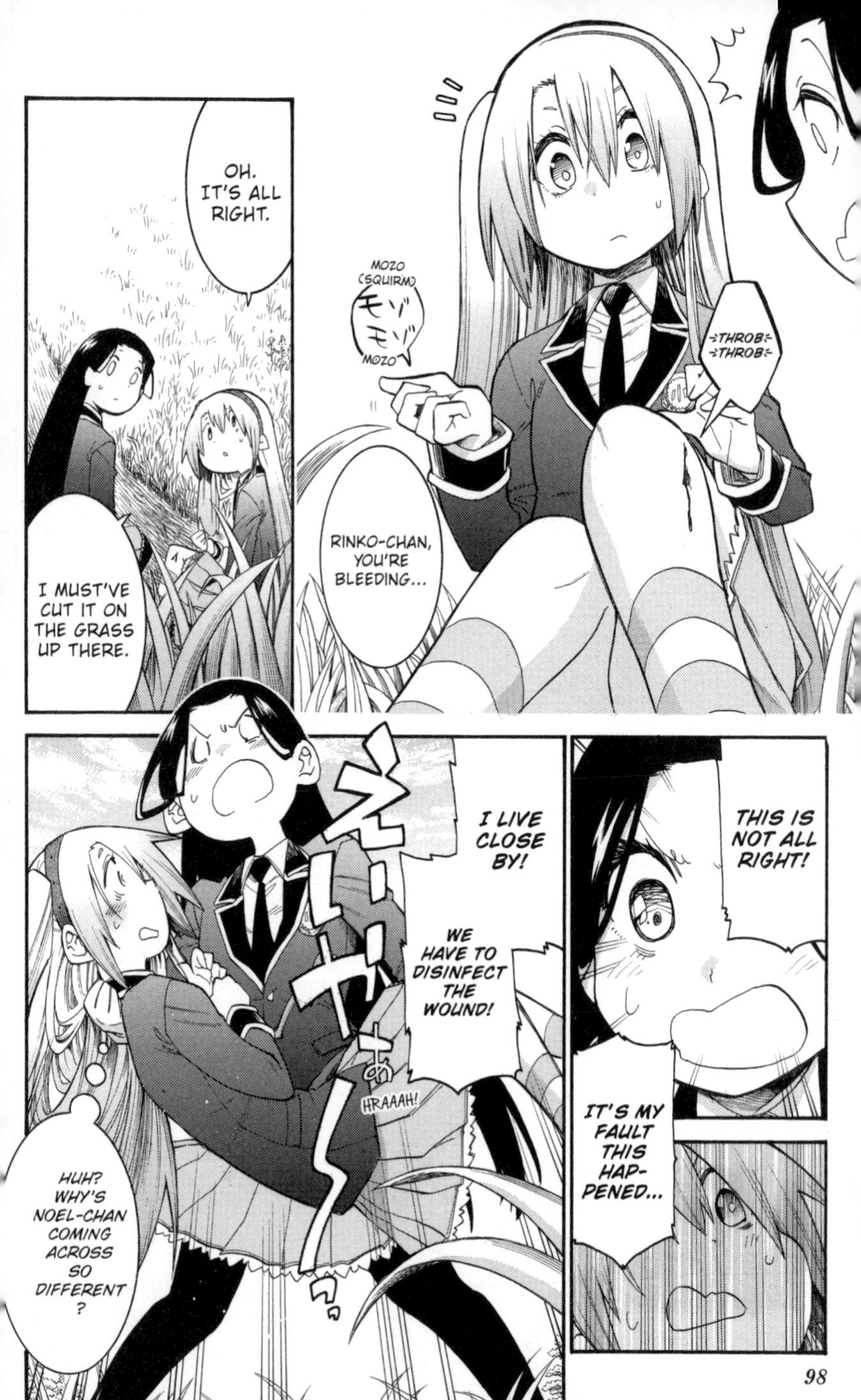

THROB THROB
MOZO (SQUIRM) モゾモゾ MOZO
RINKO-CHAN, YOU'RE BLEEDING...
OH. IT'S ALL RIGHT.
I MUST'VE CUT IT ON THE GRASS UP THERE.
THIS IS NOT ALL RIGHT!
IT'S MY FAULT THIS HAPPENED...
I LIVE CLOSE BY!
WE HAVE TO DISINFECT THE WOUND!
HRAAAH!
HUH? WHY'S NOEL-CHAN COMING ACROSS SO DIFFERENT?

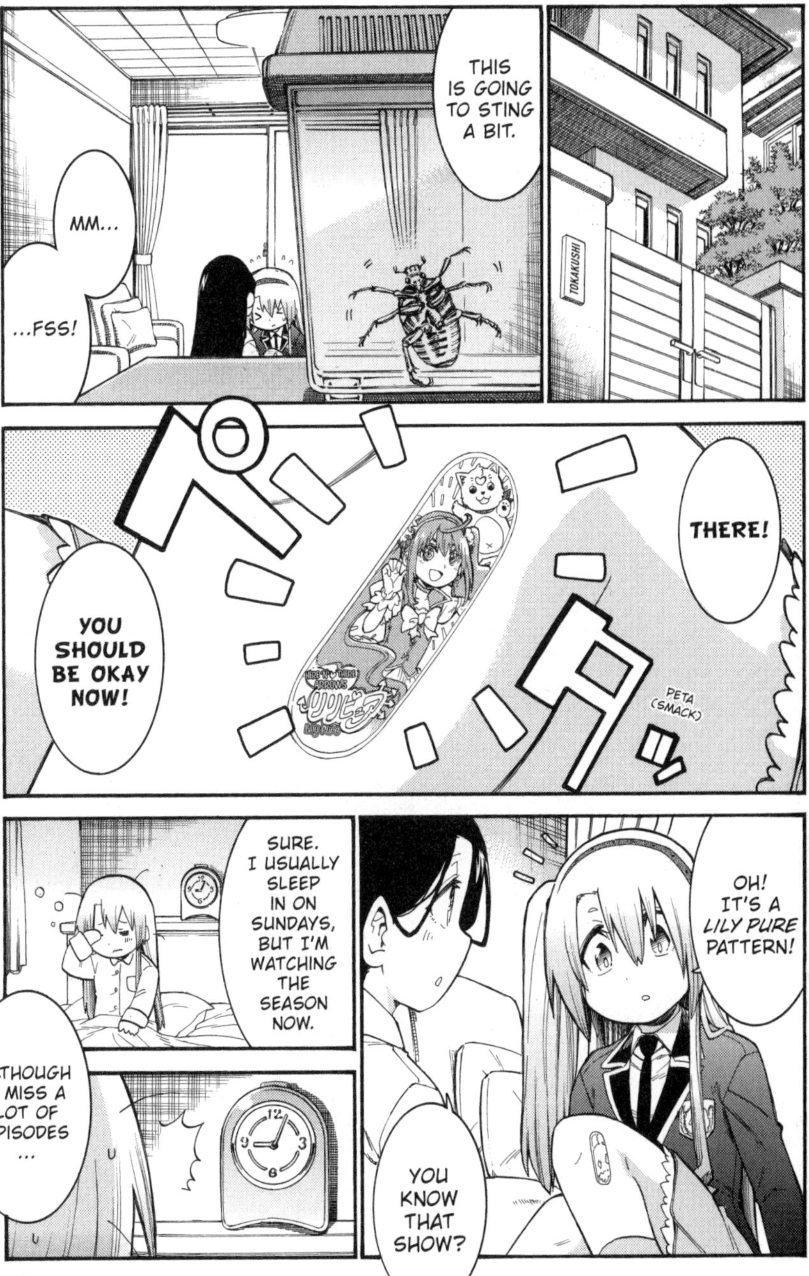
TOKAKUSHI
THIS IS GOING TO STING A BIT.
MM...
...FSS!
THERE!
PETA (SMACK)
HERE 'N' THERE ARROWS
Lily Pure
YOU SHOULD BE OKAY NOW!
OH! IT'S A *LILY PURE* PATTERN!
YOU KNOW THAT SHOW?
SURE. I USUALLY SLEEP IN ON SUNDAYS, BUT I'M WATCHING THE SEASON NOW.
ALTHOUGH I MISS A LOT OF EPISODES...

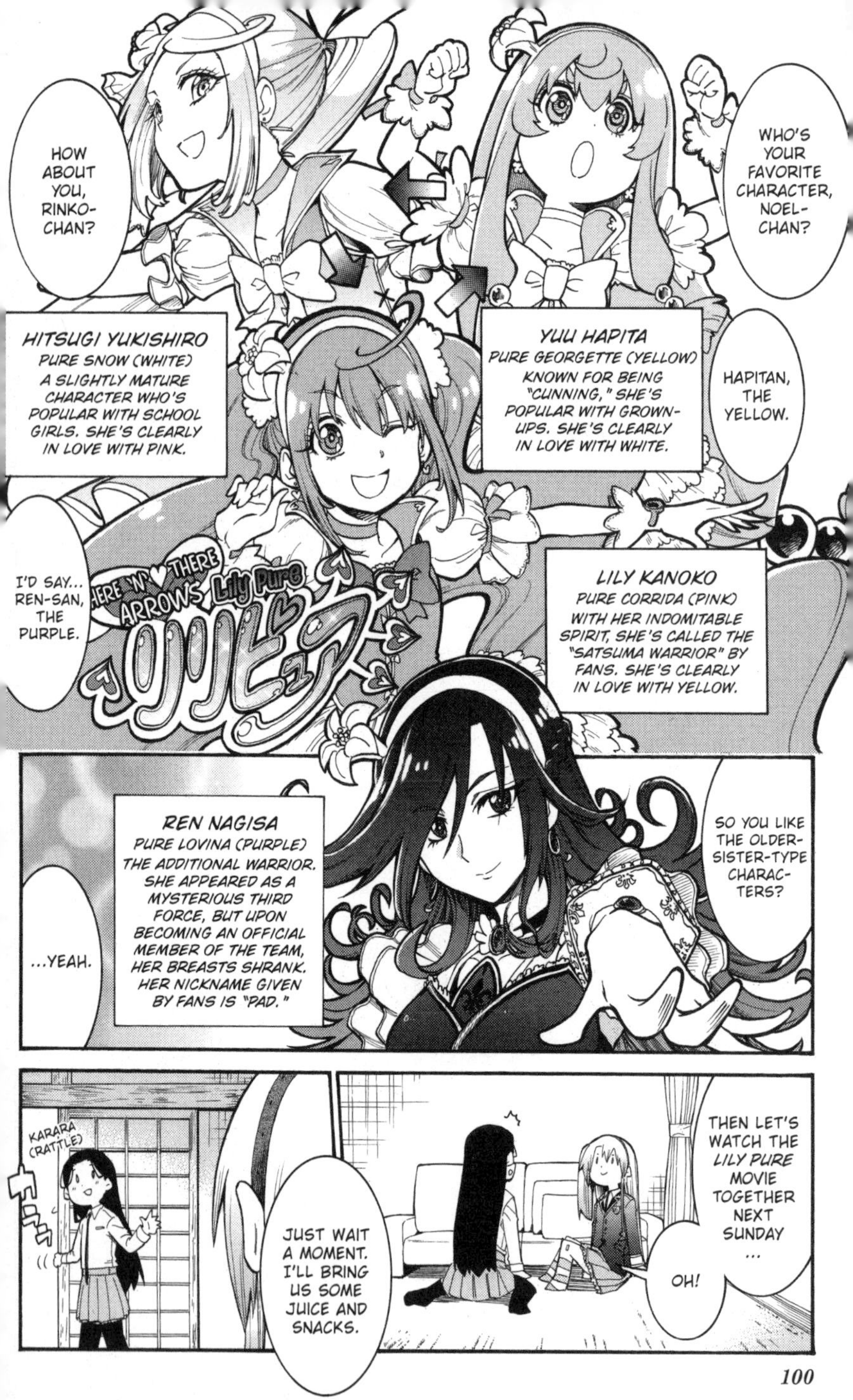
WHO'S YOUR FAVORITE CHARACTER, NOEL-CHAN?
YUU HAPITA
PURE GEORGETTE (YELLOW)
KNOWN FOR BEING "CUNNING," SHE'S POPULAR WITH GROWN-UPS. SHE'S CLEARLY IN LOVE WITH WHITE.
HAPITAN, THE YELLOW.
HOW ABOUT YOU, RINKO-CHAN?
HITSUGI YUKISHIRO
PURE SNOW (WHITE)
A SLIGHTLY MATURE CHARACTER WHO'S POPULAR WITH SCHOOL GIRLS. SHE'S CLEARLY IN LOVE WITH PINK.
LILY KANOKO
PURE CORRIDA (PINK)
WITH HER INDOMITABLE SPIRIT, SHE'S CALLED THE "SATSUMA WARRIOR" BY FANS. SHE'S CLEARLY IN LOVE WITH YELLOW.
HERE 'N' THERE ARROWS Lily Pure
リリピュア
I'D SAY... REN-SAN, THE PURPLE.
SO YOU LIKE THE OLDER-SISTER-TYPE CHARACTERS?
REN NAGISA
PURE LOVINA (PURPLE)
THE ADDITIONAL WARRIOR. SHE APPEARED AS A MYSTERIOUS THIRD FORCE, BUT UPON BECOMING AN OFFICIAL MEMBER OF THE TEAM, HER BREASTS SHRANK. HER NICKNAME GIVEN BY FANS IS "PAD."
...YEAH.
THEN LET'S WATCH THE *LILY PURE* MOVIE TOGETHER NEXT SUNDAY ...
OH!
KARARA (RATTLE)
JUST WAIT A MOMENT. I'LL BRING US SOME JUICE AND SNACKS.

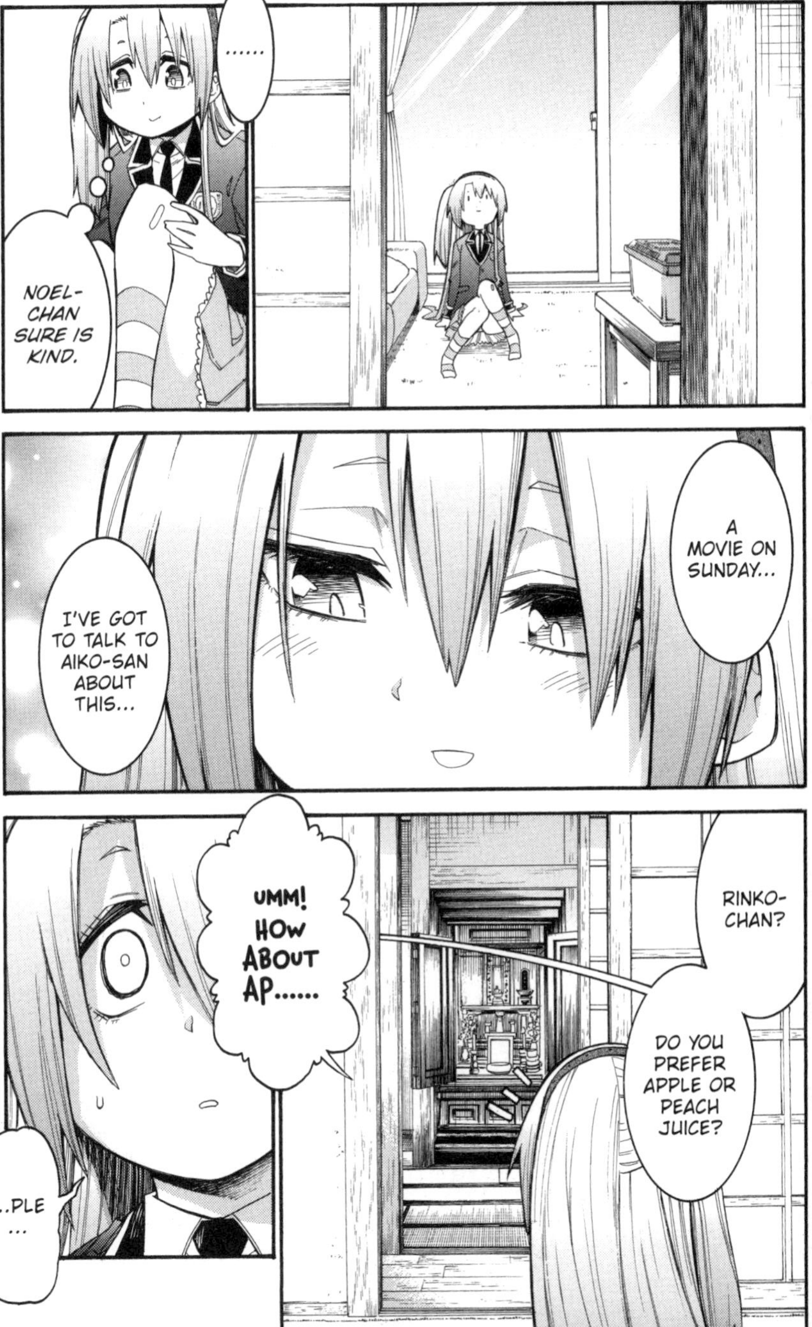
......
NOEL-CHAN SURE IS KIND.
A MOVIE ON SUNDAY...
I'VE GOT TO TALK TO AIKO-SAN ABOUT THIS...
RINKO-CHAN?
DO YOU PREFER APPLE OR PEACH JUICE?
UMM! HOW ABOUT AP......
...PLE ...

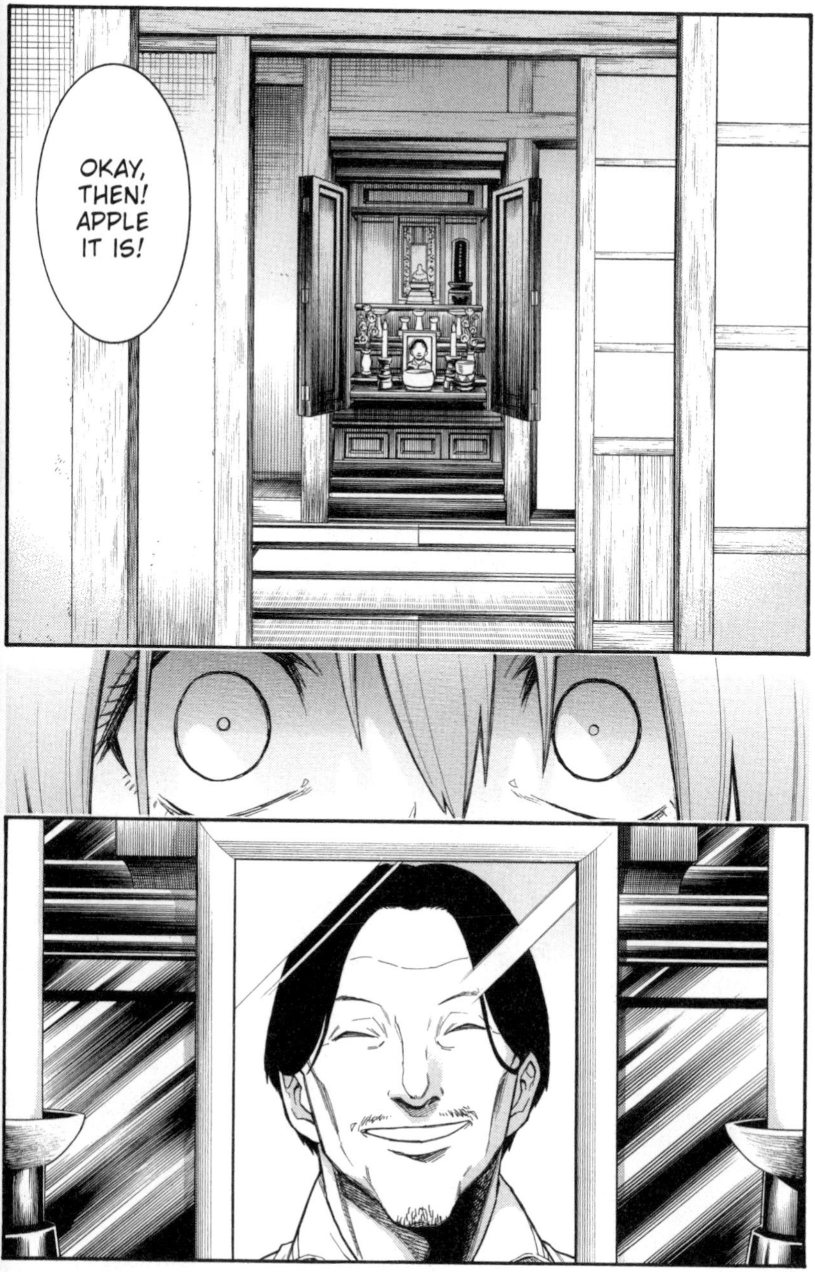
OKAY, THEN! APPLE IT IS!

MURCIÉLAGO

MURCIÉLAGO

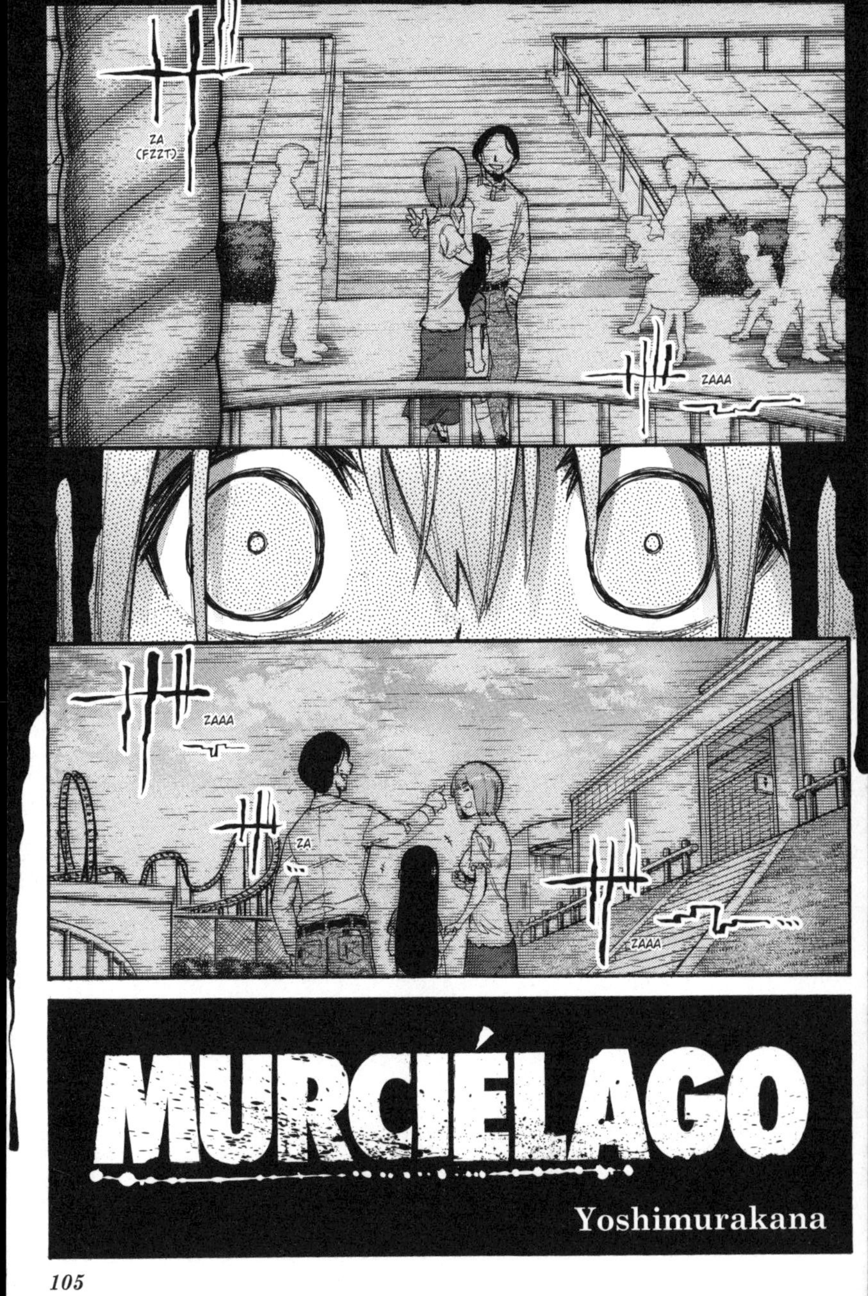
ZA
(FZZT)
ZAAA
ZAAA
ZA...
ZAAA

MURCIÉLAGO

Yoshimurakana

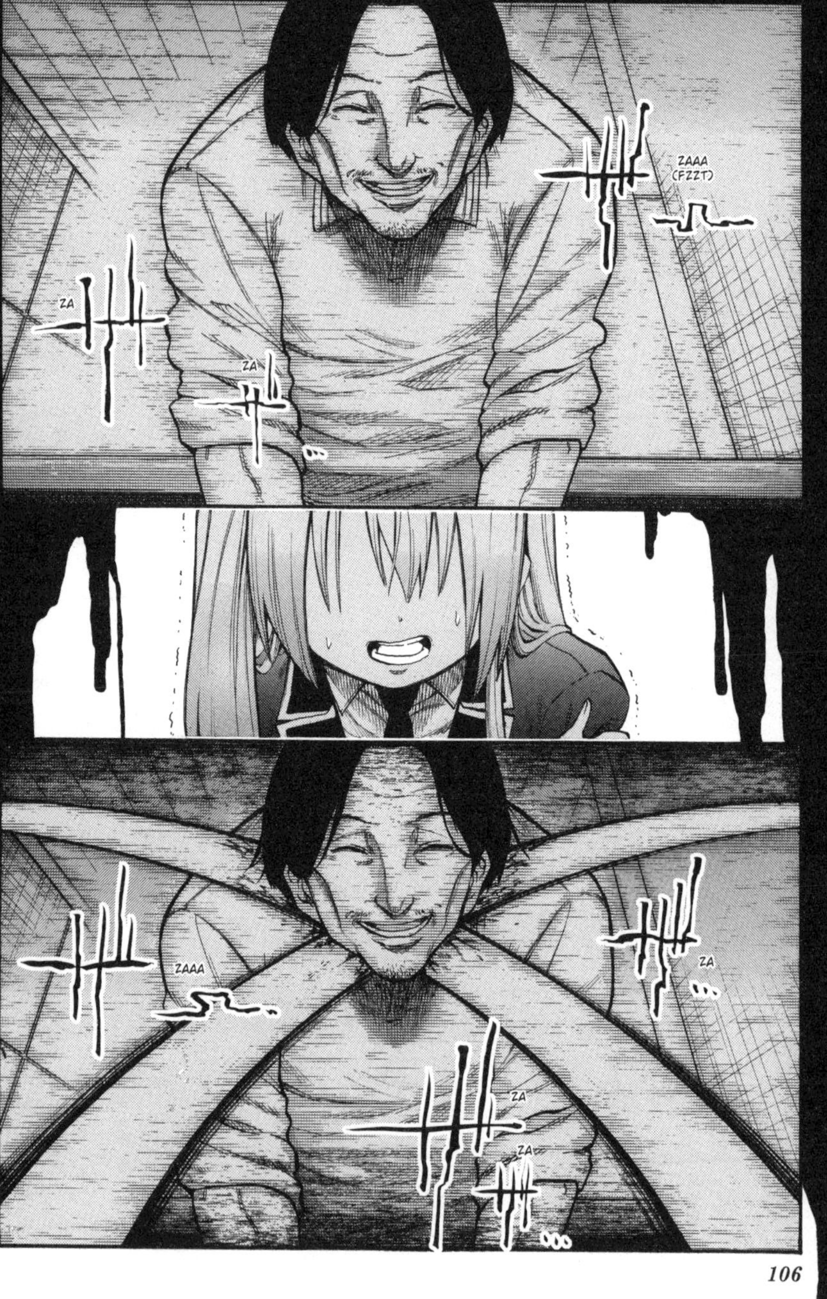
ZAAA (FZZT)
ZA
ZA
ZA
ZAAA
ZA
ZA

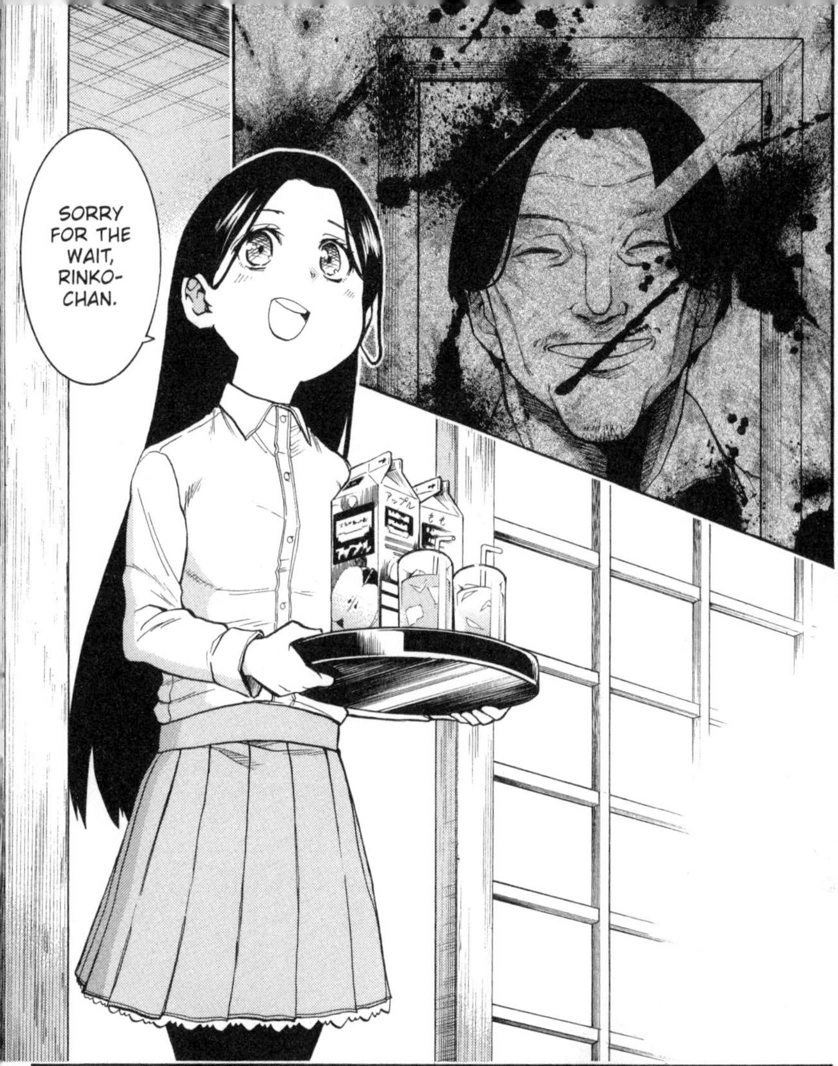
SORRY FOR THE WAIT, RINKO-CHAN.

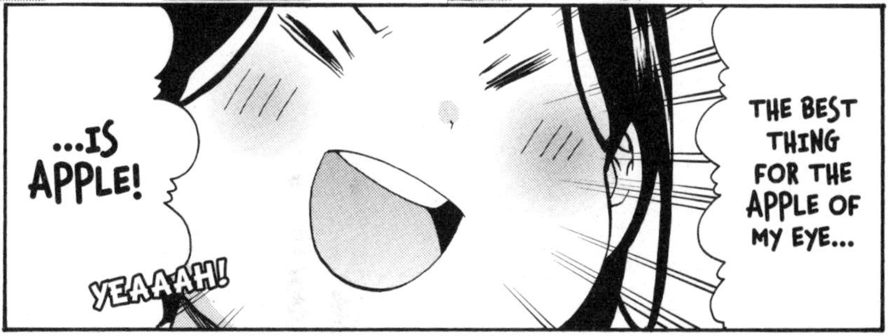
THE BEST THING FOR THE APPLE OF MY EYE...
...IS APPLE!
YEAAAH!

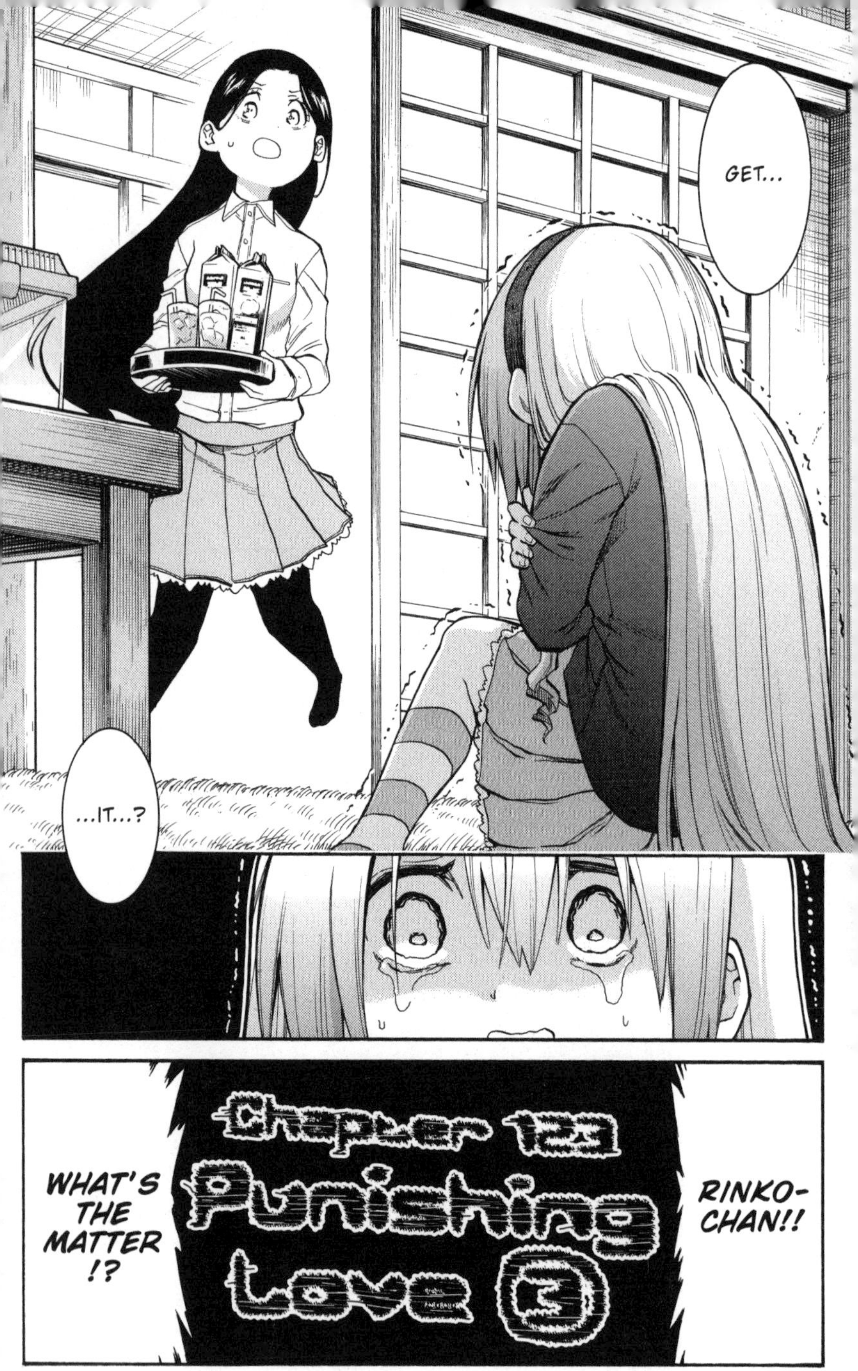
GET...
...IT...?
Chapter 123
Punishing Love ③
RINKO-CHAN!!
WHAT'S THE MATTER!?

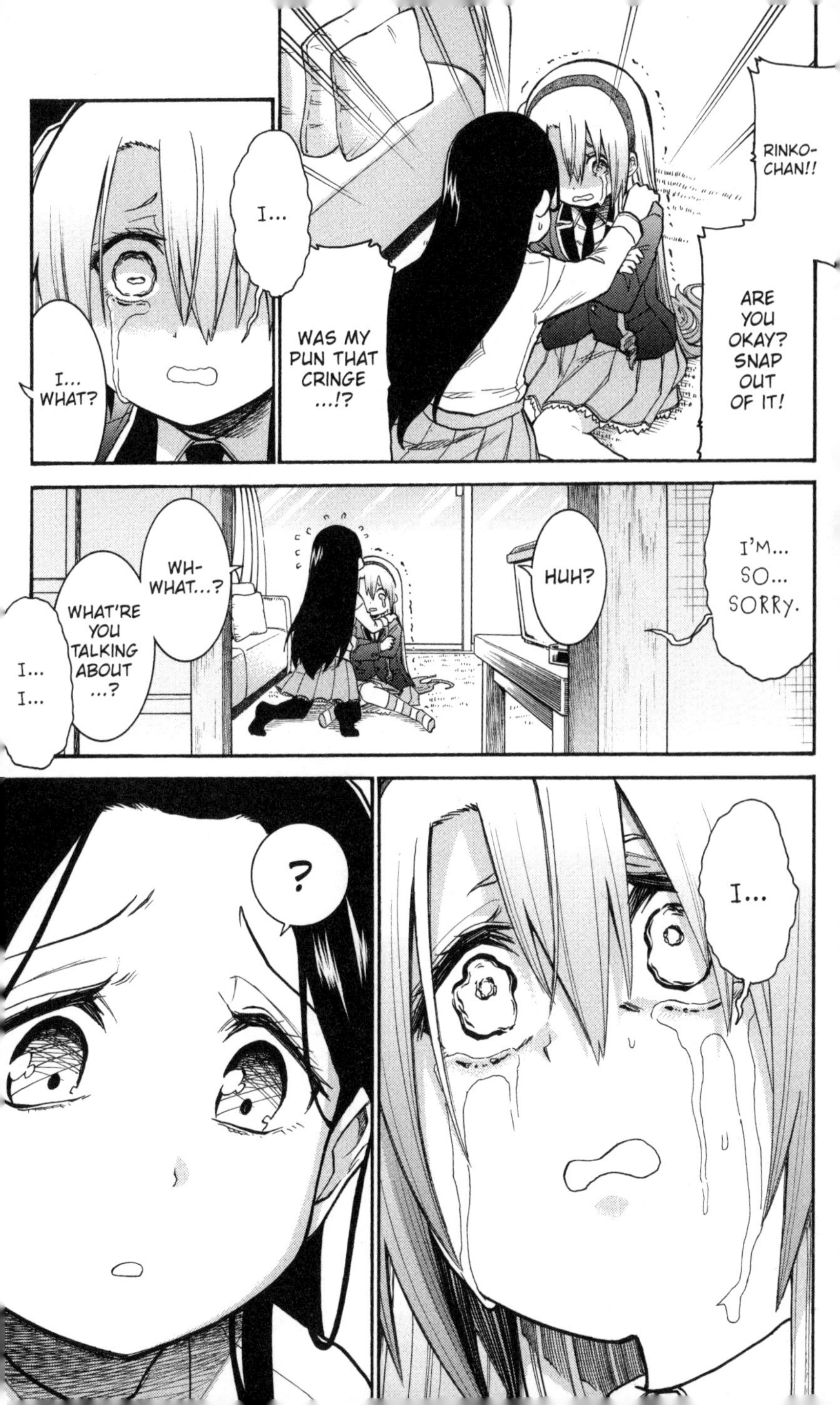
RINKO-CHAN!!
ARE YOU OKAY? SNAP OUT OF IT!
WAS MY PUN THAT CRINGE ...!?
I...
I... WHAT?
I'M... SO... SORRY.
HUH?
WH- WHAT...?
WHAT'RE YOU TALKING ABOUT ...?
I... I...
I...
?

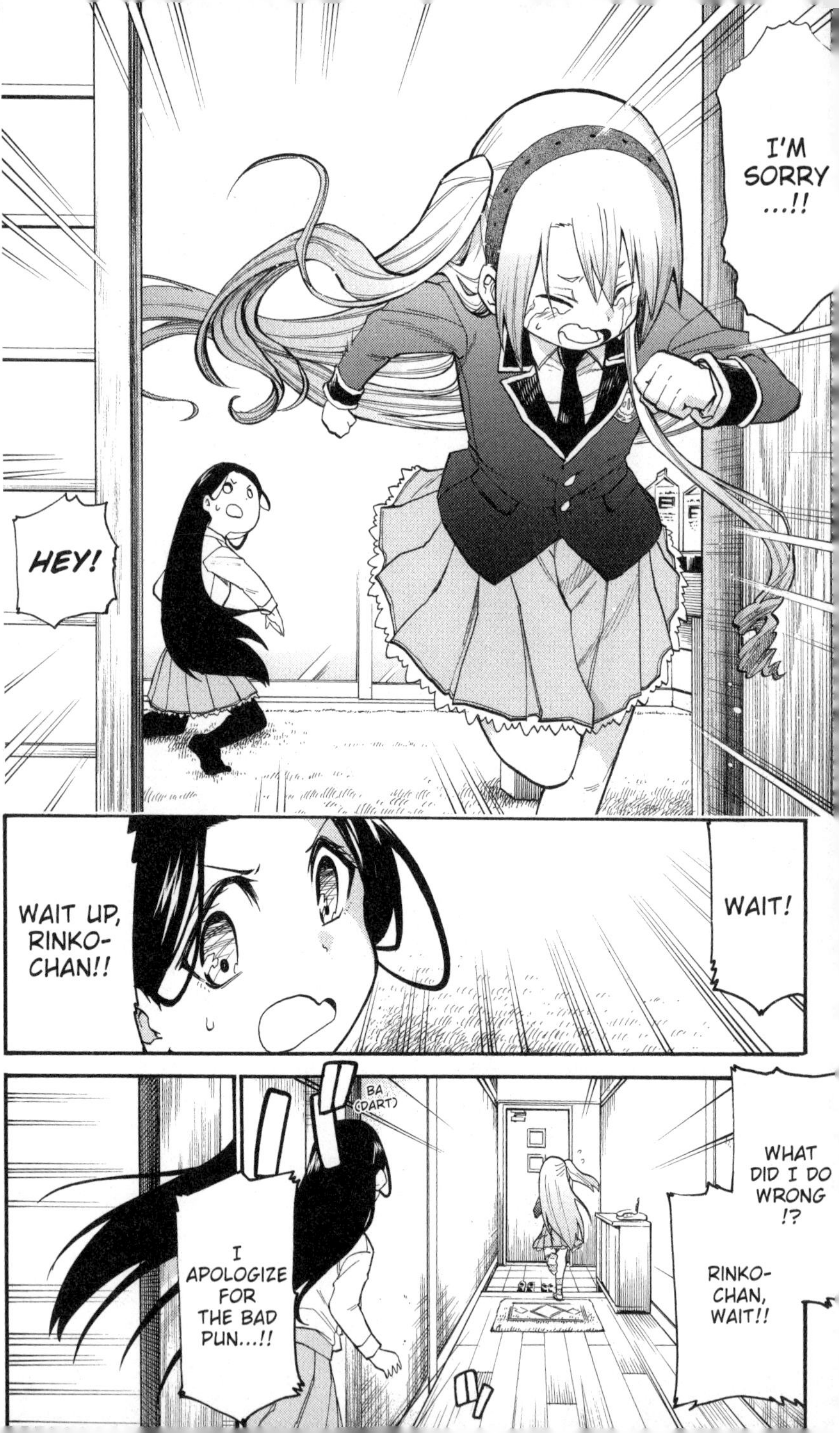
I'M SORRY...!!
HEY!
WAIT!
WAIT UP, RINKO-CHAN!!
WHAT DID I DO WRONG!?
BA (DART)
RINKO-CHAN, WAIT!!
I APOLOGIZE FOR THE BAD PUN...!!

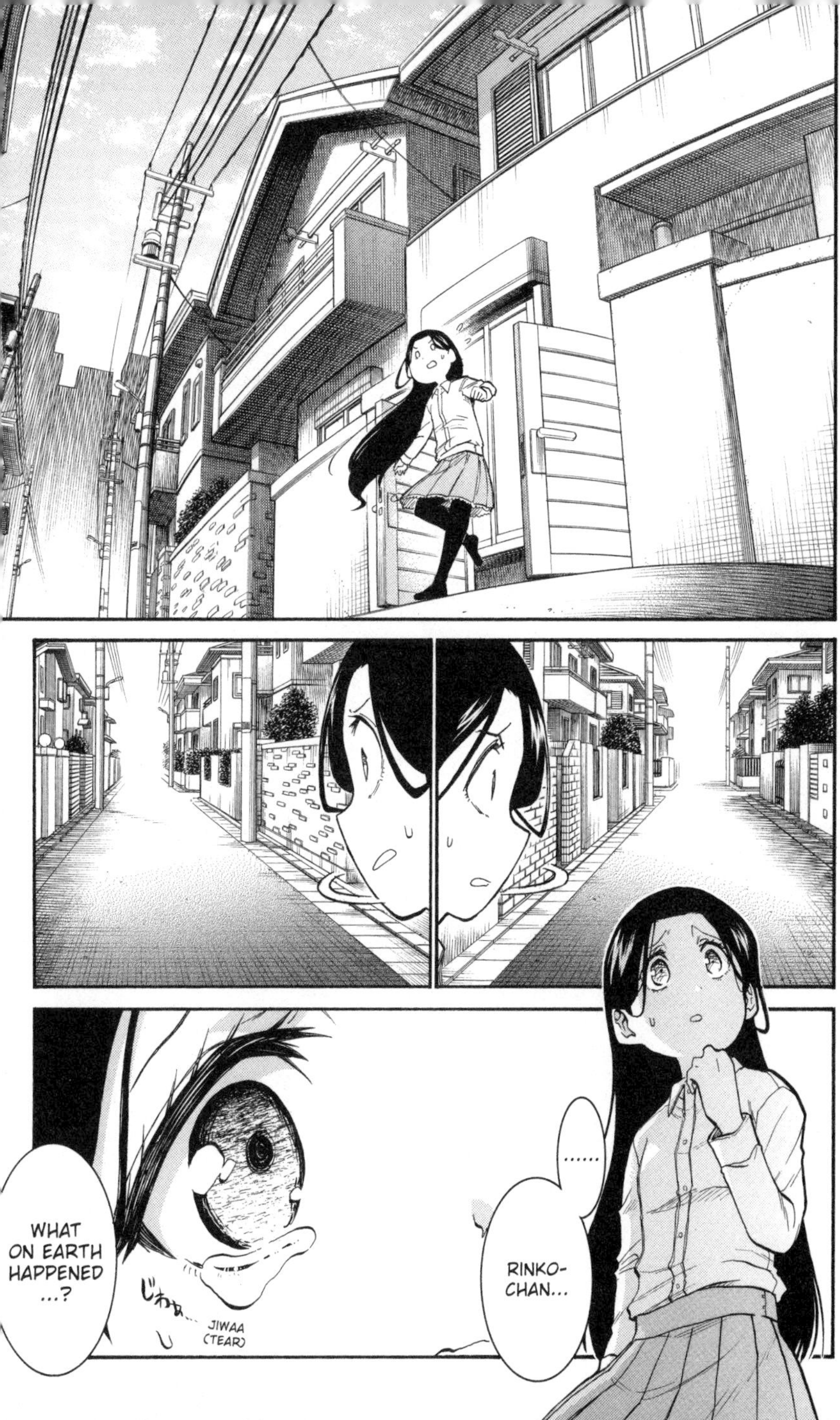

......
RINKO-CHAN...
WHAT ON EARTH HAPPENED ...?
じわぁ…
JIWAA (TEAR)

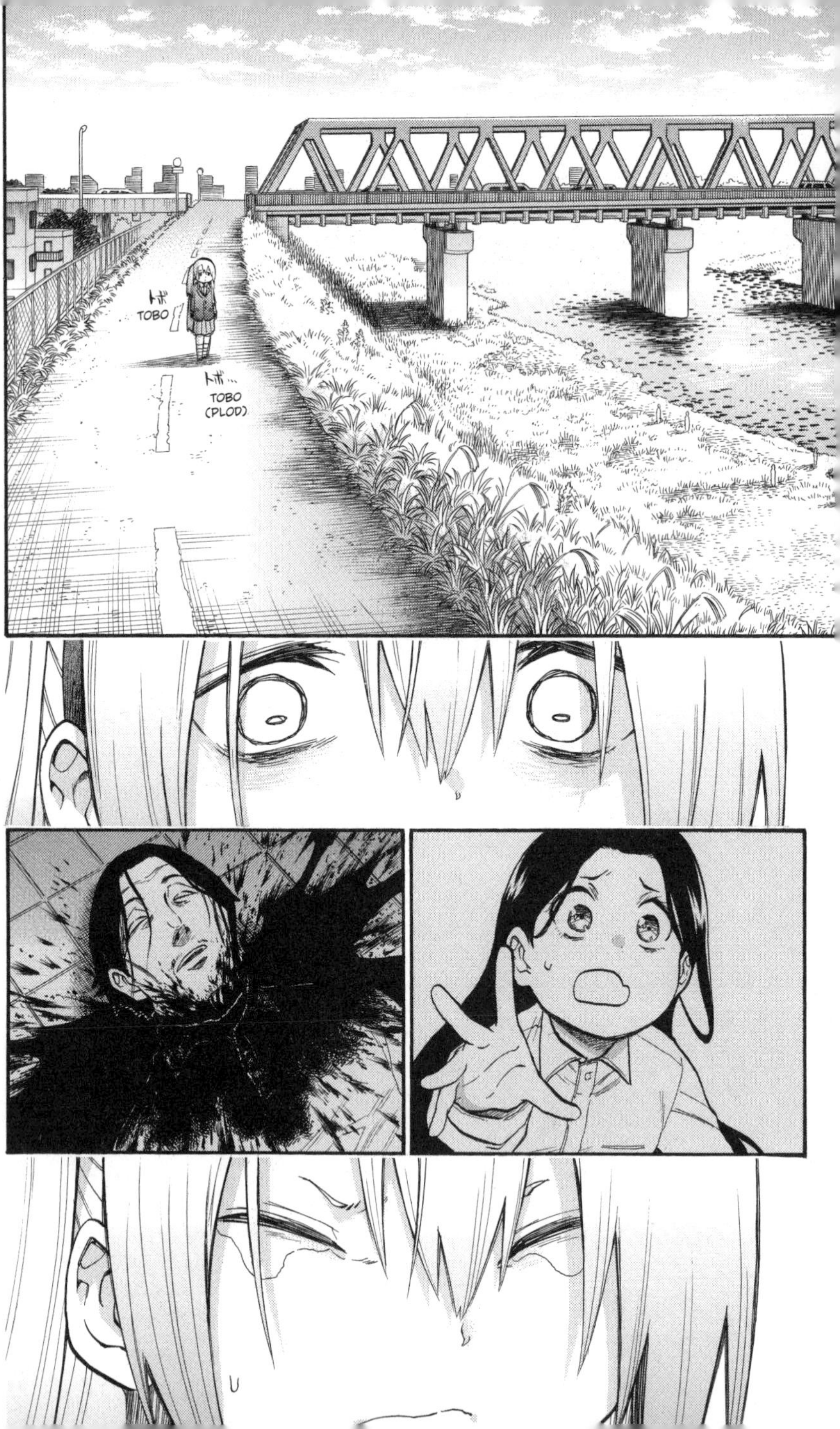

トボ
TOBO
トボ…
TOBO
(PLOD)

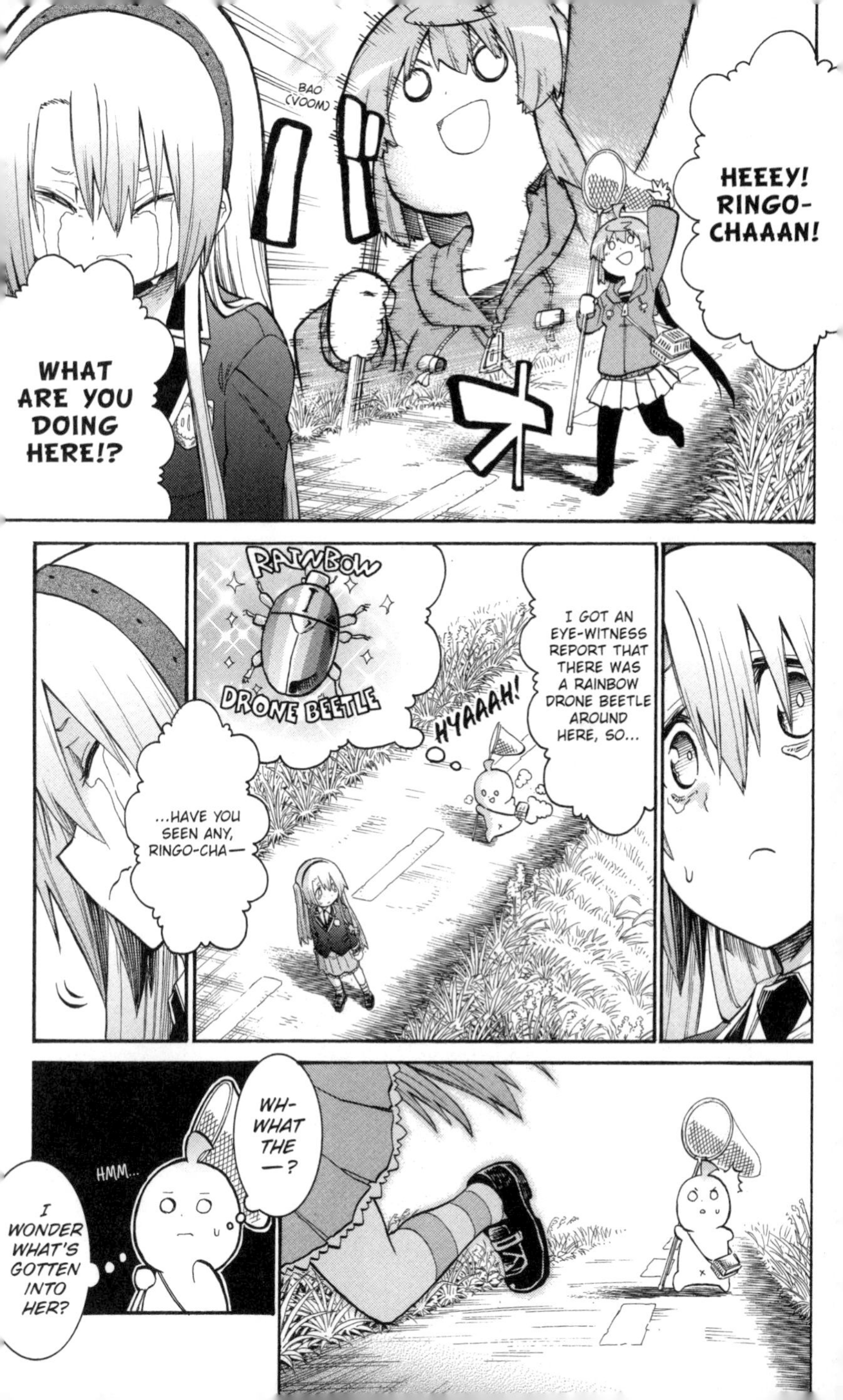
HEEEY! RINGO-CHAAAN!
BAO (VOOM)
WHAT ARE YOU DOING HERE!?
I GOT AN EYE-WITNESS REPORT THAT THERE WAS A RAINBOW DRONE BEETLE AROUND HERE, SO...
HYAAAH!
RAINBOW DRONE BEETLE
...HAVE YOU SEEN ANY, RINGO-CHA—
WH- WHAT THE —?
HMM...
I WONDER WHAT'S GOTTEN INTO HER?

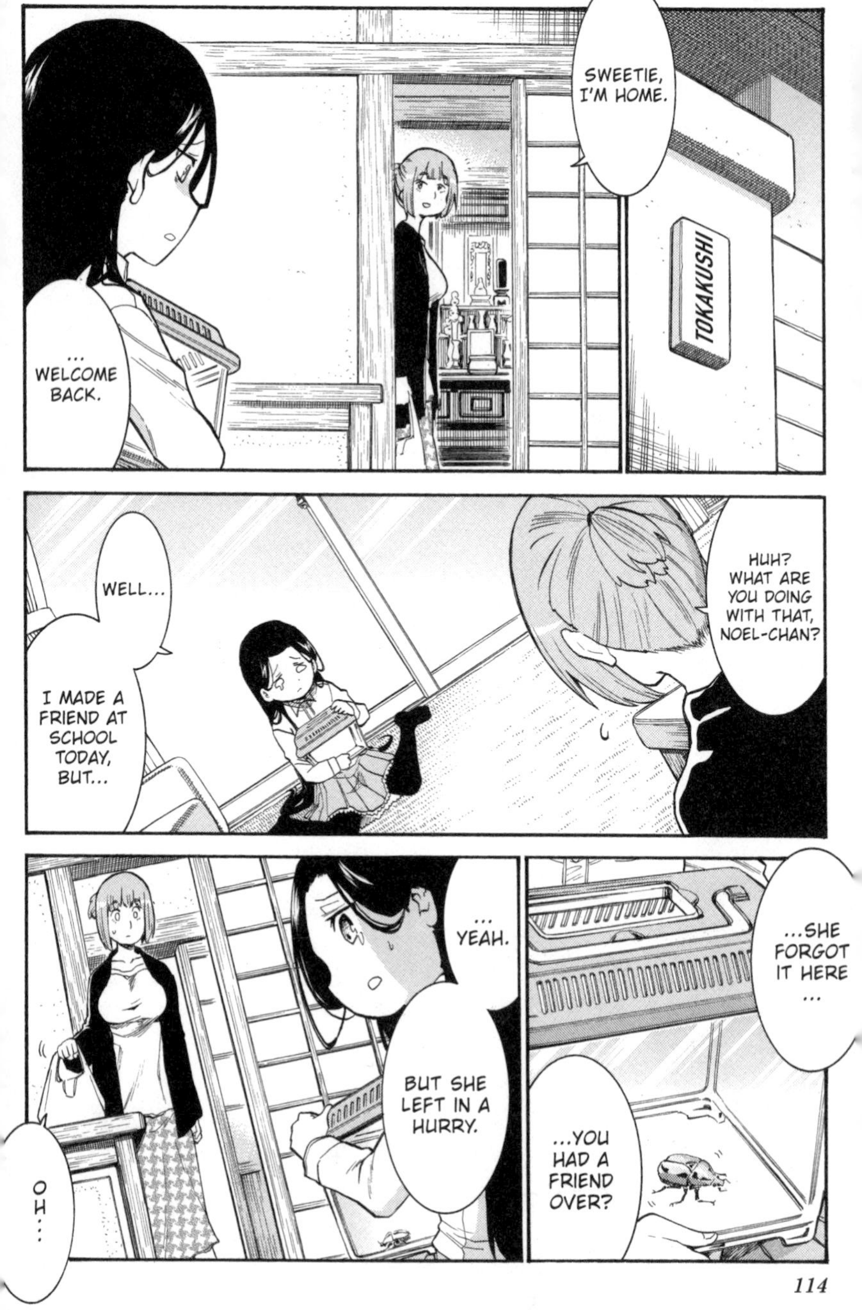

SWEETIE, I'M HOME.
TOKAKUSHI
...WELCOME BACK.
HUH? WHAT ARE YOU DOING WITH THAT, NOEL-CHAN?
WELL...
I MADE A FRIEND AT SCHOOL TODAY, BUT...
...SHE FORGOT IT HERE...
...YOU HAD A FRIEND OVER?
...YEAH.
BUT SHE LEFT IN A HURRY.
OH...

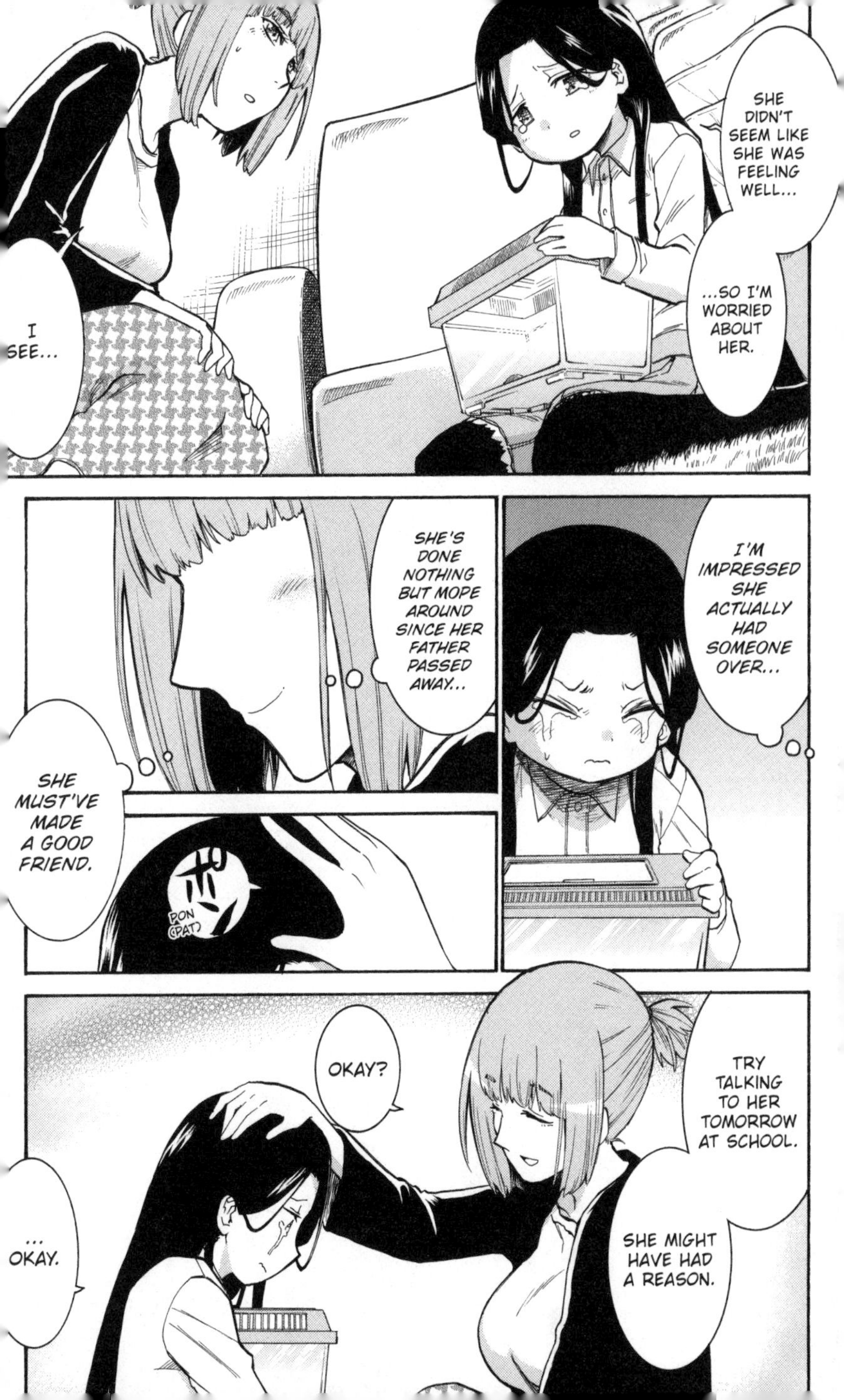
SHE DIDN'T SEEM LIKE SHE WAS FEELING WELL...
...SO I'M WORRIED ABOUT HER.
I SEE...
I'M IMPRESSED SHE ACTUALLY HAD SOMEONE OVER...
SHE'S DONE NOTHING BUT MOPE AROUND SINCE HER FATHER PASSED AWAY...
SHE MUST'VE MADE A GOOD FRIEND.
PON (PAT)
TRY TALKING TO HER TOMORROW AT SCHOOL.
SHE MIGHT HAVE HAD A REASON.
OKAY?
...OKAY.

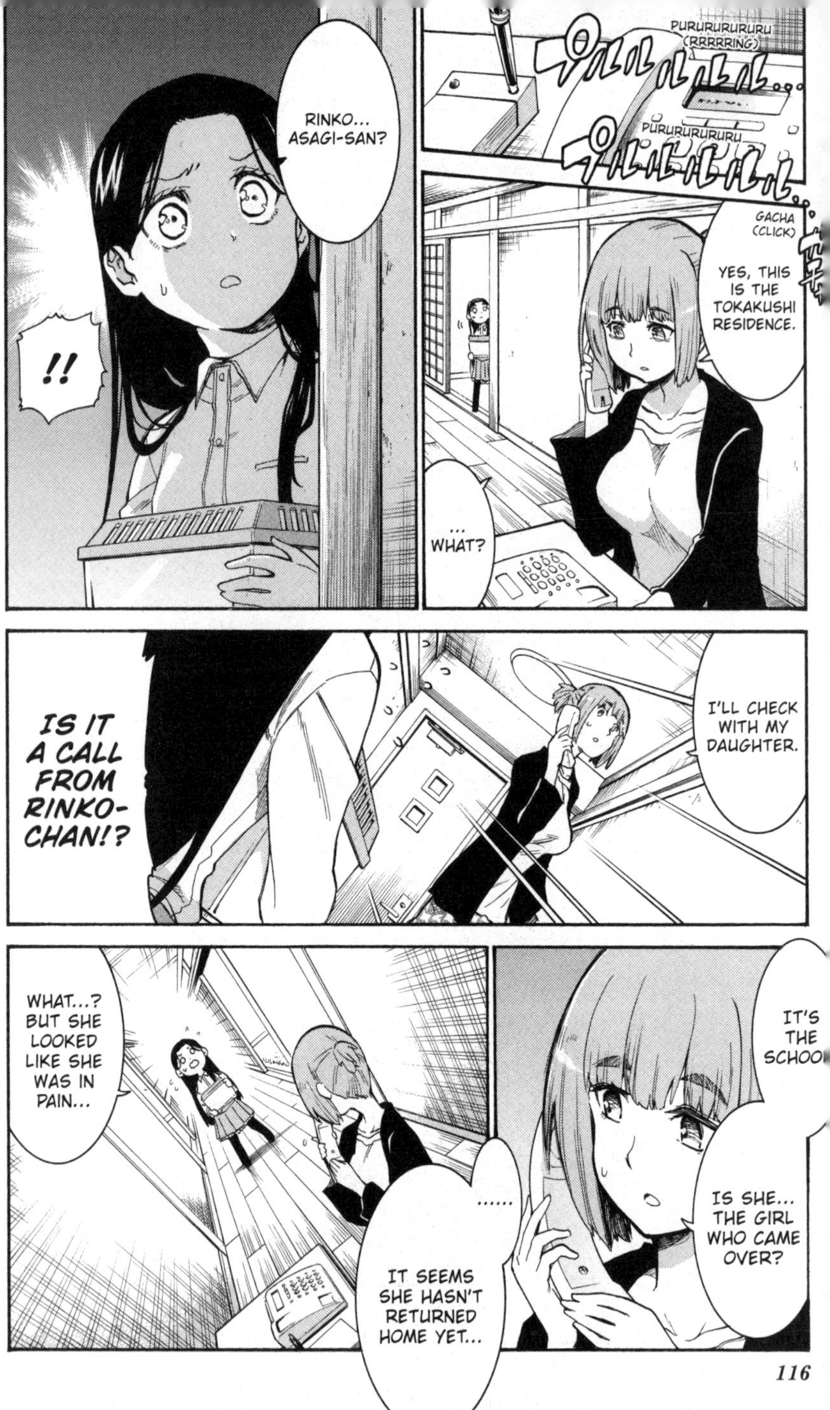
PURURURURURU (RRRRRING)
PURURURURURU
GACHA (CLICK)
YES, THIS IS THE TOKAKUSHI RESIDENCE.
... WHAT?
RINKO... ASAGI-SAN?
!!
I'LL CHECK WITH MY DAUGHTER.
IS IT A CALL FROM RINKO-CHAN!?
IT'S THE SCHOO
IS SHE... THE GIRL WHO CAME OVER?
......
IT SEEMS SHE HASN'T RETURNED HOME YET...
WHAT...? BUT SHE LOOKED LIKE SHE WAS IN PAIN...

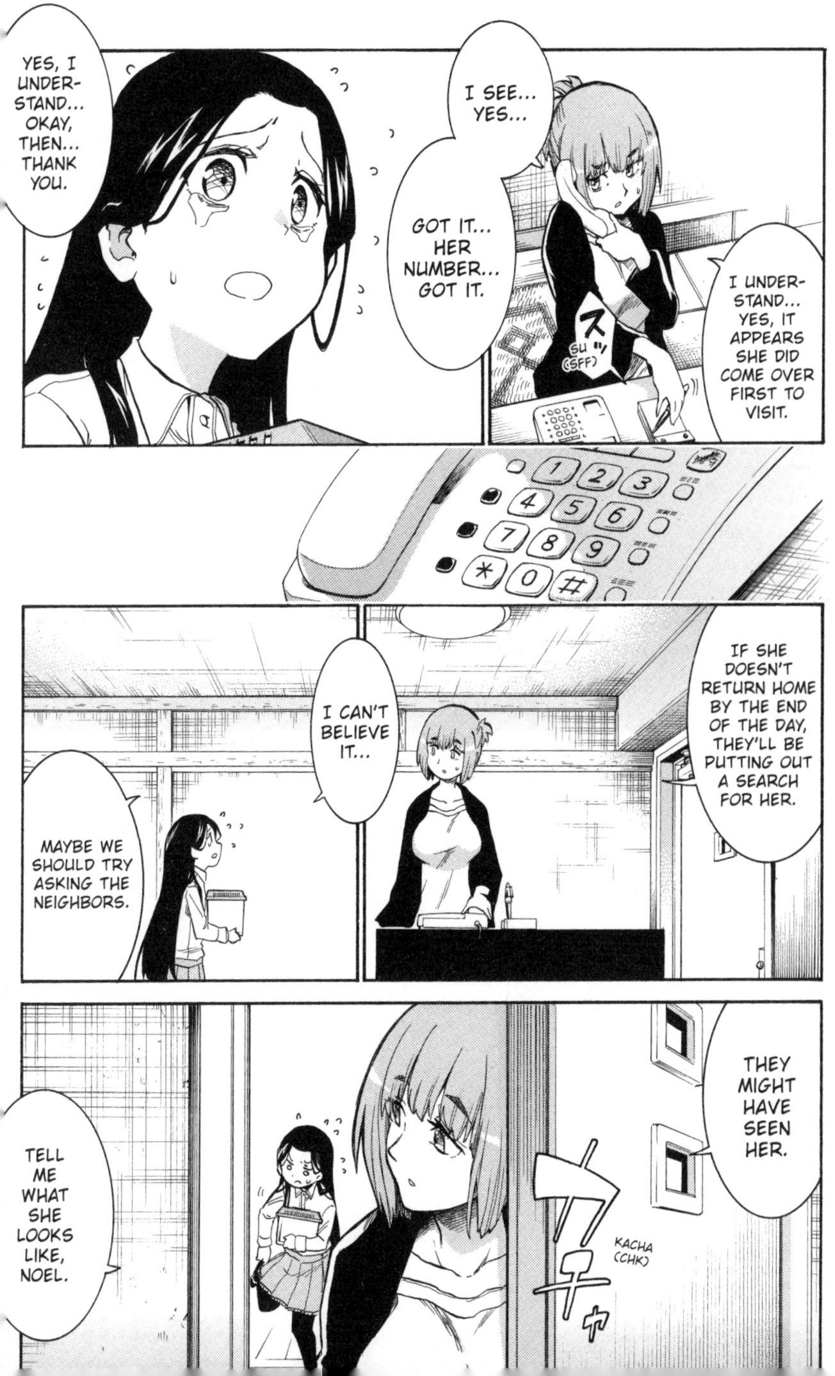

I SEE... YES...
SU (SFF)
I UNDERSTAND... YES, IT APPEARS SHE DID COME OVER FIRST TO VISIT.
GOT IT... HER NUMBER... GOT IT.
YES, I UNDERSTAND... OKAY, THEN... THANK YOU.
IF SHE DOESN'T RETURN HOME BY THE END OF THE DAY, THEY'LL BE PUTTING OUT A SEARCH FOR HER.
I CAN'T BELIEVE IT...
MAYBE WE SHOULD TRY ASKING THE NEIGHBORS.
THEY MIGHT HAVE SEEN HER.
KACHA (CHK)
TELL ME WHAT SHE LOOKS LIKE, NOEL.

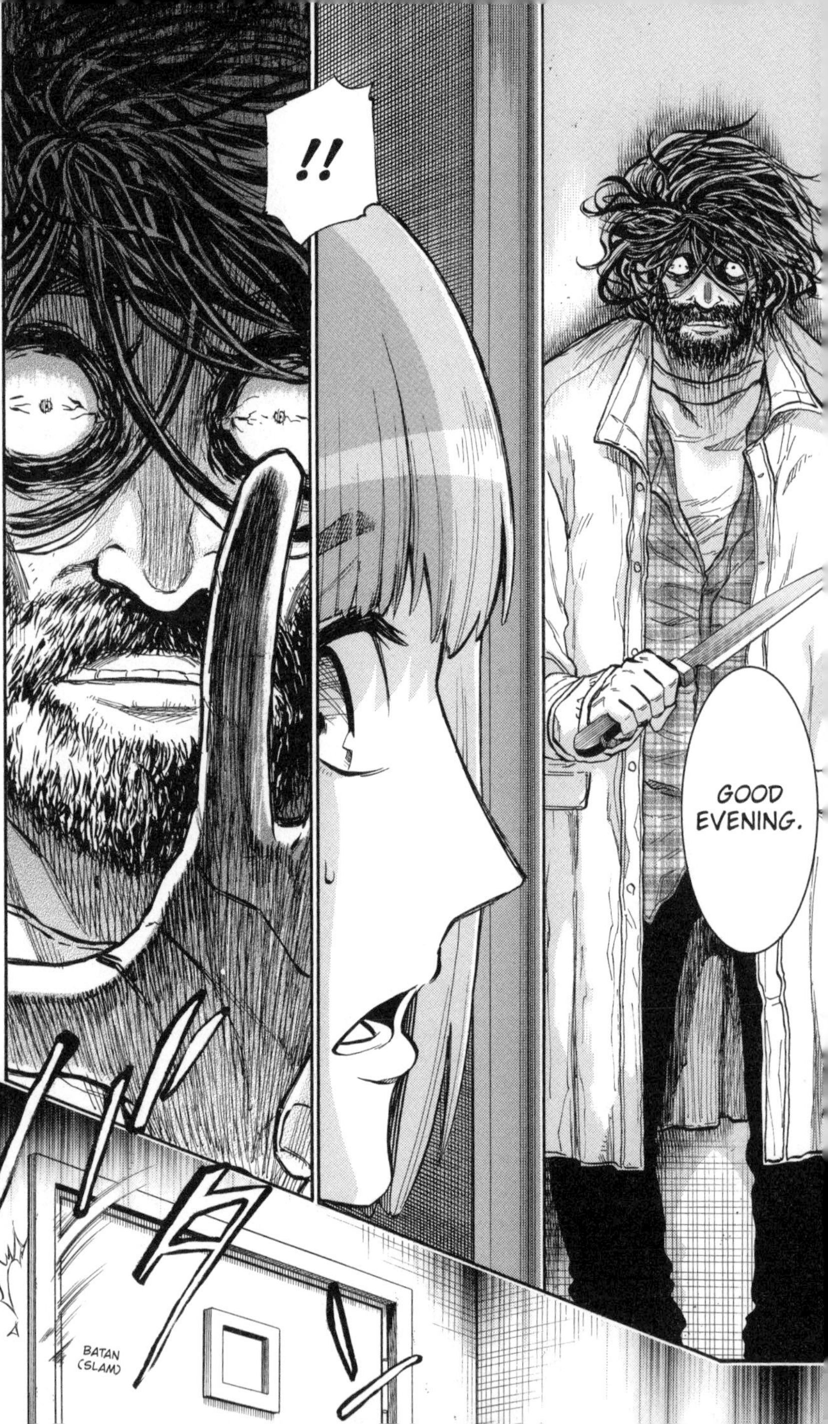
GOOD EVENING.
!!
BATAN
(SLAM)

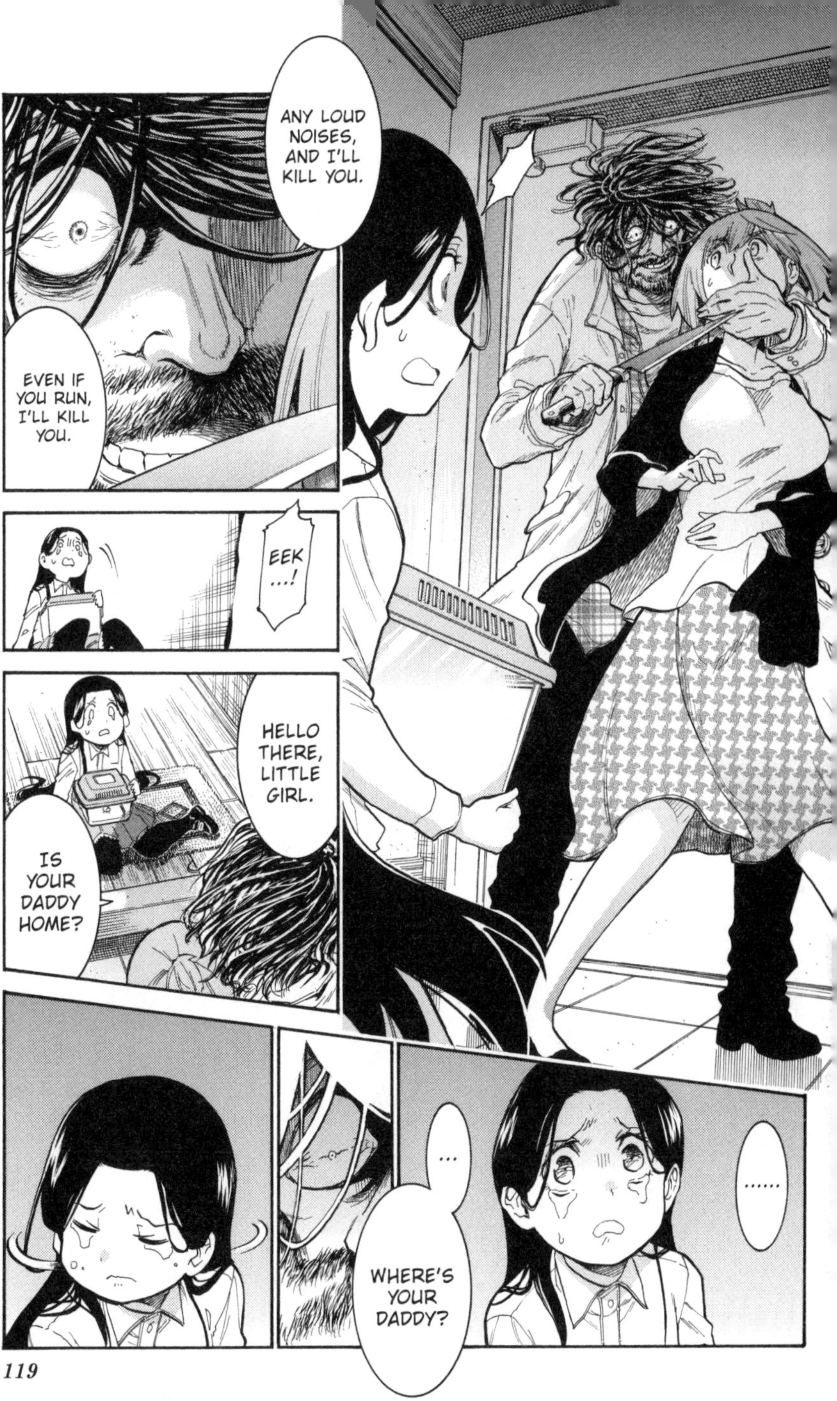
ANY LOUD NOISES, AND I'LL KILL YOU.
EVEN IF YOU RUN, I'LL KILL YOU.
EEK ...!
HELLO THERE, LITTLE GIRL.
IS YOUR DADDY HOME?
......
...
WHERE'S YOUR DADDY?

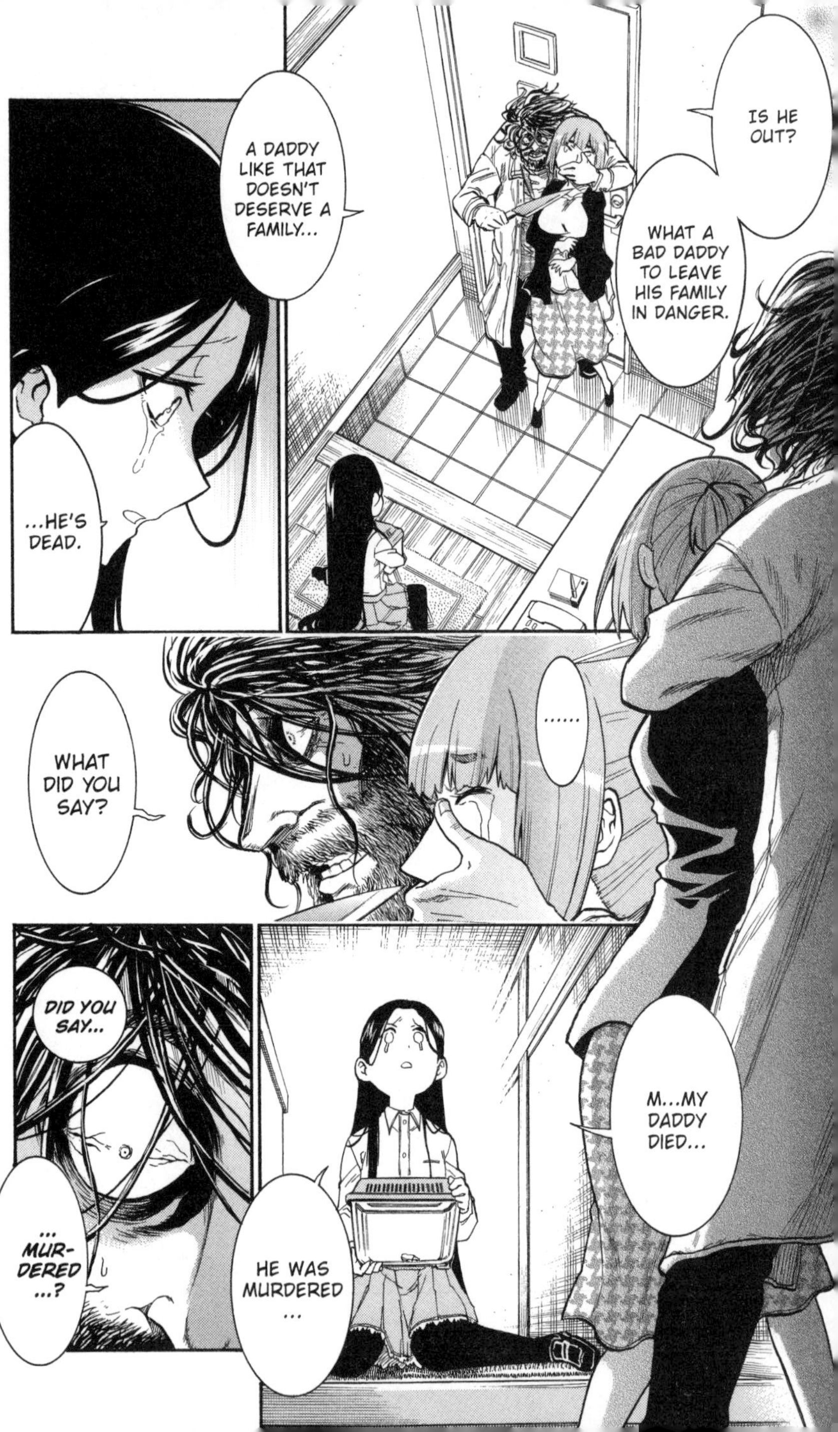
IS HE OUT?
WHAT A BAD DADDY TO LEAVE HIS FAMILY IN DANGER.
A DADDY LIKE THAT DOESN'T DESERVE A FAMILY...
...HE'S DEAD.
......
WHAT DID YOU SAY?
M...MY DADDY DIED...
HE WAS MURDERED...
DID YOU SAY...
...MURDERED...?

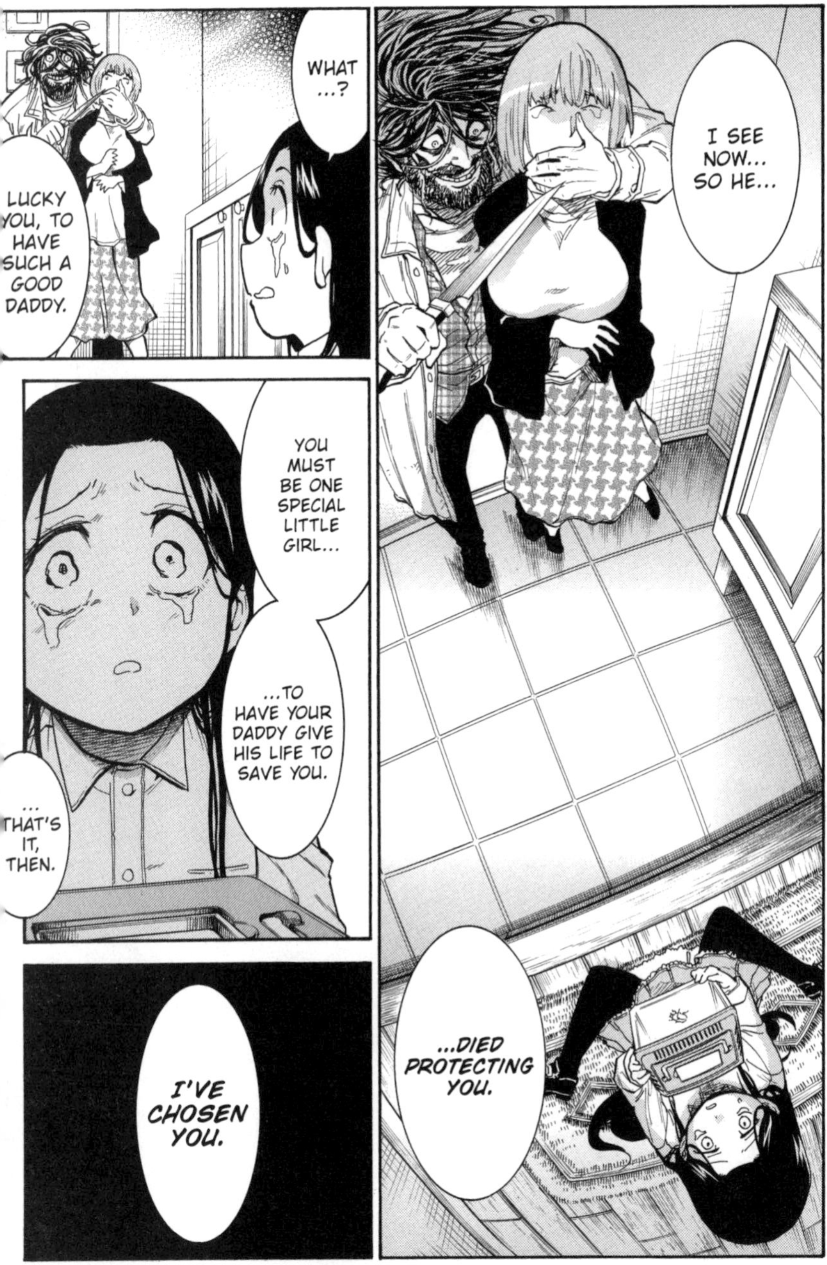
I SEE NOW... SO HE...
...DIED PROTECTING YOU.
WHAT ...?
LUCKY YOU, TO HAVE SUCH A GOOD DADDY.
YOU MUST BE ONE SPECIAL LITTLE GIRL...
...TO HAVE YOUR DADDY GIVE HIS LIFE TO SAVE YOU.
...THAT'S IT, THEN.
I'VE CHOSEN YOU.

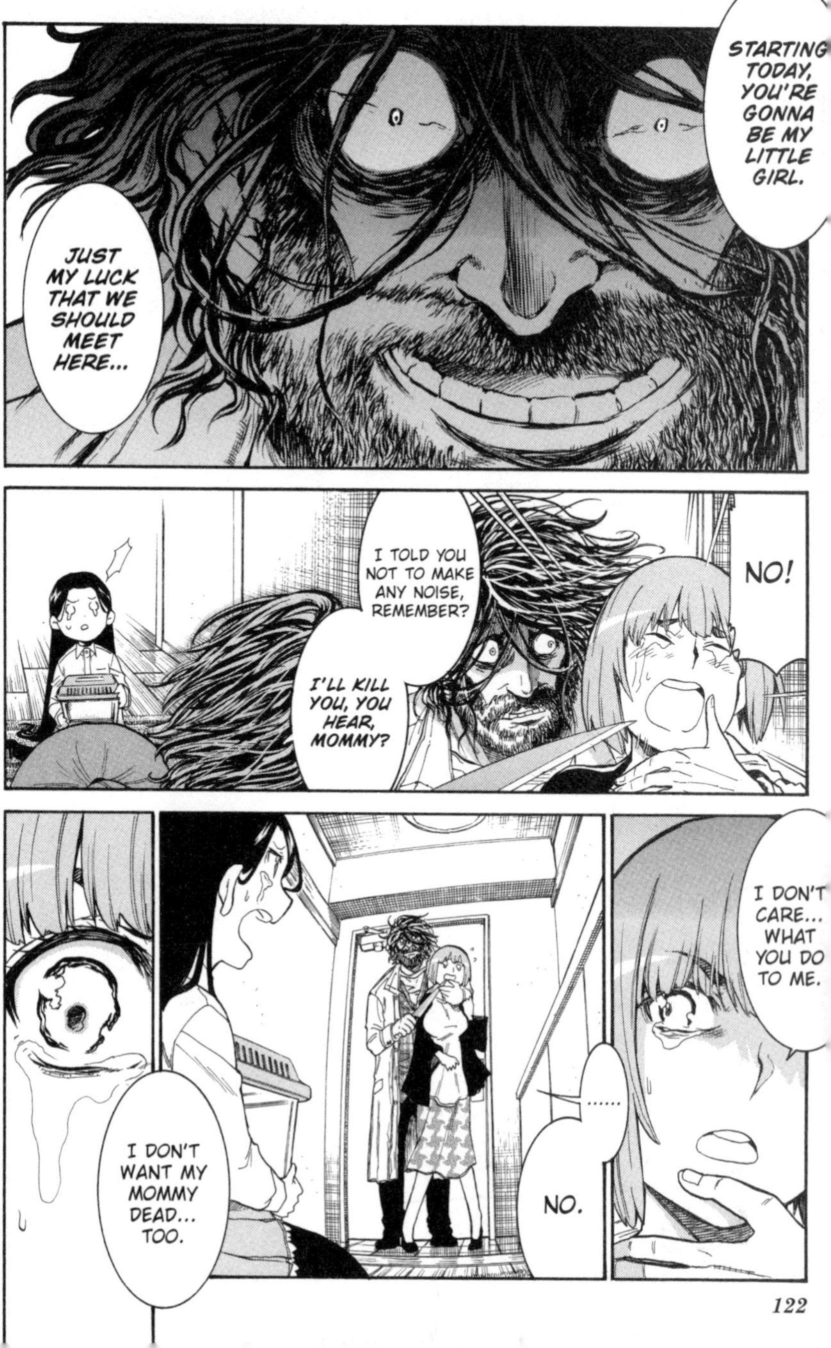
STARTING TODAY, YOU'RE GONNA BE MY LITTLE GIRL.
JUST MY LUCK THAT WE SHOULD MEET HERE...
NO!
I TOLD YOU NOT TO MAKE ANY NOISE, REMEMBER?
I'LL KILL YOU, YOU HEAR, MOMMY?
I DON'T CARE... WHAT YOU DO TO ME.
......
NO.
I DON'T WANT MY MOMMY DEAD... TOO.

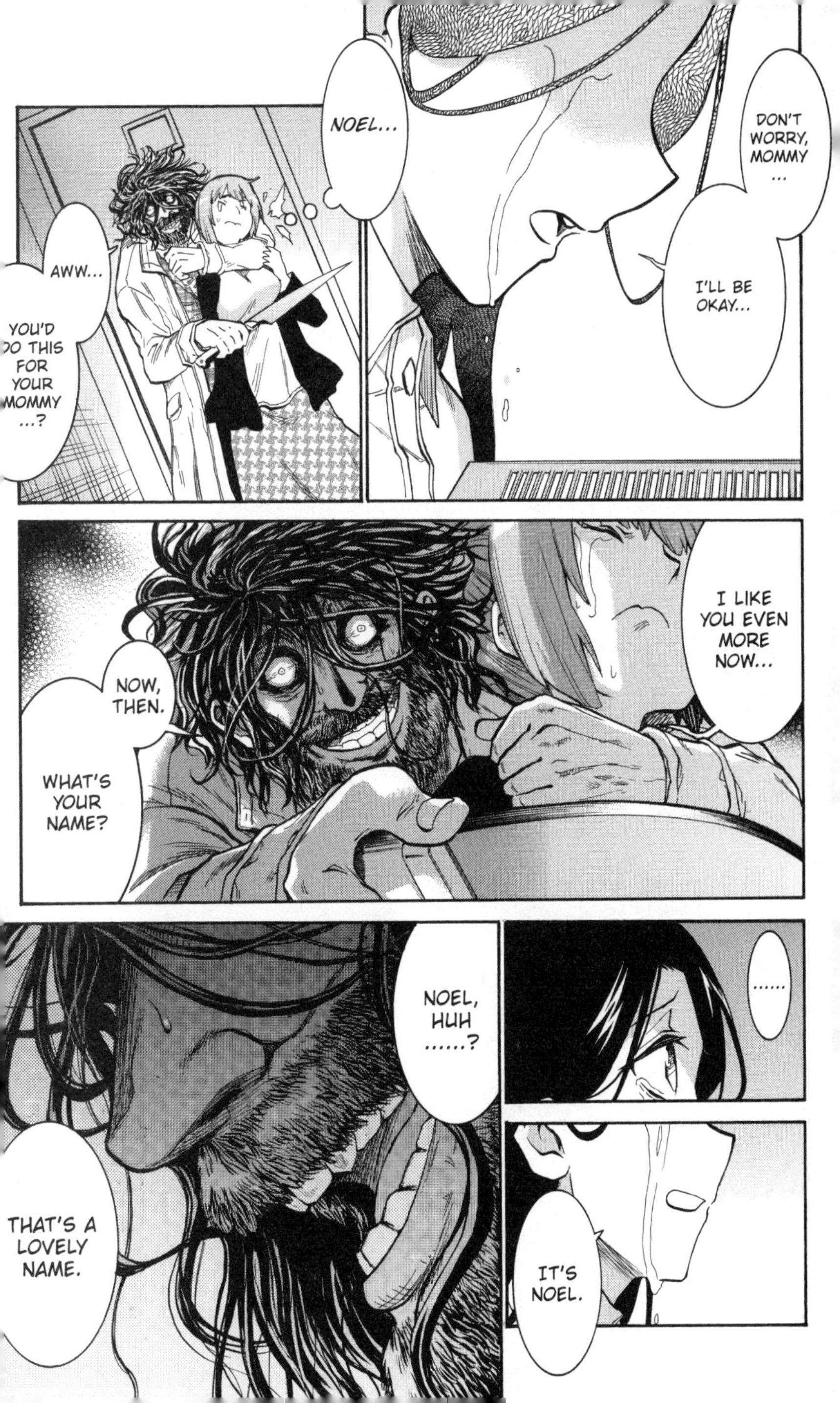
DON'T WORRY, MOMMY ...
I'LL BE OKAY...
NOEL...
AWW...
YOU'D DO THIS FOR YOUR MOMMY ...?
I LIKE YOU EVEN MORE NOW...
NOW, THEN.
WHAT'S YOUR NAME?
......
IT'S NOEL.
NOEL, HUH ......?
THAT'S A LOVELY NAME.

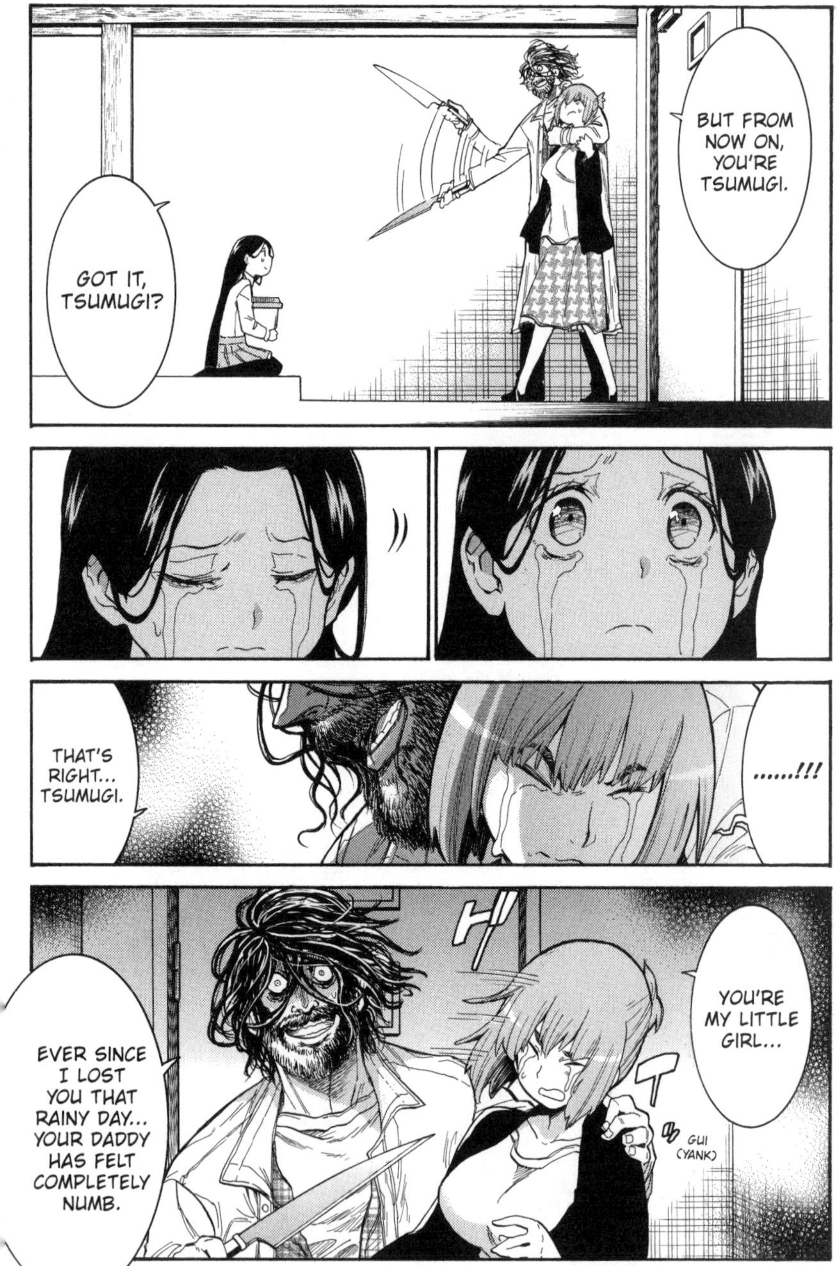
BUT FROM NOW ON, YOU'RE TSUMUGI.
GOT IT, TSUMUGI?
......!!!
THAT'S RIGHT... TSUMUGI.
YOU'RE MY LITTLE GIRL...
GUI (YANK)
EVER SINCE I LOST YOU THAT RAINY DAY... YOUR DADDY HAS FELT COMPLETELY NUMB.

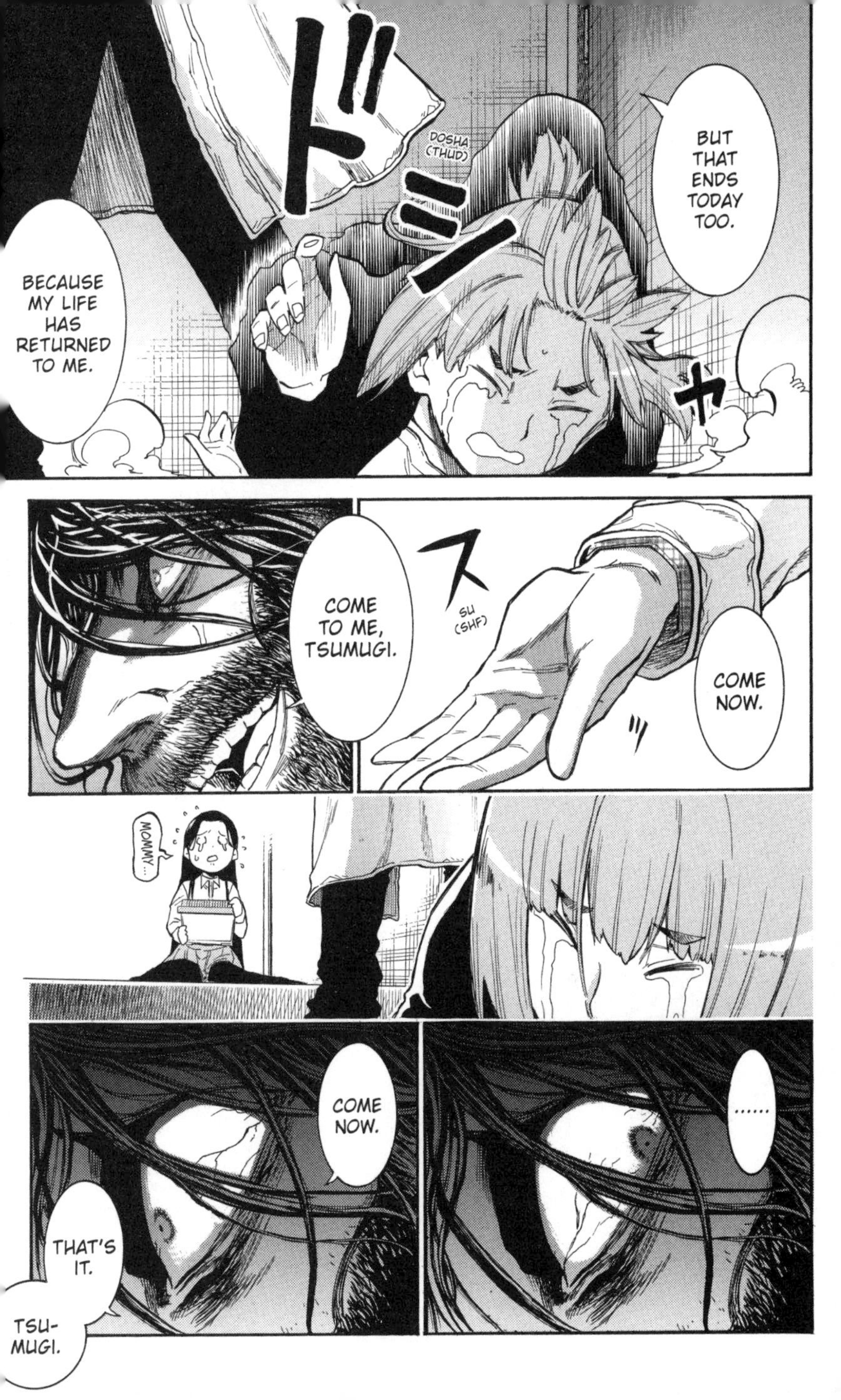
BUT THAT ENDS TODAY TOO.
DOSHA (THUD)
BECAUSE MY LIFE HAS RETURNED TO ME.
SU (SHF)
COME TO ME, TSUMUGI.
COME NOW.
MOMMY...
......
COME NOW.
THAT'S IT.
TSU-MUGI.

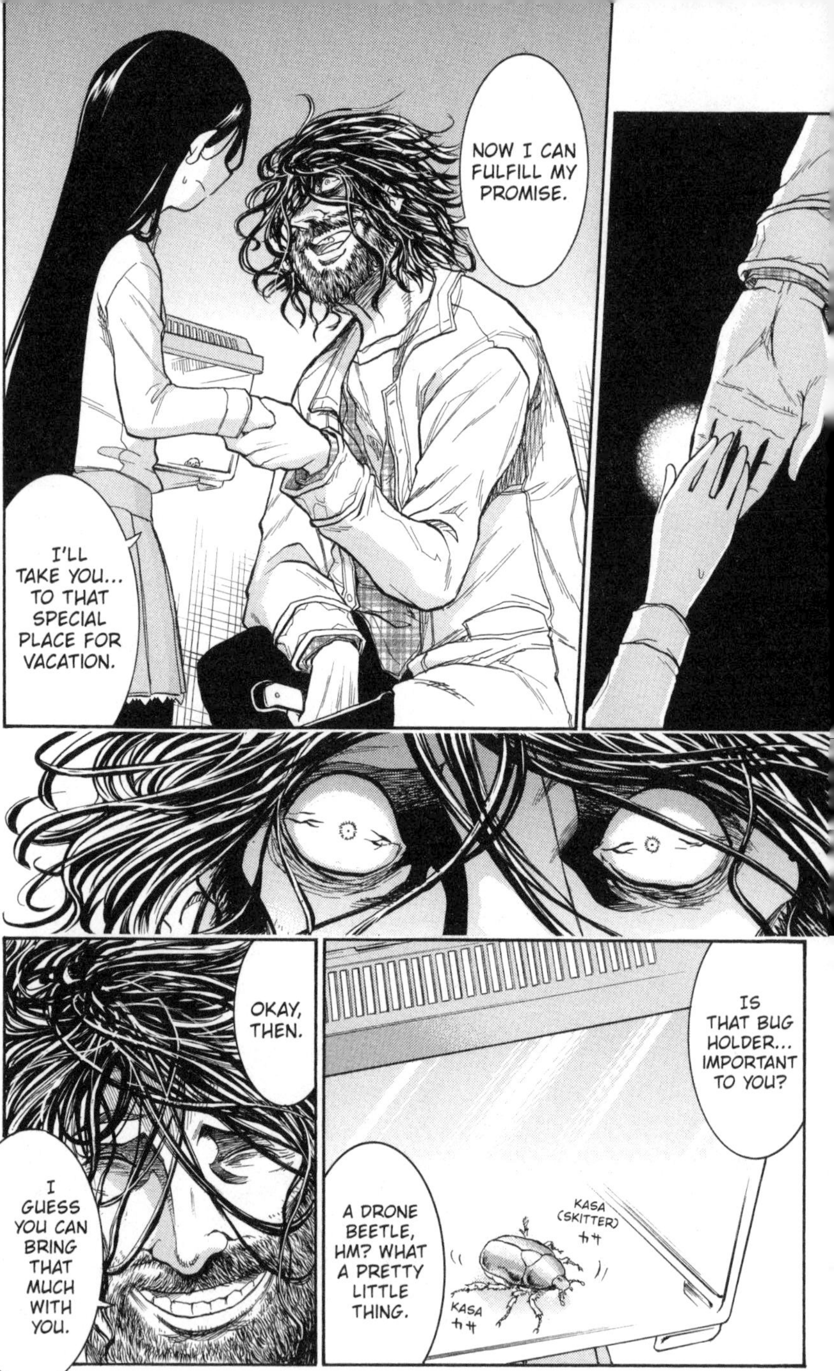
NOW I CAN FULFILL MY PROMISE.
I'LL TAKE YOU... TO THAT SPECIAL PLACE FOR VACATION.
IS THAT BUG HOLDER... IMPORTANT TO YOU?
A DRONE BEETLE, HM? WHAT A PRETTY LITTLE THING.
KASA (SKITTER)
KASA
OKAY, THEN.
I GUESS YOU CAN BRING THAT MUCH WITH YOU.

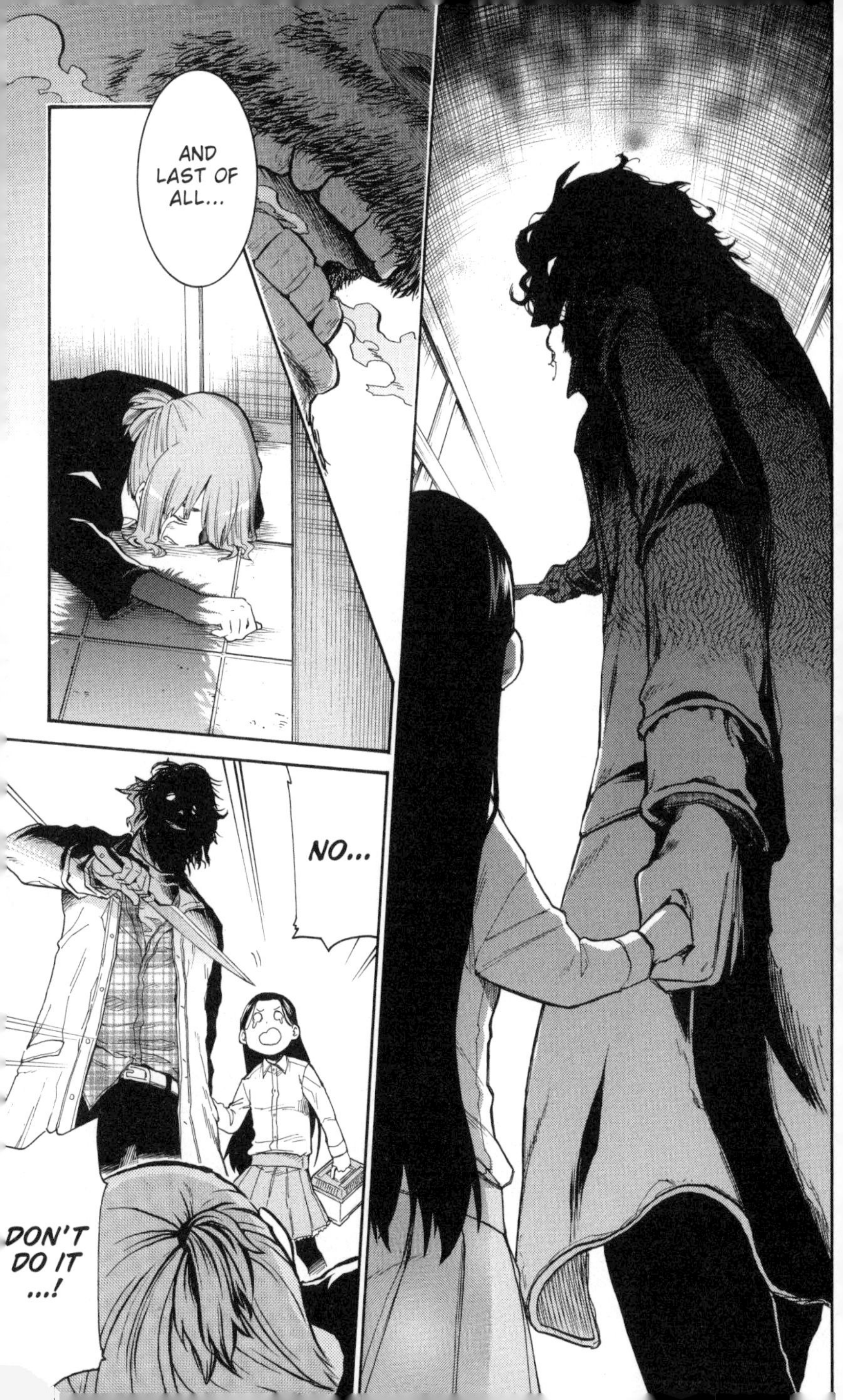
AND LAST OF ALL...
NO...
DON'T DO IT ...!

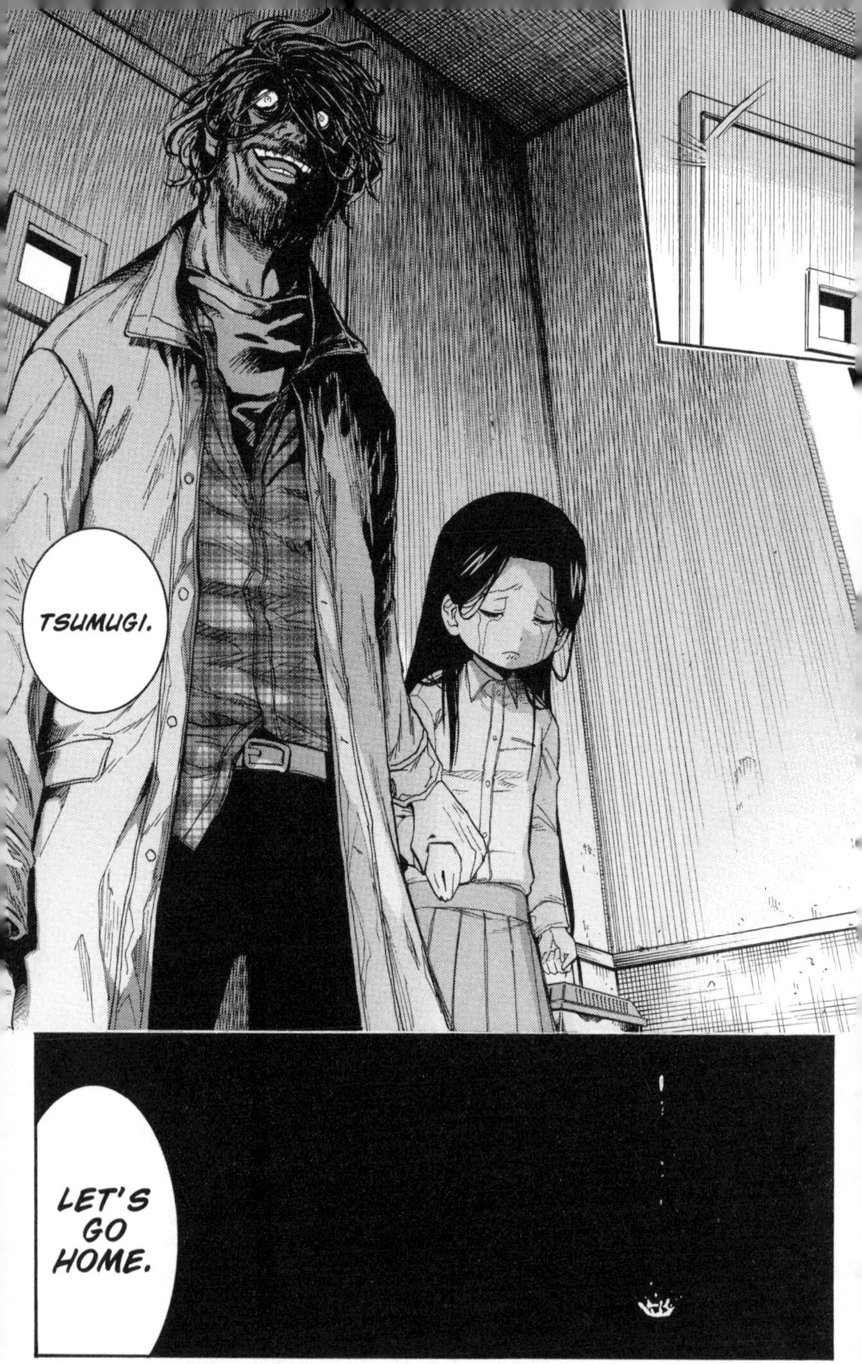
TSUMUGI.
LET'S GO HOME.

MURCIÉLAGO

MURCIÉLAGO

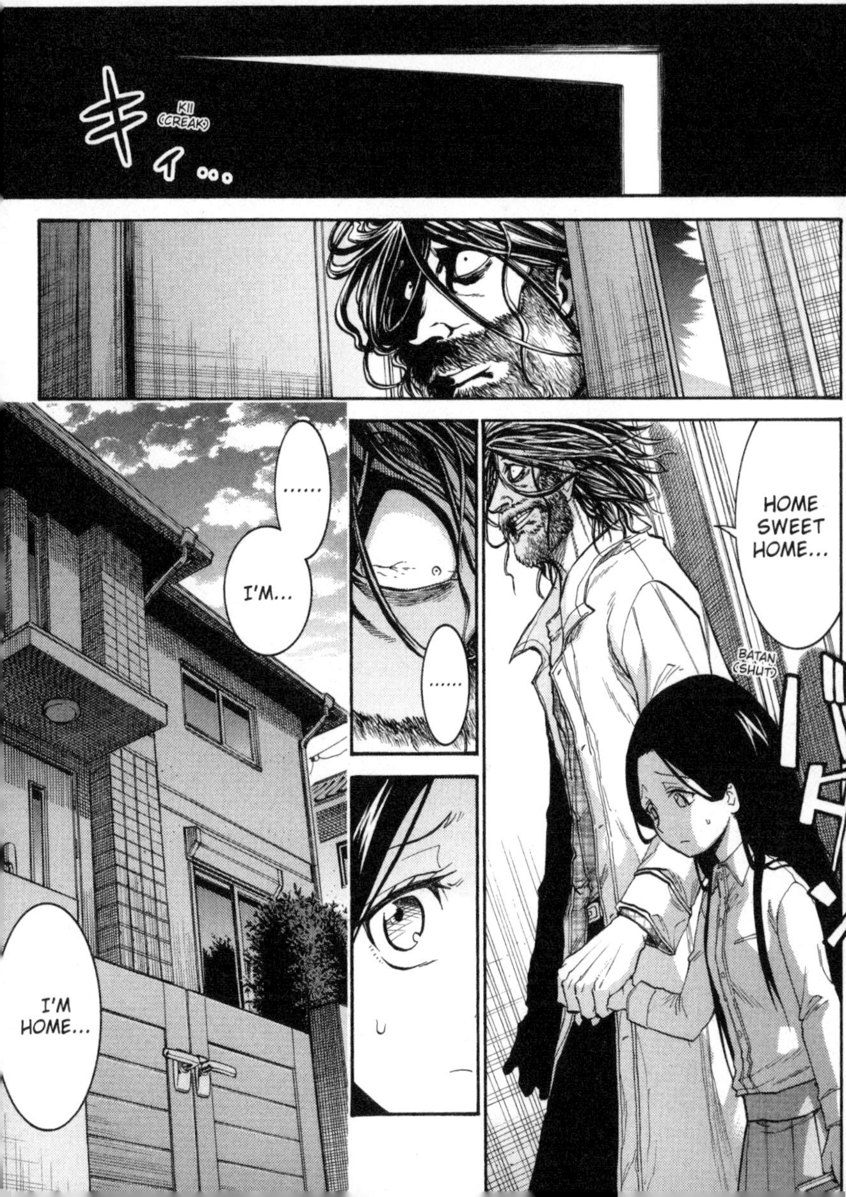
キィ…
KII (CREAK)
HOME SWEET HOME...
BATAN (SHUT)
......
......
I'M...
I'M HOME...

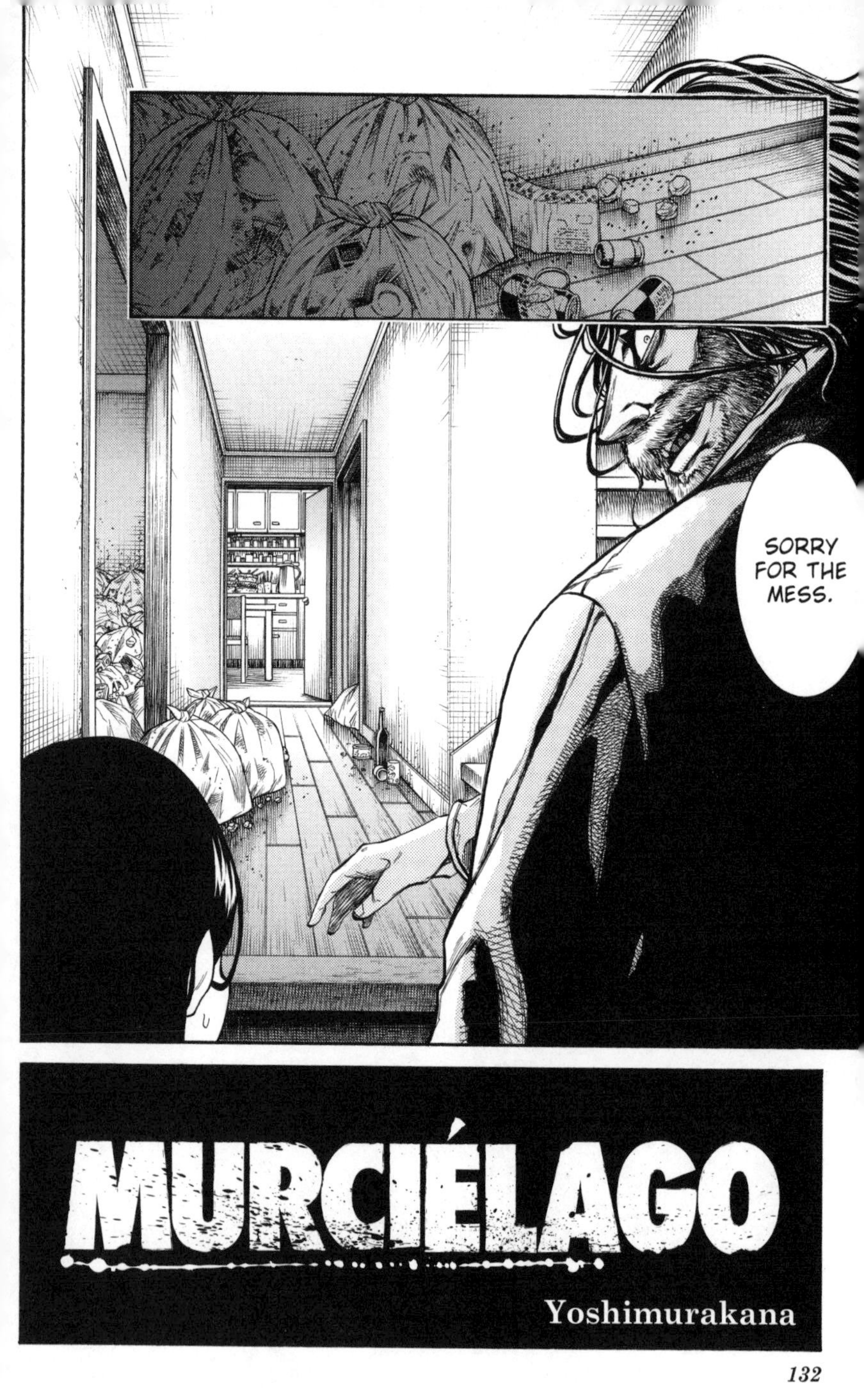
SORRY FOR THE MESS.

MURCIÉLAGO

Yoshimurakana

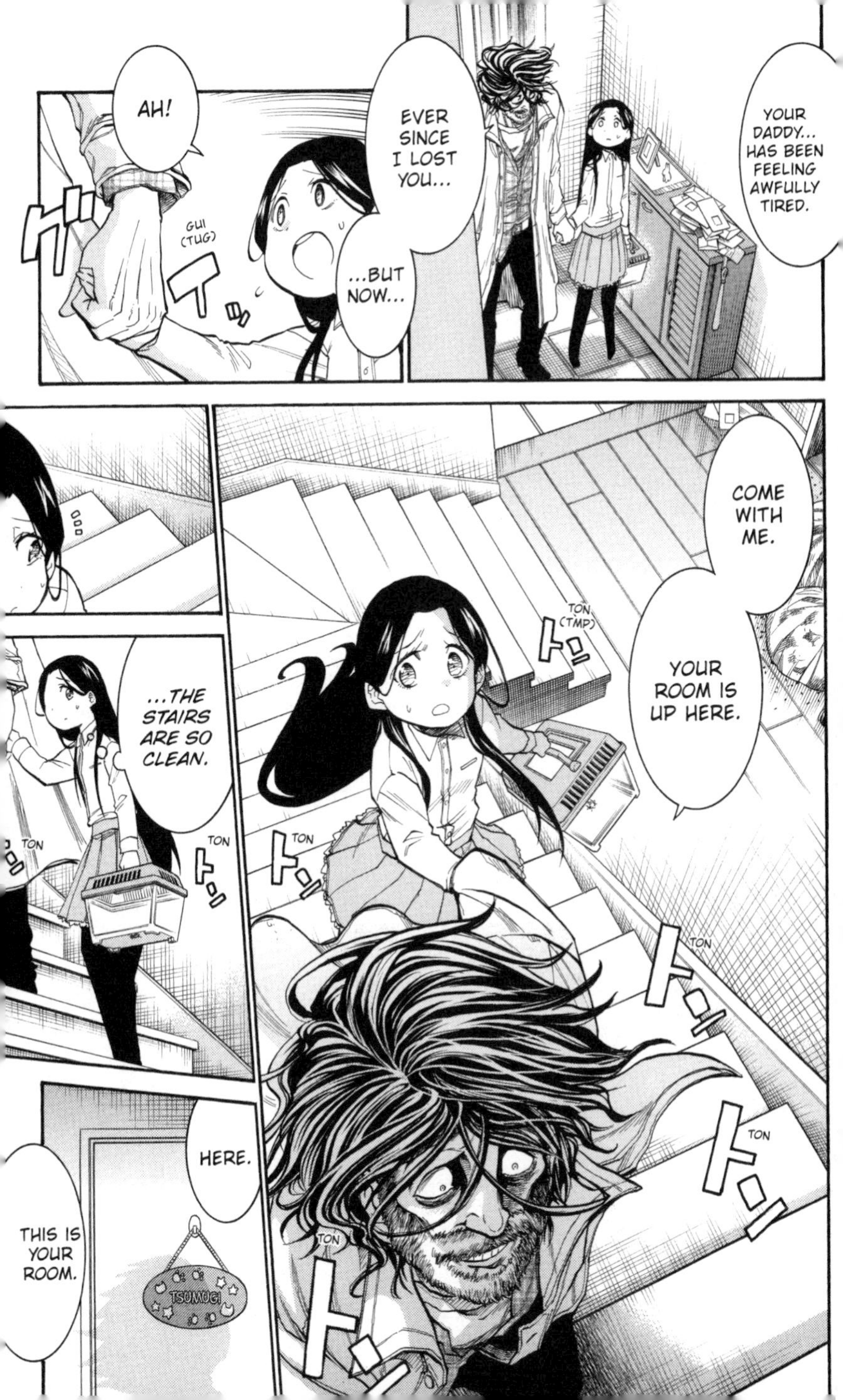
YOUR DADDY... HAS BEEN FEELING AWFULLY TIRED.
EVER SINCE I LOST YOU...
...BUT NOW...
AH!
GUI (TUG)
COME WITH ME.
TON (TMP)
YOUR ROOM IS UP HERE.
TON
TON
TON
TON
TON
TON
...THE STAIRS ARE SO CLEAN.
HERE.
THIS IS YOUR ROOM.
TSUMUGI

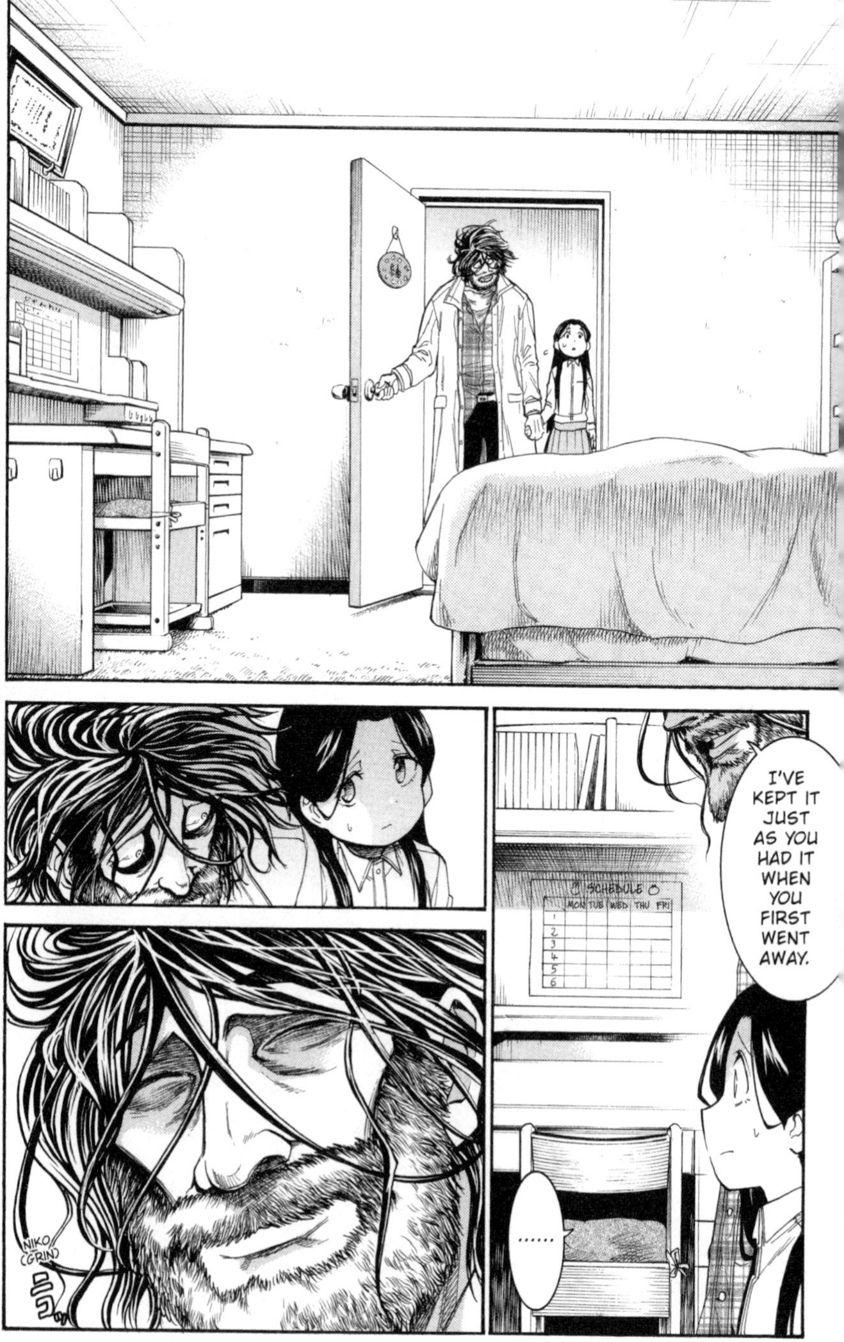
SCHEDULE
MON TUE WED THU FRI
1
2
3
4
5
6
I'VE KEPT IT JUST AS YOU HAD IT WHEN YOU FIRST WENT AWAY.
......
NIKO (GRIN)

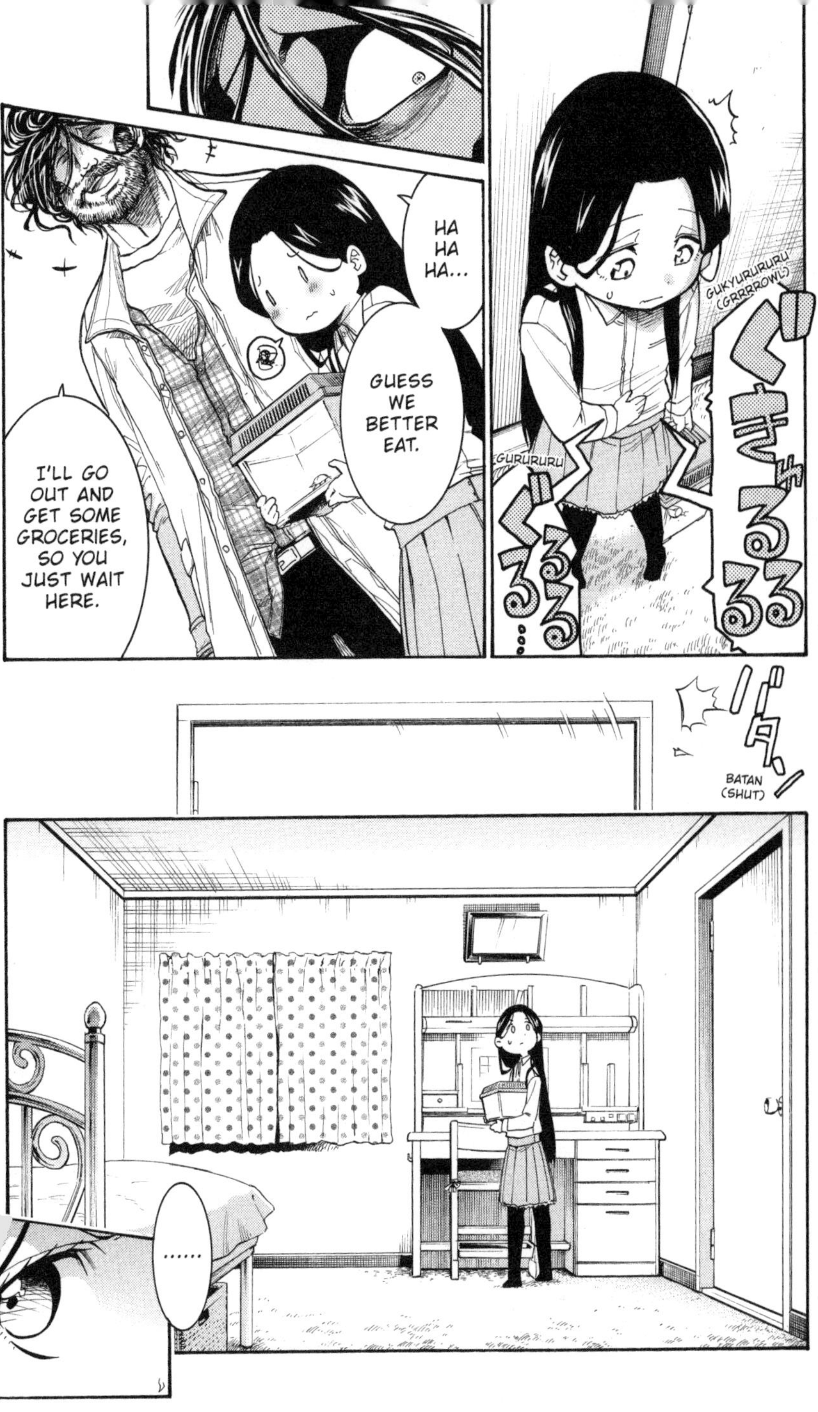

ぐきゅるるる
GUKYURURURU (GRRRROWL)
ぐるるる…
GURURURU
HA HA HA...
GUESS WE BETTER EAT.
I'LL GO OUT AND GET SOME GROCERIES, SO YOU JUST WAIT HERE.
バタン
BATAN (SHUT)
......

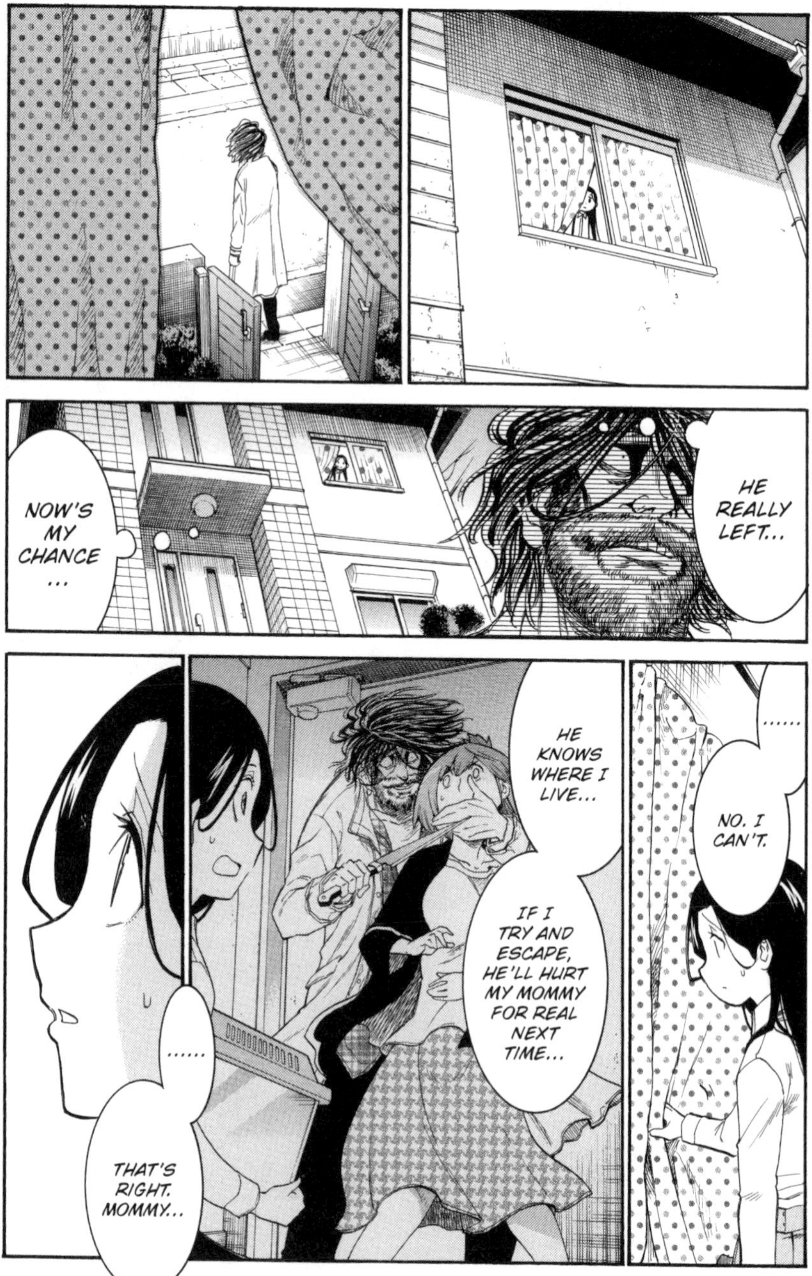
HE REALLY LEFT...
NOW'S MY CHANCE ...
......
NO. I CAN'T.
HE KNOWS WHERE I LIVE...
IF I TRY AND ESCAPE, HE'LL HURT MY MOMMY FOR REAL NEXT TIME...
......
THAT'S RIGHT. MOMMY...

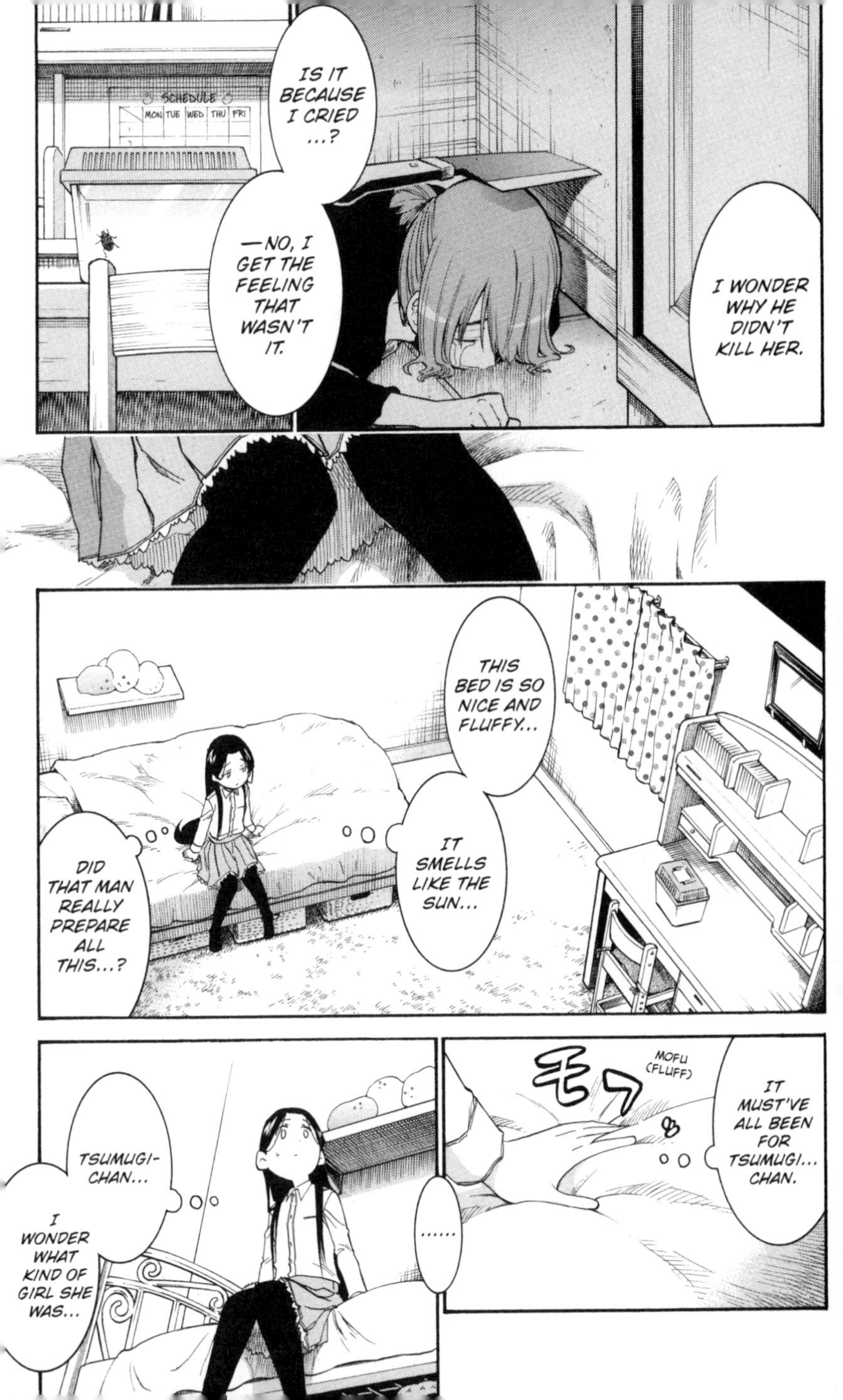
I WONDER WHY HE DIDN'T KILL HER.
SCHEDULE
MON TUE WED THU FRI
IS IT BECAUSE I CRIED ...?
—NO, I GET THE FEELING THAT WASN'T IT.
THIS BED IS SO NICE AND FLUFFY...
IT SMELLS LIKE THE SUN...
DID THAT MAN REALLY PREPARE ALL THIS...?
MOFU (FLUFF)
IT MUST'VE ALL BEEN FOR TSUMUGI... CHAN.
......
TSUMUGI-CHAN...
I WONDER WHAT KIND OF GIRL SHE WAS...

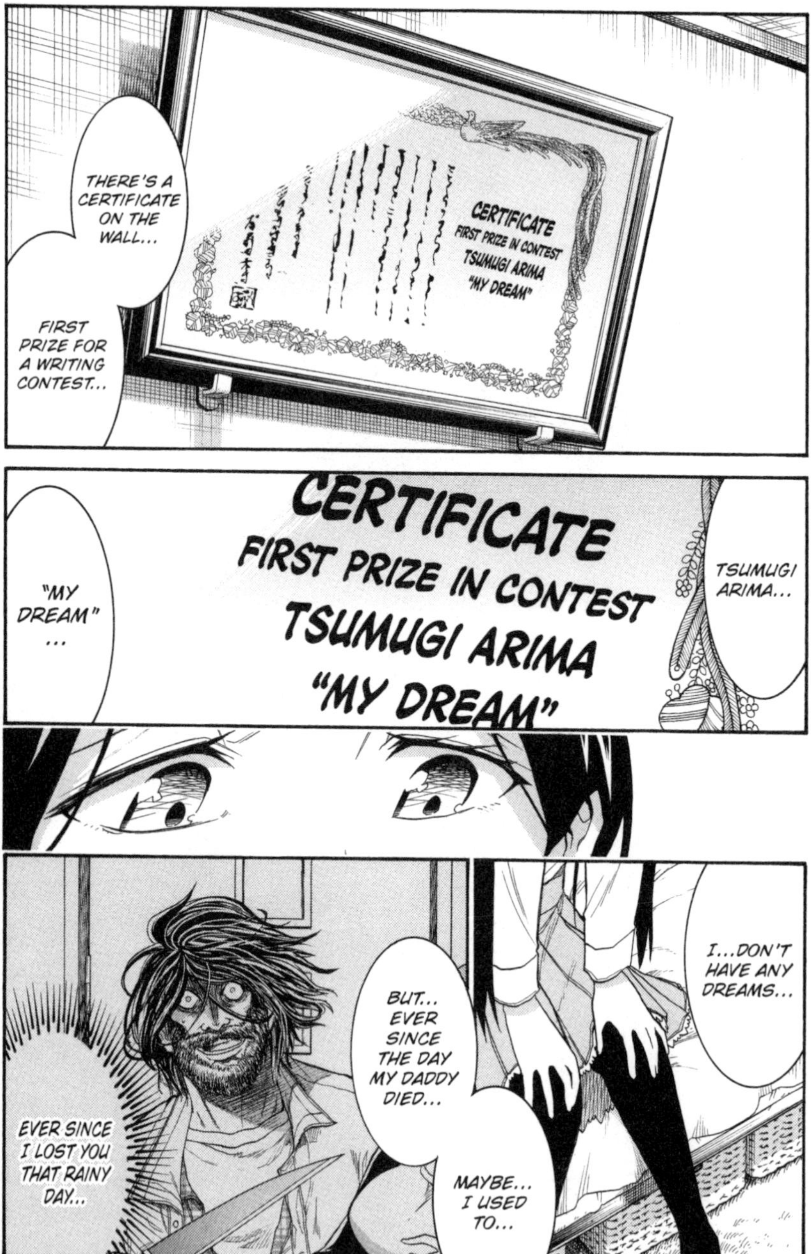
THERE'S A CERTIFICATE ON THE WALL...
FIRST PRIZE FOR A WRITING CONTEST...
CERTIFICATE
FIRST PRIZE IN CONTEST
TSUMUGI ARIMA
"MY DREAM"
TSUMUGI ARIMA...
CERTIFICATE
FIRST PRIZE IN CONTEST
TSUMUGI ARIMA
"MY DREAM"
"MY DREAM" ...
I...DON'T HAVE ANY DREAMS...
BUT... EVER SINCE THE DAY MY DADDY DIED...
MAYBE... I USED TO...
EVER SINCE I LOST YOU THAT RAINY DAY...

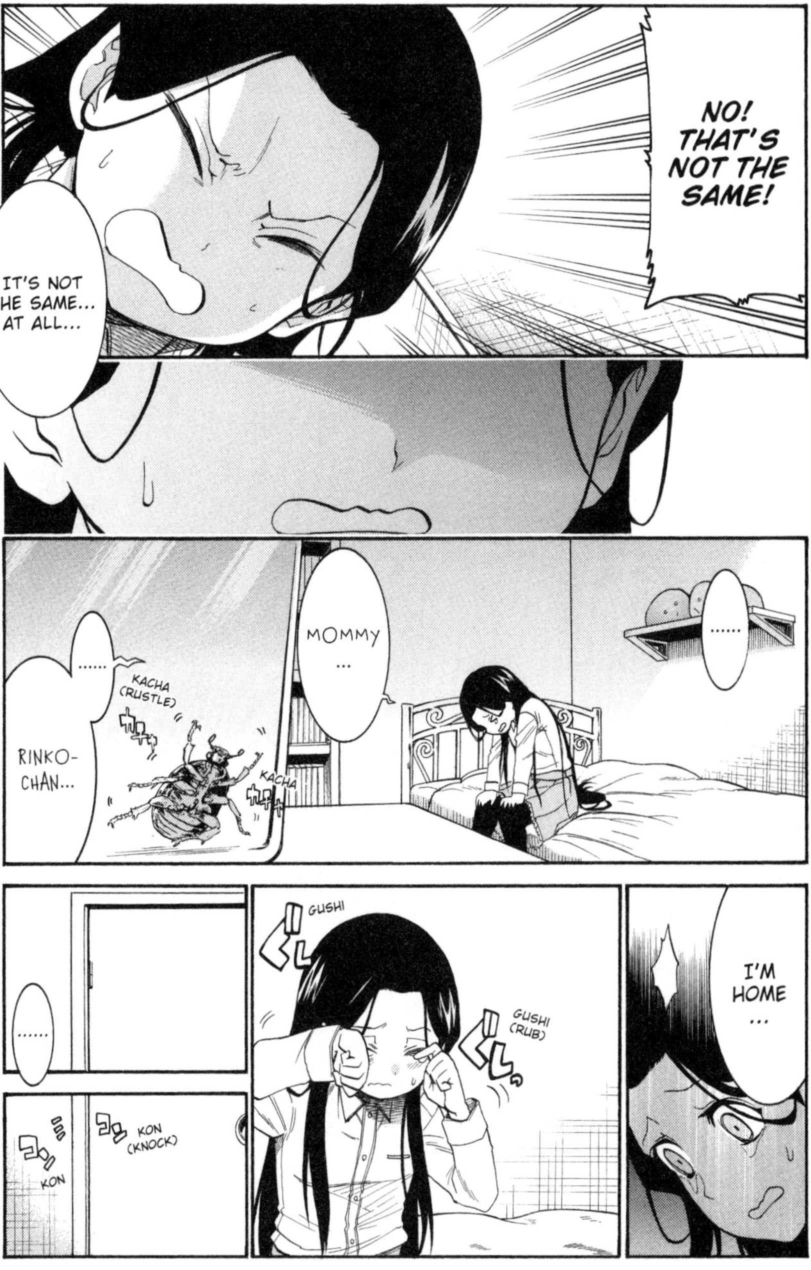
NO! THAT'S NOT THE SAME!
IT'S NOT THE SAME... AT ALL...
......
MOMMY ...
......
RINKO-CHAN...
KACHA (RUSTLE)
KACHA
I'M HOME ...
GUSHI
GUSHI (RUB)
......
KON (KNOCK)
KON

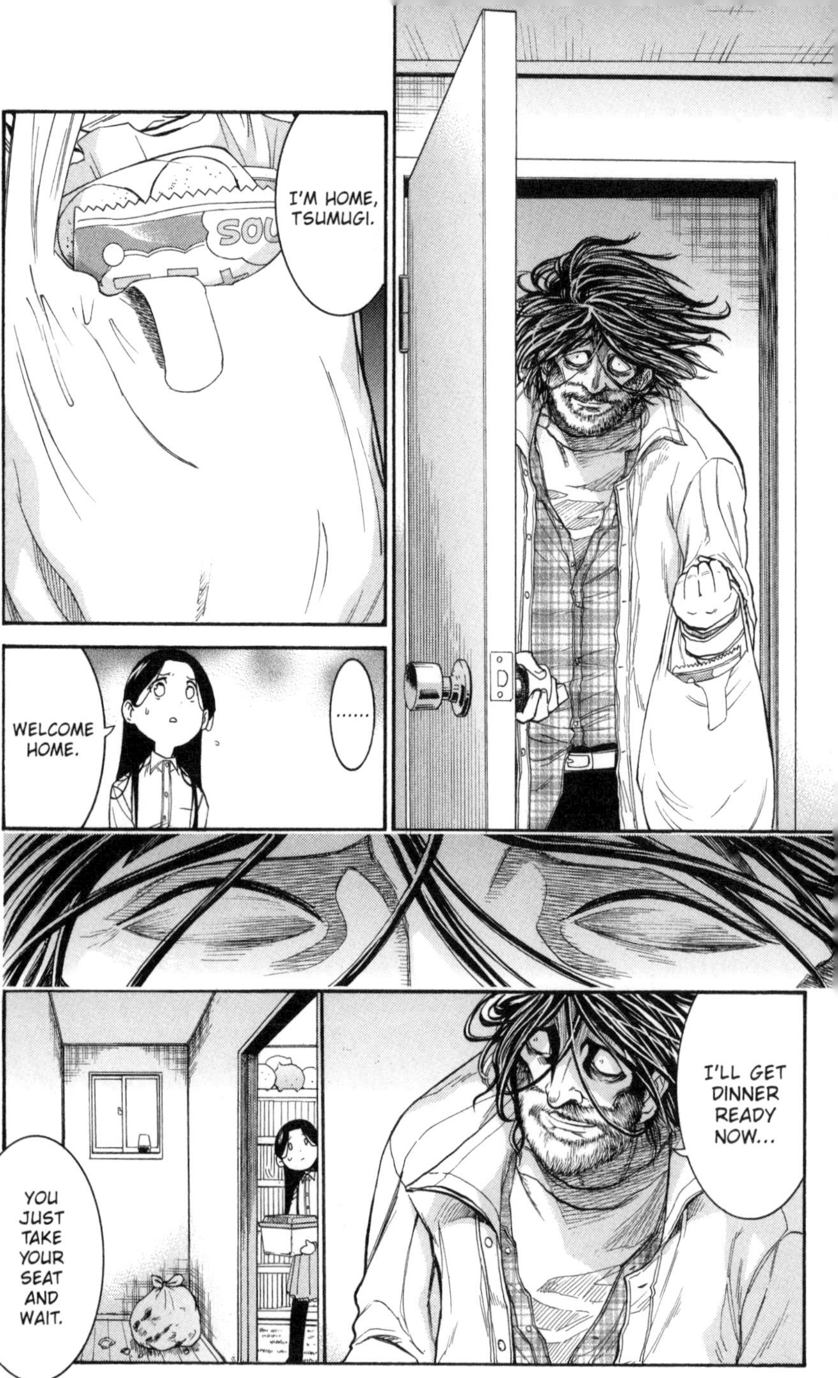

I'M HOME, TSUMUGI.
......
WELCOME HOME.
I'LL GET DINNER READY NOW...
YOU JUST TAKE YOUR SEAT AND WAIT.

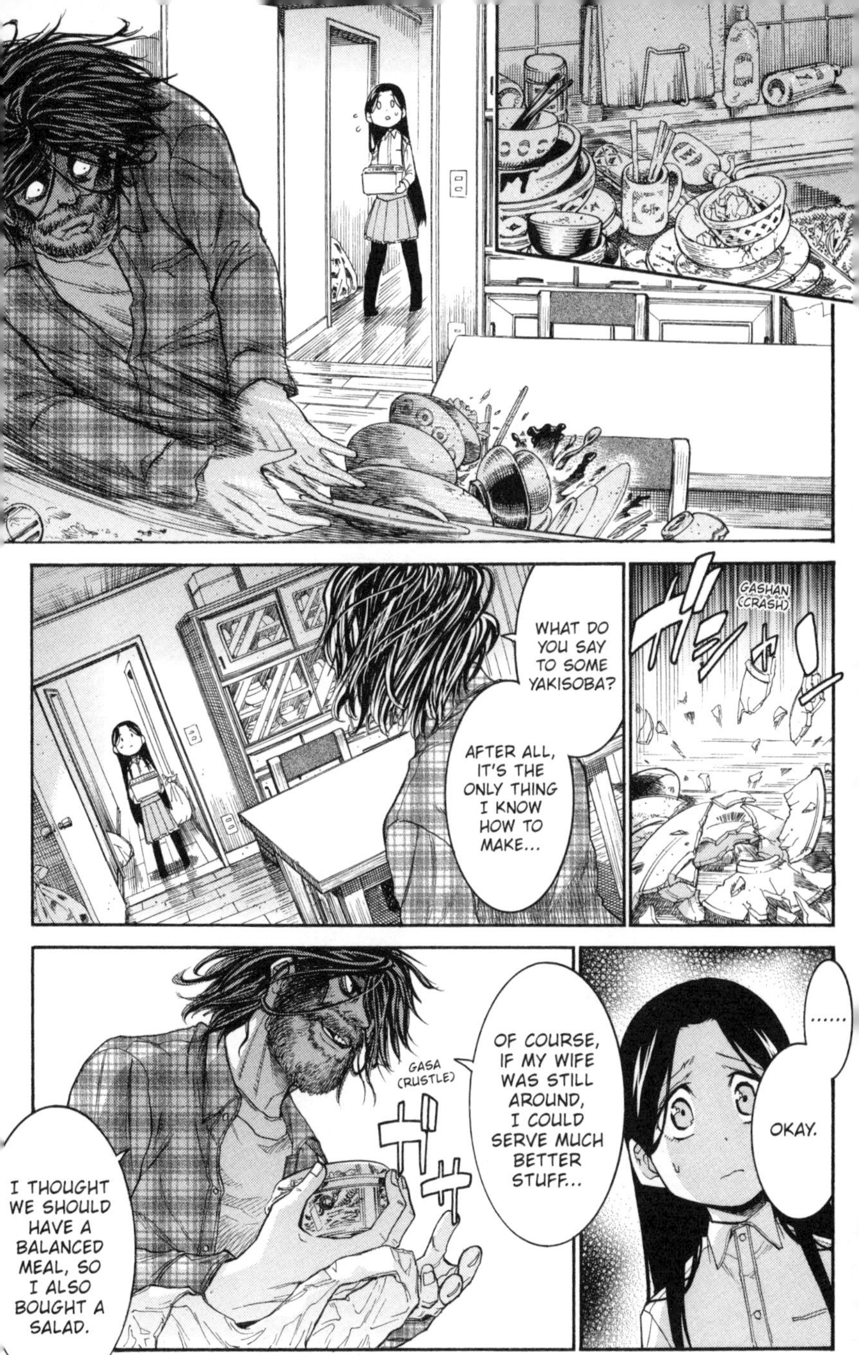
GASHAN (CRASH)
WHAT DO YOU SAY TO SOME YAKISOBA?
AFTER ALL, IT'S THE ONLY THING I KNOW HOW TO MAKE...
......
OKAY.
OF COURSE, IF MY WIFE WAS STILL AROUND, I COULD SERVE MUCH BETTER STUFF...
GASA (RUSTLE)
I THOUGHT WE SHOULD HAVE A BALANCED MEAL, SO I ALSO BOUGHT A SALAD.

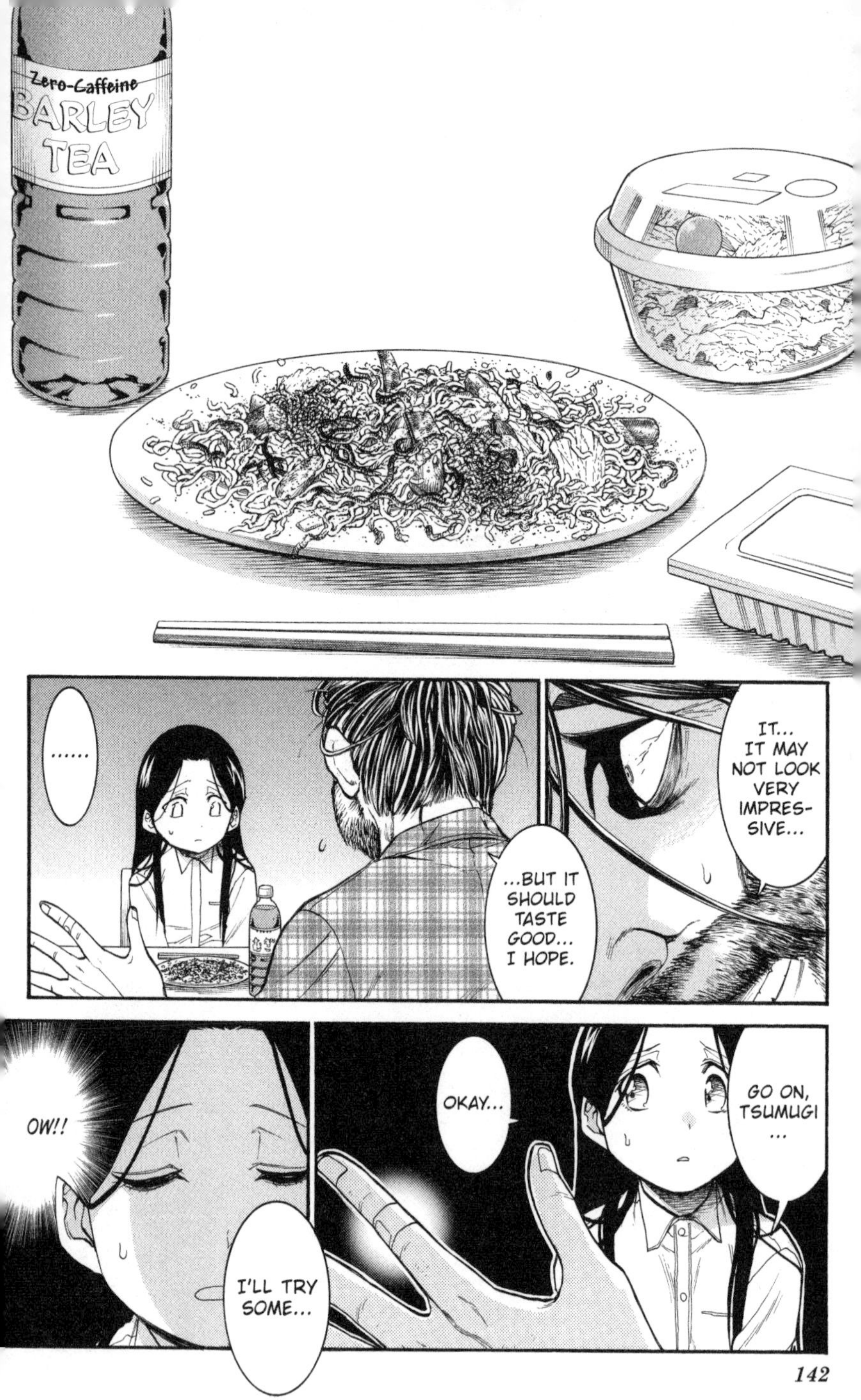
Zero-Caffeine
BARLEY TEA
IT... IT MAY NOT LOOK VERY IMPRES-SIVE...
...BUT IT SHOULD TASTE GOOD... I HOPE.
......
GO ON, TSUMUGI ...
OKAY...
I'LL TRY SOME...
OW!!

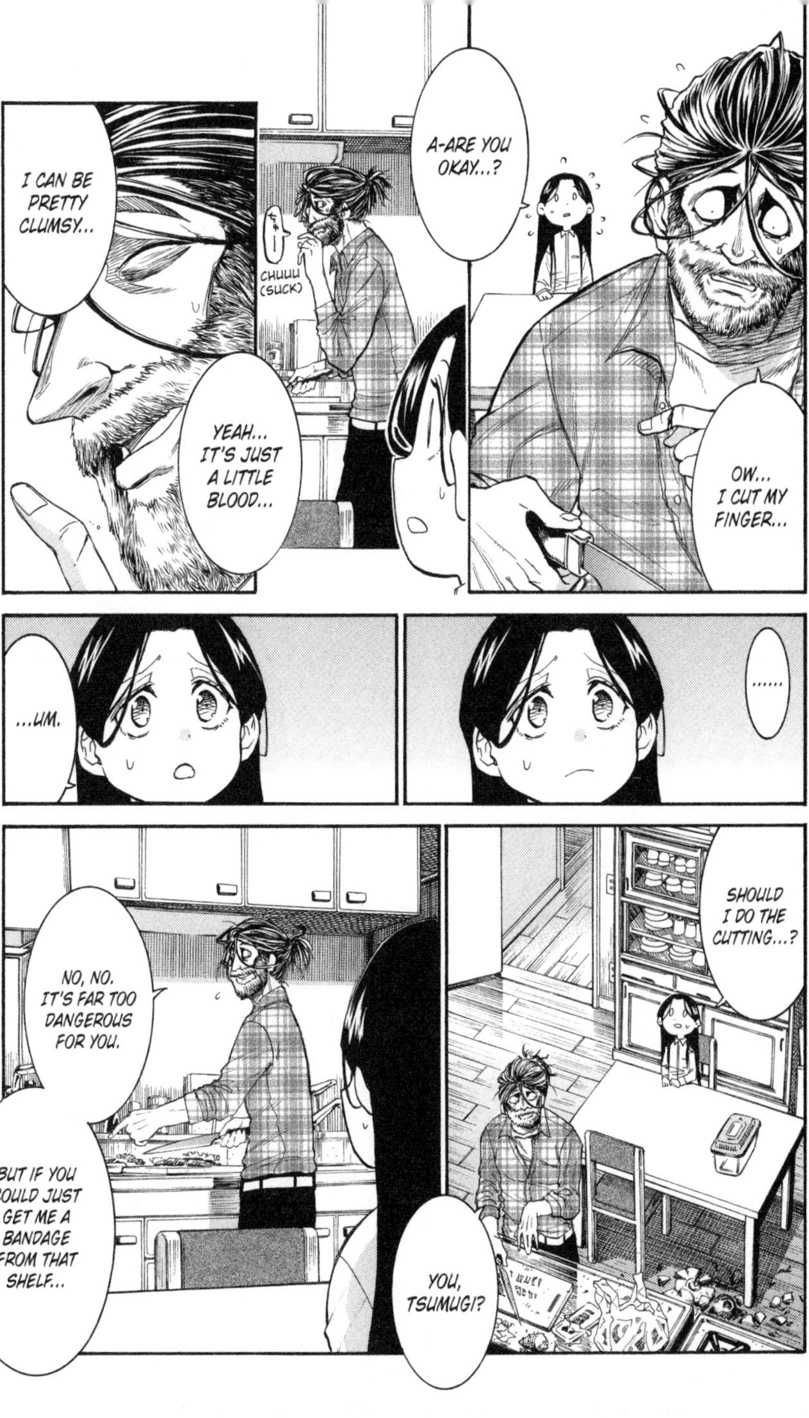

OW... I CUT MY FINGER...
A-ARE YOU OKAY...?
CHUUU (SUCK)
YEAH... IT'S JUST A LITTLE BLOOD...
I CAN BE PRETTY CLUMSY...
......
...UM.
SHOULD I DO THE CUTTING...?
YOU, TSUMUGI?
NO, NO. IT'S FAR TOO DANGEROUS FOR YOU.
BUT IF YOU COULD JUST GET ME A BANDAGE FROM THAT SHELF...

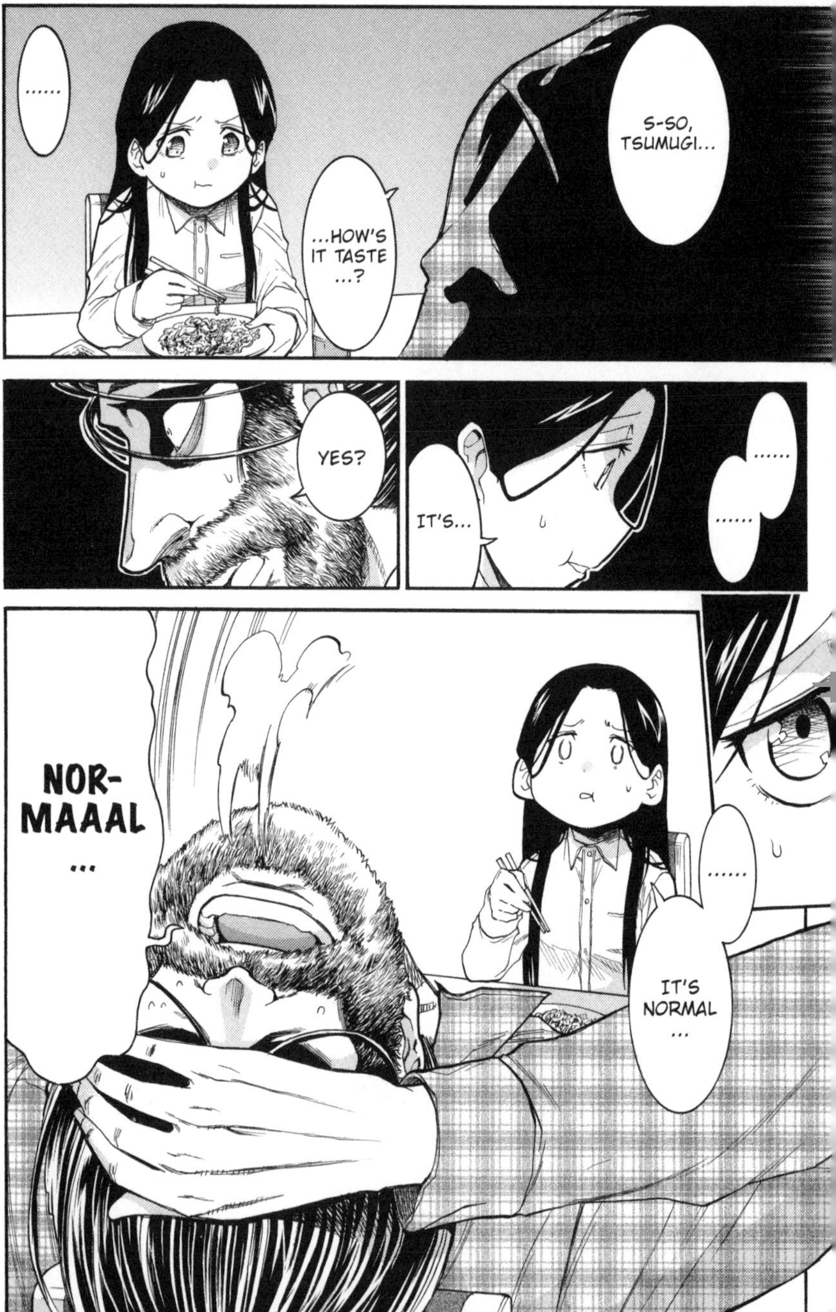
S-SO, TSUMUGI...
...HOW'S IT TASTE ...?
......
......
......
IT'S...
YES?
......
IT'S NORMAL ...
NOR-MAAAL ...

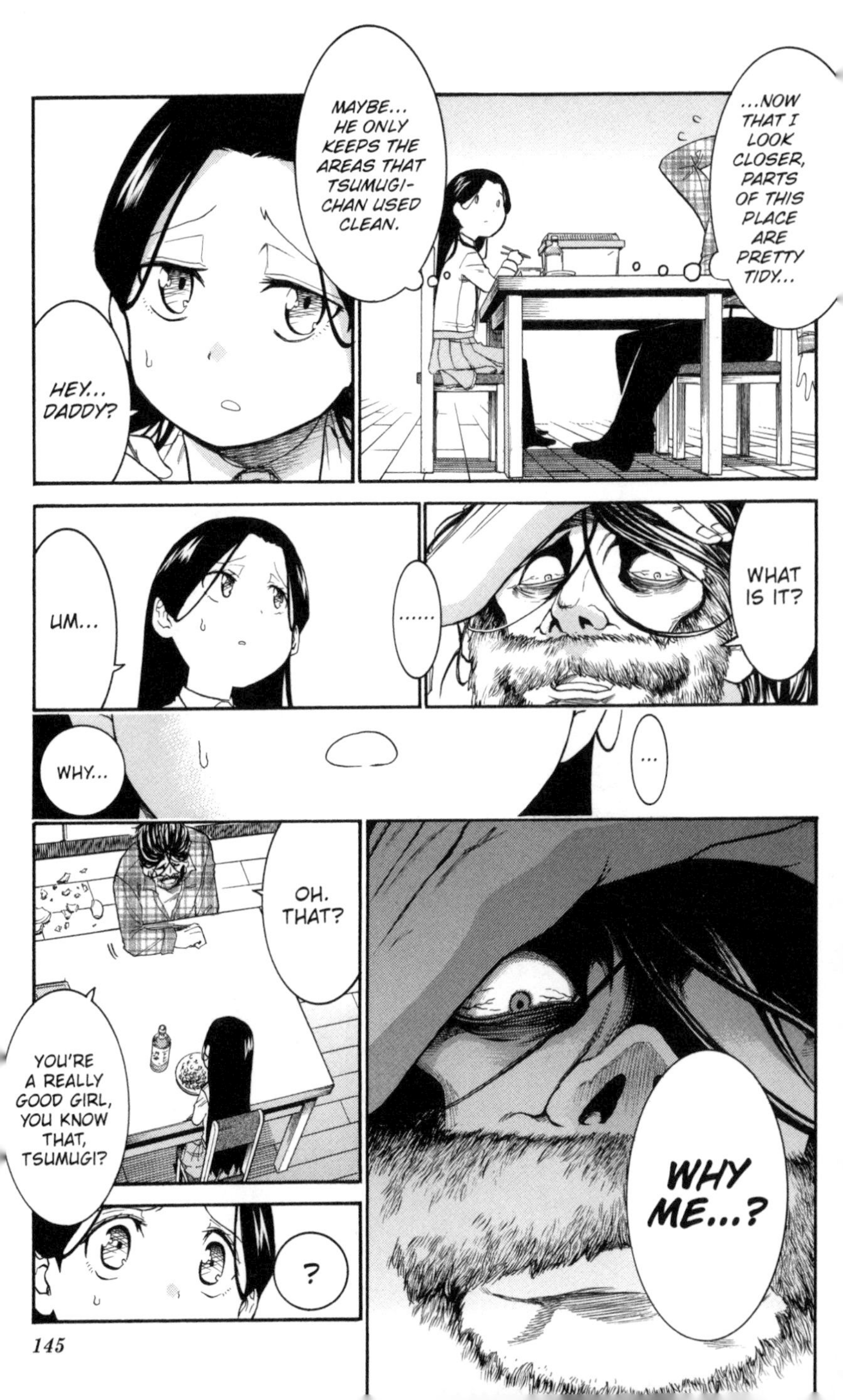
...NOW THAT I LOOK CLOSER, PARTS OF THIS PLACE ARE PRETTY TIDY...
MAYBE... HE ONLY KEEPS THE AREAS THAT TSUMUGI-CHAN USED CLEAN.
HEY... DADDY?
WHAT IS IT?
......
UM...
...
WHY...
WHY ME...?
OH. THAT?
YOU'RE A REALLY GOOD GIRL, YOU KNOW THAT, TSUMUGI?
?

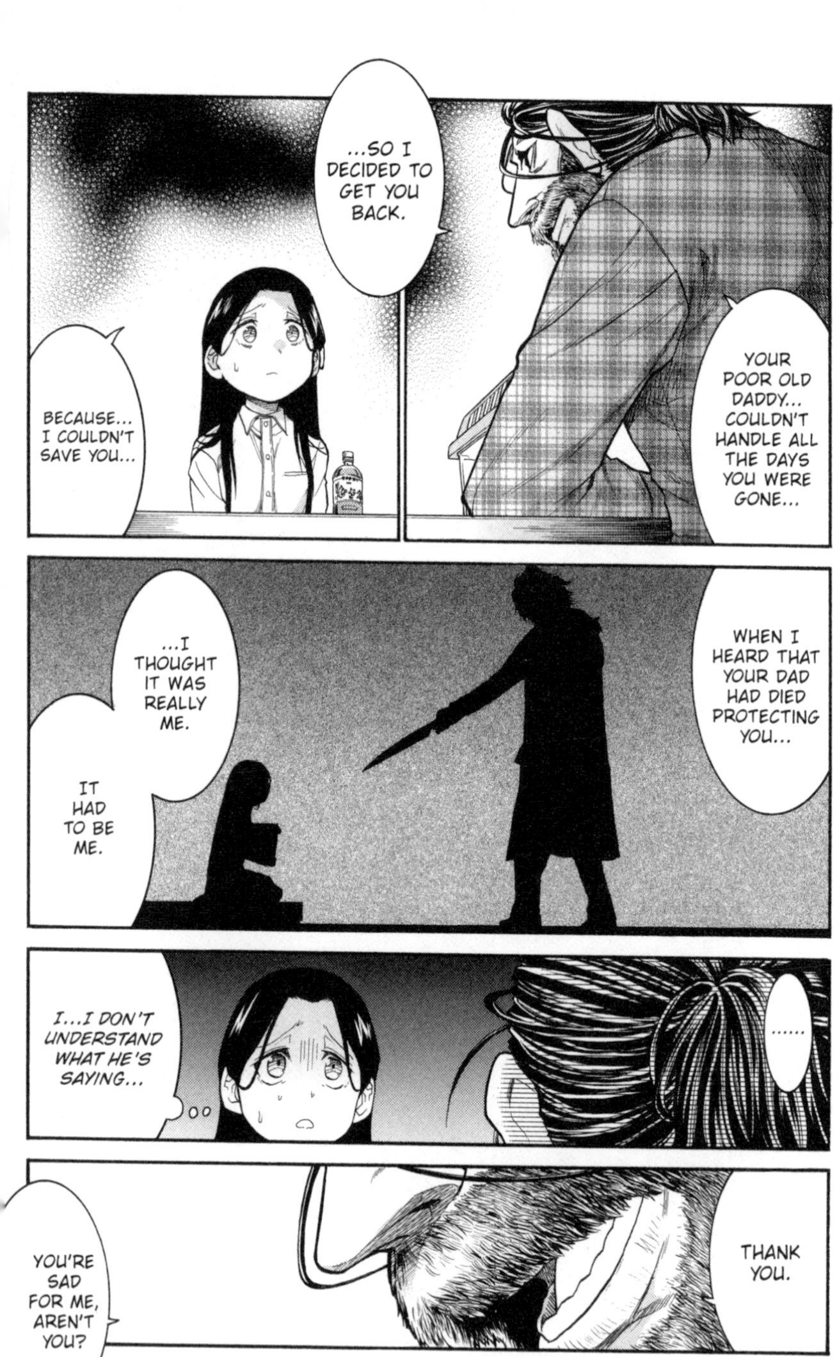
YOUR POOR OLD DADDY... COULDN'T HANDLE ALL THE DAYS YOU WERE GONE...
...SO I DECIDED TO GET YOU BACK.
BECAUSE... I COULDN'T SAVE YOU...
WHEN I HEARD THAT YOUR DAD HAD DIED PROTECTING YOU...
...I THOUGHT IT WAS REALLY ME.
IT HAD TO BE ME.
......
I...I DON'T UNDERSTAND WHAT HE'S SAYING...
THANK YOU.
YOU'RE SAD FOR ME, AREN'T YOU?

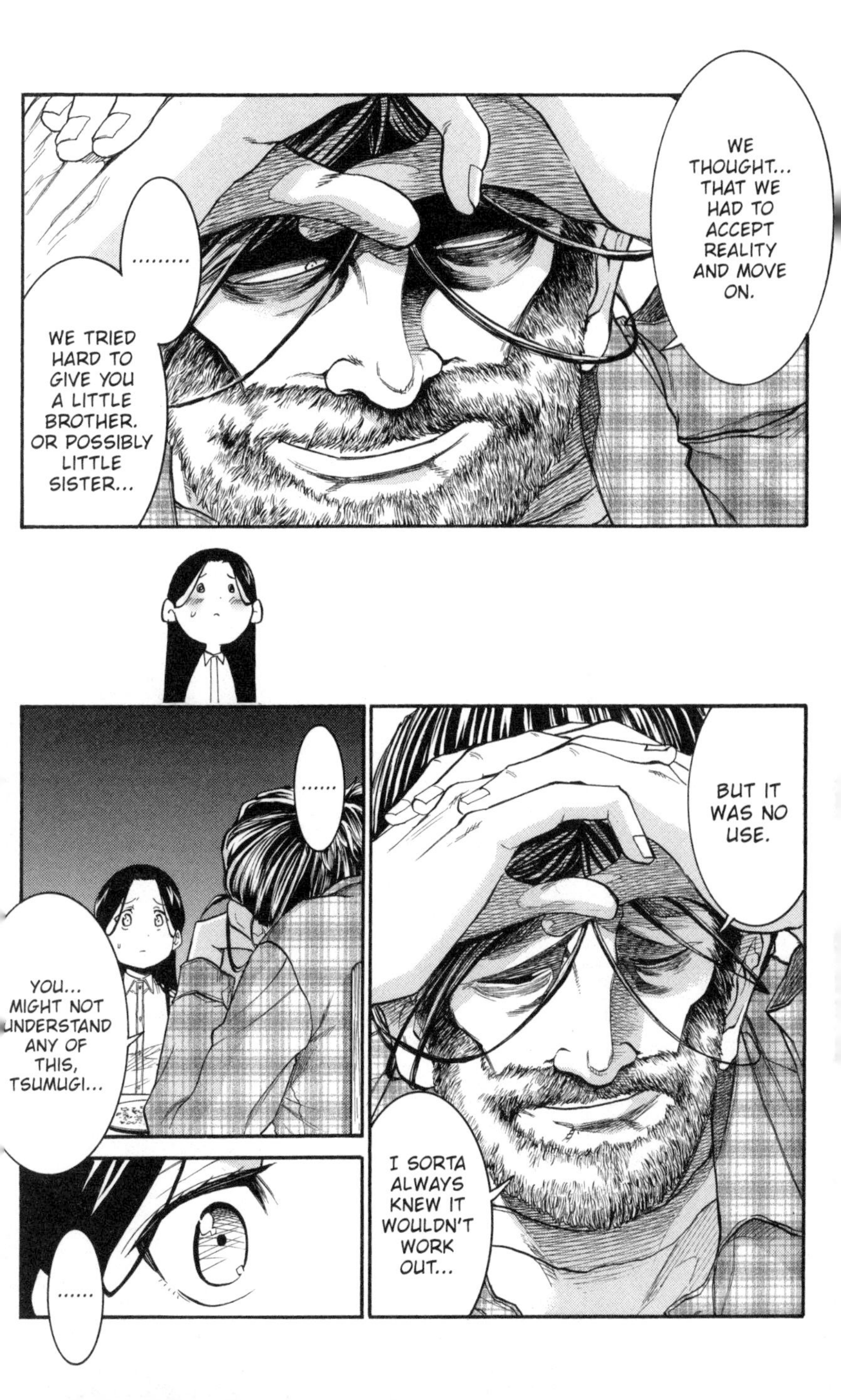
WE THOUGHT... THAT WE HAD TO ACCEPT REALITY AND MOVE ON.
....
WE TRIED HARD TO GIVE YOU A LITTLE BROTHER. OR POSSIBLY LITTLE SISTER...
BUT IT WAS NO USE.
I SORTA ALWAYS KNEW IT WOULDN'T WORK OUT...
....
YOU... MIGHT NOT UNDERSTAND ANY OF THIS, TSUMUGI...
......

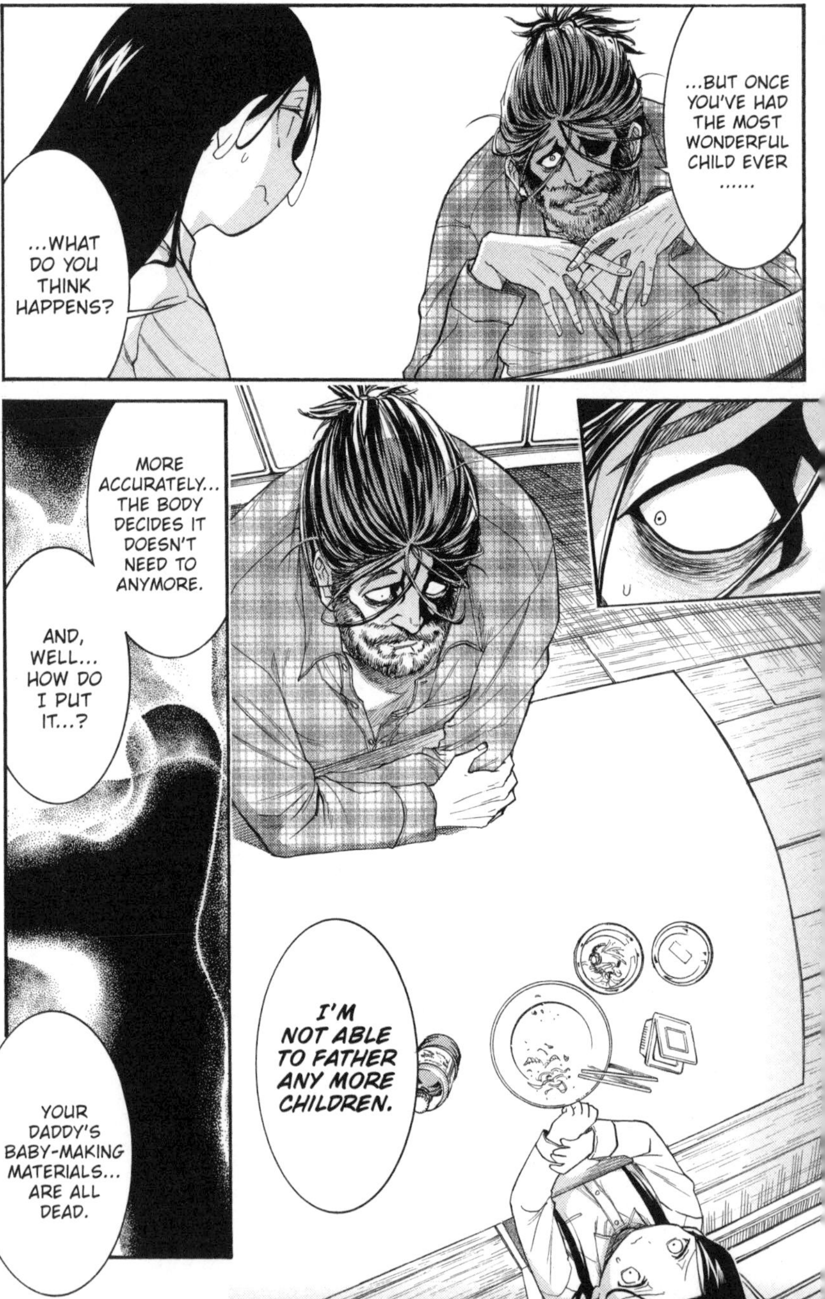
...BUT ONCE YOU'VE HAD THE MOST WONDERFUL CHILD EVER ......
...WHAT DO YOU THINK HAPPENS?
MORE ACCURATELY... THE BODY DECIDES IT DOESN'T NEED TO ANYMORE.
AND, WELL... HOW DO I PUT IT...?
YOUR DADDY'S BABY-MAKING MATERIALS... ARE ALL DEAD.
I'M NOT ABLE TO FATHER ANY MORE CHILDREN.

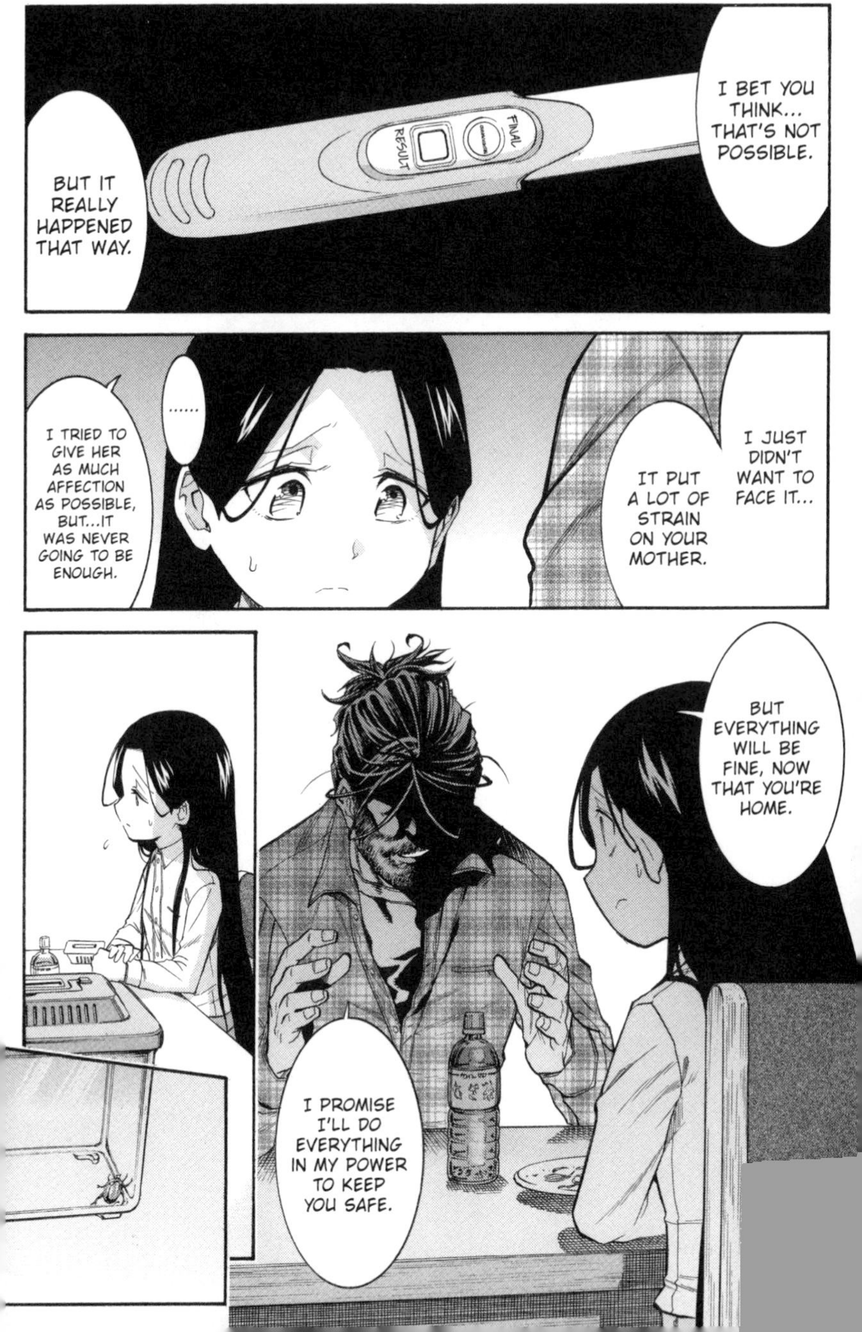
I BET YOU THINK... THAT'S NOT POSSIBLE.
FINAL
RESULT
BUT IT REALLY HAPPENED THAT WAY.
I JUST DIDN'T WANT TO FACE IT...
IT PUT A LOT OF STRAIN ON YOUR MOTHER.
......
I TRIED TO GIVE HER AS MUCH AFFECTION AS POSSIBLE, BUT...IT WAS NEVER GOING TO BE ENOUGH.
BUT EVERYTHING WILL BE FINE, NOW THAT YOU'RE HOME.
I PROMISE I'LL DO EVERYTHING IN MY POWER TO KEEP YOU SAFE.

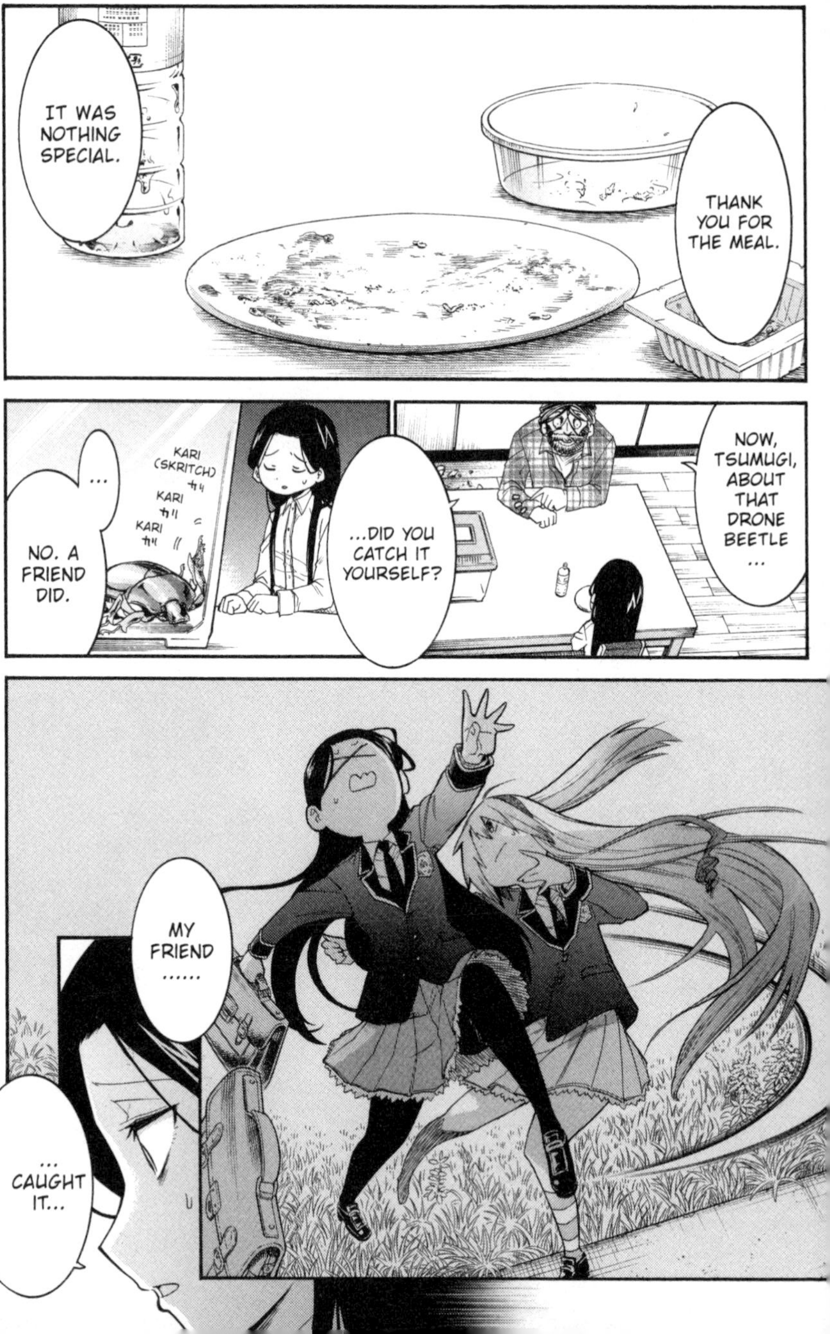
THANK YOU FOR THE MEAL.
IT WAS NOTHING SPECIAL.
NOW, TSUMUGI, ABOUT THAT DRONE BEETLE ...
...DID YOU CATCH IT YOURSELF?
KARI (SKRITCH) カリ
KARI カリ
KARI カリ
...
NO. A FRIEND DID.
MY FRIEND ......
... CAUGHT IT...

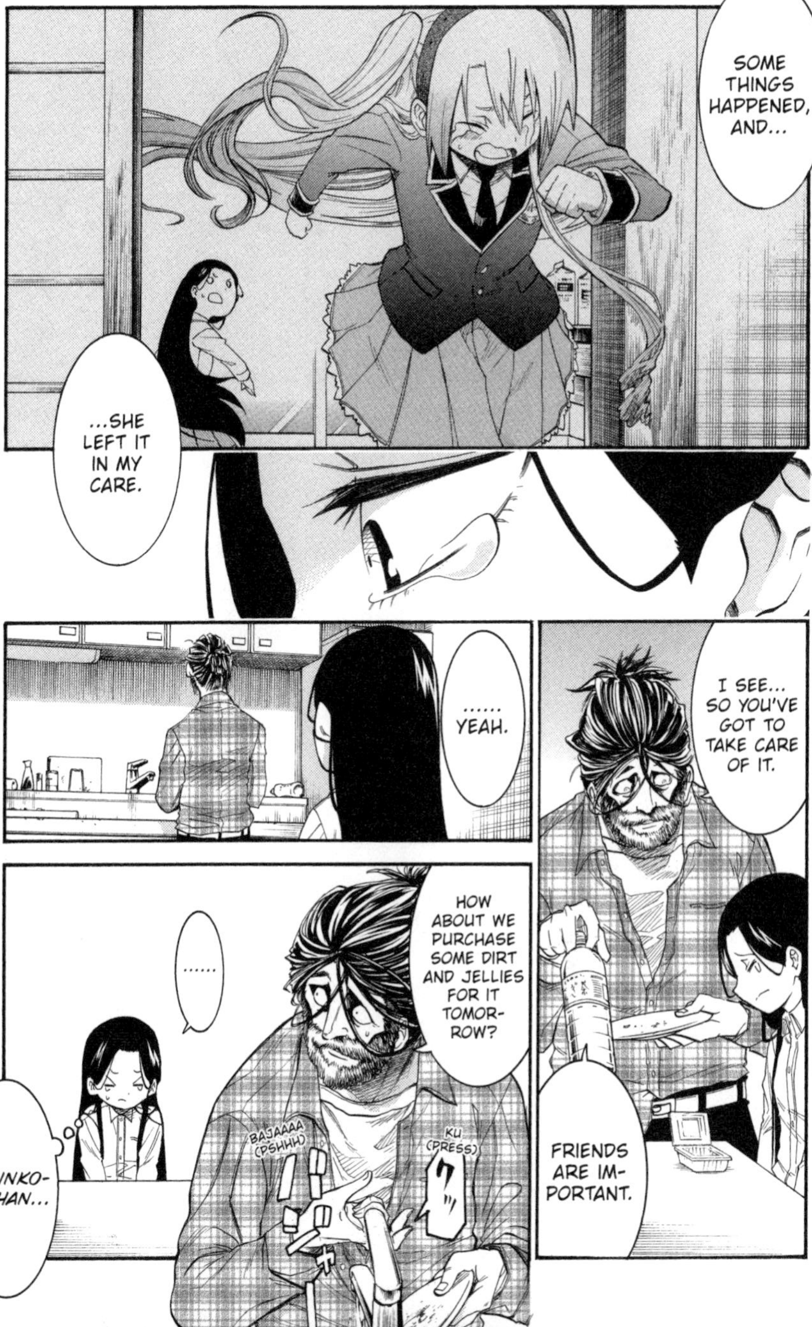
SOME THINGS HAPPENED, AND...
...SHE LEFT IT IN MY CARE.
I SEE... SO YOU'VE GOT TO TAKE CARE OF IT.
FRIENDS ARE IMPORTANT.
......YEAH.
HOW ABOUT WE PURCHASE SOME DIRT AND JELLIES FOR IT TOMORROW?
KU (PRESS)
BAJAAAA (PSHHH)
......
RINKO-CHAN...

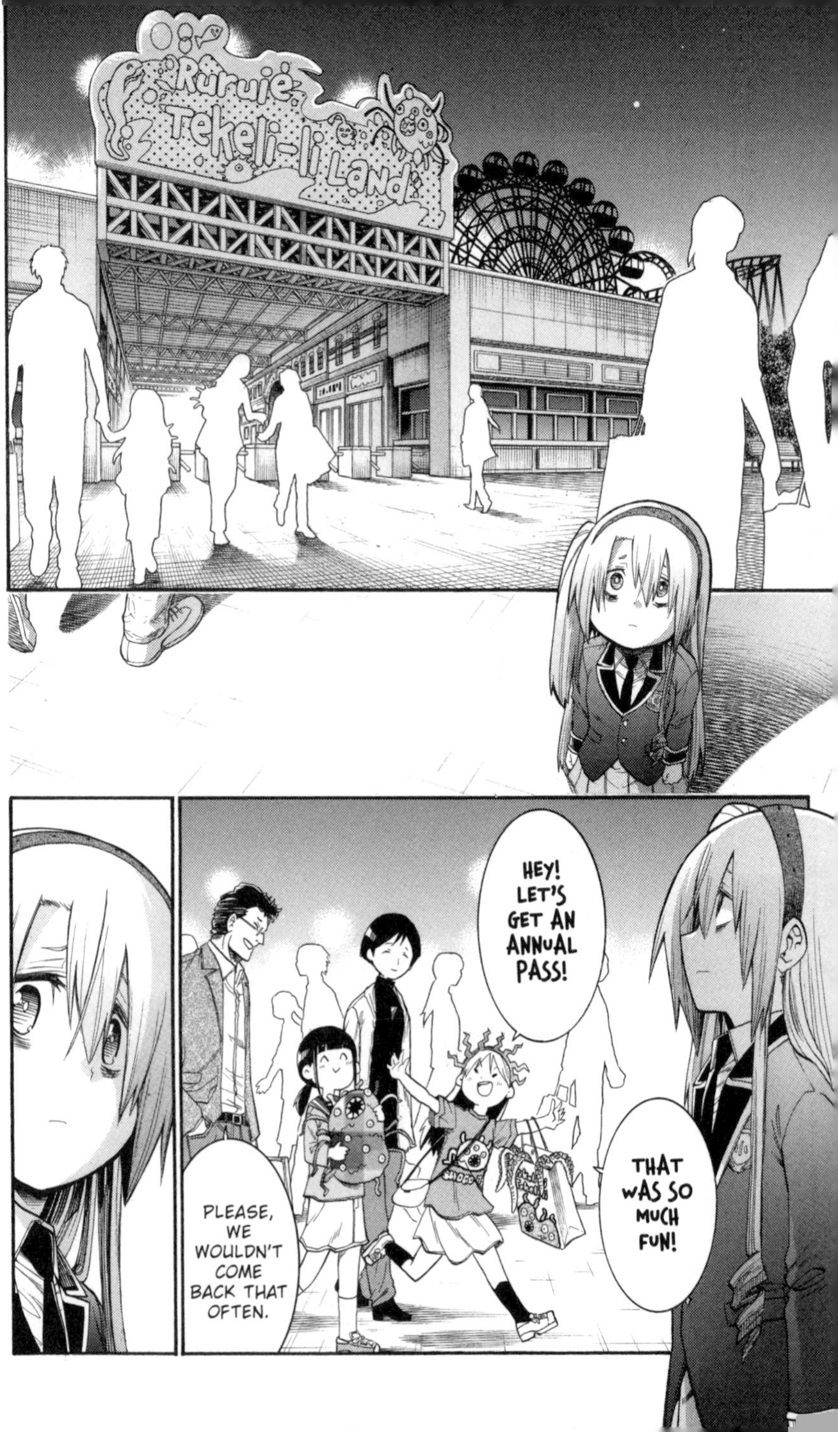
Ruruie Tekeli-li Land
THAT WAS SO MUCH FUN!
HEY! LET'S GET AN ANNUAL PASS!
PLEASE, WE WOULDN'T COME BACK THAT OFTEN.

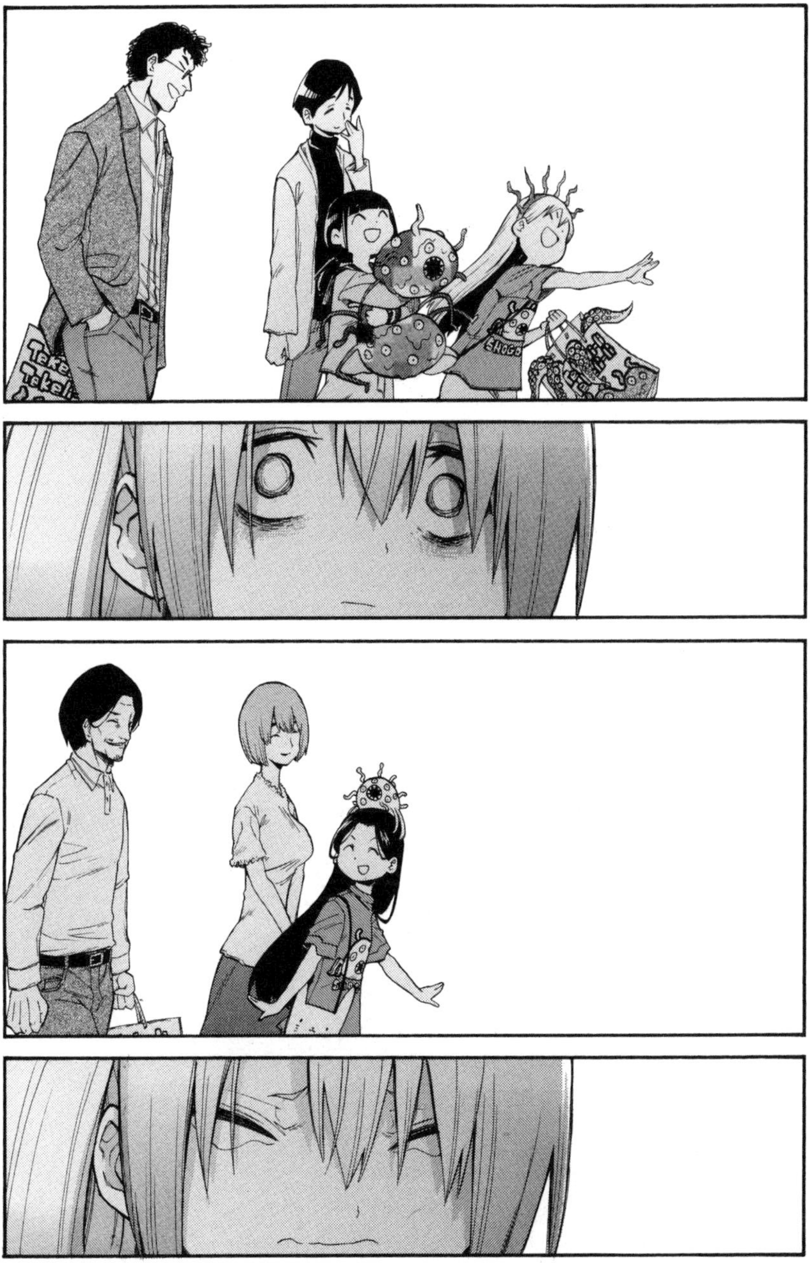

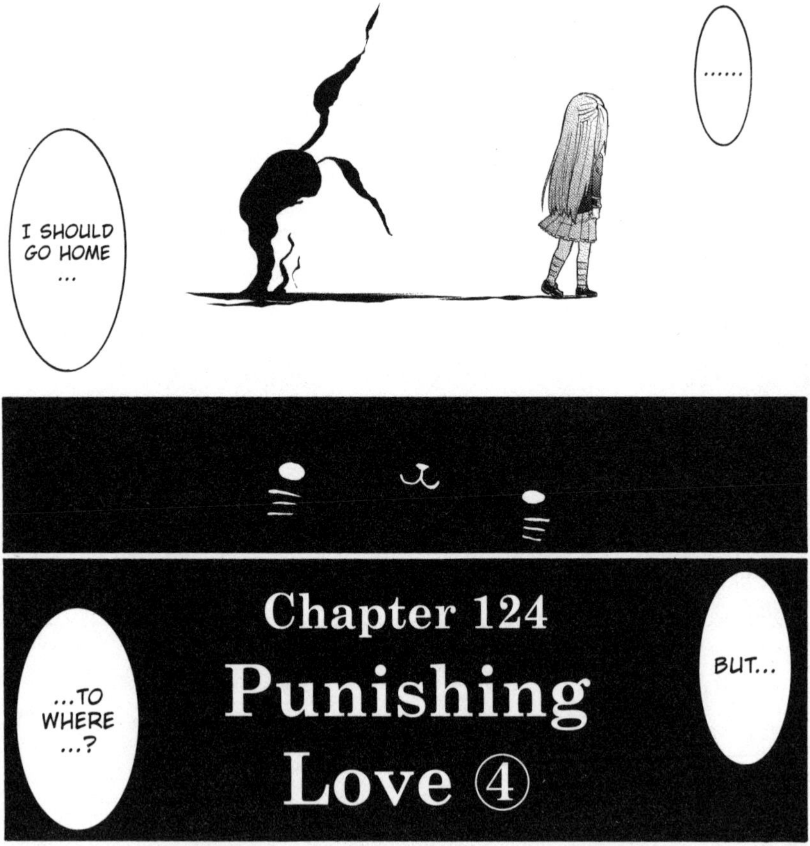
......
I SHOULD GO HOME ...
BUT...
...TO WHERE ...?

Chapter 124 Punishing Love ④

MURCIÉLAGO

MURCIÉLAGO

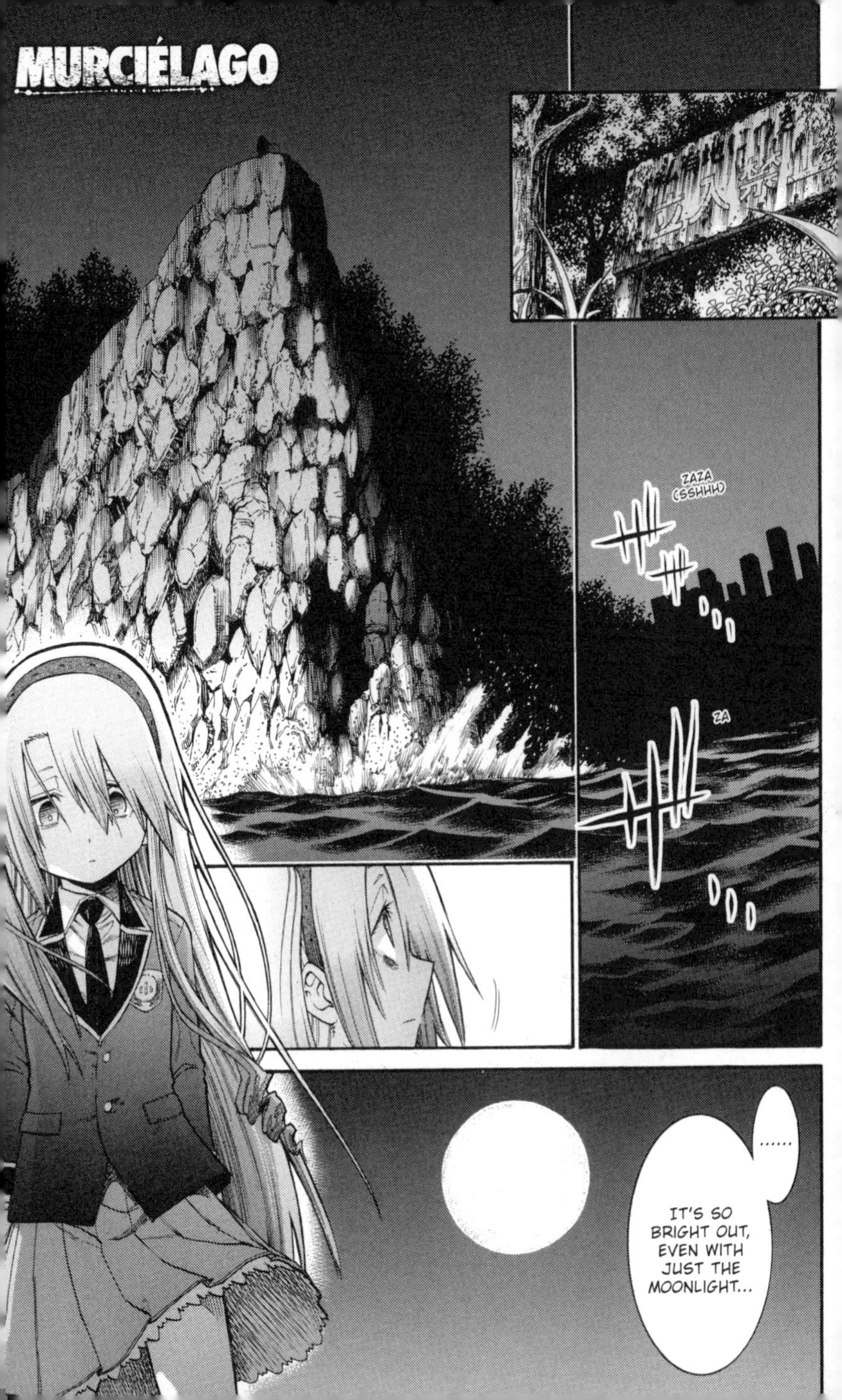
ZAZA (SSHHH)
ZA
……
IT'S SO BRIGHT OUT, EVEN WITH JUST THE MOONLIGHT...

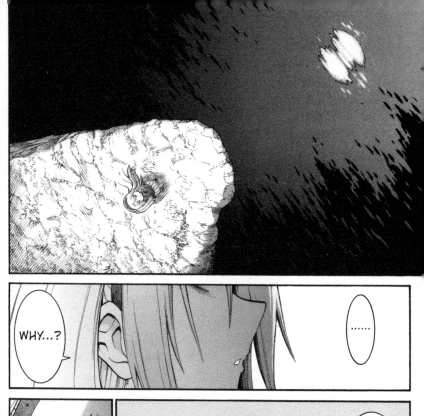

WHY...?

......

WHY AM I EVEN ALIVE?

I'M A MURDERER...

THAT'S RIGHT.

...I SHOULD'VE DIED BACK THEN...

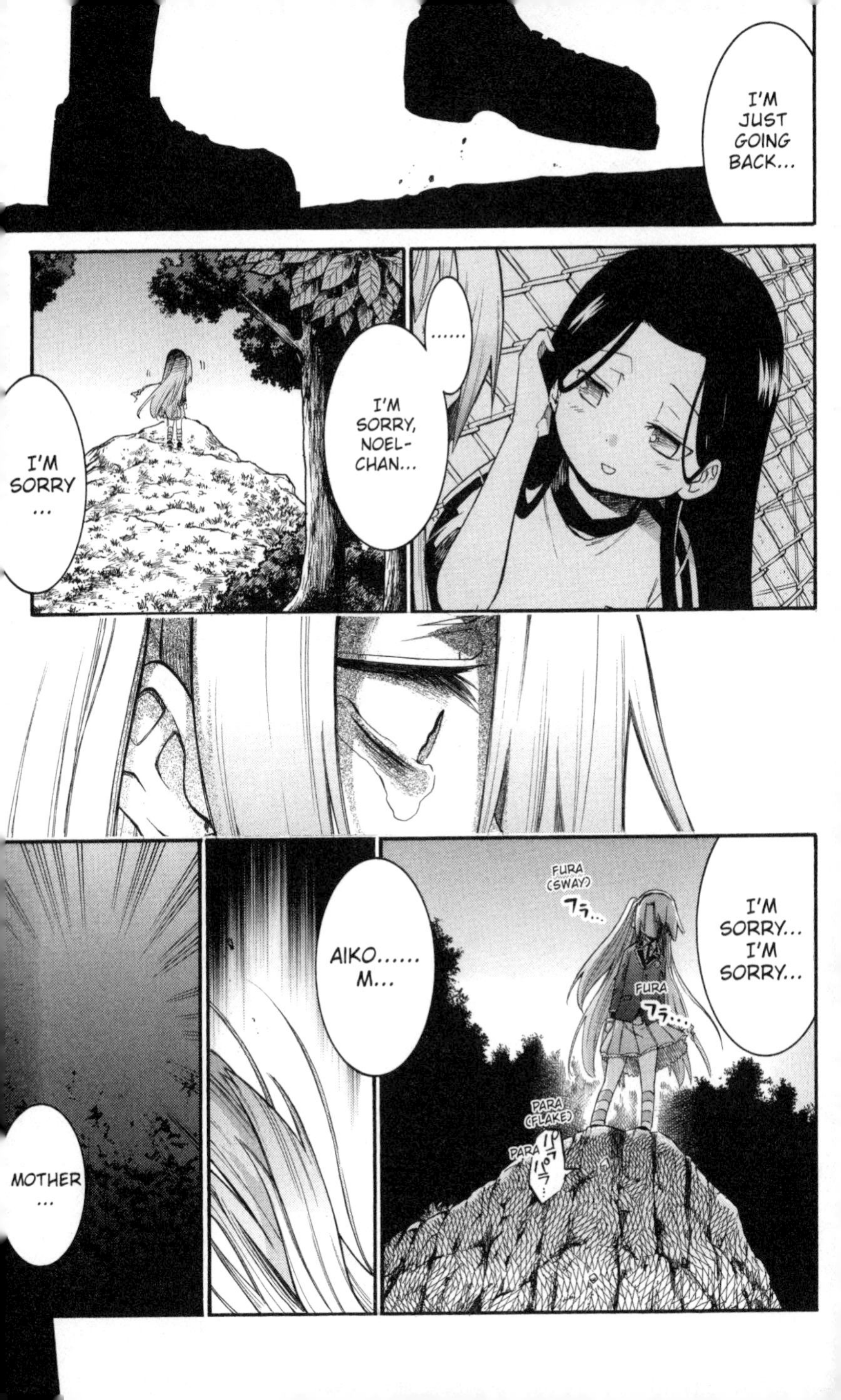
I'M JUST GOING BACK...
......
I'M SORRY, NOEL-CHAN...
I'M SORRY...
I'M SORRY... I'M SORRY...
FURA (SWAY)
フラ...
FURA
フラ...
PARA (FLAKE)
パラ
PARA
パラ...
AIKO...... M...
MOTHER...

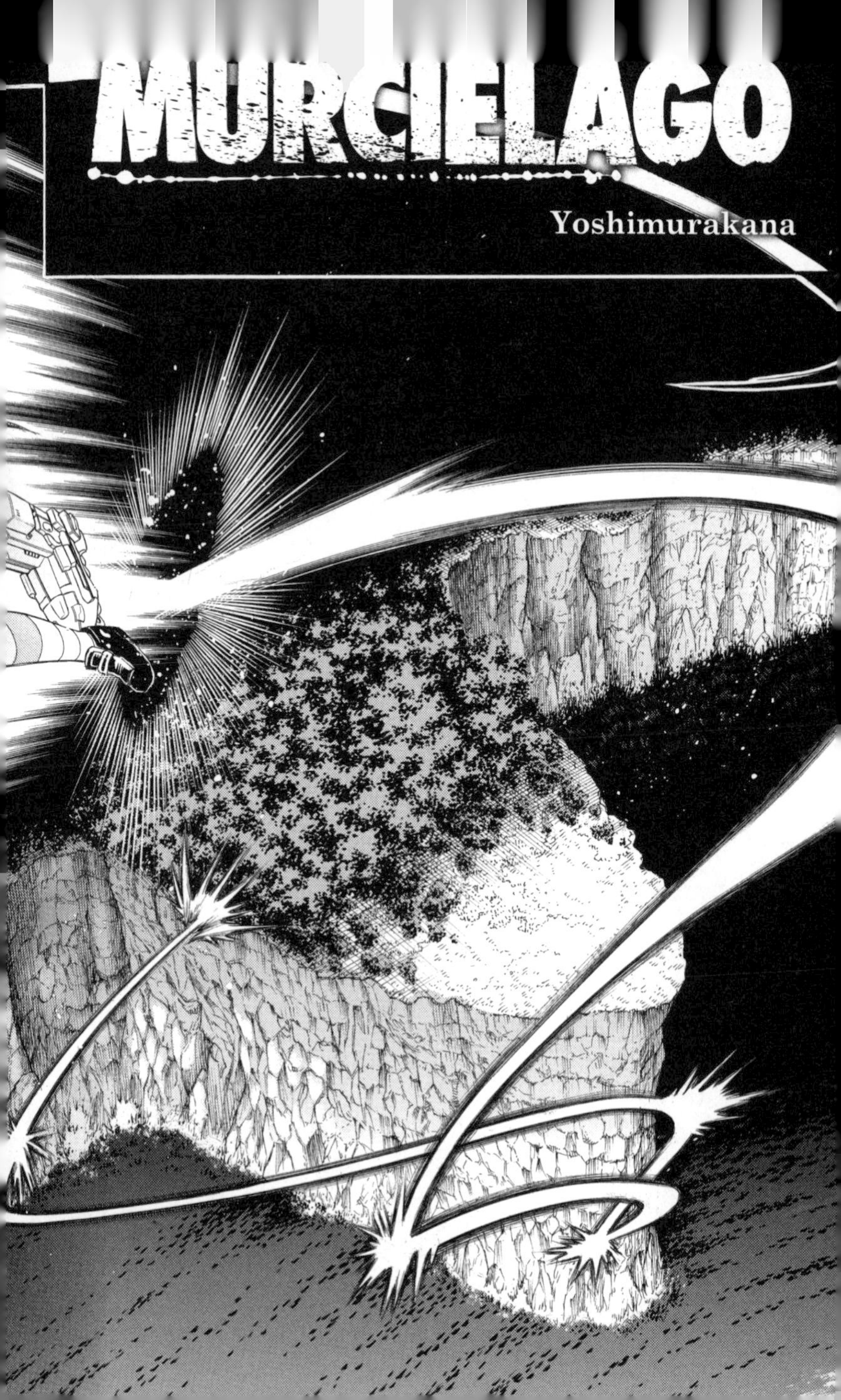
MURCIELAGO
Yoshimurakana

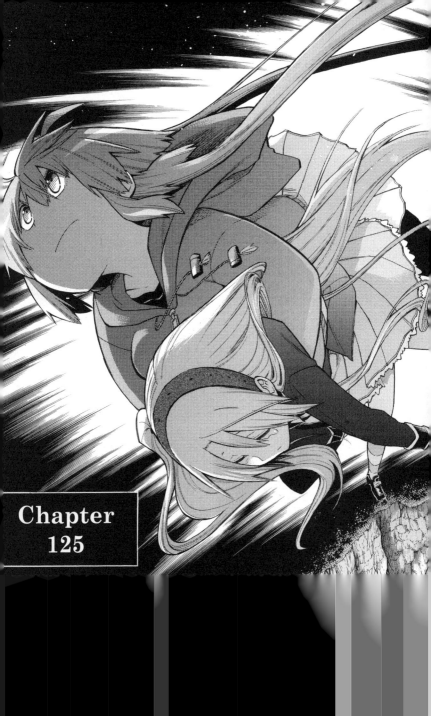

Chapter 125

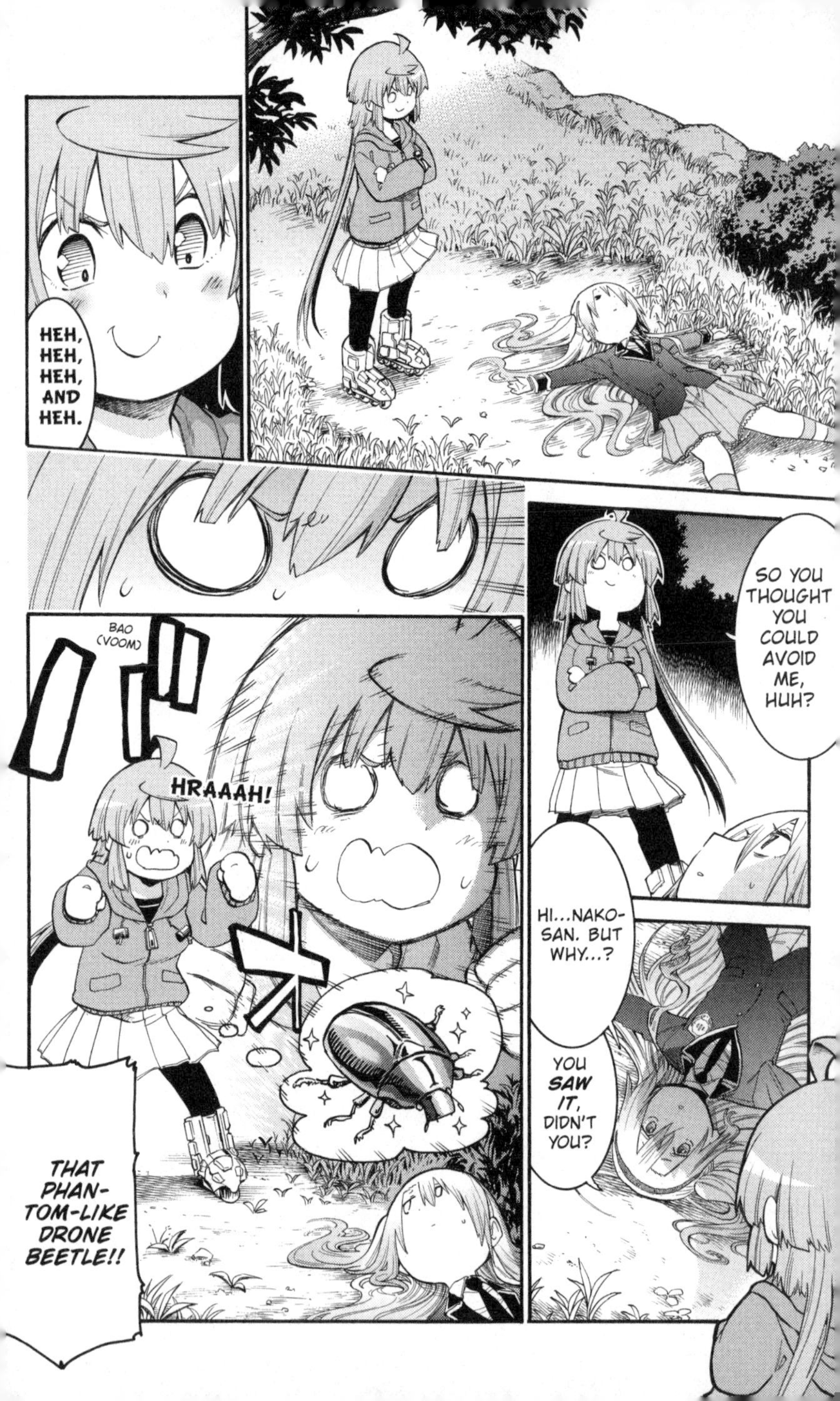
HEH, HEH, HEH, AND HEH.
SO YOU THOUGHT YOU COULD AVOID ME, HUH?
HI...NAKO-SAN. BUT WHY...?
YOU SAW IT, DIDN'T YOU?
BAO (VOOM)
HRAAAH!
THAT PHAN-TOM-LIKE DRONE BEETLE!!

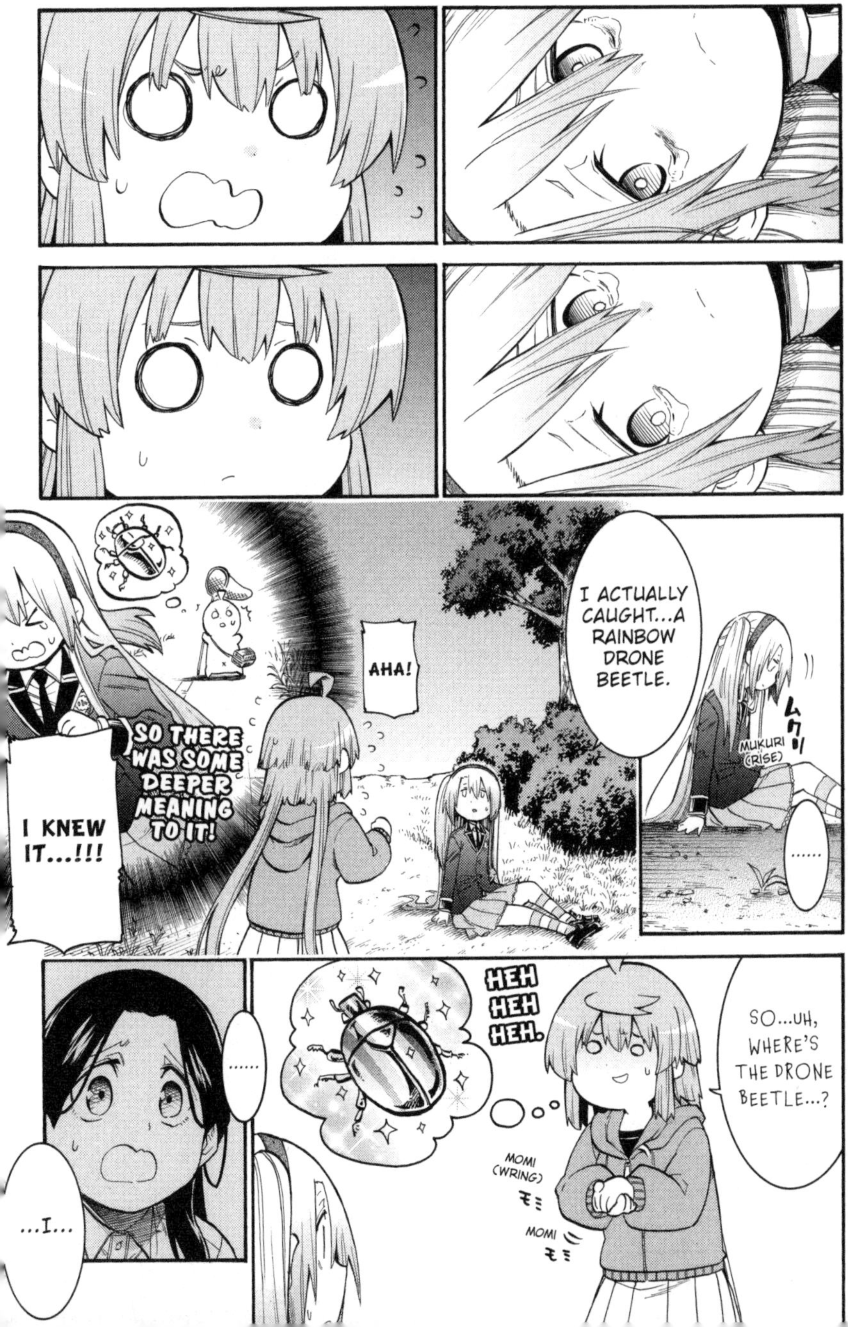
I ACTUALLY CAUGHT...A RAINBOW DRONE BEETLE.
ムクリ
MUKURI (RISE)
......
AHA!
SO THERE WAS SOME DEEPER MEANING TO IT!
I KNEW IT...!!!
SO...UH, WHERE'S THE DRONE BEETLE...?
HEH HEH HEH.
MOMI (WRING)
モミ
MOMI
モミ
......
...I...

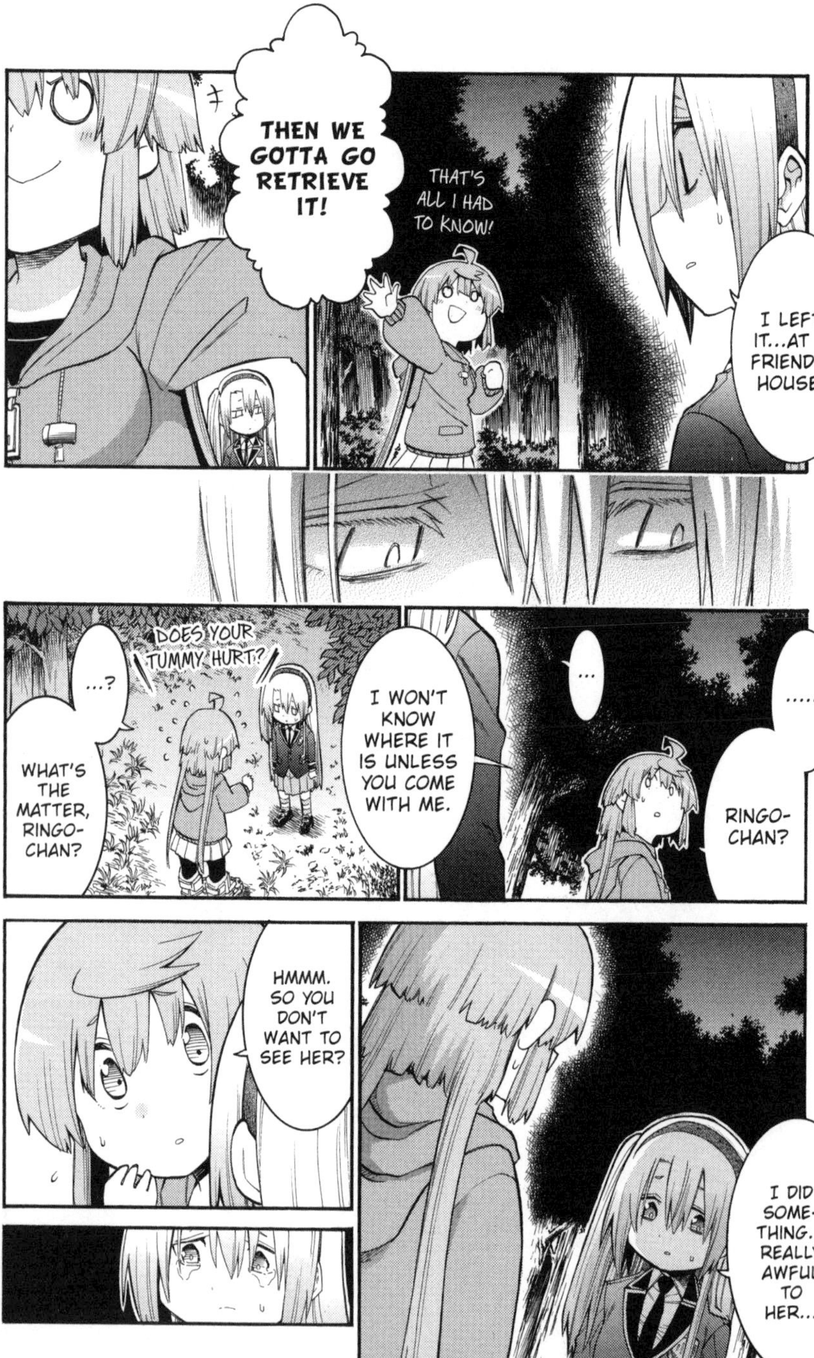
I LEFT IT...AT A FRIEND'S HOUSE.
THAT'S ALL I HAD TO KNOW!
THEN WE GOTTA GO RETRIEVE IT!
......
RINGO-CHAN?
...
I WON'T KNOW WHERE IT IS UNLESS YOU COME WITH ME.
...?
DOES YOUR TUMMY HURT?
WHAT'S THE MATTER, RINGO-CHAN?
I DID SOMETHING... REALLY AWFUL TO HER...
HMMM. SO YOU DON'T WANT TO SEE HER?

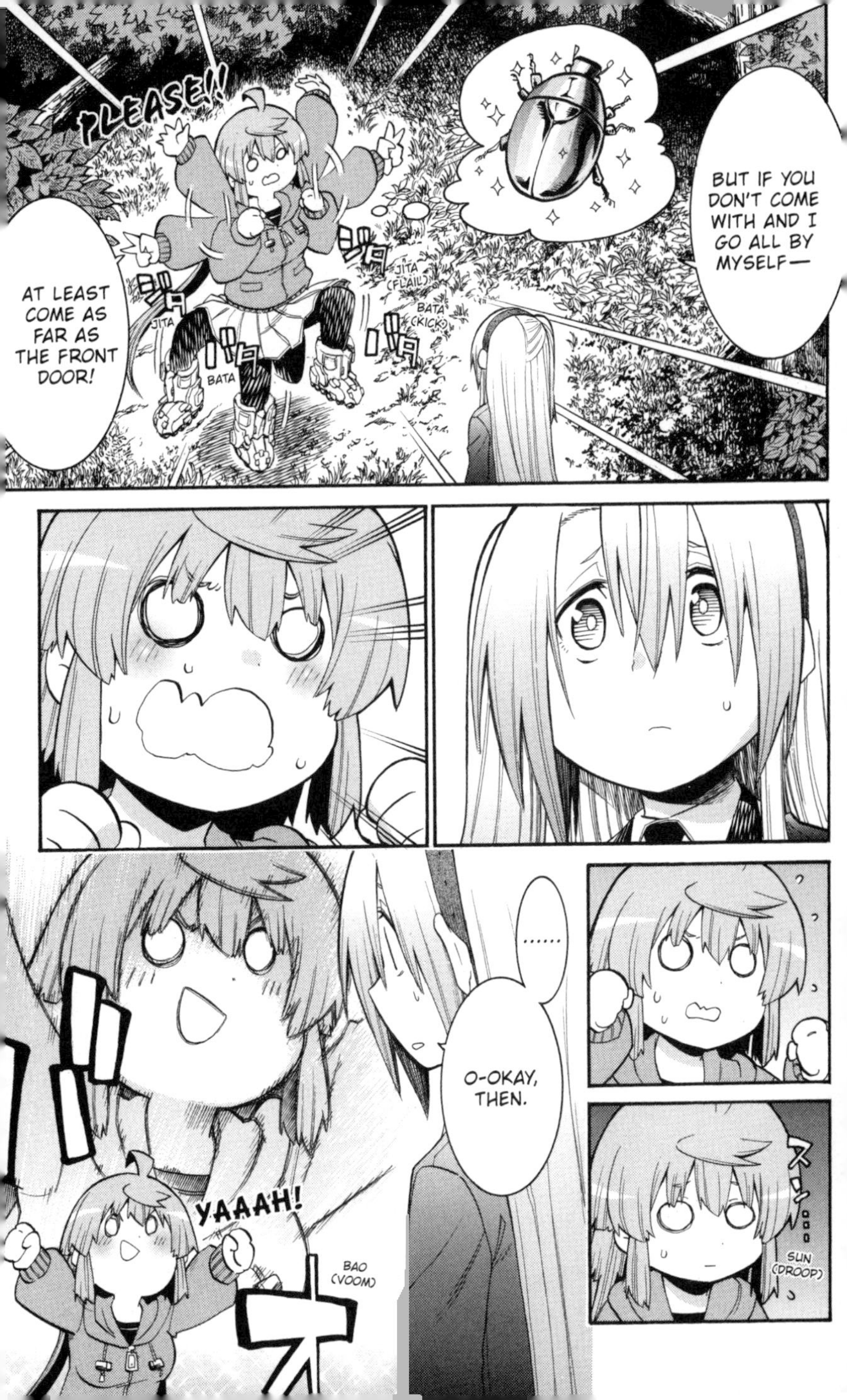
BUT IF YOU DON'T COME WITH AND I GO ALL BY MYSELF—
PLEASE!!
AT LEAST COME AS FAR AS THE FRONT DOOR!
JITA (FLAIL)
BATA (KICK)
JITA
BATA
SUN (DROOP)
......
O-OKAY, THEN.
YAAAH!
BAO (VOOM)

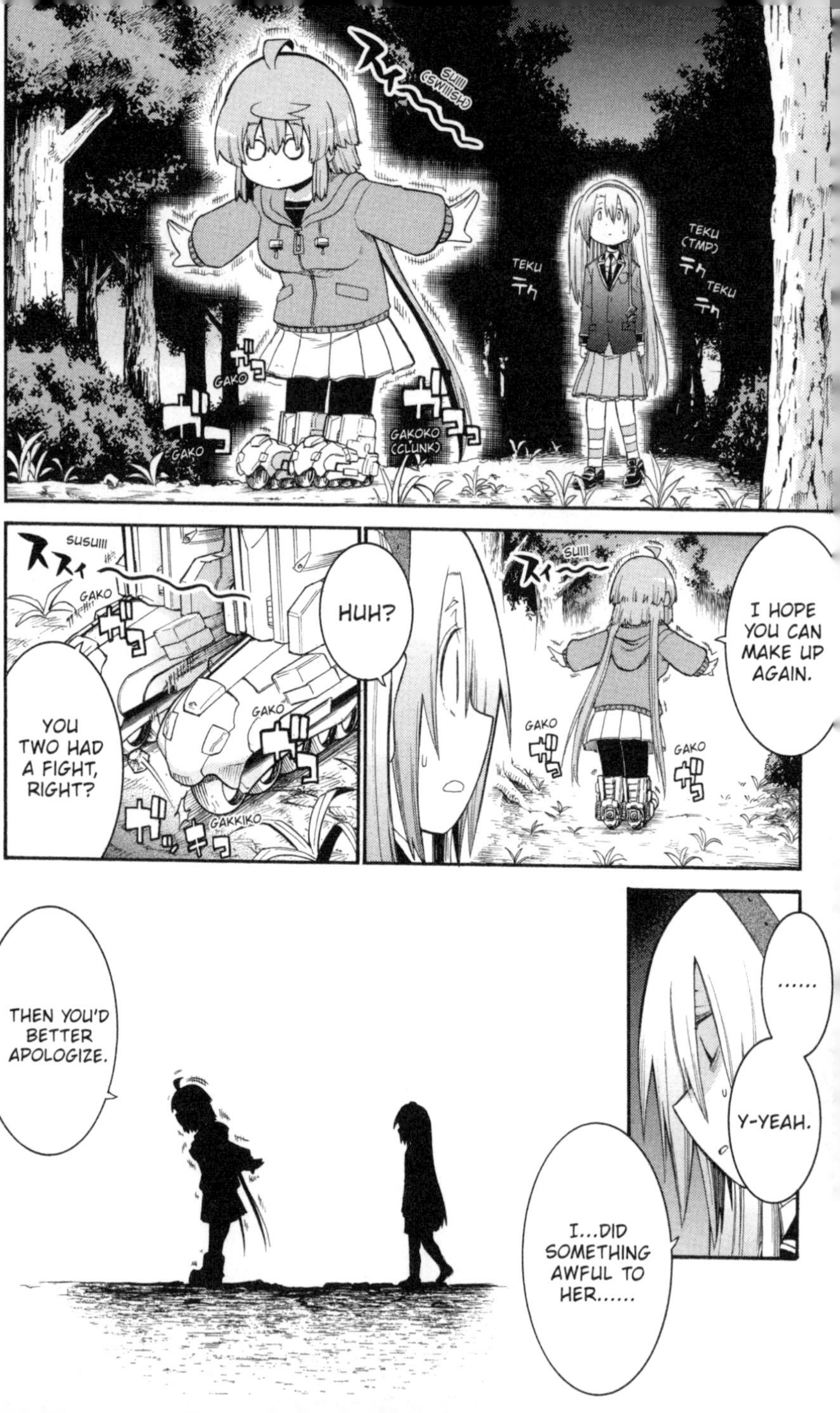
SUIII (SWIIISH)
TEKU (TMP)
TEKU
TEKU
GAKOKO (CLUNK)
GAKO
GAKO
SUIII
I HOPE YOU CAN MAKE UP AGAIN.
GAKO
GAKO
HUH?
SUSUIII
GAKO
YOU TWO HAD A FIGHT, RIGHT?
GAKO
GAKKIKO
......
Y-YEAH.
I...DID SOMETHING AWFUL TO HER......
THEN YOU'D BETTER APOLOGIZE.

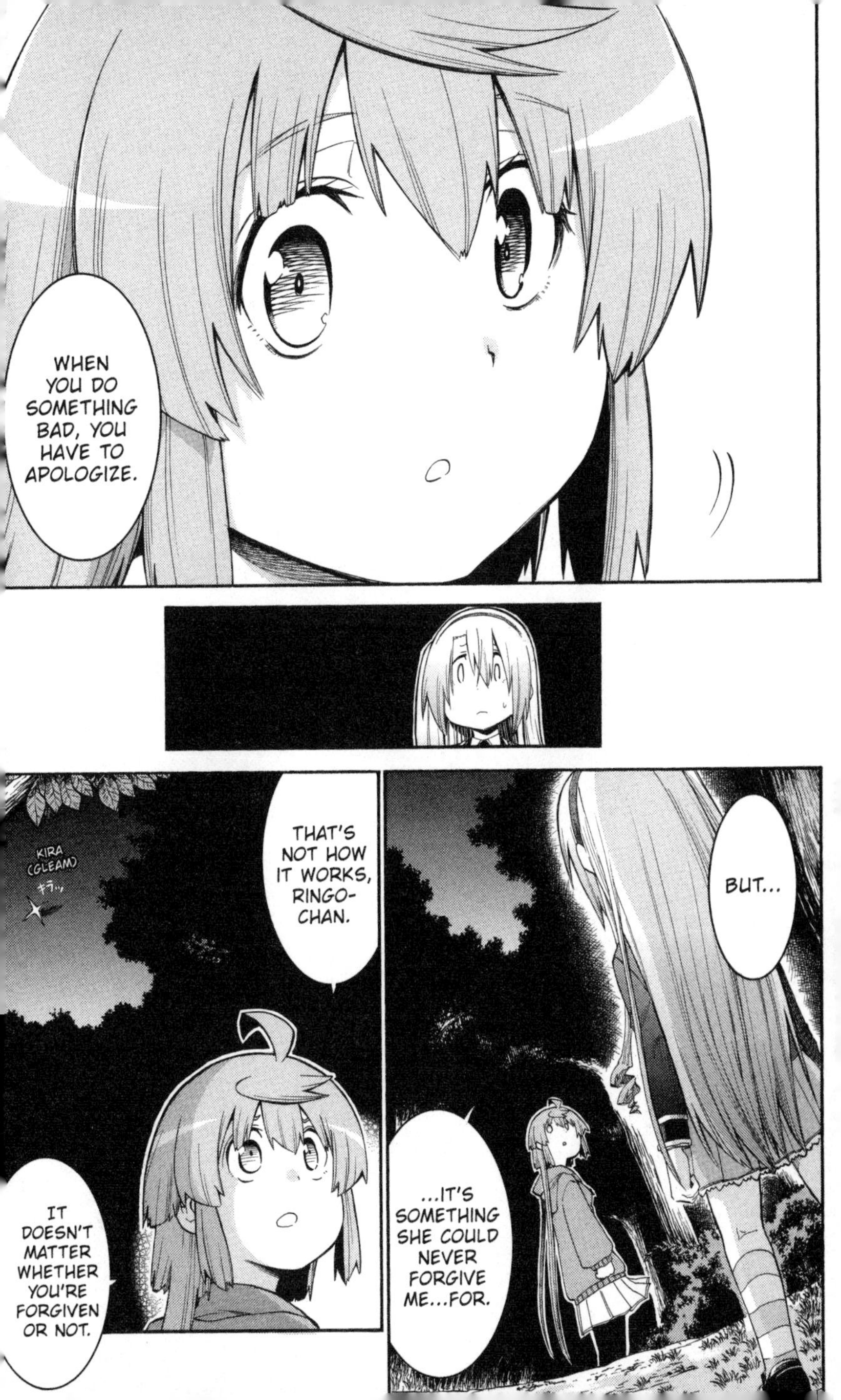
WHEN YOU DO SOMETHING BAD, YOU HAVE TO APOLOGIZE.
BUT...
...IT'S SOMETHING SHE COULD NEVER FORGIVE ME...FOR.
THAT'S NOT HOW IT WORKS, RINGO-CHAN.
KIRA (GLEAM)
キラッ
IT DOESN'T MATTER WHETHER YOU'RE FORGIVEN OR NOT.

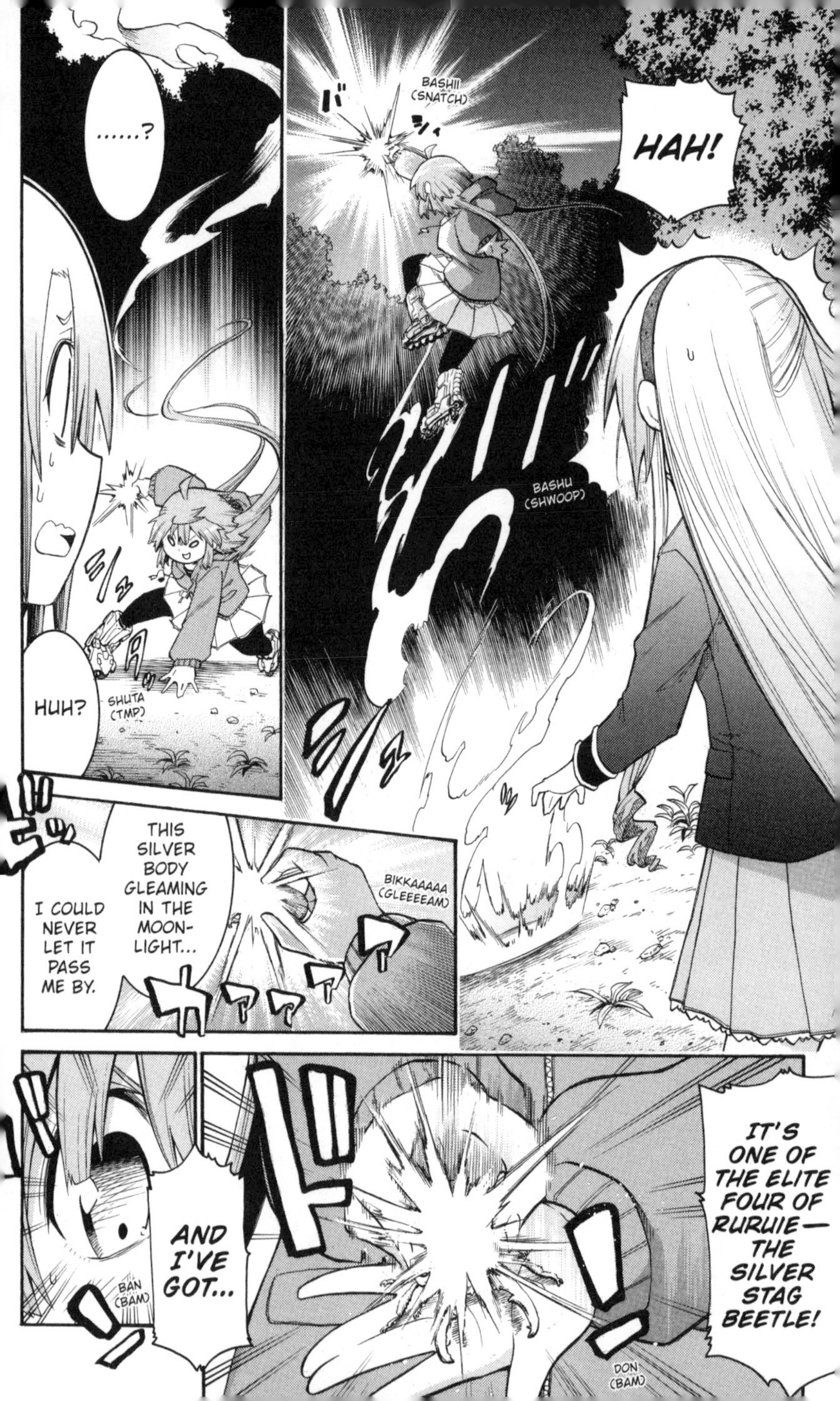
HAH!
BASHII (SNATCH)
BASHU (SHWOOP)
......?
HUH?
SHUTA (TMP)
BIKKAAAAA (GLEEEEAM)
THIS SILVER BODY GLEAMING IN THE MOON-LIGHT...
I COULD NEVER LET IT PASS ME BY.
IT'S ONE OF THE ELITE FOUR OF RURUIE—THE SILVER STAG BEETLE!
DON (BAM)
AND I'VE GOT...
BAN (BAM)

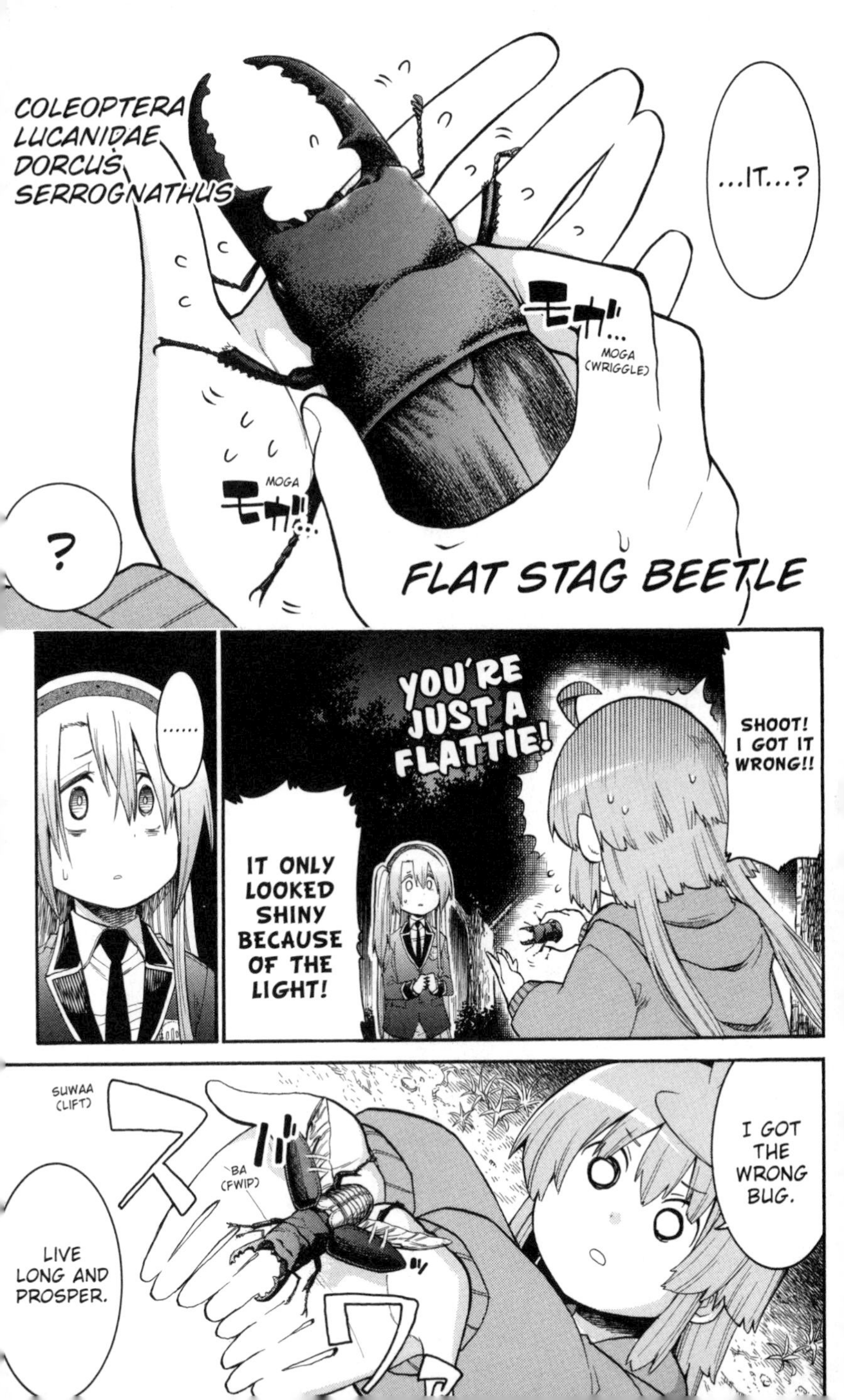
...IT...?
MOGA (WRIGGLE)
COLEOPTERA LUCANIDAE DORCUS SERROGNATHUS
MOGA
?
FLAT STAG BEETLE
SHOOT! I GOT IT WRONG!!
YOU'RE JUST A FLATTIE!
IT ONLY LOOKED SHINY BECAUSE OF THE LIGHT!
......
I GOT THE WRONG BUG.
BA (FWIP)
SUWAA (LIFT)
LIVE LONG AND PROSPER.

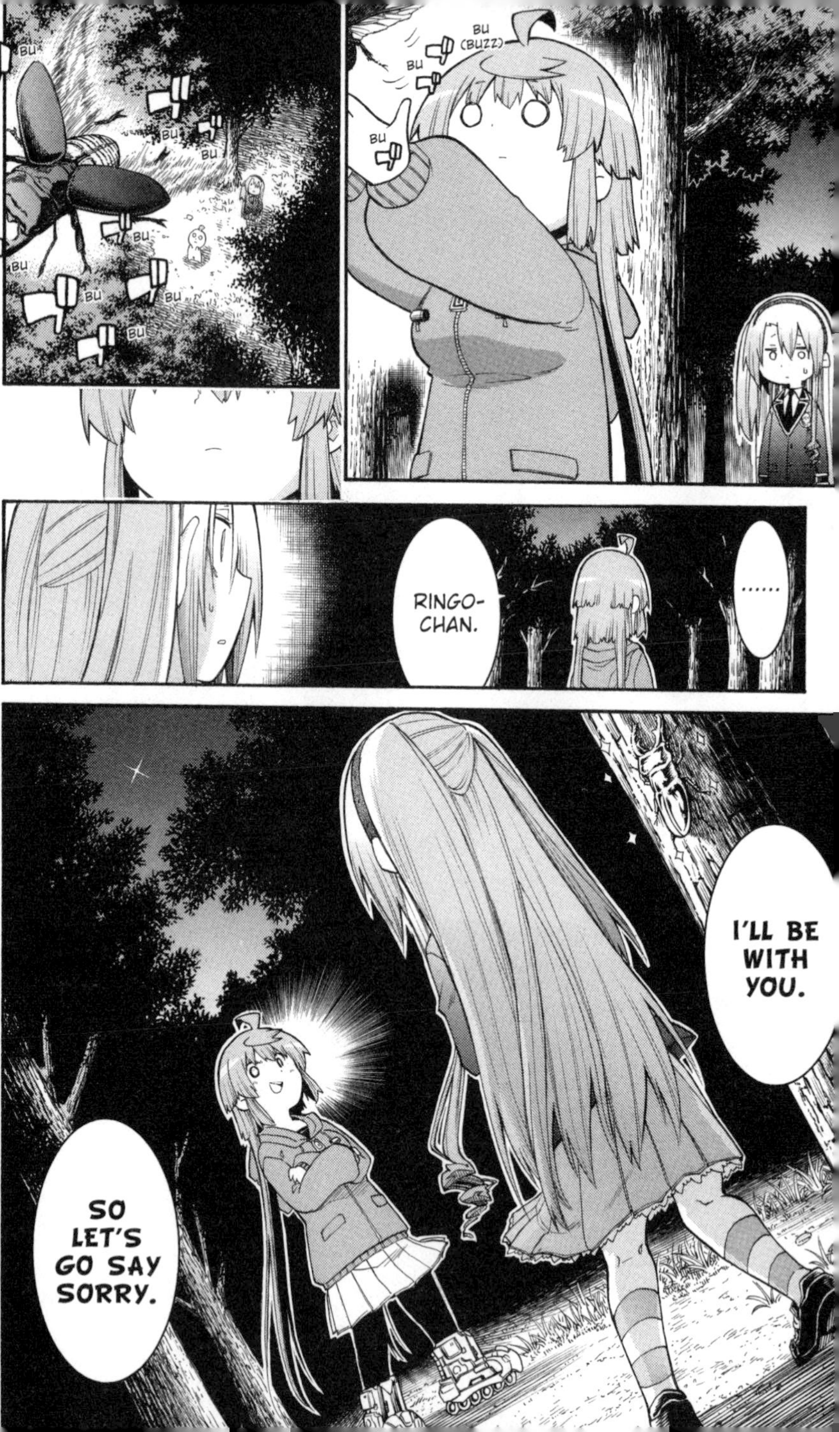
BU (BUZZ)
BU
BU
BU
BU
BU
BU
BU
BU
BU
BU
BU
......
RINGO-CHAN.
I'LL BE WITH YOU.
SO LET'S GO SAY SORRY.

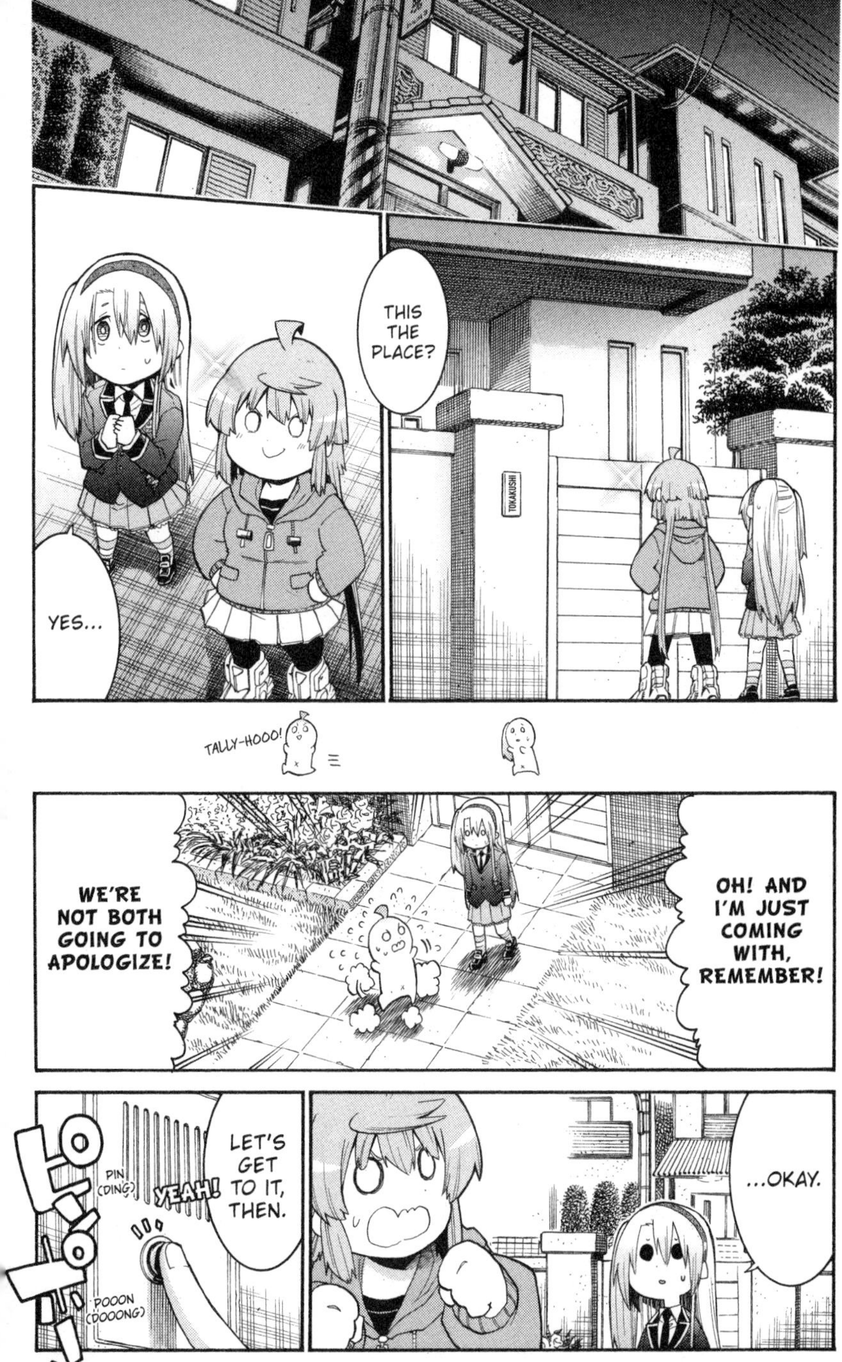
THIS THE PLACE?
TOKAKUSHI
YES...
TALLY-HOOO!
OH! AND I'M JUST COMING WITH, REMEMBER!
WE'RE NOT BOTH GOING TO APOLOGIZE!
...OKAY.
LET'S GET TO IT, THEN.
YEAH!
PIN (DING)
POOON (DOOONG)

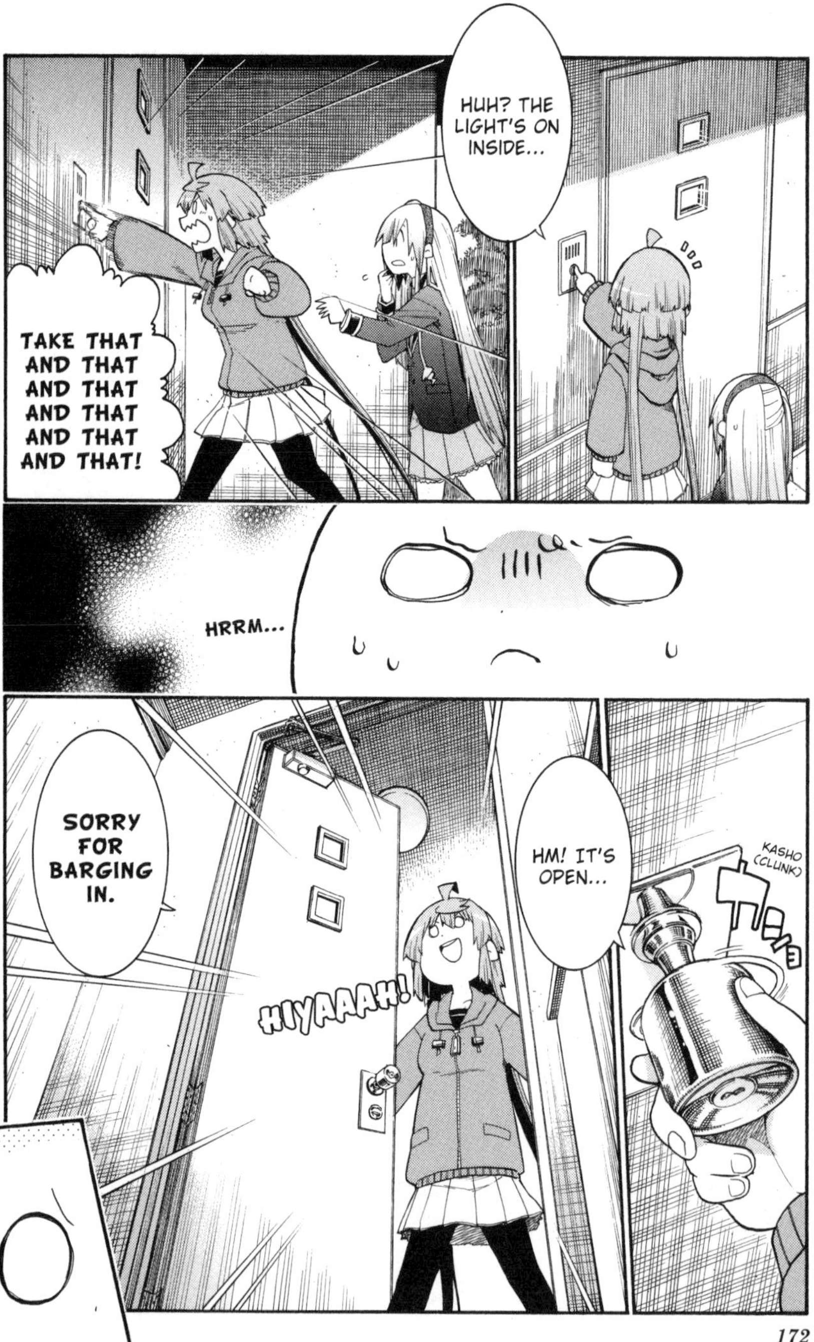
HUH? THE LIGHT'S ON INSIDE...
TAKE THAT AND THAT AND THAT AND THAT AND THAT AND THAT!
HRRM...
KASHO (CLUNK)
HM! IT'S OPEN...
HIYAAAH!
SORRY FOR BARGING IN.

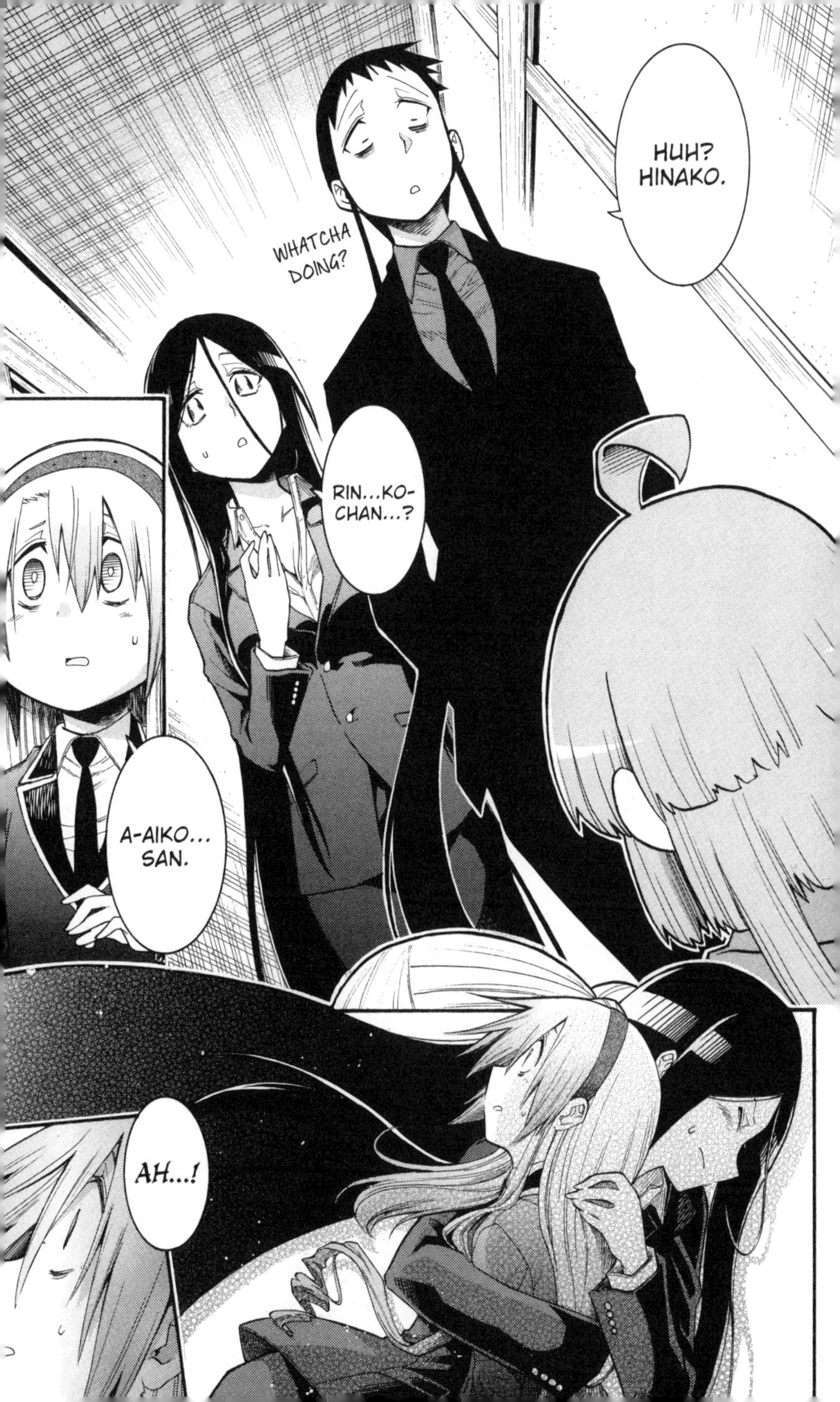
HUH? HINAKO.
WHATCHA DOING?
RIN...KO-CHAN...?
A-AIKO... SAN.
AH...!

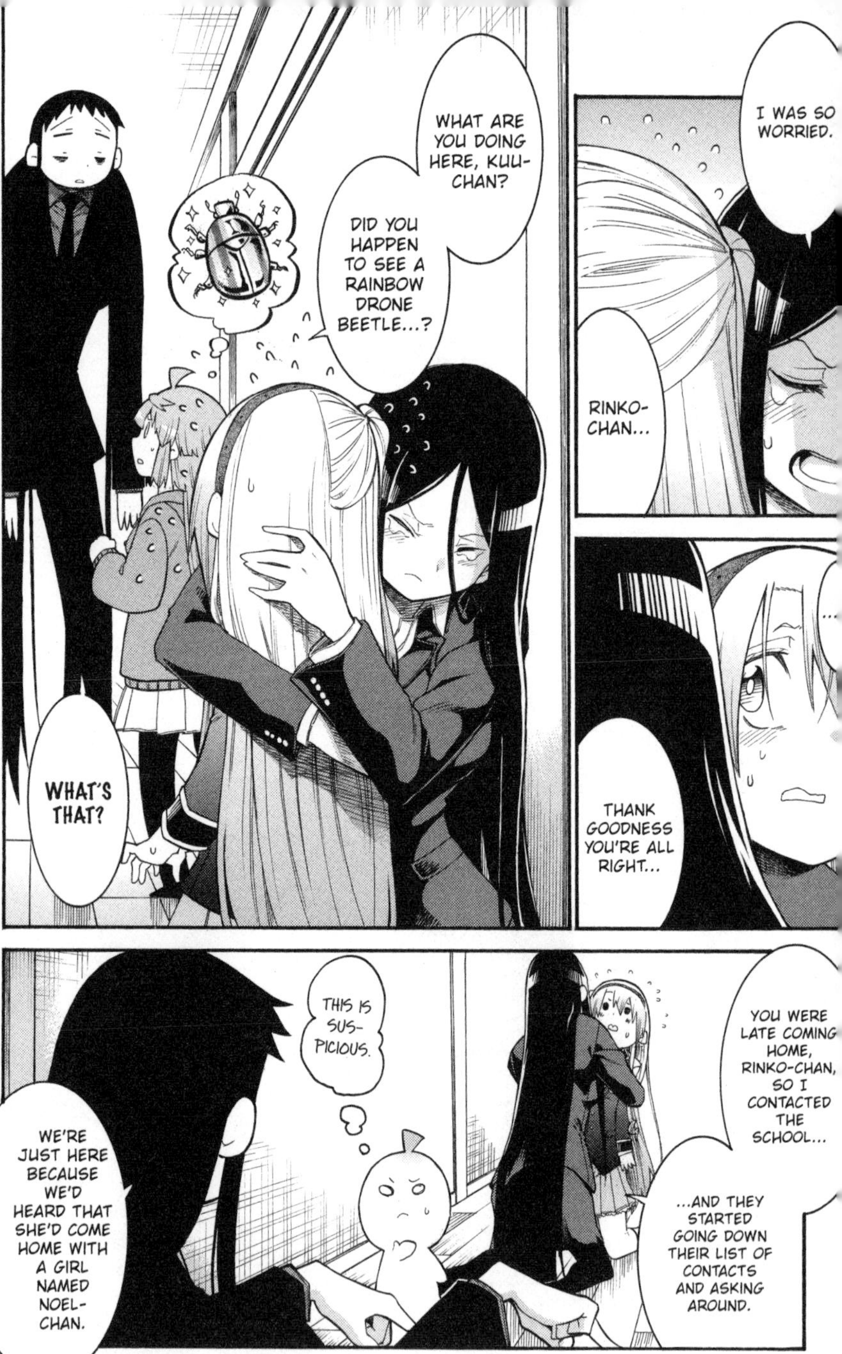
I WAS SO WORRIED.
RINKO-CHAN...
...
THANK GOODNESS YOU'RE ALL RIGHT...
WHAT ARE YOU DOING HERE, KUU-CHAN?
DID YOU HAPPEN TO SEE A RAINBOW DRONE BEETLE...?
WHAT'S THAT?
YOU WERE LATE COMING HOME, RINKO-CHAN, SO I CONTACTED THE SCHOOL...
...AND THEY STARTED GOING DOWN THEIR LIST OF CONTACTS AND ASKING AROUND.
THIS IS SUS-PICIOUS.
WE'RE JUST HERE BECAUSE WE'D HEARD THAT SHE'D COME HOME WITH A GIRL NAMED NOEL-CHAN.

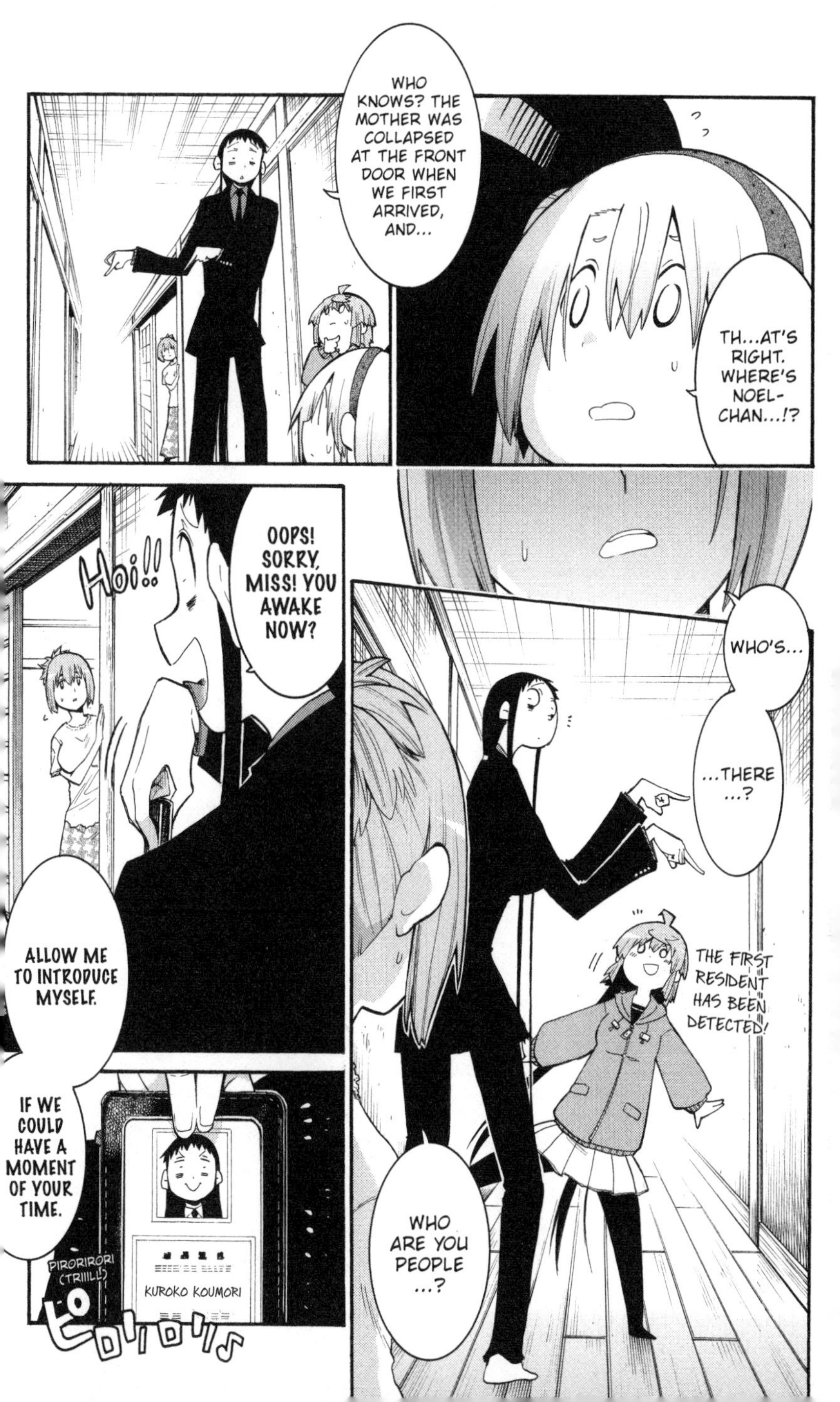
TH...AT'S RIGHT. WHERE'S NOEL-CHAN...!?
WHO KNOWS? THE MOTHER WAS COLLAPSED AT THE FRONT DOOR WHEN WE FIRST ARRIVED, AND...
WHO'S...
...THERE ...?
THE FIRST RESIDENT HAS BEEN DETECTED!
WHO ARE YOU PEOPLE ...?
Hoi!!
OOPS! SORRY, MISS! YOU AWAKE NOW?
ALLOW ME TO INTRODUCE MYSELF.
IF WE COULD HAVE A MOMENT OF YOUR TIME.
KUROKO KOUMORI
PIRORIRORI (TRIIIL!)

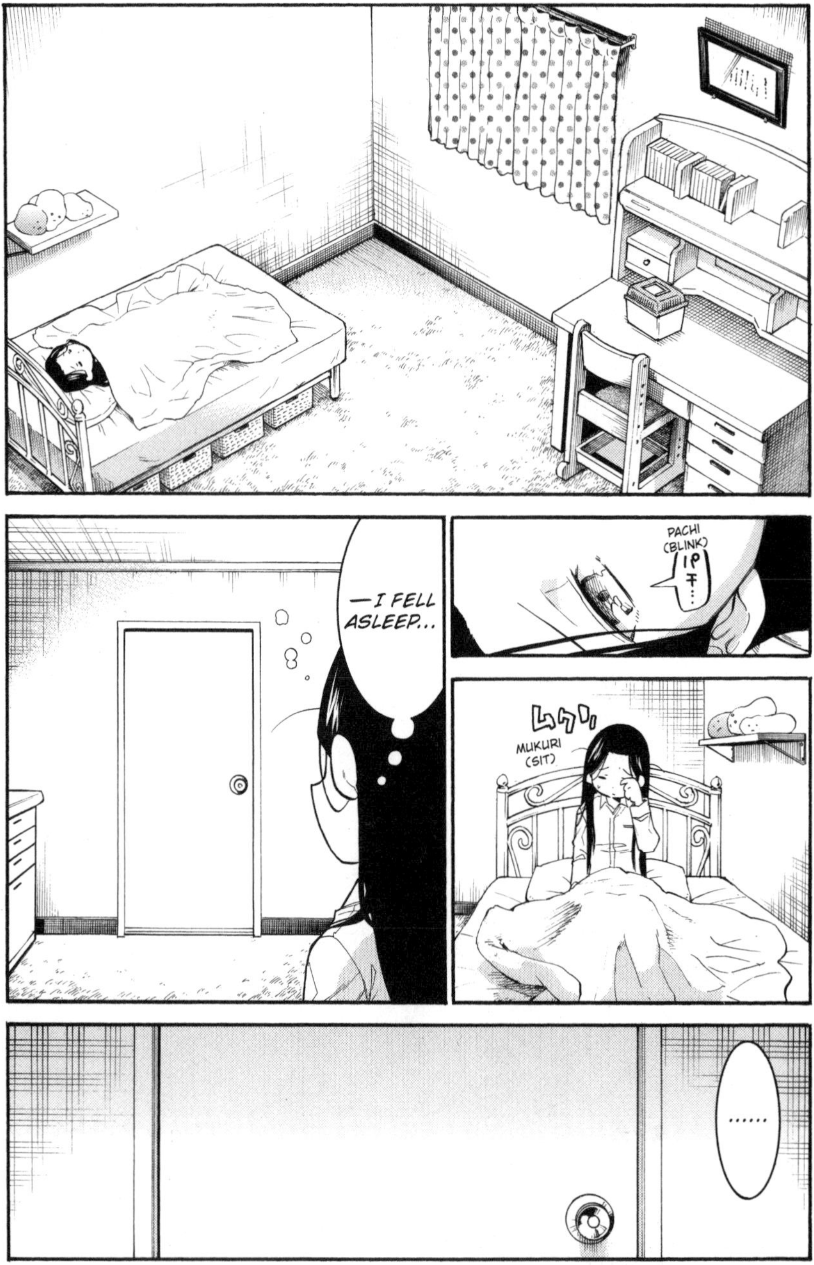
PACHI (BLINK)
MUKURI (SIT)
—I FELL ASLEEP...
......

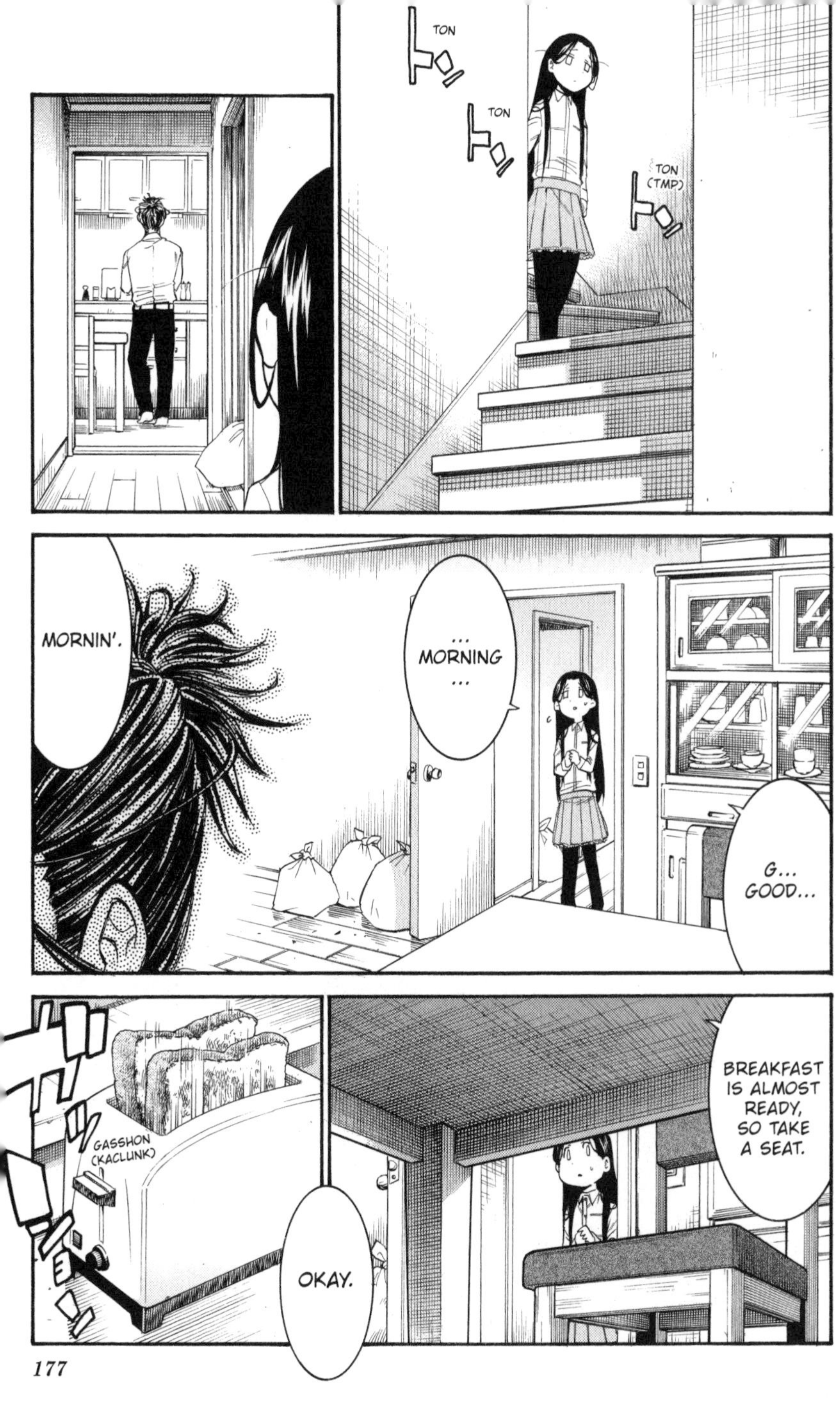
TON
TON
TON (TMP)
G... GOOD...
... MORNING ...
MORNIN'.
BREAKFAST IS ALMOST READY, SO TAKE A SEAT.
OKAY.
GASSHON (KACLUNK)

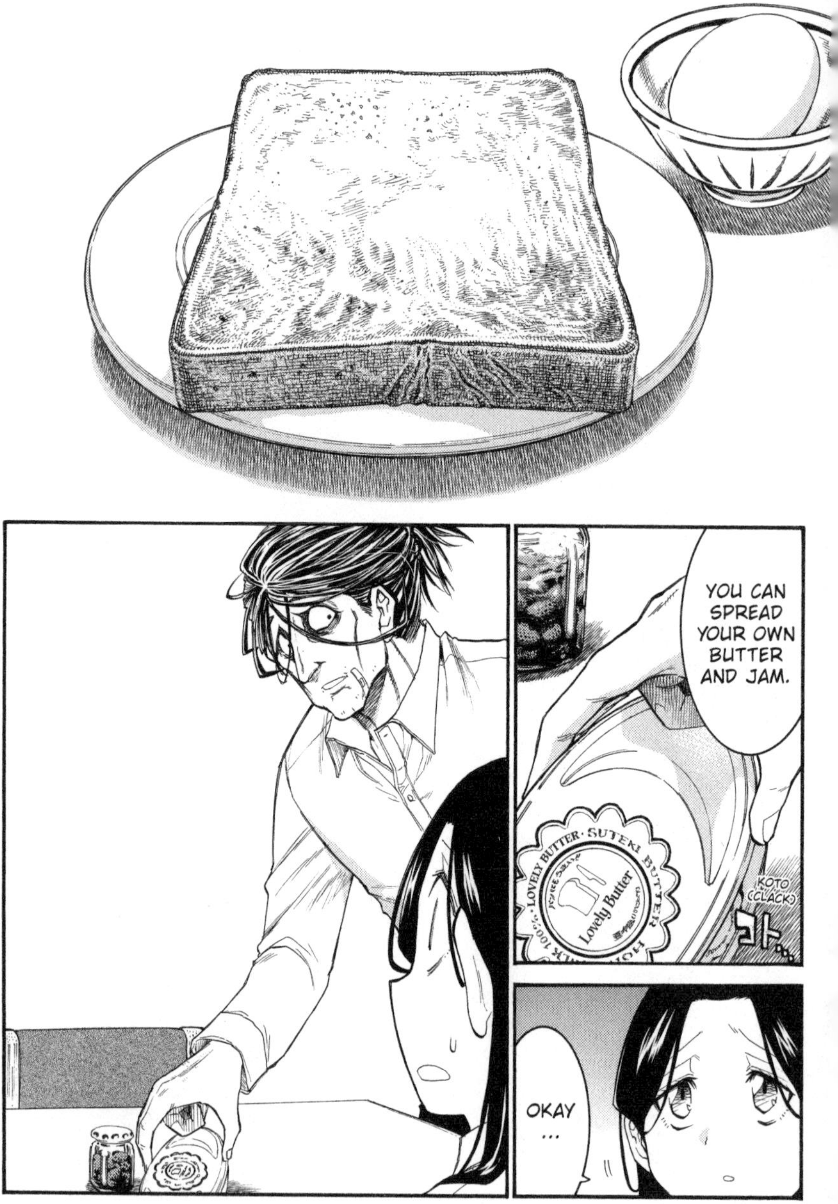
YOU CAN SPREAD YOUR OWN BUTTER AND JAM.
LOVELY BUTTER · SUTEKI BUTTER
Lovely Butter
KOTO (CLACK)
OKAY ...

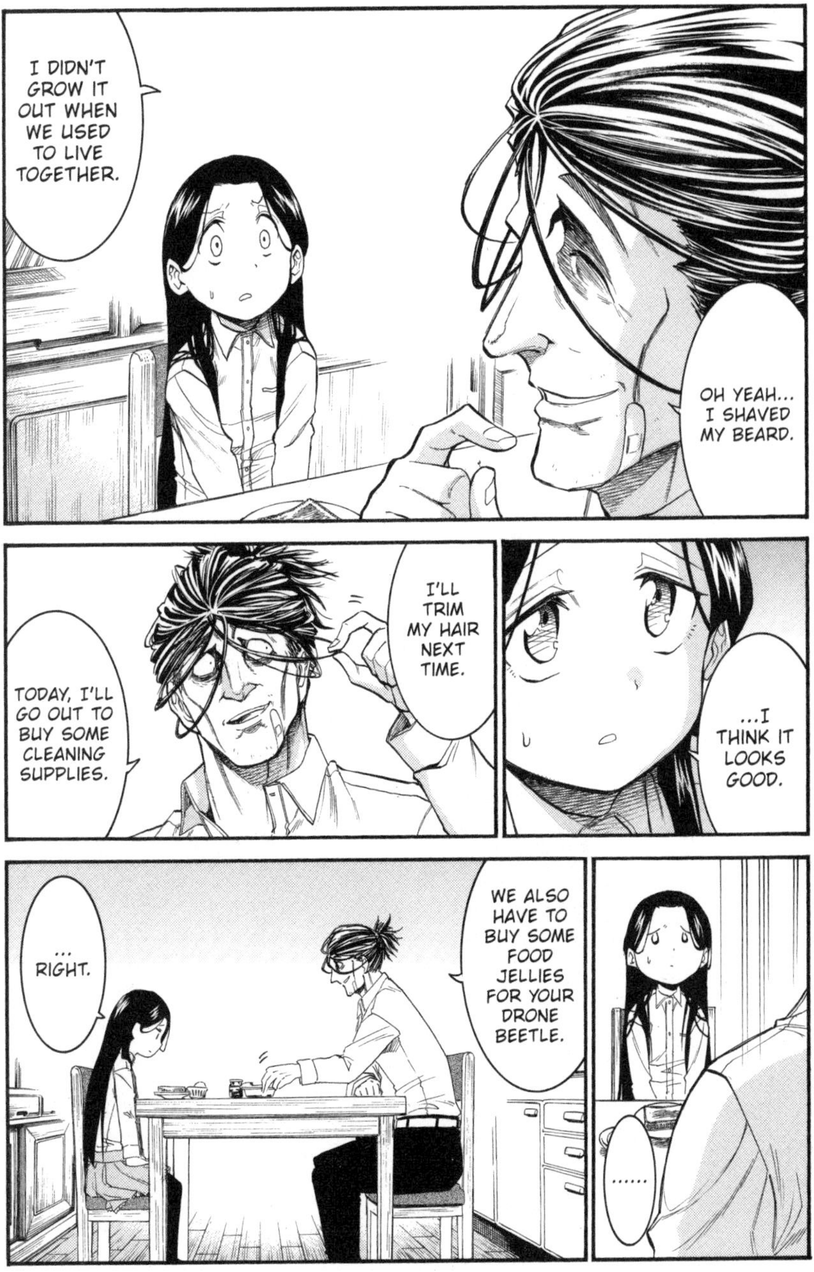
OH YEAH... I SHAVED MY BEARD.
I DIDN'T GROW IT OUT WHEN WE USED TO LIVE TOGETHER.
...I THINK IT LOOKS GOOD.
I'LL TRIM MY HAIR NEXT TIME.
TODAY, I'LL GO OUT TO BUY SOME CLEANING SUPPLIES.
......
WE ALSO HAVE TO BUY SOME FOOD JELLIES FOR YOUR DRONE BEETLE.
... RIGHT.

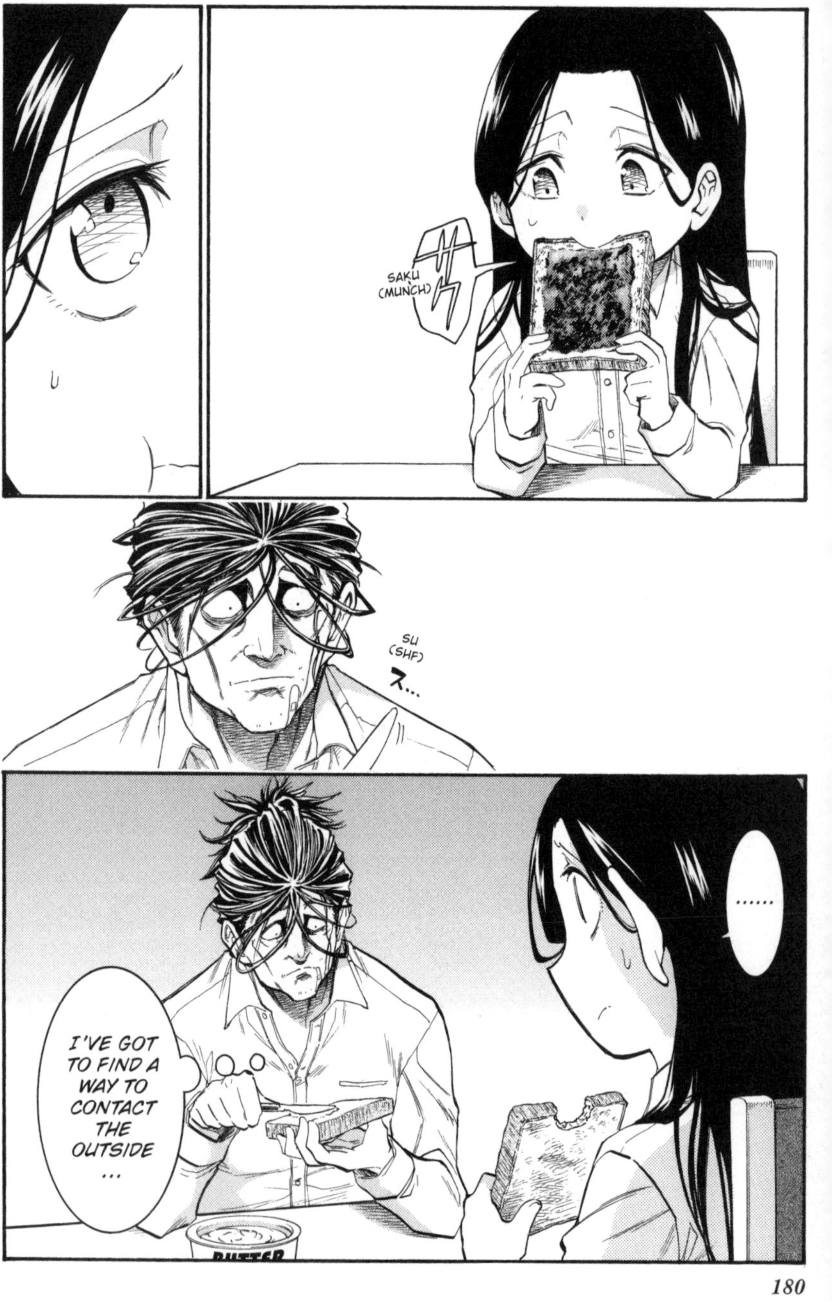
SAKU (MUNCH)
SU (SHF)
ス...
......
I'VE GOT TO FIND A WAY TO CONTACT THE OUTSIDE ...

MURCIÉLAGO

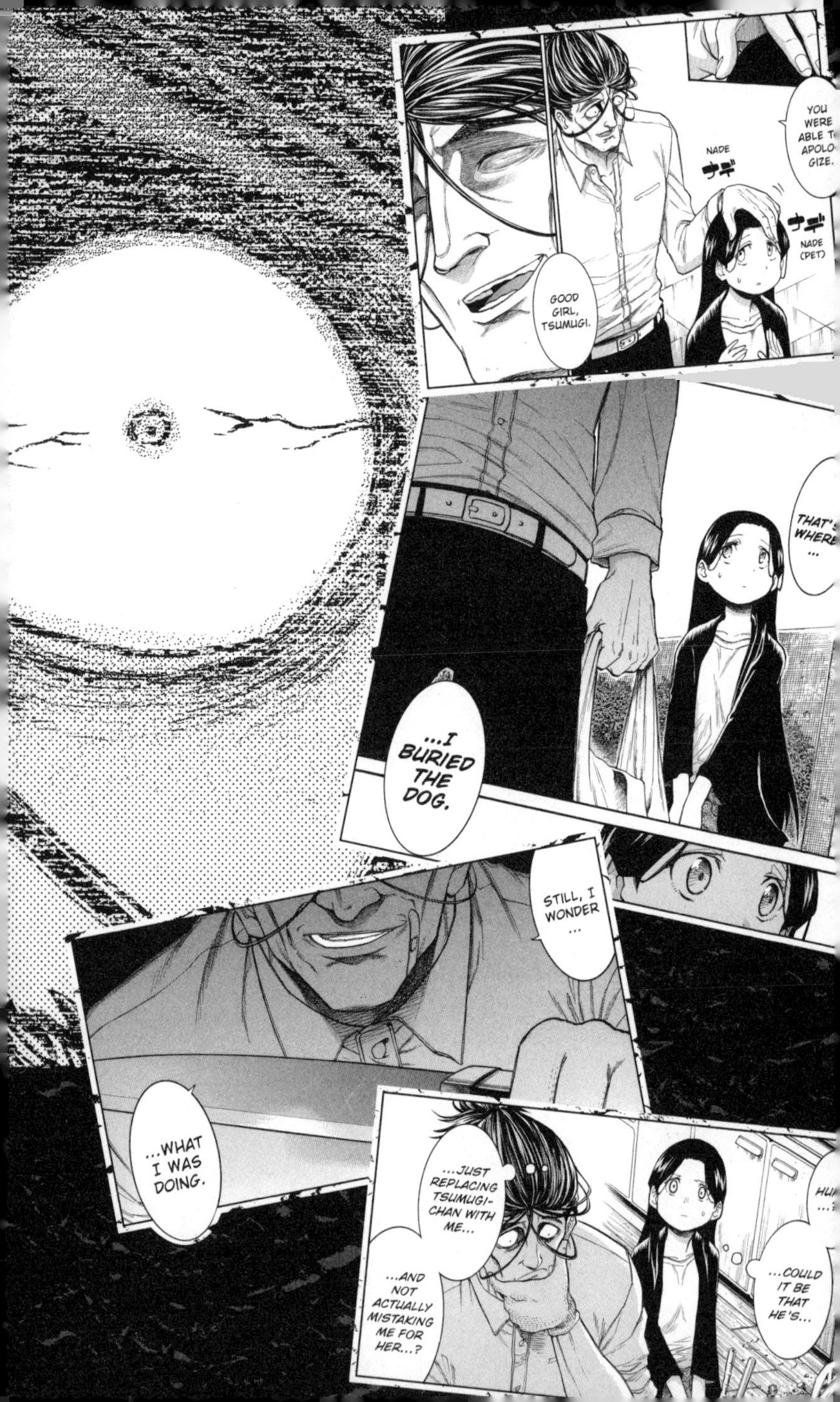
YOU WERE ABLE T APOLO GIZE.
NADE
ナデ
ナデ
NADE (PET)
GOOD GIRL, TSUMUGI.
THAT'S WHERE ...
...I BURIED THE DOG.
STILL, I WONDER ...
...WHAT I WAS DOING.
HUH ...
...COULD IT BE THAT HE'S...
...JUST REPLACING TSUMUGI-CHAN WITH ME...
...AND NOT ACTUALLY MISTAKING ME FOR HER...?

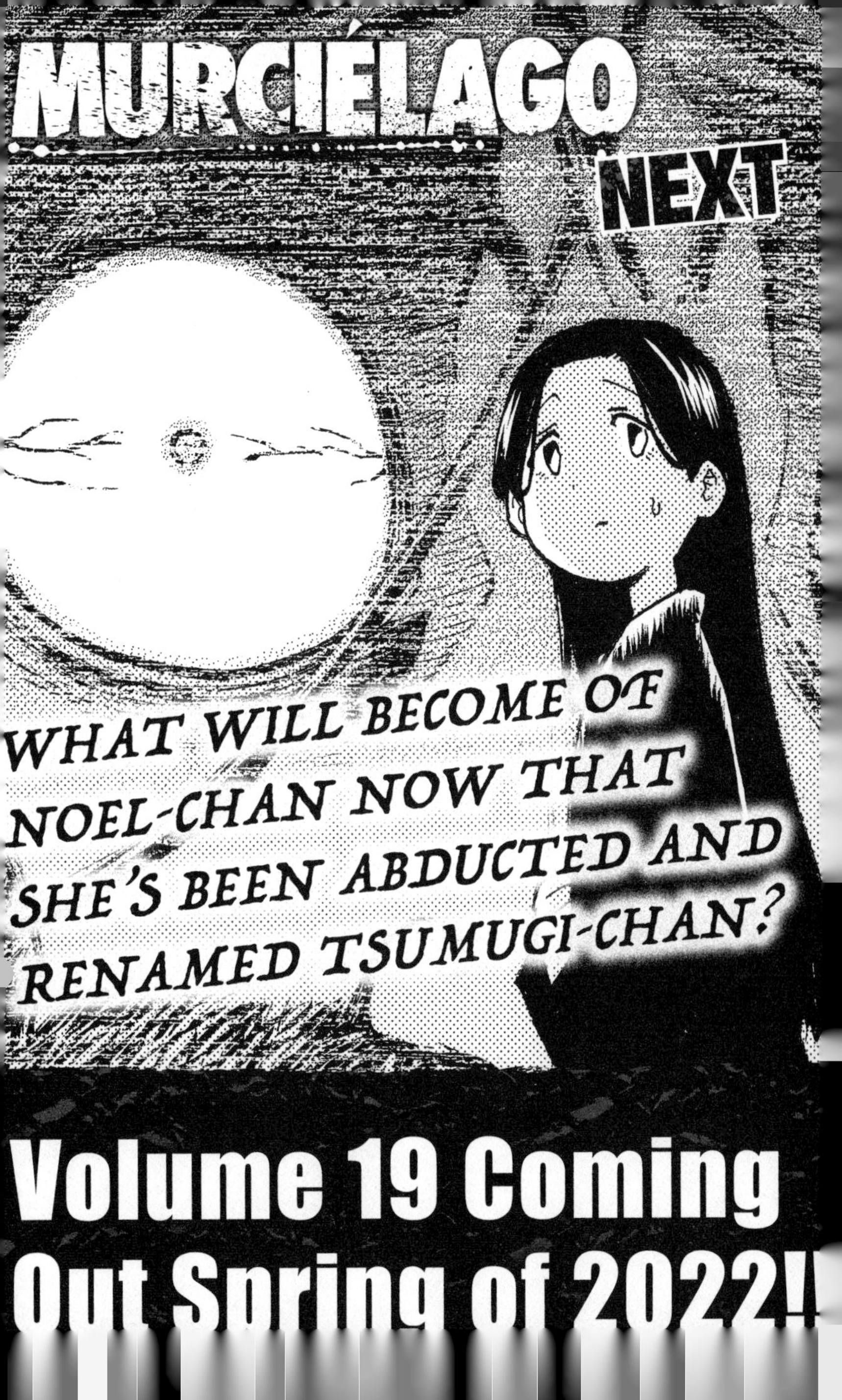
MURCIÉLAGO
NEXT
WHAT WILL BECOME OF NOEL-CHAN NOW THAT SHE'S BEEN ABDUCTED AND RENAMED TSUMUGI-CHAN?
Volume 19 Coming Out Spring of 2022!!

MURCIÉLAGO

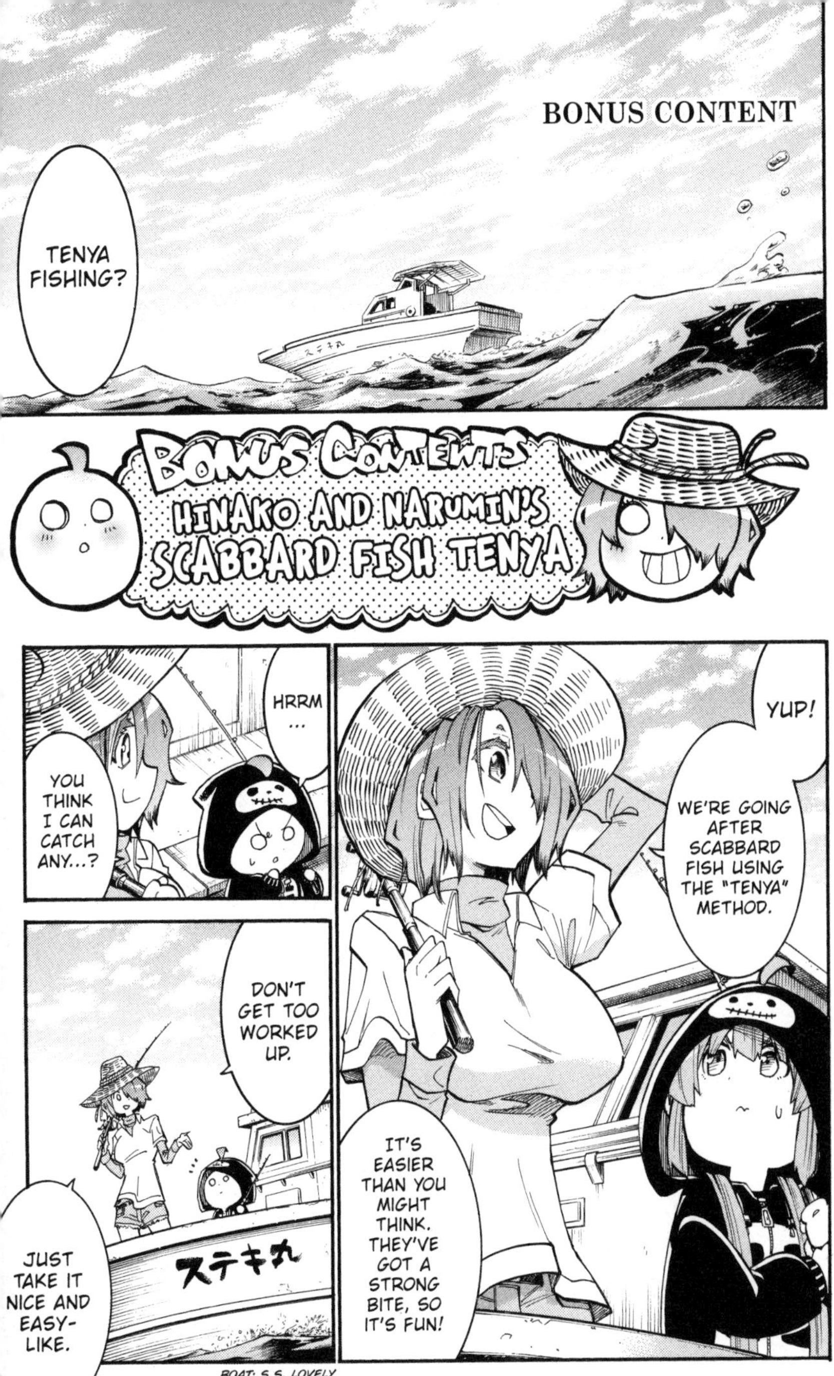
BONUS CONTENT
TENYA FISHING?
BONUS CONTENTS
HINAKO AND NARUMIN'S SCABBARD FISH TENYA
YUP!
WE'RE GOING AFTER SCABBARD FISH USING THE "TENYA" METHOD.
IT'S EASIER THAN YOU MIGHT THINK. THEY'VE GOT A STRONG BITE, SO IT'S FUN!
HRRM...
YOU THINK I CAN CATCH ANY...?
DON'T GET TOO WORKED UP.
JUST TAKE IT NICE AND EASY-LIKE.
ステキ丸
BOAT: S.S. LOVELY

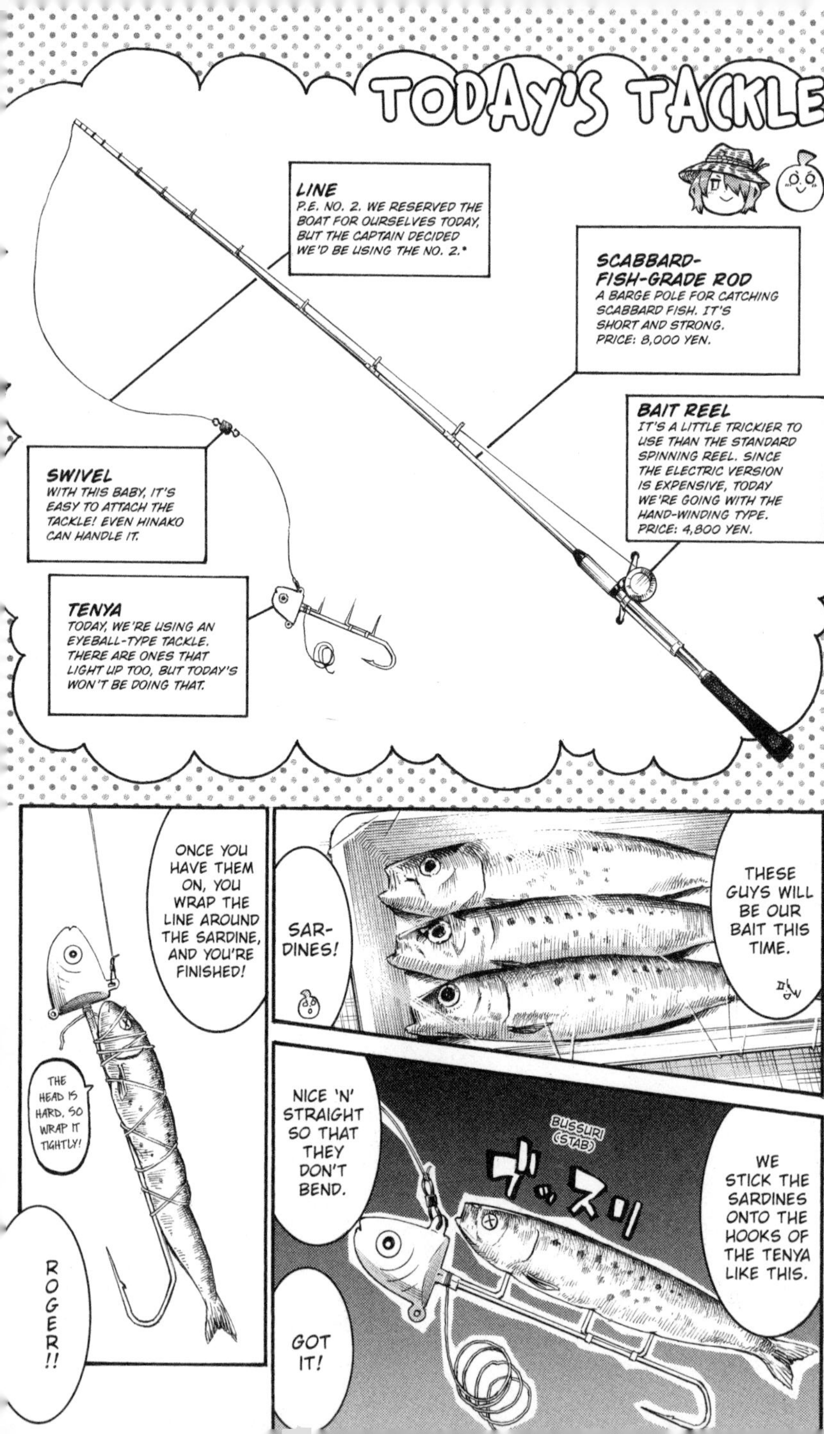
TODAY'S TACKLE
LINE
P.E. NO. 2. WE RESERVED THE BOAT FOR OURSELVES TODAY, BUT THE CAPTAIN DECIDED WE'D BE USING THE NO. 2.*
SCABBARD-FISH-GRADE ROD
A BARGE POLE FOR CATCHING SCABBARD FISH. IT'S SHORT AND STRONG. PRICE: 8,000 YEN.
BAIT REEL
IT'S A LITTLE TRICKIER TO USE THAN THE STANDARD SPINNING REEL. SINCE THE ELECTRIC VERSION IS EXPENSIVE, TODAY WE'RE GOING WITH THE HAND-WINDING TYPE. PRICE: 4,800 YEN.
SWIVEL
WITH THIS BABY, IT'S EASY TO ATTACH THE TACKLE! EVEN HINAKO CAN HANDLE IT.
TENYA
TODAY, WE'RE USING AN EYEBALL-TYPE TACKLE. THERE ARE ONES THAT LIGHT UP TOO, BUT TODAY'S WON'T BE DOING THAT.
THESE GUYS WILL BE OUR BAIT THIS TIME.
SAR-DINES!
WE STICK THE SARDINES ONTO THE HOOKS OF THE TENYA LIKE THIS.
BUSSURI (STAB)
NICE 'N' STRAIGHT SO THAT THEY DON'T BEND.
GOT IT!
ONCE YOU HAVE THEM ON, YOU WRAP THE LINE AROUND THE SARDINE, AND YOU'RE FINISHED!
THE HEAD IS HARD, SO WRAP IT TIGHTLY!
ROGER!!

*WHEN FISHING IN A GROUP, IF EVERYONE USES DIFFERENT THICKNESSES OF LINE, THE TACKLE WILL DRAG AT DIFFERENT SPEEDS ACCORDING TO THE CURRENT. SO SOMETIMES, IN ORDER TO PREVENT AN OMATSURI (WHEN THE LINES GET ALL TANGLED UP), THE CAPTAIN JUST DECIDES FOR YOU.

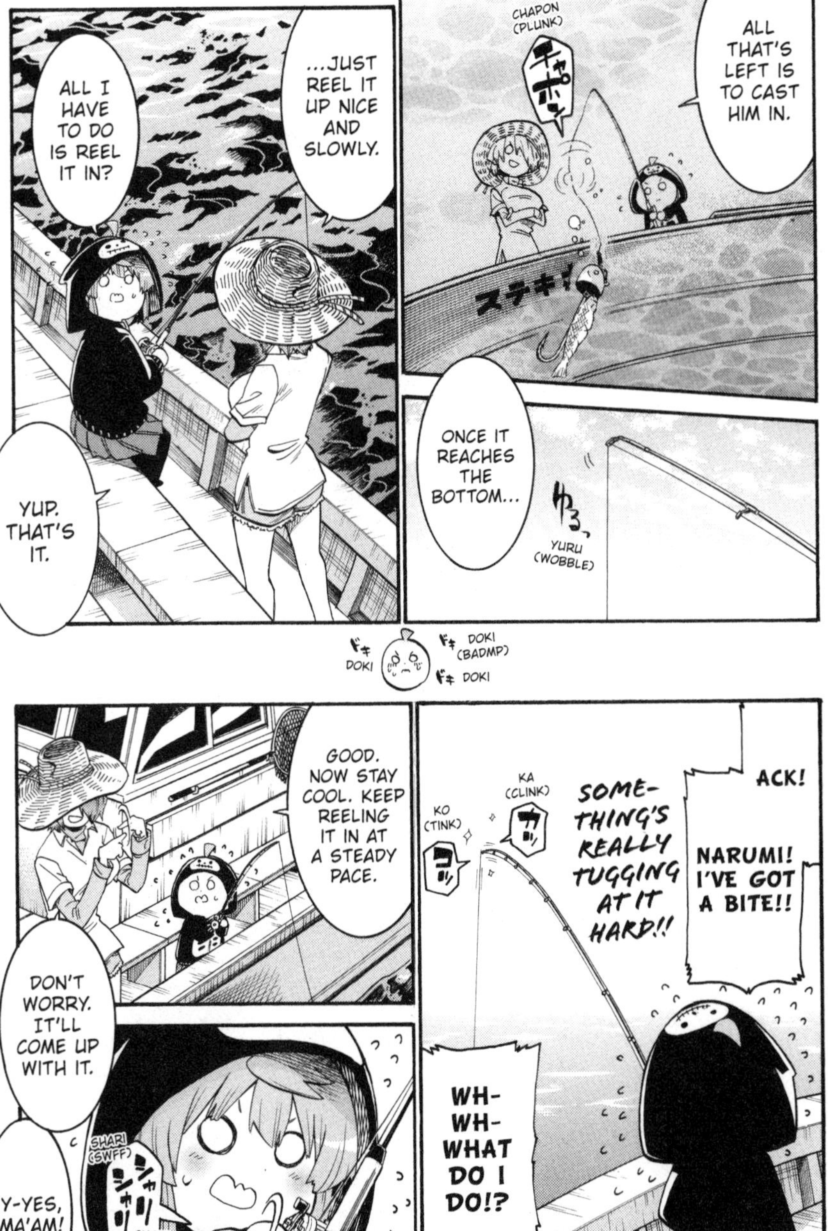
ALL THAT'S LEFT IS TO CAST HIM IN.
CHAPON (PLUNK)
ONCE IT REACHES THE BOTTOM...
YURU (WOBBLE)
...JUST REEL IT UP NICE AND SLOWLY.
ALL I HAVE TO DO IS REEL IT IN?
YUP. THAT'S IT.
DOKI (BADMP)
DOKI
DOKI
ACK!
NARUMI! I'VE GOT A BITE!!
SOME-THING'S REALLY TUGGING AT IT HARD!!
KA (CLINK)
KO (TINK)
WH-WH-WHAT DO I DO!?
GOOD. NOW STAY COOL. KEEP REELING IT IN AT A STEADY PACE.
DON'T WORRY. IT'LL COME UP WITH IT.
Y-YES, MA'AM!
SHARI (SWFF)
SHARI

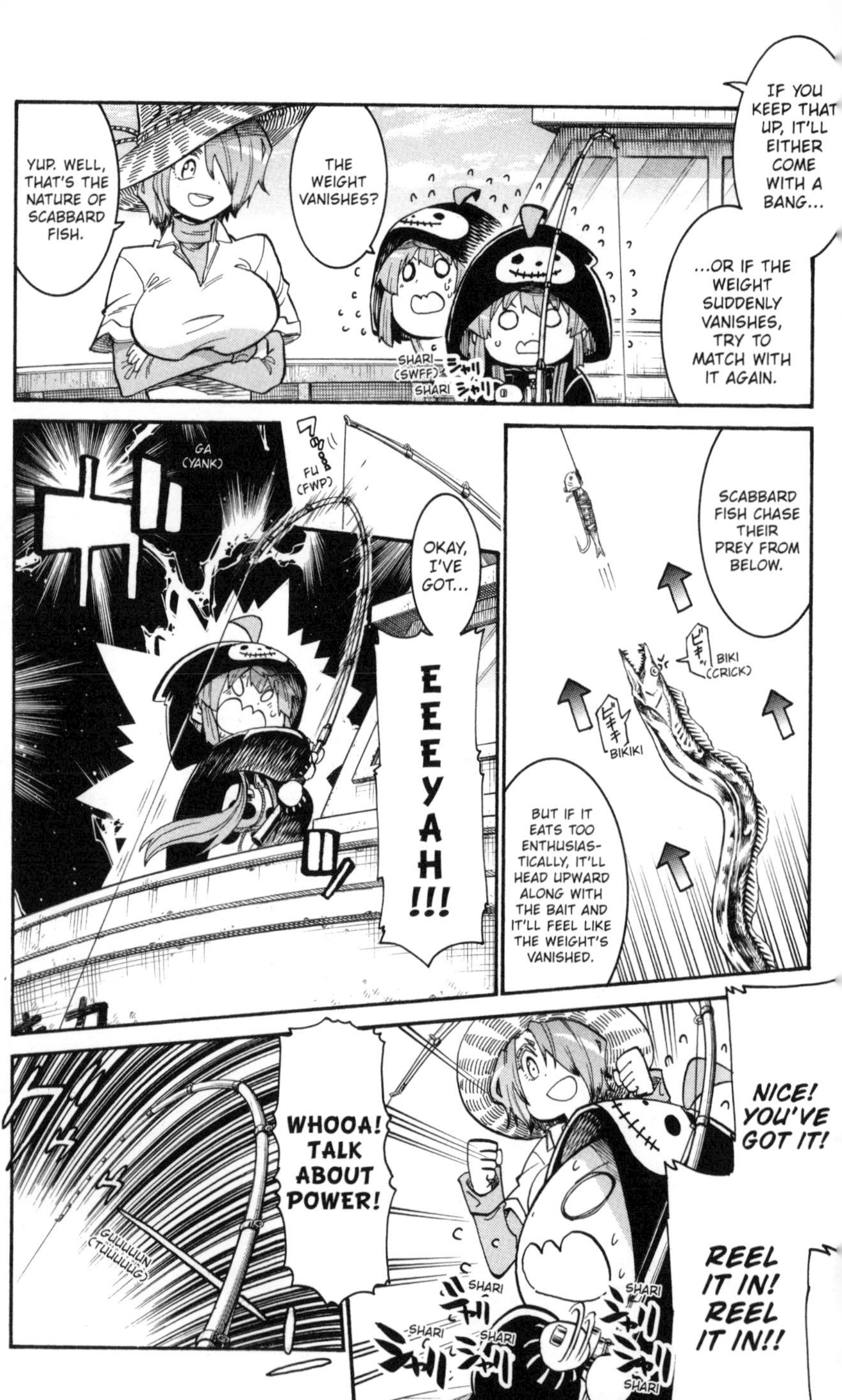
IF YOU KEEP THAT UP, IT'LL EITHER COME WITH A BANG...
...OR IF THE WEIGHT SUDDENLY VANISHES, TRY TO MATCH WITH IT AGAIN.
THE WEIGHT VANISHES?
SHARI (SWFF)
SHARI
YUP. WELL, THAT'S THE NATURE OF SCABBARD FISH.
SCABBARD FISH CHASE THEIR PREY FROM BELOW.
BIKI (CRICK)
BIKIKI
BUT IF IT EATS TOO ENTHUSIASTICALLY, IT'LL HEAD UPWARD ALONG WITH THE BAIT AND IT'LL FEEL LIKE THE WEIGHT'S VANISHED.
OKAY, I'VE GOT...
EEEYAH!!!
FU (FWP)
GA (YANK)
NICE! YOU'VE GOT IT!
REEL IT IN! REEL IT IN!!
SHARI
SHARI
SHARI
SHARI
SHARI
WHOOA! TALK ABOUT POWER!

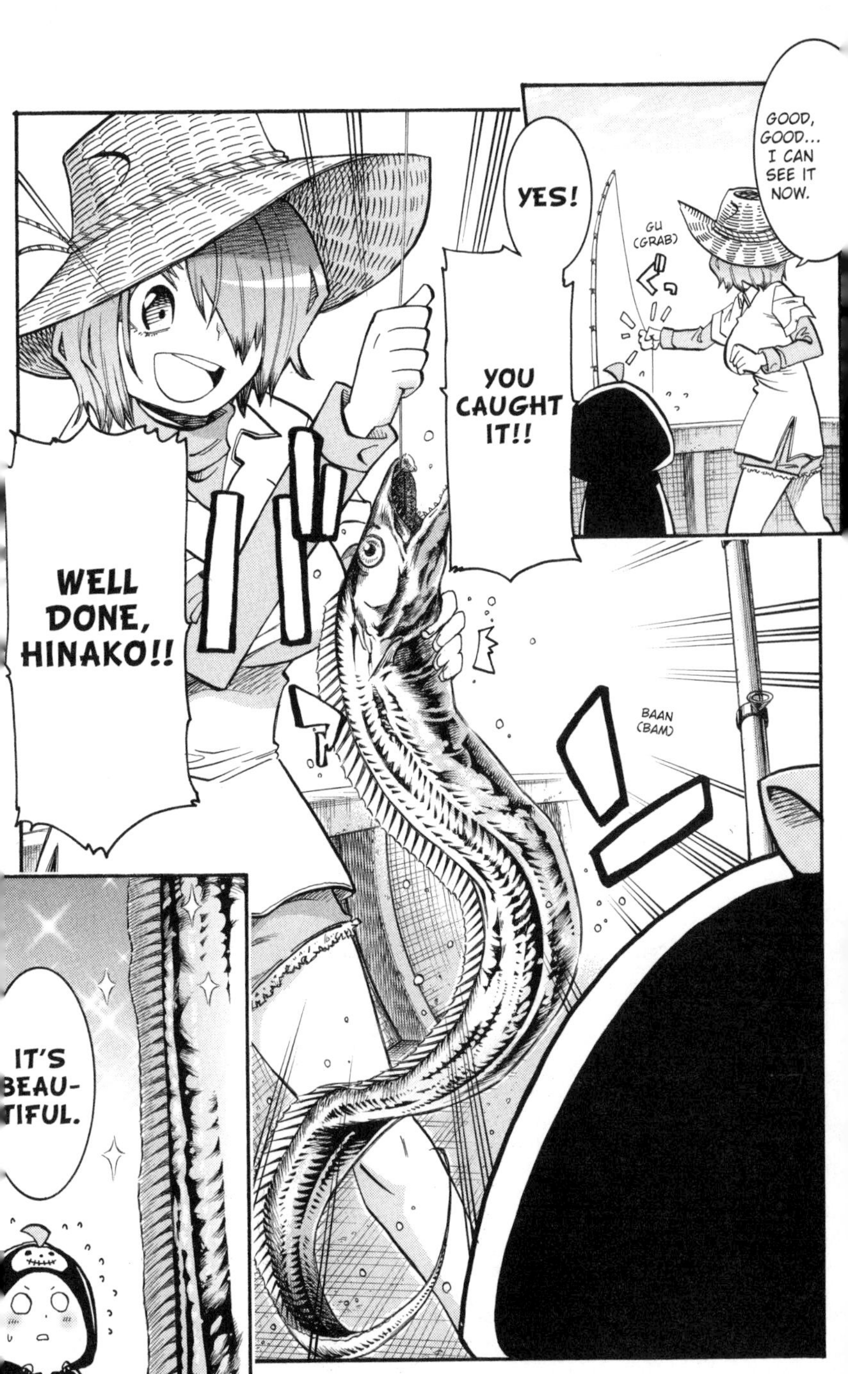
GOOD, GOOD... I CAN SEE IT NOW.
GU (GRAB)
YES!
YOU CAUGHT IT!!
WELL DONE, HINAKO!!
BAAN (BAM)
IT'S BEAU-TIFUL.

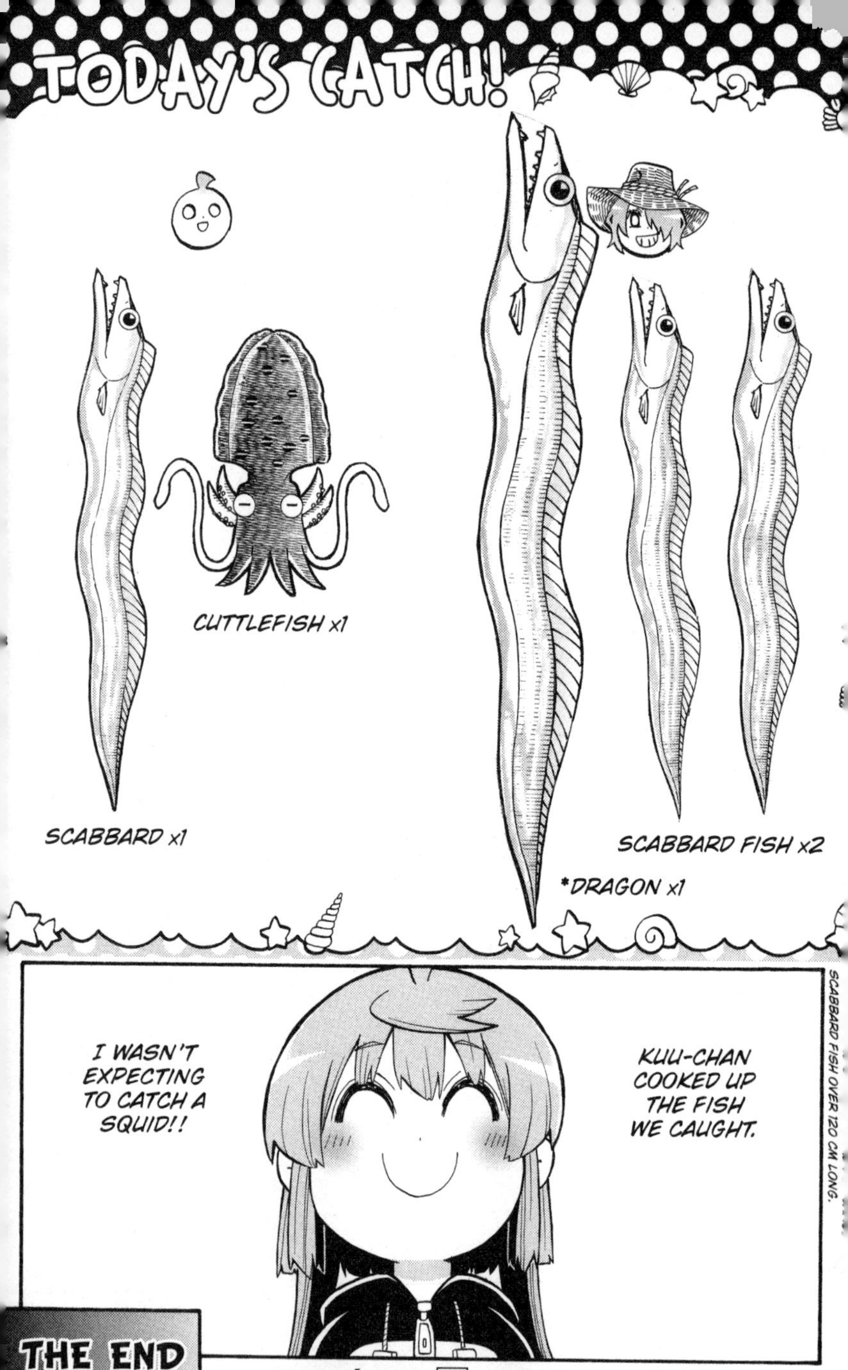
TODAY'S CATCH!
SCABBARD FISH x2
*DRAGON x1
CUTTLEFISH x1
SCABBARD x1
SCABBARD FISH OVER 120 CM LONG.
KUU-CHAN COOKED UP THE FISH WE CAUGHT.
I WASN'T EXPECTING TO CATCH A SQUID!!
THE END

MURCIÉLAGO 18 THE END

Translation Notes

Common Honorifics

no honorific: Indicates familiarity or closeness; if used without permission or reason, addressing someone in this manner would constitute an insult.

-san: The Japanese equivalent of Mr./Mrs./Miss. If a situation calls for politeness, this is the fail-safe honorific.

-sama: Conveys great respect; may also indicate that the social status of the speaker is lower than that of the addressee.

-kun: Used most often when referring to boys, this indicates affection or familiarity. Occasionally used by older men among their peers, but it may also be used by anyone referring to a person of lower standing.

-chan: An affectionate honorific indicating familiarity used mostly in reference to girls; also used in reference to cute persons or animals of either gender.

-senpai: A suffix used to address upperclassmen or more experienced coworkers.

-sensei: A respectful term for teachers, artists, or high-level professionals.

-shi: A formal honorific used to show respect, now primarily used in written language. When spoken today, it sounds a bit archaic.

General

Murciélago is Spanish for "bat."

Suteki is Japanese for "lovely."

Kuroko means "black lake" in Japanese, and is a Cthulhu Mythos reference to the Lake of Hali, where the dark god Hastur dwells.

The city of **Ruruie** is a reference to R'lyeh, a fictional lost city in H. P. Lovecraft's "The Call of Cthulhu."

Page 72
Danichi is a reference to Dunwich, a fictional village of inbred and superstitious people in the Cthulhu Mythos and the setting of the story *The Dunwich Horror*.

Page 88
Kutaato refers to Cthäat, the shape-shifting Dark Water God from the Cthulhu Mythos.

Page 99
Here 'n' There Arrows Lily Pure is a parody of the popular and long-running magical franchise *Pretty Cure*.

Page 107
In the original Japanese, the "**apple of my eye**" wordplay is a pun on Rinko's name and *ringo* (apple).

Page 152
Tekeli-li is the sound made by Shoggoths, shape-shifting creatures in the Cthulhu Mythos.

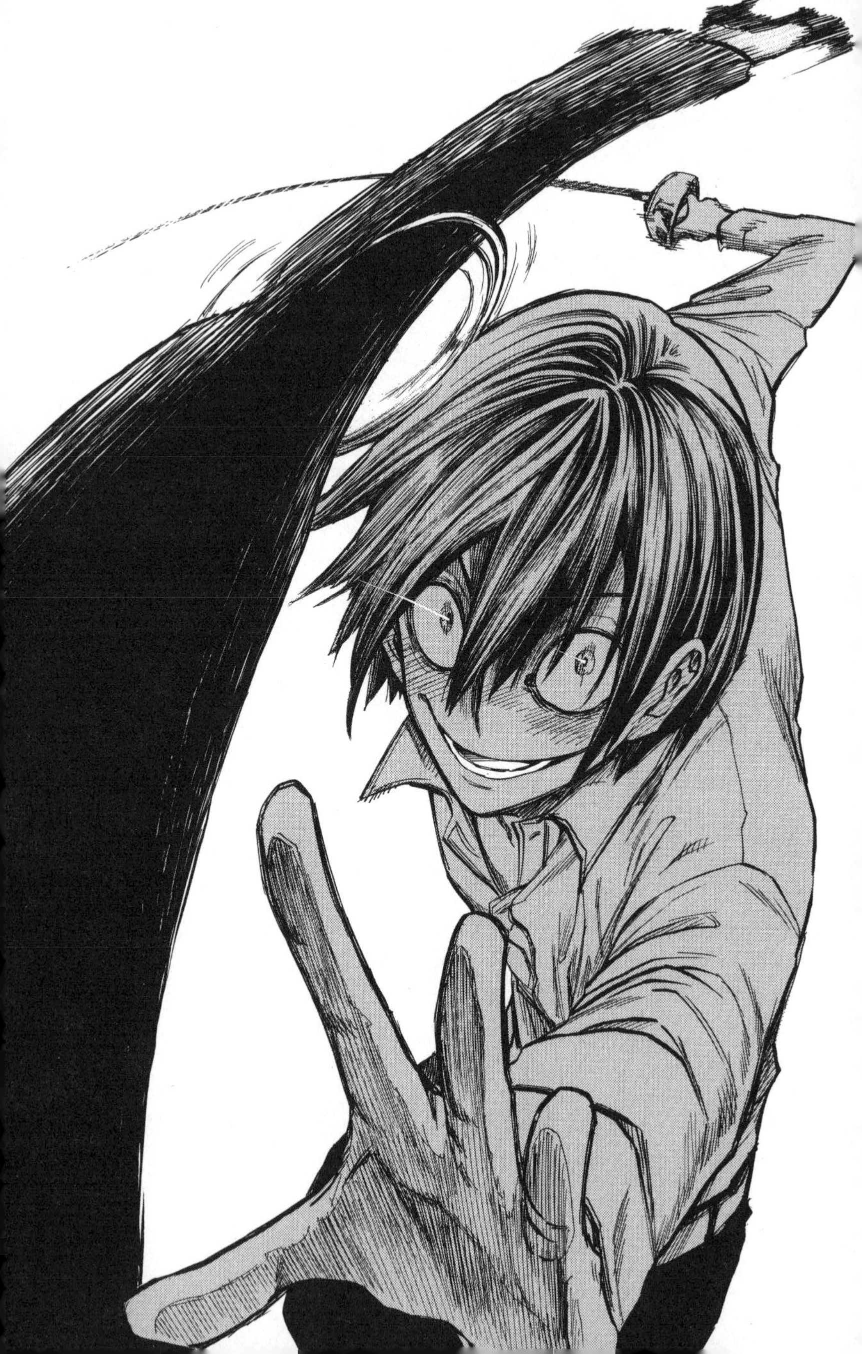

"TODAY'S BADDIE" WITH KOUMORI-SENSEI

NAME	HAZUKI SENDOU
VICTIM COUNT	27
GOAL	A HEART-POUNDING BATTLE
LIKES	ZENPACHI KUROGANE, BATTLES
DISLIKES	LIES, WEAK OPPONENTS
TREATMENT	HE INCURRED THE WRATH OF KURONO MIYAMOTO, AND AFTER HAVING HIS MIND BROKEN, THEIR FIGHT WAS INTERRUPTED BY A SNIPER WHO TOOK HIM OUT.
NOTES	THE BOY WAS A FORMER FENCING PRODIGY. HIS GENIUS IS UNDENIABLE, BUT HIS PERSONALITY ISSUES MADE HIM DISAPPEAR FROM THE CENTER STAGE. IF NOT FOR THE ONE WORD "LIAR," HE MIGHT HAVE HAD A BRILLIANT FUTURE TO LOOK FORWARD TO, BUT ONLY CHANGING THE PAST COULD HAVE MADE THAT POSSIBLE. SURPRISINGLY, NOBODY WHO EVER TOOK ON SENDOU IN A "PROXY BATTLE" LOST THEIR LIFE.

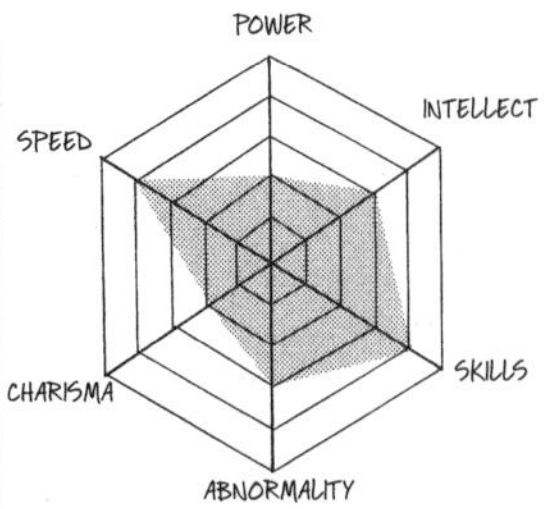

POWER
INTELLECT
SKILLS
ABNORMALITY
CHARISMA
SPEED

HINAKO'S IMPRESSIONS

ONCE SENSEI GOT MAD AT HIM, HE WAS ALL FLOPPING ON THE FLOOR AND A PANICKED MESS. MY CHESTNUT BOMB HIT ITS MARK, BUT IT WAS TOO LATE BY THEN. REST IN PEACE...

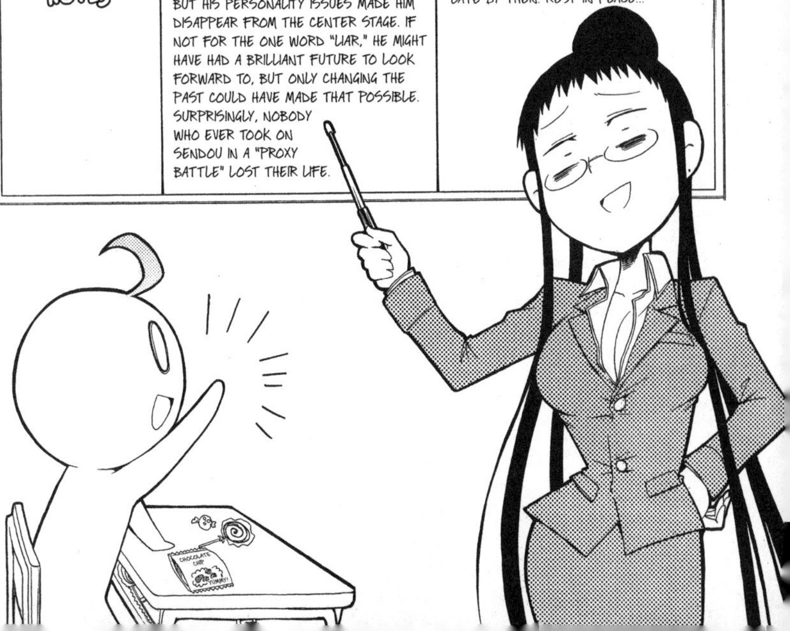

CHOCOLATE CHIP
YUMMY!

MURCIÉLAGO

Yoshimurakana

Translation: Christine Dashiell ✦ Lettering: Alexis Eckerman

MURCIÉLAGO vol. 18
© 2020 Yoshimurakana / SQUARE ENIX CO., LTD.
First published in Japan in 2020 by SQUARE ENIX CO., LTD.
English translation rights arranged with SQUARE ENIX CO., LTD. and Yen Press, LLC through Tuttle-Mori Agency, Inc.

English translation © 2021 by SQUARE ENIX CO., LTD.

Yen Press
150 West 30th Street, 19th Floor
New York, NY 10001

Visit us at yenpress.com
facebook.com/yenpress
twitter.com/yenpress
yenpress.tumblr.com
instagram.com/yenpress

Yen Press is an imprint of Yen Press, LLC.
The Yen Press name and logo are trademarks of Yen Press, LLC.

First Yen Press Edition: November 2021

Library of Congress Control Number: 2016958266

ISBNs: 978-1-9753-3641-7 (paperback)
978-1-9753-3642-4 (ebook)

10 9 8 7 6 5 4 3 2 1

LSC-C

Printed in the United States of America